Justice, Crime and Ethics

Michael C. Braswell
East Tennessee State University

Belinda R. McCarthy
University of Central Florida

Bernard J. McCarthy
University of Central Florida

anderson publishing co.
2035 reading road
cincinnati, ohio 45202
(513) 421-4142

JUSTICE, CRIME AND ETHICS

Copyright © 1991 by Anderson Publishing Co./Cincinnati, OH

ISBN 0-87084-093-2
Library of Congress Catalog Number 90-82316

Kelly Humble *Managing Editor*

Cover Design by Leanne M. Johnson

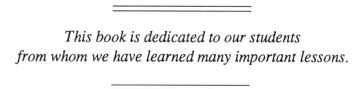

*This book is dedicated to our students
from whom we have learned many important lessons.*

Acknowledgments

We would like to thank the following publishers and journals for allowing us to reprint portions of their materials:

Criminal Justice Ethics, published by The Institute for Criminal Justice Ethics
Criminal Law Bulletin, published by Warren, Gorhan and Lamont
Criminology, published by The American Society of Criminology
Journal of Criminal Justice, published by Pergamon Journals, Ltd.
Justice Quarterly, published by the Academy of Criminal Justice Sciences

We would like to thank the following colleagues for their helpful suggestions and encouragement in reading selected portions of the manuscript: Steve Bader, Morton Brown, Frank Cullen, Richard Quinney, and John Whitehead.

In addition, a special thank you goes to Sharon Elliott for her typing of the manuscript and to Bill Simon and Kelly Humble of Anderson Publishing for their support and confidence.

Finally, we are particularly indebted to Narda Boggs for her tireless commitment to the many tasks that are essential to manuscript preparation and completion. Thank you, Narda.

Contributors

Robert Bohm—
Department of Criminal Justice, University of North Carolina at Charlotte

Michael C. Braswell—
Department of Criminal Justice and Criminology,
East Tennessee State University

Gray Cavender—
Arizona State University

Howard Cohen—
Associate Dean, College of Arts and Sciences,
University of Massachusetts, Boston

Elliot D. Cohen—
Professor of Philosophy, Indian River Community College

Franics T. Cullen—
Department of Criminal Justice, University of Cincinnati

Bennett L. Gershman—
Professor of Law, Pace University Law School

Jeffrey Gold—
Department of Philosophy, East Tennessee State University

Paul Jesilow—
University of California

Robert Johnson—
College of Criminal Justice, The American University

Dennis R. Longmire—
Sam Houston State University

William J. Maakestad—
Western Illinois University

Belinda R. McCarthy—
University of Central Florida

Bernard J. McCarthy—
Department of Criminal Justice, University of Central Florida

Harold Pepinsky—
Department of Criminal Justice, Indiana University

Joycelyn Pollock-Byrne—
University of Houston, DnTn/ Criminal Justice

Lawrence Sherman—
Crime Control Institute, Washington, D.C.

Jerome H. Skolnick—
Director of Center for the Study of Law and Society,
University of California at Berkeley

Dean J. Spader—
Department of Political Science/Criminal Justice,
University of South Dakota

Lawrence F. Travis, III—
Department of Criminal Justice, University of Cincinnati

Ernest Van den Haag—
School of Law, Fordham University

John T. Whitehead—
Department of Criminal Justice and Criminology,
East Tennessee State University

Foreword

This book is badly needed in criminal justice because some academic criminologists are timid about approaching burning ethical dilemmas, and because practitioners are often adamant that their uses of authority are beyond question. The stakes are high, particularly in the United States, where we punish people as criminals at a growing, world-leading rate. For example, one in four black men between the ages of 20 and 29 is in some form of criminal justice custody at any given time in the United States. Still, politicians, law enforcers, the media and many criminologists clamor that most offenders are not receiving the punishment they deserve.

I hope readers will do the kind of soul searching called for in the first and last chapters of this work. The fact is that many people in the United States, out of long and proud traditions (practicing Mennonites and Quakers, for instance) reject coercion and punishment altogether, and oppose taking any collective actions, save with absolute consensus. In a larger sense, they cannot justify any context for violence and believe deeply in non-violent resistance to any form of violence. It might be said that their motto is "Better dead than having blood on one's hands." As you will see in the chapter of this book that I co-authored, I am one of these pacifists. In more than twenty years of teaching, I have struggled with my conscience about how to give grades.

I can scarcely imagine that any reader of this book will not face the moral choice of whether to accept punishment of offenders. I invite you, as you read the diverse perspectives represented in this book, to ask yourself whether, or how, you would do the job of policing, prosecuting, sentencing or guarding. Could you in good conscience be a judge or recognize anyone else's competence to be one? Within every soul and every religious and political tradition lies a basic ambivalence on this issue. One side of each of us believes, and one body of religious and political thought teaches, that no earthly figure is competent to sit in judgment of any other. Neither Laotze nor Buddha nor Christ would ever have thrown the switch on an electric chair. The other side of us, and another body of religious and political thought, says that some of us are wiser, more virtuous or more learned in the laws of God, nature or the legislature than others, and that God, nature or the body politic demands they put sinners and incompetents in their rightful place. Although I try to be a pacifist in thought and deed, I struggle with the violent side of my nature. I infer that even the most fervent polemicists for punishment must also have twinges and episodes of mercy and compassion. We can try to deny the issue, but we cannot escape it. The morally responsible and accountable thing to do is to confront the issue, as have the authors in this volume, and open your own feelings and doubts to public discourse. The authors in this volume take at least implicit stands on this ever debatable issue, and you should feel free to debate with each of them as you read. If this book is the vehicle you use to begin your own soul searching on punishment and on passing judgments, I hope that such soul searching continues for a lifetime. To do so, the Buddhists tell us, is to open ourselves to suffering, which helps explain why we avoid seriously thinking about whether punishing, judging and grading ought to be done. However, avoiding the issue (following orders or the job description without questioning whether the job ought to be done) carries a price: the denial of one's personal moral responsibility for all that one does amounts to an addiction to violence.

It helps to put the basic moral issue in situational contexts, and the readings in this book do that nicely. The recurrent form of the issue is whether "they" are really different from "us"—whether criminals are basically different from or the same as law-abiding people, whether corrupt police are basically different from honest police, whether unethical prosecutors are basically different from zealously honest prosecutors, whether guards are basically different from prisoners, and whether ethical researchers are basically different from their unethical colleagues. Insofar as you believe that they are basically different, you believe that some people are closer to God, political legitimacy or scientific truth than others, and it follows that their will should prevail, and the will of their counterparts be subdued, in a just and peaceful world. Insofar as you believe they are basically the same, you believe no one is virtuous, wise or knowledgeable enough to use force, especially absolute force, to put others in their place. It is a good exercise to put yourself in the places described in the readings that follow, and ask yourself whether, if you were given the job of enforcer, you would personally feel morally qualified to pull the switch or otherwise punish or discipline the transgressors. More to the point, ask yourself how you would justify the moral position you take upon yourself—as superior to or comparable to the transgressor. The toughest part may be getting in touch with the way in which you feel superior and accounting for it. Thereafter, you will have an easier time picking up your ethical position where you last left it and reevaluating it in light of new circumstances. As Mickey Braswell closes by telling us, moral responsibility is a way of living rather than the rightness or wrongness of any particular moral decision we make. Moral responsibility means accounting for yourself. This book is a fine asset to use—use it well.

Hal Pepinsky
Bloomington, Indiana
July 1990

Contents

I. INTRODUCTION

Our personal and social values shape and color the way we perceive the world in which we live. While we are concerned with achieving personal goals and ambitions, we also come to realize at a rather early age that the needs and desires of others are also forces to be reckoned with. The question for us then becomes one of reconciling the pursuit of our individual dreams within the context of the larger community. Maintaining our individual integrity, our personal sense of right and wrong, and at the same time, conforming to what is best for the majority of persons in our society can often become a perplexing challenge. Yet we are all connected to each other in one way or another, such as with parents and children, and inmates and correctional staff. We are even connected to our physical environment as evidenced in the quality of air we breathe and water we drink. As potential criminal justice practitioners, our professional choices and policies will emanate from our personal beliefs and values—from our personal philosophies. How much do we care about trying to honestly and effectively address the pressing justice issues of the day? Are we truly mindful of the ways we are connected to our problems? Do we have a long-term as well as short-term sense of what the costs of our proposed solutions will be?

Cultivating a greater understanding of our own philosophical perspectives can provide us with a foundation for making more informed decisions about the diverse social issues we face and the way our system of justice responds to such issues.

CRIMINAL JUSTICE ETHICS:
A SURVEY OF
PHILOSOPHICAL THEORIES   1

Jeffrey Gold, Michael C. Braswell & Belinda R. M^{C}Carthy

Over the past ten to fifteen years, interest in professional ethics has grown steadily. Business ethics, medical ethics, and environmental ethics are all flourishing as components in most college and university curricula. Despite this fact, until recently, "higher education programs in criminology and criminal justice have largely neglected the systematic study of ethics."[1] This is unfortunate because the ethical issues that arise in the area of criminal justice are significant and complex. And, even though many of the ethical issues that arise in criminal justice are common to other professions, there are other issues that are specifically tailored to criminology and criminal justice. The most significant example of this involves the use of force and physical coercion. Sherman points out: "Force is the essence of criminal justice...The decisions of whether to use force, how much to use, and under what conditions are confronted by police officers, juries, judges, prison officials, probation and parole officers and others. All of them face the paradox, noted earlier, of using harm to prevent harm."[2] The use of force, which is central to criminal justice, distinguishes criminal justice from other professions.

In addition to the issue concerning the use of force, there are other factors that seem to distinguish the moral decisions of criminal justice agents from other professionals. Sherman discusses two of them:

First, criminal justice decisions are made on behalf of society as a whole, a collective moral judgment made in trust by a single person. That would entail a far greater responsibility than what other vocations are assigned. Second, the decisions criminal justice agents make are not just incidentally, but are primarily, moral decisions. An engineer designs a building that may or may not kill people, but the decision is primarily a physical one and only incidentally a moral one. When a police officer decides to arrest someone...when a judge decides to let that person out on a suspended sentence, the decisions are primarily moral ones.[3]

As we can see, the moral issues that arise in the field of criminal justice are both distinctive and significant.

It is sometimes helpful, when trying to solve certain specific ethical issues, to begin with more general, more theoretical questions. When we get a handle on the more theoretical issue, we can apply that to a specific moral problem. So, with respect to criminal justice, we might begin by raising more general questions about the nature of justice. Theories of justice address broad social issues including human rights, equality, and distribution of wealth. We might even go up one more level of generality. Justice is itself a branch of an even wider sphere, that of ethics. It seems important that we view issues in criminal justice from the larger framework of ethics and morality. It would be a mistake to assume that issues in criminal justice could emerge outside of the larger social and ethical context of our culture. Therefore, this essay will explore the field of ethics with the hope that such a study will provide us with a set of concepts that will shed some light on specific moral issues in the field of criminal justice. That shall be done by presenting a survey of some of the major philosophical theories in the field of normative ethics.

Normative ethics is the study of right and wrong. A normative ethical theorist tries to discover whether or not there are any basic, fundamental principles of right and wrong. If such principles are discovered, they are held to be the ground or foundation of all of our ethical judgments. For example, we ordinarily say lying, cheating, stealing, raping, and killing are wrong. The ethical theorist asks: Do these very different activities of lying, stealing, and killing all have something in common which makes them all wrong? If so, what is that common characteristic?

One of the most important figures in the history of Western philosophy, Socrates, was famous for seeking the universal in ethical matters.[4] In other words, when Socrates asked "What is Justice?" or "What is Virtue?" he was not asking for a list of actions which are just or list of examples of virtue, rather, he was seeking the universal characteristic that all just or virtuous actions had in common.[5] Just as all squares, no matter how large they are or what color they are, have something in common (four equal sides and four right angles), the ethical theorist wants to know if all morally right actions (whether they are cases of honesty, charity, or benevolence) also have something in common. If such a common characteristic is found, it is held to be the ground or foundation or fundamental principle of ethics. We shall now turn to our survey of some standard ethical theories, in an effort to locate such a foundation for ethics.

Utilitarianism

The most famous version of utilitarianism was developed in Great Britain in the 18th and 19th centuries by Jeremy Bentham and John Stuart Mill.[6] Utilitarianism is classified as a consequentialist ethical theory. In other words, the utilitarian holds that we judge the morality of an action in terms of the consequences or results of that action. Mill states: "All action is for the sake of some end, and rules of action, it seems natural to suppose, must take their whole character and color from the end to which they are subservient."[7] The insight that motivates consequentialism is this: A moral action produces something good; an immoral action produces a bad or harmful result. Put in the simplest possible way, cheating, stealing and murder are all wrong because they produce bad or harmful consequences and charity and benevolence are good because they produce something beneficial. To summarize, the consequentialist holds that the morality of an action is determined by the consequences of that action; actions which are moral produce good consequences, actions which are immoral produce bad consequences.

At this point, two questions come up:

1) What do we mean by good consequences (and bad consequences)?
2) Consequences for whom?

Actions have consequences for many different people. Which people should we consider when contemplating the consequences of our actions? By giving concrete answers to these two questions, the utilitarian carves out a unique and specific version or type of consequentialist moral theory.

In order to explain utilitarianism, we shall begin with the first question. How does the utilitarian define or characterize good and bad consequences? The most famous version of utilitarianism (the one advocated by Bentham and Mill) is called hedonistic utilitarianism. According to Mill, the fundamental good that all humans seek is happiness. Aristotle agrees with that point even though he is not a utilitarian. In his discussion of the highest good Aristotle says: "As far as its name is concerned, most people would agree, for both the common run of people and cultivated men call it happiness."[8] Mill holds that "there is in reality nothing desired except happiness."[9] Mill's view is that all people desire happiness and everything else they desire is either a part of happiness or a means to happiness. Thus, the basic and fundamental good, according to hedonistic utilitarianism (hereafter called utilitarianism) is happiness.

According to both Bentham and Mill, happiness is identified with pleasure. Mill claims: "By happiness is intended pleasure and the absence of pain; by unhappiness, pain and the privation of pleasure."[10] In his discussion of pleasure, Mill includes not only the pleasures of food, drink, and sex, but also the intellectual and aesthetic pleasures. In fact, Mill considers the "higher order" pleasures, that is the intellectual, emotional, and aesthetic pleasures that non-human animals are not capable of experiencing, to be of a higher quality than the "lower order" pleasures that many species of animals experience. The pleasures of poetry and opera are, on Mill's view, qualitatively superior to the pleasures of drinking and playing pinball.

Consequentialism holds that the morality of an action is determined by the consequences produced by the action. For the utilitarian, the morally right action produces happiness (pleasure and the absence of pain) and the morally wrong action produces unhappiness (pain and suffering). Mill states: "The creed which accepts as the foundation of morals 'utility' or 'the greatest happiness principle' holds that actions are right in proportion as they tend to promote happiness; wrong as they tend to produce the reverse of happiness."[11] Bentham states: "By the principle of utility is meant that principle which approves or disapproves of every action whatsoever, according to the tendency which it appears to have to augment or diminish the happiness of the party whose interest is in question: or, what is the same thing in other words, to promote or to oppose the happiness."[12]

Before we examine the theory in any more sophistication, we can already feel the intuitive appeal of the theory. Why do we think that murder, rape, cheating, and lying are immoral? because those actions cause pain to the victims and the families of the victims. Why do we think that charity and benevolence are righteous actions? because they produce pleasure or happiness.

Let us now move to the second question. Since utilitarianism holds that we ought to produce happiness or pleasure, whose happiness or pleasure ought we consider? After all, the thief gets a certain amount of pleasure from a successful burglary. The utilitarian answer to this is that we ought to consider all parties affected by the action, calculate the pain and pleasure of everyone who is influenced. After due consideration, the action which is morally correct is the one which produces the greatest good (amount of happiness) for the greatest number of people. If all the alternatives involve more pain than pleasure, the morally right action is the one which produces the least amount of pain.

For example, the thief wants money to accord himself a certain lifestyle. Stealing will bring him jewelry or other valuable items which he can trade for money which will make him feel good. However, such actions would also have as their consequence that those persons who were stolen from would become victims with the accompanying feelings of sorrow, anger, or perhaps even fear. As a result, their pain outweighs his pleasure. "The greatest good for the greatest number" creates the context for community. The proportionality of pain and pleasure must be judged in this context.

In calculating the amount of pleasure and pain produced by any action, many factors are relevant. Bentham creates a hedonistic calculus in which he lists those factors.[13] I shall briefly describe some of the major elements in Bentham's calculus. First of all, we must consider the *intensity* or strength of the pleasure or pain. A minor inconvenience is much less important than a major trauma. We must also consider the *duration* of the pleasure or pain. For example, in the case of a rape psychological scars may last a lifetime. Additionally, we must consider the *long-term consequences* of an action. Certain actions may produce short-term pleasures but in the long run prove to be more harmful than good (for example, alcohol and drugs). Finally, we must consider the *probability* or likelihood that our actions will produce the consequences we intend. For example, the prisons are full of thieves who in a personal (and not merely community) context did not make a good utilitarian choice. For instance, a certain offender commits an armed robbery to acquire money to spend on a lavish lifestyle which would make him or her feel good. Instead, because the offender did not consider the probability of being caught, he or she spends 15 years experiencing the pain of imprisonment.

Let me briefly summarize. The ethical theorist is interested in discovering the basic, fundamental principle of morality, a foundation upon which all moral judgments rest. The utilitarian claims to have found such a principle and identifies it as the greatest happiness principle. According to utilitarianism, an action ought to be done if and only if that action maximizes the total amount of pleasure (or minimizes the total amount of pain) of all parties affected by the action.

The entire criminal justice system can be justified on utilitarian grounds. Why do we need a police force? to serve and protect. That is to say, it is in the long-term interests of a society (produces the greatest amount of happiness for the greatest number of people) to pay police officers to protect the community from burglars, murderers, rapists, and drunk drivers. The utilitarian would argue that what we call criminal activities tend to produce much more pain than pleasure. Therefore, a criminal justice system is instituted in order to lower the amount of crime thereby lowering the amount of pain produced by crime.

Despite that fact that utilitarianism can be used successfully to justify the criminal justice system, there are certain times when we say a police officer is justified in arresting (or ticketing) a citizen even though that arrest does not lead to the greatest good for the greatest number. For example, suppose a man is in a rush to pick up his daughter at school. He is driving on the freeway on a bright, sunny day and there is virtually no traffic. Suppose he exceeds the speed limit by 15 miles per hour (the speed limit is 55 mph and he is driving at 70 mph). The police officer stops him and gives him a ticket for $75. One might argue that in this case the painful consequences of giving a ticket outweigh the pleasurable consequences. First of all, the driver is caused pain by having to pay the ticket. Secondly, by getting the ticket, the driver is late to pick up his daughter, which causes the daughter anxiety. The delay also causes inconvenience for the principal at school. What are the pleasurable consequences for giving the ticket? Who is made happier? really, no one. Had the officer just given the driver a warning, the driver, the principal and the child would all be happier and no one would be less happy. So, on utilitarian grounds, the officer should not issue a ticket in the set of circumstances just described.

The previous example leads some people to say that the officer has a *duty* to issue the ticket regardless of the consequences. And this leads us to our next moral theory, namely, deontological ethics.

DEONTOLOGICAL ETHICS

The word 'deontology' comes from two Greek roots, 'deos' meaning duty, and 'logos' meaning study. Deontology is therefore the study of duty. Deontologists have argued that human beings sometimes have duties to perform certain actions regardless of the consequences. Police officers have a duty to issue traffic tickets even when it does not produce the greatest good for the greatest number. Teachers have the obligation or duty to fail students who do failing work even if failing than student produces more misery than happiness.

The most famous deontologist is Immanuel Kant, an 18th century German philosopher. Kant believed that all consequentialist theories missed something crucial to ethics by neglecting the concept of duty. But that is not all. Kant also believed that by focusing solely on consequences, utilitarian type theories missed something even more basic to morality, namely, a good will or the intention to do what is right. He begins his treatise on ethics as follows: "It is impossible to conceive anything at all in the world, or even out of it, which can be taken as good without qualification, except a *good will.*"[14] In other words, the key to morality is human will or intention, not consequences.

Consider the following example: Suppose John is driving down the road and sees someone on the side of the road having difficulty with a flat tire. John notices that the car is a brand new Cadillac and the driver of the car (an elderly woman) is wearing a mink coat. John thinks to himself "If I help this woman, she will give me a large reward." So, John stops his car and helps the woman fix her flat tire. In the second case, Mary drives down the road and sees someone on the side of the road having difficulty with a flat tire. Mary says to herself "That woman seems to be in trouble. I think I should help her," and she does help her. Kant would argue that there is a moral difference between case one and case two, despite the fact that the consequences in the two cases are identical. In both cases, John and Mary (on a utilitarian view) did the right thing by helping the woman, thereby producing the greatest good for the greatest number. However, Kant would argue that even though John and Mary both did the right thing (Kant would say they both acted in accordance with duty), there is still a moral difference. Mary did the act because it was her duty, whereas John was motivated by self-interest. Kant would not say that John was immoral. After all, he didn't do anything wrong. In fact, he did the right thing. But, because he didn't do it for the right reason, his action has no moral worth. He did the right thing for selfish reasons (which is still better than doing the wrong thing, that is to say, performing an action inconsistent with duty). Kant draws a distinction between actions that are merely in accordance with duty and actions which are done for the sake of duty.[15] And he holds that only actions that are done for the sake of duty have moral worth.

Having established the importance of a good will (doing an act for the right reason), Kant moves to the question: What is our duty? In other words, just as the utilitarians have a fundamental principle of morality (act so as to produce the greatest good for the greatest number), Kant argues for a different fundamental principle of morality.

Kant calls the fundamental principal of morality "the categorical imperative." An imperative is a command. It tells us what we ought to do or what we should do. The categorical imperative contrasts with what Kant calls hypothetical imperatives. A hypothetical imperative is a command that begins with "if," for example, *if* you want to get a good grade, you ought to study, or *if* you want to make a lot of money, you should work hard, or *if* you want to stay out of jail, you should not break the law. The categorical imperative is unhypothetical, no ifs whatsoever. Just do it! You ought to behave morally, period. Not: *if* you want people to like you, you should behave morally. Not: *if* you want to go to heaven, you should behave morally. Just: you ought to behave morally. In other words, the categorical imperative commands absolutely and unconditionally.

What is the categorical imperative? Kant gives several formulations of it. We will focus on two formulations. The first formulation emphasizes a basic concept in ethics called "universalizability." The basic idea of universalizability is that for my action to be morally justifiable, I must be able to will that *anyone* in relevantly similar circumstances act in the same way. For example, I would like to cheat on my income tax, but could I will that *everyone* cheat on their income taxes, thereby leaving the government insufficient funds to carry out programs I support? I would like to tell a lie to extricate myself from an uncomfortable situation, but could I will that someone else lie to me in order to get him or herself out of a difficult situation? Kant's formulation of the categorical imperative is as follows: "Act only on that maxim [a maxim is a principle of action] through which you can at the same time will that it should become a universal law."[16]

Kant's insight is that morality involves fairness or equality, that is, a willingness to treat everyone in the same way. I am acting immorally when I make myself an exception ("I wouldn't want others behaving this way, but it is fine for me to behave this way.") Put in that way, we see a similarity to the Golden Rule which states "Do unto others only as you would have them do unto you."[17] Kant's idea is that you should do only what you are willing to permit anyone else to do. The idea is that there is something inconsistent or irrational about saying that it is fine for me to lie to you, cheat you, steal from you, but it is not justified for you to do those things to me.

The next formulation of the categorical imperative focuses on the fact that human beings have intrinsic value (that is value in and of themselves). Because human beings have intrinsic value, they ought always to be treated with reverence and never to be treated as mere things. When I treat someone as a thing, an object, a tool, or an instrument, I am treating that person as a means to my own ends. For example, if I marry someone to get her money, I am using her as a means to my own ends. I am not treating her with dignity, respect, or reverence, but as a mere thing. It is the classic case of using someone. When I was about 10 years old, a friend and I wanted to go to a movie. My mother could drive one way, but my friend's mother was busy and couldn't drive that day. So we decided to call a neighbor (Richard). I still remember the conversation. I said "Hi, Richard. Would you like to go to a movie with me and Kenny?" Richard responded affirmatively, saying he would enjoy that very much. I then said "Could your mother drive one way?" Well, Richard exploded. Richard immediately recognized that we were not inviting him because we especially wanted him to come, rather we were using him to get a ride from his mother. Unfortunately Richard was right. That was precisely why we called him.

Kant speaks of human beings as "something whose existence has in itself an absolute value."[18] He goes on to say that "man, and in general every rational being, exists as an end in himself, not merely as a means for arbitrary use by this or that will."[19] On the basis of this, he offers the following formulation of the categorical imperative: "Act in such a way that you always treat humanity, whether in your own person or in the person of any other, never simply as a means but always at the same time as an end."[20]

Kant believed that these two seemingly different formulations of the categorical imperative really come to the same thing. Perhaps the reasoning goes as follows: What maxims or principles of action would I be willing to universalize? only those that treated others as ends in themselves and not as things. Why? because I want to be treated with reverence, respect, and dignity. Since I want to be treated as a being with intrinsic value, I can only universalize maxims that treat other people as having intrinsic value.

Before moving to our third type of ethical theory, let us contrast deontological ethics with utilitarianism on a specific issue related to criminal justice. The issue is: What are the legitimate restraints a society should impose on police officers in the apprehension of suspected criminals? To limit this rather broad topic somewhat, let us focus on the use of techniques of deceit including entrapment, bugging telephones, and undercover operations. In this example I will not try to predict the answer that a utilitarian or a deontologist will give. Instead I will simply contrast the approach or the strategy they will use in thinking about the issue.

Let's begin with utilitarianism. Utilitarianism is a consequentialist moral theory. We decide on the legitimacy of deceptive tactics on the basis of the consequences of using those tactics. In particular, we must weigh the positive results against the negative results in deciding what to do. On the positive side, entrapment, bugging operations, and undercover operations work. As a result of the use of such tactics, we are able to apprehend some criminals that might otherwise go free. And as a result of apprehending those criminals, we deter future crime in two ways:

1) We keep known criminals behind bars where they are unable to commit further crimes; and
2) we show, by example, what happens when someone breaks the law, thereby deterring other citizens from risking incarceration.

On the negative side, we have certain individuals' right to privacy being violated by the use of deceptive tactics. The utilitarian will now weigh the positive benefits of apprehending criminals and thereby protecting society against the negative consequence of violating certain citizens' right to privacy.

Kant would approach the issue from a very different reference point. As a deontologist he would not approach this issue from the perspective of "What consequences are likely to occur?" Rather than focus on the results or ends of the behavior, he or she would look at the behavior itself and see if it conforms to the categorical imperative. Concentrating on the universalizability formulation of the categorical imperative, a Kantian might ask himself or herself "Would I consent to having my telephone bugged if there was reason to suspect that I was guilty of a crime?"

Or, if we were to attend to the second formulation of the categorical imperative, a Kantian might ask: "Does the use of manipulative techniques in law enforcement constitute treating suspected criminals as mere means to our ends (by manipulating them we are using them) or does it constitute treating them as ends in themselves (mature, responsible citizens who must answer to their behavior)?"

These are difficult questions to answer. The point of the example was not to show how a utilitarian or deontologist would solve an ethical issue in criminal justice, but to illustrate how they would approach or think about such an issue. Let us now turn to our third ethical theory.

CONNECTEDNESS

The next set of ethical theories to be studied has no standard name or designation. And though these theories are found predominantly in the East (especially in Hinduism and Yoga), there are also Western representatives of the theories (most notably, Plato). Although the theories are diverse, they seem to share a common metaphysical assumption. (By metaphysics, I mean a theory of or view of the nature of reality.) The metaphysical assumption that these theories share is what I shall call the assumption of connectedness. The idea is that human beings are not simply isolated, atomistic creatures, rather each one of us is integrally connected and bonded to other human beings and to the environment. Chief Seattle of the Duwamish Tribe, in a letter to the President of the United States in 1852, wrote the following:

> Every part of this earth is sacred to my people. Every shining pine needle, every sandy shore, every mist in the dark woods, every meadow, every humming insect...We know the sap which courses

through the trees as we know the blood that courses through our veins. *We are part of the earth and it is part of us.* The perfumed flowers are our sisters. The bear, the deer, the great eagle, these are our brothers. The rocky crests, the juices in the meadow, the body heat of the pony, and man, all belong to the same family...This we know: the earth does not belong to man, man belongs to the earth. *All things are connected like the blood that unites us all.* Man did not weave the web of life, he is merely a strand in it. Whatever he does to the web, he does to himself."[21] (Emphasis mine.)

In that letter, Chief Seattle emphasizes our connection to the natural world. One can find a similar position in several different Eastern philosophies. Bo Lozoff, articulating the position found in Yoga, states: "In Truth, we (everybody and everything in the Universe) are all connected; most of us just can't see the glue."[22]

The idea that we just can't see the glue (that is, we can't see the connection linking ourselves to others) is the Hindu concept that we misperceive ourselves as isolated and disconnected from one another and the world. Alan Watts says:

We suffer from a hallucination, from a false and distorted sensation of our own existence as living organisms. Most of us have the sensation that 'I myself' is a separate center of feeling and action, living inside and bounded by the physical body—a center which 'confronts' an 'external' world of people and things...[we] continue to be aware of ourselves as isolated 'egos' inside bags of skin."[23]

Watts, following the Hindu Vedantic tradition, calls this an "illusion" and maintains that that illusion is responsible for our estranged and hostile attitude towards the environment, as evidenced by the expressions "conquering nature" and "the conquest of space." Insofar as we see ourselves as apart from nature rather than a part of nature, we end up with pollution, acid rain, destruction of forests, and the depletion of the ozone layer.

In this regard, it is interesting to contrast two metaphors concerning the earth. The more "primitive" metaphor "mother earth" contrasts dramatically with the contemporary metaphor of the earth as a collection of "natural resources." A mother is someone to whom we feel connected and bound. To perceive the earth as one's mother is to see oneself as coming out of the earth. The connection could not be any more intimate. To perceive the earth as an assortment of natural resources is another matter entirely. To conceive of the earth as merely a provider of goods for our own purposes is, to borrow

Kant's expression, to see the earth as merely a means to our own ends. The danger in that attitude is now obvious. Insofar as we do not consider the earth to be sacred or precious (as Chief Seattle did), but instead see it as a commodity with no intrinsic worth, we find ourselves in a world with places like Prince William Sound, Three Mile Island, Love Canal, and Chernobyl.

Once we accept the assumption that we are connected to everyone and everything around us, it becomes clear that our actions do not take place in a vacuum but within a complex web of interconnected people and things. Whatever I do has an impact upon those around me. My actions have consequences. This is the Hindu and Buddhist concept of karma. The law of karma is the law of cause and effect. All actions have effects or consequences.

When we integrate the notion of karma (lawful consequences) with the notion of connectedness, it becomes clear that, since we are connected to everyone around us, our actions affect those who are connected to us. Insofar as we have an impact on someone we are connected with, we have an impact upon ourselves. In other words, our actions ultimately come back to us. What goes around comes around. It is the Biblical idea that we reap what we sow. It is Chief Seattle's idea "Man did not weave the web of life, he is merely a strand in it. *Whatever he does to the web, he does to himself.*" (Emphasis mine.) Plant seeds of violence and reap violent fruits. Plant seeds of compassion and reap compassionate fruits. Bo Lozoff states: "Every thought, word, and deed is a seed we plant in the world. All our lives, we harvest the fruits of those seeds. If we plant desire, greed, fear, anger and doubt, then that's what will fill our lives. Plant love, courage, understanding, good humor, and that's what we get back. This isn't negotiable; it's a law of energy, just like gravity."[24]

When we speak of karma, we are not talking about retribution, revenge, or punishment. Rather, we are speaking of the consequences of actions. We do not say of someone who jumps from a third-story window that his broken leg is a punishment for jumping. It is simply a consequence. Rather than thinking of karma as retribution, it is better to think of it as the principle "You've made your bed, now you must lie in it." We must inhabit the world we create. If we pollute the world, we must live in a polluted world. If we act violently, we must live in a violent world.

According to proponents of the idea of karma (the idea that each one of us reaps what he sows), no one can ever get away with one's actions. Perhaps we won't get caught by the police, but the action still has an impact on our own life. For a philosopher like Plato the consequences are consequences for our own psyche. In Plato's *Gorgias*, Socrates compares physical health with psychological health. To understand this comparison, consider the following example. I live a sedentary life, eat a diet of junk food and soda pop, smoke cigarettes, and drink alcohol excessively. This life of no exercise, poor nutrition, cigarettes, and alcohol will eventually catch up with me. After I become adjusted and acclimated to it, I may believe that I feel just fine. But from the fact that I believe that I feel fine, it does not follow that I am in an optimal state of physical health. The reason that I believe that I feel fine is precisely because I no longer even know what it is like to feel healthy. This is also true in bad or unhealthy marriages, even in some cases of spouse abuse. It is like a severely nearsighted child who has never worn glasses. He will not know that his sight is not optimal; he will think the world is supposed to look the way he sees it. He will not know that there is a better way to see. Similarly, the person who lives a sedentary life and eats exclusively at fast food restaurants may not know that there is a better way to feel. But the fact that he doesn't know it does not stop the junk food and cigarettes from continuing to affect his physical condition. One simply cannot avoid the consequences of an unhealthy diet and lifestyle.

In the *Gorgias*, Plato argues that the same is true with injustice and psychological health. One can never escape the consequences of injustice. As I said earlier, one may escape detection by the police; one may never be brought to trial; one may never go to prison. But injustice continues to affect one's psyche, whether we know it or not. We must inhabit the unjust world that we have created. According to Plato, injustice brings strife, disharmony, and conflict.[25] There will be strife and conflict in an unjust city. Similarly, there will be strife and conflict in an unjust individual (a lack of psychic health and wholeness). Just as the physically unhealthy man may not know he is unhealthy and the nearsighted child may not know his eyesight is poor, the unjust man may not know that he is in a state of psychic disharmony and imbalance. That is because he has become adjusted and acclimated to an unjust and violent life. He simply doesn't know what it is like to feel balanced and harmonious.

To summarize, according to what I am calling theories of connectedness, people are not isolated, disconnected, atomic beings. Rather, we are earthly beings and social beings, that is, we are creatures integrally connected to the earth and to other people on the earth. What we do has direct consequence on those to whom we are connected whether or not we see the connection. Our actions directly affect the world in which we live. We must live in the world created by our own actions. If we act violently, cruelly and unjustly, we will live in a world filled with violence, cruelty and injustice. If we act compassionately and benevolently, we will live in a world filled with compassion and benevolence.

This metaphysical view naturally leads to an ethics of nonviolence. The Sanskrit word, ahimsa, meaning nonviolence, is a fundamental concept in Hinduism and Buddhism. Mahatma Ghandi, who advocated an ethic of nonviolence is a contemporary representative of that idea. A Christian representative is Martin Luther King. Both believed in changing the world and rectifying the injustices they saw, but both insisted on using nonviolent strategies. Martin Luther King, accepting the Nobel Peace Prize, said: "The nonviolent resisters can summarize their message in the following simple terms: We will not obey unjust laws or submit to unjust practices. We will do this peacefully, openly, cheerfully, because our aim is to persuade. *We adopt the means of nonviolence because our end is a community at peace with itself.*"[26] (Emphasis mine.) The idea is that violence breeds violence. You don't fight fire with fire, rather you put out fire with water. You don't end violence by violently resisting it. Perhaps that is what Jesus meant by "resist not evil."[27] A 1960s bumper sticker read "Fighting for peace is like screwing for chastity." You don't end violence by creating more of it. If we must inhabit the world we create and we want to live in a world which is just and peaceful, we ought to act in just and peaceful ways.

The relevance of this to criminal justice is to be found in our contemporary prisons. Bo Lozoff states: "Prison systems throughout the world are generally ugly, barbaric, counterproductive, and insane."[28] Contemporary prisons are violent institutions which tend to perpetuate rather than diminish violence. According to the theories presented in this section, we must begin to treat criminals in less violent and more compassionate ways. We must stop thinking in terms of revenge, retribution and recrimination, and begin to think in terms of compassion and forgiveness. Richard Quinney states: "The peacemaking perspective is steadily making its way into criminology. In recent years, there have been proposals and programs on mediation, conflict resolution, reconciliation, and community. They are part of an emerging *criminology of peacemaking*, a criminology that seeks to alleviate suffering and thereby reduce crime."[29]

The following Zen story presents this philosophy *in its most radical form:*

One evening as Shichiri Kojun was reciting sutras a thief with a sharp sword entered, demanding either his money or his life. Shichiri told him: 'Do not disturb me. You can find the money in that drawer.' Then he resumed his recitation. A little while afterwards he stopped and called: 'Don't take it all. I need some to pay taxes with tomorrow.' The intruder gathered up most of the money and started to leave. 'Thank a person when you receive a gift,' Shichiri added. The man thanked him and made off. A few days afterwards the fellow was caught and confessed, among others, the offence against Shichiri. When Shichiri was called as a witness he said: 'This man is no thief, at least as far as I am concerned. I gave him the money and he thanked me for it.' After he had finished his prison term, the man went to Shichiri and became his disciple.[30]

Along the same lines, Jesus teaches that if anyone sues you for your coat, let him also have your cloak.[31] He goes on to say: "Love your enemies, bless them that curse you, do good to them that hate you, and pray for them who despitefully use you, and persecute you"[32] The radical message of these philosophies is that we should cease to repay violence with violence, whether that repayment be called "retribution" or "just deserts." Instead, we must learn to, as Paul puts it, "overcome evil with good."[33] In terms of criminal justice, that would involve a total and complete reform of what we now call "corrections."

CARING

The preceding three ethical theories attempt to justify a specific ethical rule or principle as the foundation of morality. Utilitarians produce reasons in support of their version of the fundamental rule of morality, namely that we ought to produce the greatest good for the greatest number. Kant advances arguments for what he considers to be the basic moral principle, that we ought to treat others as ends in themselves and not as mere means. Theories of connectedness defend the moral absolute of nonviolence. Though each of the three theories differ from one another, all share a similarity of approach. All attempt to *prove*, by means of *argument, justification,* and *reason,* a specific moral *rule,* or *principle.* According to Nel Noddings, proving, justifying, and arguing for rules and principles is a masculine approach to ethics. In *Caring: A Feminine Approach to Ethics & Moral Education,* she outlines an alternative. Noddings claims:

Ethics, the philosophical study of morality, has concentrated for the most part on moral reasoning...Even though careful philosophers have recognized the difference between 'pure' or logical reason and 'practical' or moral reason, ethical argumentation has frequently proceeded as if it were governed by the logical necessity characteristic of geometry. It has concentrated on the establishment of principles and that which can be logically derived from them. One might say that ethics has been discussed largely in the language of the father: in principles and propositions, in terms such as justification, fairness, justice. The mother's voice has been silent. Human caring and the memory of caring and being cared for, which I shall argue form the foundation of ethical response, have not received attention except as outcomes of ethical behavior. One is tempted to say that ethics has so far been guided by Logos, the masculine spirit, whereas the more natural and perhaps stronger approach would be through Eros, the feminine spirit.[34]

According to Noddings, the masculine approach (the approach of the father) is a detached perspective that focuses on law and principle, whereas the feminine approach (the approach of the mother) is rooted in receptivity, relatedness, and responsiveness.[35] Noddings advocates the feminine perspective. She goes on to point out that "this does not imply that all women will accept it [the feminine perspective] or that men will reject it; indeed, there is no reason why men should not embrace it."[36]

The masculine perspective is an approach to ethics, an approach through justification and argument. The feminine perspective, on the other hand, "shall locate the very wellspring of ethical behavior in human affective response."[37] Noddings' point is that ethical caring is ultimately grounded in natural caring, for example, the natural caring a mother has for her child. Noddings' emphasis on natural caring leads her to the conclusion "that in truth, the moral viewpoint is prior to any notion of justification."[38] In other words, rather than viewing reason and justification as the process by which one comes to the moral perspective, Noddings indicates that the moral perspective is a natural perspective, as natural as a mother caring for her infant.

An ancient Chinese philosophy, Taoism, advocates a position that is similar to the one we find in Noddings. The two major Taoist philosophers, Lao Tzu and Chuang Tzu, suggest that not only is natural caring prior to reason, justification, and principle, it is superior to those activities. In fact, the Taoists claim that principles of ethics actually interfere with caring. Just as Nel Noddings is responding to a particular masculine tradition in Western ethics, the Taoists are responding to a particular tradition in Chinese ethics, namely, Confucianism. The Confucianists were very rule and principle oriented: rules for filial piety, rules for those who govern, rules for those who are governed. The Taoists responded by claiming that those rules, because of their artificiality, destroyed true, natural caring and replaced it with forced or legislated "caring."

From the Taoist perspective, the danger of advocating ethical rules and principles is that they will replace something far superior to those principles, namely natural caring. Chuang Tzu says: "Because [the doctrine of] right and wrong appeared, the Way was injured."[39]

Lao Tzu makes a similar, but weaker claim. Lao Tzu doesn't make the strong claim that the doctrine of right and wrong destroyed the Way (the Tao). However, he does claim that only in unnatural states does the doctrine of right and wrong arise. In the *Tao-te-Ching*, Lao Tzu says:

> Therefore, when Tao [the natural Way] is lost, only then does the doctrine of virtue arise.
> When virtue is lost, only then does the doctrine of humanity arise.
> When humanity is lost, only then does the doctrine of righteousness arise.
> When righteousness is lost, only then does the doctrine of propriety arise.
> Now, propriety is a superficial expression of loyalty and faithfulness, and the beginning of disorder.[40]

Notice how Lao Tzu concludes by discussing the superficiality of notions of propriety and how such notions are the beginning of disorder. In another section of the *Tao-te-Ching*, Lao Tzu summarizes the preceding by saying: "When the great Tao [natural Way] declined, the doctrine of humanity and righteousness arose."[41] Lao Tzu is saying that artificial doctrines of virtue, humanity, and righteousness, doctrines that tell us how we ought to behave, arise only in unhealthy situations. Something is already terribly wrong when we tell a mother she ought to feed her child or that she has a duty to feed her child. Feeding one's child is a natural, caring response. Lao Tzu says: "When the six family relationships are not in harmony, there will be the advocacy of filial piety and deep love to children."[42]

Given that we live in and are inculcated into a patriarchal society, a society of rules, principles, and laws, do the Taoists have any suggestions as to how to break free from patriarchal modes of thought, how to return to a more natural and caring way of living in the world? As you might expect, the answer to this is yes. The Taoist position can be put in the following way: Moral reasoning is the product of a mind that discriminates and draws distinctions (between right and wrong, good and bad, just and unjust). According to Taoism, these categories and distinctions are artificial and conventional, not natural. To put oneself into a more natural state, which according to the Taoist view on human nature, would be a more caring state, one must undo, erase, or transcend all the conventional, artificial dualisms that have been inculcated into us. We perceive the world the way we have been taught to perceive the world. So, we must begin to unlearn the categories that have been programmed into us.

We unlearn these categories by emptying the mind. The process of emptying the mind is accomplished through a technique called meditation. Meditation is a practice through which the meditator quiets or stills the contents of the mind: the thoughts, the emotions, the desires, the inner chatter. Successful meditation culminates in the cessation of mental activity, a profound inner stillness.

Recall that Taoism teaches us to return to a more natural state, a state in which we are not controlled by the artificial modes of thought that have been inculcated into us by our society. The practice of meditation teaches us to control and still those modes of thought. By freeing ourselves from conventional ways of thinking, we return to a more natural state, a more caring state.

The relevance of this approach in ethics to criminal justice can be seen in the work of Bo Lozoff, Director of the Prison Ashram Project. Lozoff works with prisoners, teaching them techniques of meditation. Lozoff is "helping prisoners to use their cells as ashrams [places of spiritual growth], and do their time as 'prison monks' rather than convicts."[43] In his book *We're All Doing Time*, Lozoff has a chapter on meditation in which he describes and teaches a number of meditation techniques. Much of his work in prisons involves teaching these techniques to convicts.

Lozoff describes meditation as "sitting perfectly still—Silence of body, silence of speech and silence of mind. The Buddha called this 'The Noble Silence.' It's just a matter of STOPPING."[44] To connect this with Taoism, we might say that by achieving a state of inner silence in which we stop all the conventional modes of thinking and reasoning that have been inculcated into us, we return to a more natural state, a more caring state.

It goes without saying that caring is not the exclusive property of Taoism or Yoga. Mother Theresa, a recipient of the Nobel Peace Prize, encompasses this ethic of caring from a Christian perspective. She started her work as a one-woman mission in Calcutta, India, ministering to and caring for the dying. Generally speaking, in some ways we might consider the dying poor even more undesirable than incarcerated offenders. Yet Mother Theresa's Sisters of Charity have grown from a one-woman operation to active missions all over the world. When asked how she could emotionally handle constantly being around so many dying persons, she responded that when she looked into the eyes of the dying she saw "Christ in a distressing disguise."[45]

CONCLUSION

In this essay, we have surveyed four very different ethical theories: utilitarianism, deontology, connectedness, and caring. Each theory presents a different approach to moral problems. It is not the purpose of this essay to solve ethical issues in criminal justice. Rather, the point is to present a number of different theoretical perspectives from which we can consider the difficult issues in criminal justice. Criminal justice is not an isolated discipline disconnected from other systems of thought. Criminal justice is a branch of justice. And justice is a part of the larger discipline of value theory or ethics. The hope is that this essay will provide some tools which we can use in trying to understand and solve some of the tough ethical decisions facing our criminal justice system.[46]

NOTES

1. Lawrence W. Sherman, *The Study of Ethics in Criminology and Criminal Justice Curricula*, Chicago: Publications of the Joint Commission of Criminology and Criminal Justice Education and Standards, 1981, p.7.

2. Sherman, p. 30.

3. Sherman, p. 14.

4. In the *Metaphysics* (987b1), Aristotle states: "Now Socrates was engaged in the study of ethical matters but not at all in the study of nature as a whole, yet in ethical matters he sought the universal and was the first to fix his thought on definitions."

5. See Plato, *Laches* 191c, *Euthyphro* 5c-d, *Meno* 72a.

6. See Jeremy Bentham, *The Principles of Morals and Legislation* (Darien, Connecticut: Hafner Publishing Company, 1970); and John Stuart Mill, *Utilitarianism* (Indianapolis: Hackett Publishing Company, 1979).

7. Mill, p. 2.

8. Aristotle, *Nicomachean Ethics* 1095a15-20.

9. Mill, p. 37.

10. Mill, p. 7.

11. *Id.*

12. Bentham, p. 2.

13. Bentham, pp. 29-32.

14. Immanuel Kant, *Groundwork of the Metaphysic of Morals*, translated by H. J. Paton (New York: Harper and Row, 1964), p. 61.

15. Kant, pp. 65-67.

16. Kant, p. 88.

17. Matthew 7:12; Luke 6:31.

18. Kant, p. 95.

19. *Id.*

20. Kant, p. 96.

21. The entire letter can be found in Joseph Campbell, *The Power of Myth* (New York: Doubleday, 1988), pp. 32-35.

22. Bo Lozoff, *We're All Doing Time* (Durham, North Carolina: Hanuman Foundation, 1987), p. 11.

23. Alan Watts, *The Book* (New York: Random House, 1972), p.8.

24. Bo Lozoff, p. 9.

25. Plato, *Republic* 351d-352a.

26. Carl Cohen, *Civil Disobedience* (New York: Columbia University Press, 1971), p. 40.

27. Matthew 5:39.

28. Bo Lozoff, p. viii.

29. Richard Quinney, "Forward" in *Inner Corrections: Finding Peace and Peace Making,* by Bo Lozoff and Michael Braswell (Cincinnati: Anderson Publishing, 1989), p. vii.

30. Paul Reps, editor, *Zen Flesh, Zen Bones* (Garden City: Doubleday and Company), p. 41.

31. Matthew 5:40.

32. Matthew 5:44.

33. Romans 12:21. The entire passage 12:17-12:21 is relevant.

34. Nel Noddings, *Caring: A Feminine Approach to Ethics & Moral Education* (Berkeley: University of California Press, 1986), p. 1.

35. Noddings, p. 2.

36. *Id.*

37. Noddings, p. 3.

38. Noddings, p. 95.

39. Chuang Tzu, *Basic Writings* (New York: Columbia University Press, 1964), p. 37. The entire Section 2 is an extended commentary on this topic.

40. Lao Tzu, *The Way of Lao Tzu (Tao-te-Ching)* (Indianapolis: Bobbs-Merrill, 1963), p. 167.

41. Lao Tzu, p. 131.

42. *Id.*

43. Bo Lozoff, *We're All Doing Time,* p. xvii.

44. Bo Lozoff, *We're All Doing Time,* p. 29.

45. From the documentary film, *Mother Theresa,* directed by Richard Attenborough.

46. I would like to express my gratitude to Mickey Braswell, Hugh LaFollette, Dan Turner, Gail Stenstad, Wendie Jekabsons, and Kim Rogers for reading a previous version of this essay and providing helpful comments and suggestions for improvement.

INDIVIDUAL RIGHTS VS. SOCIAL UTILITY: THE SEARCH FOR THE GOLDEN ZIGZAG BETWEEN CONFLICTING FUNDAMENTAL VALUES

2

Dean J. Spader

Numerous practitioners, judges, researchers, and theorists have noted the existence of conflicts between fundamental values within law and criminal justice (Cardozo, 1928; Packer, 1968; Freund, 1968; Stein and Shand, 1974; Ely, 1978, 1980; Richards, 1981a, 1981b; Beardsley, 1982; Sherman, 1982; Walzer, 1931). These fundamental conflicts between opposite values appear to have at least four qualities. These conflicts seem to be

1) ancient, perhaps ageless and "eternal" conflicts (Pittman, 1960; Mill, 1959);
2) conflicts that involve opposing and logically inconsistent values (Adler, 1981:138);
3) inherent, inevitable, and essential conflicts (Cardozo, 1928); and
4) dynamic conflicts, in that they seem to "coexist in uneasy and perpetual tension, moving toward no natural equilibrium" (Feeley, 1983:150).

John Stuart Mill (1966) noted long ago the dynamism and necessity of these conflicts between opposite values and the need for an adversarial system in order to find truth, which lies in the balance:

Truth, in the great practical concerns of life, is so much a question of the reconciling and combining of opposites, that very few have the minds sufficiently capacious and impartial to make the adjustment with an approach to corrections, and it has to be made by the rough process of a struggle between combatants fighting under hostile banners. (p. 63)

The pattern of resolutions of these fundamental value conflicts within any justice system looks more like a golden zigzag than a golden mean.[1]

Klockars (1983:423), in his discussion of the "Dirty Harry Problem," used classical ethical theories to illustrate the moral dilemmas of police. Klockars concluded that these dilemmas are "insoluble." Dirty Harry's temptation to use dirty means (torture) to obtain good ends (saving a young girl's life) is an extreme example. The temptation to justify dirty means with just ends is a problem that does not only confront the police; rather, it is a temptation at the base of most all criminal justice debates. The purpose of the present article is to generalize from the means/end debate to the rights/utility question and show that most criminal justice issues are "insoluble" precisely because they involve key conflicts between conflicting fundamental values. The following examination of the individual rights vs. social utility conflict[2] as one of these unending conflicts includes

1) an outline of the conflict;
2) an analysis of the conflict;
3) a clarification of the conflict;
4) functions of the conflict;
5) types of conflicts;
6) trends and history of the conflict; and
7) the "rocks and shoals" of the conflict.

OUTLINE OF THE CONFLICT

The conflict between the rights and social utility theories suggests that both sides of the conflict protect fundamental values while simultaneously possessing fundamental weaknesses. In the present article, the strengths of each side are termed "positive values" and the weaknesses of each side "negative values." Figure 1 outlines some of the dichotomous positive and negative values associated with rights and utility. Figure 1 merely attempts to describe, and not prescribe, "two separate value systems that compete for priority in the operation of the criminal process" (Packer, 1968:153). Richards

(1981a:326) noted that "any serious philosophical controversy…rests on the assumption that one or the other must be right. And, both may be useful." Figure 1 does not suggest that one is right and the other not; rather, it suggests why there is a serious philosophical controversy, namely because each perspective represents opposite positive fundamental values and each perspective carries the baggage of opposite negative values. Most theorists use polemics. Polemics occur when, for example, an advocate of more rights argues all the positive values of rights (Box A) and all the negative values of utility (Box D). Conversely, utilitarian advocates of crime control argue all the positive values of utility (Box C) and all the negative values of criminal rights (Box B). Polemics, rather than honesty, prevails in criminal justice literature today. Figure 1 tries to avoid the polemics and show "the traditional antagonism between the natural rights and utilitarian positions" (Richards, 1981b:247).

ANALYSIS OF THE CONFLICT

Three relationships exist between the set of values listed in Figure 1:

a) the horizontal value-vs.-value relationship,
b) the vertical value-vs.-disvalue relationship, and
c) the crisscrossing relationship.

The first relationship is the horizontal conflict between opposite fundamental values, which hints at why the conflict is insoluble and the classical antagonism persists. Point for point, the two theories take counter perspectives that emphasize divergent values. Equally important, though rarely noted, the two theories have opposite weaknesses, which Figure 1 lists point for point in the negative values. In short, not only are the values conflicting, but the two theories have opposite disvalues also. Later, in the crisscrossing relationship, it will be noted how the strengths (values) of the one correct the weaknesses (disvalues) of the other.

The second relationship is the vertical relationship between positive values and negative values within each theory. If the horizontal relationship of value-vs.-value presents the hard cases, the vertical relationship of value-vs.-disvalue indicates the easy cases. Easy cases involve choices between jus-

Figure 2.1

<table>
<tr><td colspan="2" align="center">POSITIVE VALUES
(Arguments For)</td></tr>
<tr>
<td>

Box A
Individual Rights

Theme: "There is nothing in the world so sacred as the rights of others." *Kant*

1. Seeks more the Rights before the Good, Principle before Policy

2. Seeks more to Preserve Rights of Individual, Individualism

3. More Autonomy, Equal Respect for Integrity of Each Person, Person as the Sovereign End

4. More emphasis on Integrity of Acts, Dignity Analysis

5. Focus on more Just Means, Fair Procedure, more emphasis on Process, seeks more Fairness and Judicialization (Due Process Model)

6. More oriented to Past, Justice Based on Proof of Past Acts, emphasis on Reliability of Past and Present Facts, Factual Truth, Accurate Assessment of Responsibility, Proportionality

7. Seeks Justice as More Past-Oriented, Proportional, Fair, Consistent, Visible, Certain, Equal Treatment Under Rule of Laws

</td>
<td>

Box C
Social Utility

Theme: "Utility is the ultimate source of moral obligations." *J.S. Mill*

1. Seeks the Good as the Right, Policy as Principle

2. Seeks More to Promote the Good of Society, Holism

3. More Satisfaction, Happpiness, Pleasure of Whole Community, Group, or Society, Social Order as Sovereign End

4. More emphasis on Consequences of Acts, Cost-Benefit Analysis

5. Focus on More Effective Results, Good Consequences, More Emphasis on Consequences of Process, seeks more Efficiency and Efficacy (Crime Control Model)

7. Seeks Justice as more Future-Oriented, Predictive, Flexible, Creative, Equitable Treatment Under Discretionary Powers

</td>
</tr>
<tr><td colspan="2" align="center">NEGATIVE VALUES
(Arguments Against)</td></tr>
<tr>
<td>

Box B
Individual Rights

Theme: "As a matter of principle, it sacrifices the good of all for the sake of one."

1. Sacrifices Good of All for Rights of Few

2. Rights Worship, "Righteousness," Too Rigid, Principled, Harsh, Too Likely to Produce Wrong Results, the Right Without the Good

3. Sacrifices Just Results for Fair Means, Means Become the Ends, Excessive Proceduralism

4. Sacrifices Efficiency and Efficacy for more Reliability and Certainty, Relies Too Much on Proof of Past Acts Only

5. Too Little Concern for Potential Future Good of Acts

6. Too Complex, too many Conflicting Rights and Rules

</td>
<td>

Box D
Social Utility

Theme: "In the serpent windings of utilitarianism, the ends justify the means."

1. Sacrifices Rights of Few for Good of All

2. Too Little Respect for Individual Rights, Less Respect for Integrity and Autonomy of Each Person, the Good Without the Right

3. Sacrifices Fair Means for Good Consequences, Ends Justify Means, Gross Injustice

4. Sacrifices Reliability and Certainty for more Efficiency and Efficacy, relies too much on Prediction or Probable Future Outcomes

5. Too little concern for Desert and Obligations of Past Acts and Promises

6. Too Simple, Too Simple-Minded for Complexity of Social Reality

</td>
</tr>
</table>

tice and injustice, right and wrong, good and bad. When rights are described with only their positive values, the choice seems clearly to demand more rights for individuals; when rights are described with only their negative values, then the choice seems clearly to limit the scope of individual rights. The same is true of the social utility theory. In truth, values come with some baggage, namely their disvalues. Benefits carry some burdens. More due process rights create less efficiency. The exclusionary rule sacrifices just ends (conviction of a guilty person) to obtain just means (constitutional searches and seizures). Rights may become rigid righteousness; standing on principle may involve the sacrifice of good results, and creating more autonomy may endanger collective order. Recognition of the vertical relationship prevents naive absolutism. If something is good, more of it may not be better.

The third relationship is the most important and the least recognized by the literature. It is, in reality, two crisscrossing relationships between the positive values of one theory and the negative values of the other. Usually, theorists focus on only one of the crisscrossing relationships. Rights advocates are quick to note the positive values of rights and the negative values of social utility theories. Social utility theorists, on the other hand, expound the positive values of utility, stressing the negative values of too many rights. Figure 2 diagrams these common sophistic stances. The polemics in the debates between rights advocates and utilitarians reflect John Stuart Mill's observation that "very few have the minds sufficiently capacious and impartial" to approach the truth (Mill, 1966:63). F. Scott Fitzgerald noted the test many contemporary theorists fail: "The test of a first-rate intelligence is the ability to hold two opposed ideas in mind at the same time and still retain the ability to function" (quoted in Peters and Waterman, 1982:89).

The golden zigzag between the conflicting values represents the dynamic tendencies of officials and entire systems to shift back and forth on the rights/utility scale in search of the proper balance. Jenkins (1980) described the zigzag between more or less rights as having

> the profile of a ride on a seesaw, with its succession of ups and downs. Somewhat more exactly, there has been a series of expansions and contractions....The meaning of natural and legal rights was continually being redefined, their reach extended here, and withdrawn there, their emphasis shifted, and their content modified. (pp. 253-4).

The reason for the seesaw or, preferably, the golden zigzag, is that rights threaten those fundamental values utilitarians seek to promote. Jeremy Bentham, who fathered modern utilitarian theories, felt that "the word *right* is the greatest enemy of reason, and the most terrible destroyer of governments" (Bentham, 1950:85). The conflict is not only insoluble logically, but it should remain unresolved on a theoretical level. It is not only a productive conflict, but also an essential and necessary conflict, which sustains the search for the golden zigzag.

In summary, the strengths and weaknesses of individual rights are intimately intertwined with the strengths and weaknesses of social utility. Many of the strengths of rights (Box A) offset the weaknesses of utility (Box D), and the strengths of utility (Box C) offset the weaknesses of rights (Box B). The positive values of individual rights are the opposite of the negative values of social utility, and the positive values of social utility are the opposite of the negative values of individual rights. Each is strong precisely where the other is weak. Each answers the weaknesses of the other, and to that degree each obtains its justifications by its ability to offset the negative values of the other:

> Each of these modes of thinking derives its utility from the deficiencies of the other, but it is in a great measure the opposition of the other that keeps each within the limits of reason and sanity. (Mill, 1966:621)

Figure 2.2

Individual Rights	Social Utility
Box A Positive Values of Rights	Box C Positive Values of Utility
Box B Negative Values of Rights	Box D Negative Values of Utility

Each set of positive values conflicts with the other, but the limitations of each make the other possible. Each is to some degree the absence of the other, and to that extent, each illustrates John Stuart Mill's observation that we define something by its opposite. Each has its limits, which are imposed by the demands of the other, and the extreme advocacy of one set of values motivates the countervailing demands from the other. Paradoxically, each threatens to produce its negative values when freed from limits imposed by the other, but, equally paradoxically, each seems not likely to produce its positive values when limited by the other. Each provides a part of justice that must be delicately balanced with the other to produce the whole of justice. Each, when joined with the other, creates a

> pair of opposites,...which put tension into the world, a tension that sharpens man's sensitivity and increases his self-awareness. No real understanding is possible without awareness of these pairs of opposites which permeate everything man does. (Schumacher, 1977:127).

The rights/utility dichotomy[3] is one of the most fundamental pairs of opposites, though certainly not the only one (Spader, 1982; 1984).

CLARIFICATION OF THE CONFLICT: THE RIGHT VS. THE GOOD

Rawls (1977:24) noted that "the two main concepts of ethics are those of the right and the good." The conflict between rights and utility may be as simple as the age-old right means/good ends debate. Utilitarian thinking focuses on the ends (telos, hence teleology), goals, good, satisfaction, efficacy, pleasure, happiness, usefulness (hence utility), and consequences (hence, consequentialism) that might result from a particular action or decision. According to Brody (1983:10), "the basic thesis of this approach is that the rightness or wrongness of an action is based solely on the consequences of performing it; the right action is that which leads to the best consequences." In short, a utilitarian is future-oriented and relies on the prediction or probability of future results to determine the correctness of the present decision. Utilitarianism seeks the greatest good for the greatest number. The ends may justify the means if, after consideration of all possible alternatives, this particular means is the one that maximizes expected utility (sometimes defined as pleasure, preference, happiness, or satisfaction) for the most people. If the prediction of future consequences suggests more disutility (pain, unhappiness, dissatisfaction) than utility for the most people, then a utilitarian, theoretically, would declare the action wrong. To the extent that people are goal-oriented, planning beings, utility is appealing. To the extent that prediction and the use of probabilities is or is not possible, utilitarianism is a highly ambiguous and controversial theory (Brody, 1983).

On the other hand, rights-based advocates and ruled-based morality (deontology) tend to focus on the present means rather than the future consequences to determine whether an action is right or wrong.[4] In ethical theories, "rule-based morality (also called the deontological approach) proposes that an action is right if it conforms with a proper moral rule" even if the action does not provide the greatest good for the greatest number of people (Brody, 1983:24). In short, future social good does not always determine a decision. In legal/criminal justice theories, the means or process must be fair irrespective of the substantive results. Convicting an innocent person cannot be right even if the conviction obtains massive deterrence. Or, conversely, freeing a factually guilty offender and incurring disutility is necessary if illegal and unfair means that violate fundamental rights were used to convict him or her.[5] Fair means, usually equated with due process rights, limit the utilitarian's demand for the maximum social good (conviction and punishment of offenders and future deterrence of other potential offenders). If utilitarians focus on the results of decisions, rights advocates and deontologists focus on the process of decision-making. The one tends to be future-oriented, the other present-oriented. Utility uses prediction and probabilities; rights advocates demand rules or rights that require accurate proof of facts. If it is the goal of most due process rules to provide procedural rights that seek more accurate proof of facts, then Packer's due-process-model-vs.-crime-control-models are another version of the rights/utility conflict.

The degree to which a criminal justice official gives priority to fair means or future good in critical decisions may be the ultimate test to determine if he or she is a utilitarian or rights advocate. However, Sherman (1982:59) suggested that "at the level of specific decisions, it may even be appropriate to use different frameworks for different kinds of decisions." At the most critical level, the conflict between utility and rights may reduce itself to the conflict between the good and the right or, more particularly, the good of the community and the legal right of the individual. The following example will clarify the conflict. This example is an extreme situation, in which the choice is also extreme; however, it clearly illustrates the dilemma faced by practitioners of criminal justice in less extreme choices.

During his travels in another country, Bill happens to enter a city square at the time when a military firing squad is about to execute a dozen rebels who were randomly selected from among hundreds of rebels imprisoned without trial. The purpose of the execution is to deter other protestors and rebels against the local government. The commander of the execution squad sees Bill and decides the government can obtain more deterrence by having an American execute just one of the rebels. If Bill accepts the offer, only one rebel will be executed; the other eleven will be spared. If Bill refuses, all twelve will be executed. The crowd surrounding the execution is begging Bill to accept the offer. What should he do?

A utilitarian who seeks the greatest good for the greatest number theoretically will accept the offer and sacrifice one potentially innocent individual for the good of eleven others, their families, and (if he or she agrees with the purpose of the execution and prediction of the officer), the greater deterrence of the rebels. The consequences will be less drastic if only one individual dies, though that individual is being sacrificed for the "greater good" of the other rebels, the whole community, and its government. Fried (1978) stated the primary value and prioritization scheme of utilitarians:

> The category of the good is the single overriding moral category, identifying those states of affairs we should wish to obtain. All other moral concepts are secondary and derivative. Right and wrong are the derivative categories directing choice, but they do so under the sovereign mandate of the category of the good. (p. 7)

Once it is established that an innocent person must die for the greater social good, some utilitarians have few reservations about such sacrificial use of an innocent person. As long as it does not become the "practice" of society to punish innocent persons, the sacrifice of some innocent life is justified to save others.... One can imagine, for example, the execution of a single innocent scapegoat to appease those who hold many other innocent persons hostage and threaten them with certain death. Similarly, some lesser sacrifice also in the form of criminal punishment inflicted on an innocent person might be justifiable when it is the only way to avert some greater evil. (Gross, 1979:410)

Because utilitarianism is a complex term, not all utilitarians would agree that Bill ought to accept the offer; this example merely represents the extreme choices, and space does not allow a full discussion of the many intricacies of utilitarian thought.

A deontologist who seeks the right, and a rights advocate who prioritizes the rights of individuals, presumably would not accept the offer. If Bill prioritized the right, he would not sacrifice a potentially innocent person for the greater good. He would hold that there are some acts a person cannot commit, regardless of the consequences. Killing innocent people is one of those acts "...decent people shrink from, though great good might seem to come in particular cases from resorting to them" (Fried, 1978:7). Again, Fried (1978) graphically isolated the basic dichotomy:

The difference between the views is that consequentialism subordinates the right to the good, while for deontology the two realms, while related, are distinct. The goodness of the ultimate consequences does not guarantee the rightness of the actions which produced them. The two realms are not only distinct for the deontologist, but the right is prior to the good. (p. 9)

Later, Fried noted that "the theory of rights must have as one of its points of departure the notion that there are some things we may not do to each other, no matter what, some things that are categorically wrong" (p. 28). Thus, in Bill's dilemma the fundamental conflict appears in its most classical and generalized term—the good versus the right. Does justice seek the general good of the most people? Or does justice require doing what is right (and killing an innocent person is never right)?

Most theorists of justice choose either the right or the good and give priority to the one over the other. For example, Rawls (1971) clearly stated his position:

...In justice as fairness, the concept of right is prior to that of the good....This priority of the right over the good in justice as fairness turns out to be a central feature of the conception. (pp. 31-32)

Although Rawls clearly sought the right as his priority, Holmes (1881) noted that public policy often sacrifices individual rights and autonomy for the common good:

Public policy sacrifices the individual to the general good...and justice to the individual is outweighed by the larger interests on the other side of the scales. (p. 48)

For Holmes, the general good often had priority over individual rights. Murphy (1979) rather clearly stated the conflict:

What the utilitarian theory really cannot capture, I would suggest, is the notion of persons having rights ...The Kantian will maintain that the consequentialist outlook, important as it may be, leaves out of consideration entirely that which is most morally crucial— namely, the question of right...Marx, like Kant, seems prepared to draw the important distinction between (a) what it would be good to do on grounds of utility and (b) what we have a right to do. Since we do not always have the right to do what it would be good to do, this distinction is of the greatest moral importance; and missing the distinction is the Achilles heel of all forms of utilitarianism. (p. 560)

Thus the rights/utility conflict is at its core a conflict between the demands of the right and the good, the present process and the future consequences, proof of facts and prediction of facts.

FUNCTIONS OF THE CONFLICT

Although the criminal justice and jurisprudential literature is replete with isolated observations concerning the many conflicting values, goals, and interests inherent in the system, there is little or no theory concerning the productive potential of conflict. In fact, most observations about conflict reflect the author's belief that conflict is socially stultifying, administratively counter-productive, empirically unmeasurable, or ultimately destructive. Deutsch (1969) decried the pervasive focus on the destructive aspects of conflict and urged concentration on its many productive components.

I stress the positive functions of conflict,...because many discussions of conflict cast it in the role of the villain as though conflict per se were the cause of psychopathology, social disorder, war.... It has been long recognized that conflict is not inherently pathological or destructive. Its very pervasiveness suggests that it has many positive functions. (p. 19)

Despite the strong tendency of social science literature to be preoccupied with the negative aspects of conflict, many theorists have recognized that conflict can be "integrative" and "functional" (Coser, 1956, 1967; Horton, 1966), "beneficial," "unifying," "satisfying" (Simmel, 1955:17-19), "productive" (Deutsch, 1973:359-400), and "creative" (Dewey, 1930:300). The creative and productive potential of conflict has been described in business and management (Kelley, 1970), education (Tapp and Levine, 1977:174), labor (Kerr, 1954), intergroup relations (Dobson, 1958), community organization (Alinsky, 1971), protests and social movements, and numerous other past and present social institutions or processes (Storr, 1968).

If conflict has many positive functions, then it is ironic that there is little express theory dealing with the productive potential of conflict in the very institution in American society that was established to resolve value conflicts, namely the legal system, with its civil and criminal components. Alinsky (1971) had productive conflict in mind when he wrote:

Conflict is the essential core of a free and open society. If one were to protect the democratic way of life in the form of a musical score, its major theme would be the harmony of dissonance. (p. 62)

Perhaps theorists in criminal justice cannot be blamed if their emphasis has been more on harmony than dissonance, more on orderly consensus than on productive conflict, given the often overwhelming experience of destructive conflict and the social need to prevent it. Yet the experience of destructive conflict should not stop the search for the positive functions of conflict. There should be at least an initial recognition that the conflict of ideas, as opposed to the conflict involved in over physical actions, is one of these necessary and essential conflicts:

Conflict is the gadfly of thought. It stirs us to observation and memory. It instigates to invention. Conflict shocks us out of sleep-like passivity, and sets us at noting and contriving.... It is the *sine qua non* of reflection and ingenuity. (Dewey, 1930:300)

Cardozo (1921) argued that the very nature of the legal process entails strife between conflicting views of law and justice: "For every tendency, one seems to see a counter-tendency; for every rule its antinomy" (p. 28). Cardozo listed the many fundamental conflicts inherent in the legal process, and he illustrated how the path of the law is a zig and a zag between these opposites. For Cardozo, the "task of judging is found to be a choice between antithetical extremes" (1928:62). Legal concepts and logic are not the ends, only means that must be manipulated to obtain the continuous shifting between the good and the right: "There is nothing new in this notion of subordination of legal concepts to expediency and justice" (p. 64). There is a temptation to seek a definitive solution by fleeing the conflict and retreating to one side of the polar extremes, obtaining certainty by aggrandizing its positive values and denigrating the negative values of the opposing side. Such tactics are simplistic solutions for immature minds or the tools of sophistic advocates; they are not the path to mature, creative decisionmaking. In those areas in which fundamental opposites clash, the range of choice is large and the judgment

> might be decided either way....Here come into play the balancing of judgment, that testing and sorting of considerations of...*utility and fairness*, which I have been trying to describe....I sought for certainty. I was oppressed and disheartened when I found that the quest for it was futile. I was trying to reach land, the solid land of fixed and settled rules....As the years have gone by, and as I have reflected more and more upon the nature of the judicial process, I have become reconciled to the uncertainty, because I have grown to see it as inevitable. I have grown to see that the process in its highest reaches is not discovery, but *creation*. (Cardozo, 1921:165-6, emphasis added)

Early in his classic work, Cardozo had noted: "Justice and general utility, such will be the two objectives that will direct our course" (1921:75; quoting Geny). Therefore, in his own eloquent fashion, Cardozo elaborated on the conflicting positive values underlying the individual rights ("justice") and social good dichotomy, and he concluded that often the conflict "in its highest reaches" demands creativity. Conflict produces creativity. Fundamental opposites clash and are reconciled (for the moment) in the present decision.

In summary, some types of conflict have a productive, creative function. Conflicts between "opposing opposites," each of which protect fundamental values, certainly may be of this type. Yet, before the creativity can emerge, it seems that decisionmakers must abide in the conflict and not flee it in search of certainty and certitude. Recognizing and remaining in the conflict takes courage. It is not coincidence that Rollo May (1975) titled his recent book on creativity *The Courage to Create*. In it, he noted that "the creative act is such an encounter between two poles" (p. 89). If creativity for the individual emerges from the encounter between dichotomous poles, then perhaps creativity, and life itself, involves the continuing encounter between conflicting opposites. "Everywhere society's health depends on the simultaneous pursuit of mutually opposed activities or aims" (Schumacher, 1977:127). Likewise, the health of the criminal justice system depends on the simultaneous promotion of polar opposites.

TYPES OF CONFLICTS: IN-KIND CONFLICTS AND CONFLICTS OF DEGREE

John Stuart Mill (1959:465) noted the tendency to define something "by its opposite." This tendency to create competing value systems (Packer, 1968), competing models of paradigms (Kuhn, 1970; Fletcher, 1972), or competing dichotomies and dualities exists in the legal and criminal justice system. Meador (1980) described a number of these "yins and yangs" and noted that "these dualities, if not eternal, have long appeared in Anglo-American history" (p. 122). Pittman (1960:873) termed them "eternal conflicts," and Cardozo (1928) titled his classic work *The Paradoxes of Legal Science* because at the core of most legal issues "fundamental opposites clash" (p. 5). For Cardozo, the real purpose of the legal system was the reconciliation of these ancient fundamental value conflicts:

> The reconciliation of the irreconcilable, the merger of antithesis, the synthesis of opposites, these are the great problems of the law.... We fancy ourselves to be dealing with some ultra-modern controversy, the product of the clash of interests in an industrial society. The problem is laid bare, and at its core are the ancient mysteries crying out for understanding....(p. 4)

The tendency to define something by its opposite, or to dichotomize and polarize conflicting models, is pervasive. The use of in-kind conflicts, or conflicts involving opposites of some kind, may be inherent to the nature of language and learning, and the understanding of this tendency to dichotomize may be essential to understanding the pursuit of justice. Human beings may not fully know a concept until its in-kind opposite is also fully comprehended. A complete understanding of justice, then, may require a complete understanding of the dichotomies underlying most fundamental issues.

Our neural systems seem better adapted to the binary program of yes-no responses than to the responses of yes/but or no/but.... Learning the law is not merely learning principles. In fact, we do not really "know" a principle until we know its opposing principles.... Legal thinking requires a resolution in the individual mind and encourages the finding of solutions that transcend, as by synthesis, the polar opposites of a debate.

This process is not easy, but on its cultivation may depend the pursuit of justice in society. (Freund, 1977:159)

Dichotomies are efficiency devices; they simplify vastly complex aspects of reality into two abstract terms or sets of terms. This simplifying, efficiency function of dichotomies perhaps explains their pervasiveness in our language. Dichotomies are present not only in descriptions and explanations of the physical world (e.g., up-down, in-out, black-white, front-back, and so on ad infinitum), but also in descriptions and explanations of the social world, including the philosophical and legal social world. Justice Cardozo (1928:132) concluded that "dichotomy is everywhere." Perhaps it is that dichotomies are everywhere because they are the efficient means to simplify complex issues. In this sense, then, the rights/utility issue is one of those fundamental dichotomies.

Although it is important, perhaps essential, to understand the opposite concepts contained in dichotomous models, it is also dangerous to stop there. Dichotomous models, often called paradigms (Kuhn, 1970), are distortions of reality because they are abstractions from reality. According to Packer:

There is a risk in an enterprise of this sort that is latent in any attempt to polarize. It is, simply, that values are too various to be pinned down to yes-or-no answers. (1968:153)

Between the opposites lies a continuum of degrees that may describe potentially infinite sets of variations or mixtures of the in-kind opposites. This continuum has various names; Packer (1968:153) calls it a "spectrum between the extremes." In the present article it is a "continuum of degrees" between "in-kind opposites." Figure 2.3 illustrates the in-kind dichotomies and the continuum of degrees between the in-kind opposites in the rights/utility conflict. Figure 2.3 does not purport to describe the amount of rights/utility considerations in any system, nor does it prescribe how much rights or utility ought to exist in any circumstance or system. That task lies far beyond the limitations of this article. Figure 2.3 merely schematizes Justice Cardozo's conclusions about degrees in decisionmaking.

> Our survey of judicial methods teaches us, I think, the lesson that the whole subject matter of jurisprudence is more plastic, more malleable, the moulds less definitely cast, the foundation of right and wrong less preordained and constant than most of us, without the aid of some analysis, have been accustomed to believe. We draw our little lines, and they are hardly down before we blur them. As in time and space, so here. Divisions are working hypotheses, adopted for convenience. We are tending more and more toward an appreciation of the truth that, after all, there are few rules: there are chiefly standards and degrees....So also the duty of a judge becomes itself a question of degree....If this seems a weak and inconclusive summary, I am not sure that the fault is mine. (1921:161)

If it is important to "become fully aware of these pairs of opposites" (Schumacher, 1977:127), it is also important to develop an awareness of the degrees of mixtures, because most conflicting values are limited by their opposites. The process of decisionmaking, especially in the legal and criminal justice system, is a process of balancing, synthesizing, or reconciling these opposing values. Often a resolution is in the form of a delicate synthesis that allows degrees of both sets of values.

Figure 2.3

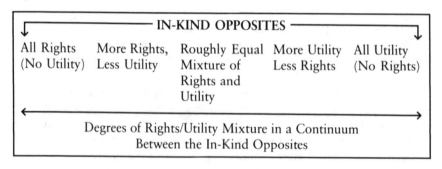

	IN-KIND OPPOSITES			
All Rights (No Utility)	More Rights, Less Utility	Roughly Equal Mixture of Rights and Utility	More Utility Less Rights	All Utility (No Rights)

Degrees of Rights/Utility Mixture in a Continuum
Between the In-Kind Opposites

Trend and History of the Conflict

A number of theorists have noted or advocated the recent shift in the philosophy of government from varying forms of utilitarianism to the advocacy of a rights perspective (Rawls, 1971; Dworkin, 1978; Fletcher, 1972, 1978; Hart, 1979; Richards, 1981b). Richards (1981b:247) noted that "we are in the midst of a major philosophical shift from…seeking the utilitarian goal of the greatest happiness of the greatest number to a natural law concern for rights." H.L.A. Hart (1979) pointed out that in England and the United States

> We are currently witnessing, I think, the progress of a transition from a once widely accepted old faith that some form of utilitarianism, if only we could discover the right form, *must* capture the essence of political morality. The new faith is that the truth must lie not with a doctrine that takes the maximisation of aggregate or average general welfare for its goal, but with a doctrine of basic human rights, protecting specific basic liberties and interests of individuals, if only we could find some sufficiently firm foundation for such rights to meet some long familiar objections. Whereas not so long ago great energy and much ingenuity of many philosophers were devoted to making some form of utilitarianism work, latterly such energies and ingenuity have been devoted to the articulation of theories of basic rights. (p. 77)

The philosophical transition certainly has its match in the legal growth of rights advocacy in many phases of the criminal justice system (von Hirsch, 1976; Palmer, 1977; Way, 1980). The philosophical and practical transition from emphasis on utilitarianism to a rights perspective is not total (some rights advocates would argue that it is in minor increments), and the present complexity exists precisely because there is an immense variety in the mixture of utility and rights in the many phases of the many criminal justice systems of the United States. In any case, the present transition reflects many historical characteristics of the conflict between utility and rights (Sidgwick, 1907; Bentham, 1950; Kant, 1959, 1965).

Commentators on legal developments and philosophers have pointed out at least five characteristics of the rights/utility conflict: its agelessness, its necessity, its contradictory nature, its many protean forms or its complexity, and its dynamism.

In 1863, when John Stuart Mill wrote *Utilitarianism*, the first observation he made concerned the agelessness of the conflict between utility and "popular morality":

From the dawn of philosophy, the question concerning...the foundation of morality,...has occupied the most gifted intellects, and divided them into sects and schools, carrying on a vigorous warfare against one another. And after more than two thousand years the same discussions continue, and philosophers are still ranged under the same contending banners, and neither thinkers nor mankind at large seem nearer to being unanimous on the subject, than when the youth Socrates listened to the old Protagoras and asserted...the theory of utilitarianism against the popular morality....(Mill, 1959:445)

The agelessness of the conflict reflects two other characteristics—its necessity and its logically inconsistent nature.

Most philosophers and practitioners who have studied the rights/utility issue have concluded that it contains "two radically conflicting moral theories" (Brody, 1983:8) or have concluded at least that "some conflicts between retributivism and utilitarianism are not resolvable" (Wertheimer, 1976:198). In his classic essay entitled "Two Concepts of Rules," Rawls (1955) stated "these two competing views very roughly to make one feel the conflict between them: one feels the force of both arguments and one wonders how they can be reconciled" (p. 4). However, not one single theorist has concluded that the value conflict itself is necessary or essential to either a complete moral theory or a complete understanding of criminal justice. Theorists from other disciplines have recognized the productive and constructive potential of conflict and have recognized that fundamental values are necessarily conflicting. For example, Williams (1979:222) stated, "It is my view, as it is Isaiah Berlin's, that value-conflict is not necessar[il]y pathological at all, but sometimes *necessarily involved in human values* and to be taken as *central by any adequate understanding of them*" (emphasis added).

Monists, who believe that a moral theory can reduce value conflicts to one monolithic principle or a logically consistent set of principles, find the thought of pluralistic conflicting values threatening because "one can easily feel pulled sometimes one way and sometimes the other" (Smart and Williams, 1973:73). Dualists, on the other hand, such as Cardozo (1928) and Williams (1979), believe that at the essential core of moral and legal conflicts lie value paradoxes. G.K. Chesterton once defined a paradox as a truth standing on its head trying to get attention. Dualists recognize the upright value that the majority may favor, but they also give some attention to its dichotomous opposite, which has been stood on its head.

Finally, the history of the rights/utility conflict indicates a variety of protean forms in which the conflict arises. Most theorists tolerate degrees of both perspectives but give priority to rights over utility or utility over rights. Therefore, most theorists recognize that the conflict is one of degrees (priorities), not dichotomy. Because the balance between utility and rights can be struck in numerous ways, there are many different rights perspectives and many different utilitarian perspectives (Brody, 1983; Narvesan, 1967). Yet, despite this complexity, most all theorists recognize and "agree on the basic theoretical framework that supports each approach to the criminal justice system" (Brody, 1983:66). In short, there are two conflicting approaches with numerous variations on the two approaches.

For purposes of clarification, a few of the many sets of dichotomous terms that characterize the rights/utility debate are listed below. At the risk of simplifying complex and subtle distinctions, these dichotomous sets are listed merely to make the point that many contemporary debates are rooted in the values underlying the rights/utility conflict. With the caveat that the relationship is not always identical, it is suggested that the following sets of dichotomous terms reflect the same conflict involved in the rights/utility issue:

1. Rights vs. Utility (Feinberg, 1970; Hart, 1979; Richards, 1981b).
2. Rule-Based Morality vs. Consequentialism (Brody, 1983).
3. Precedent vs. Instrumentalism (Summers, 1982).
4. "Justice" vs. Utilitarianism (von Hirsch, 1976; Fogel, 1975).
5. Deontology vs. Teleology (Brody, 1983).
6. Fairness vs. Expediency (Fletcher, 1972; Fogel and Hudson, 1981).
7. Conscience vs. Convenience (Rothman, 1980).
8. Retributivism vs. Utilitarianism (Rawls, 1955).
9. Due Process vs. Crime Control (Packer, 1968).

It is important to recognize the relationship between rules and rights, precedent and "justice," due process and fairness. Likewise, it is important to recognize the relationships among terms that are closely synonymous with utility, such as consequentialism, instrumentalism, teleology, efficacy. The point is that the philosophical/moral terms are closely related to the legal/criminal justice terms, and any practitioner or theorist in criminal justice should take note of the many terms that represent various perspectives on each side of the conflicting dichotomy. "If life feels the tug of these opposing opposites, so also must the law which is to prescribe the rule of life" (Cardozo, 1928:7).

In summary, the rights/utility conflict is just one of many fundamental value conflicts underlying criminal justice, and by all accounts it is one of the most central. In its logical form, the conflict is ageless, essential, paradoxical, complex, and dynamic. The dynamism of the issue is not about to subside, nor should it. The rights/utility conflict is a divergent problem. According to Schumacher,

> Divergent problems cannot be killed; they cannot be solved in the sense of establishing a "correct formula"....Divergent problems offend the logical mind, which wishes to remove tension by coming down on one side or the other....Divergent problems call not for new inventions but for the development of man's higher faculties and their application. (1977:127,131)

The real need is not to resolve the rights/utility conflict but to understand it at levels of comprehension beyond logic.

THE "ROCKS AND SHOALS" OF THE CONFLICT

This article began with a reference to Klockar's (1983) discussion of "The Dirty Harry Problem," which illustrated the classic rights/utility conflict. Klockars ended his discussion by stating that the danger lies "in thinking that one has found a way to escape a dilemma which is inescapable" (p. 428). Likewise, H.L.A. Hart (1980:60) warned, "Surely if we have learned anything from the history of morals, it is that the thing to do with a moral quandary is not to hide it." More importantly, both Hart (1979) and Klockars (1983) concluded that although a final resolution has not been achieved, a great deal can be learned by "examining some failed solutions" (Klockars, 1983:428). Hart's (1979) conclusion was somewhat more perspicacious:

> So in the rough seas which the philosophy of political morality is presently crossing between the old faith in utilitarianism and the new faith in rights, perhaps these writers' [Nozick and Dworkin] chief and very considerable service is to have shown, by running up against them, some of the rocks and shoals to be avoided, but not where the safe channels lie for a prosperous voyage. That still awaits discovery. (p. 97)

Klockar's and Hart's admonitions were quite simple yet quite elusive— becoming aware of the essential conflict between rights and utility is important to avoid the rocks and shoals upon which some practitioners (in Klockar's article, the police) or some advocates (in Hart's article, the theorists) have imperiled themselves.

Bodenheimer (1979:156) correctly noted that "genuine compromises between conflicting values presuppose an approximate parity of rank for these values." The underlying assumption of the present article is that greater awareness of logically conflicting values will lead to better, more balanced decisionmaking at any point in time when a rights/utility value conflict must be "compromised" or "resolved" by a decision, whether that decision is made by police officers, prosecutors, judges, corrections officials, legislators, or any other governmental official. The empirical claim is that many official decisions are choices somewhere on the rights-to-utility scale, and therefore official decisions are either promoting or not promoting the values underlying rights or utility. In this sense, all decisions are decisions carrying value choices. If this claim is correct, then no rights or utility-guided decision is value-free nor made in a value void. Impartiality may exist as to persons or issues that are subjects of a decision, but partiality is inherent in the values promoted by rights or utility. Because every rights/utility decision is, then, partial to one set of positive values and not the other set of positive values, the danger is not only that the decision may not be the proper balance for a particular problem at a particular point in time, but also that even if any such resolution is optimal, it will not, if institutionalized or regularized, continue to be such. Like democracy, the rights/utility issue requires eternal vigilance. Or, to paraphrase Klockars, the real danger in the rights/utility conflict is never in how it is resolved in a particular problem but "in thinking that one has found a resolution with which one can truly live in peace" (1983:438). The needs leading to golden zigs may in time produce greater needs demanding golden zags. The scales of justice may find a temporary resting place that produces a good balance for that point in time, but the dynamic nature of society and the criminal justice system will continually require new balancings. Enduring conflicts require enduring creativity.

REFERENCES

Adler, M. (1981). *Six great ideas.* New York: Macmillan Publishing Co.

Alinsky, S. (1971). *Rules for radicals.* New York: Random House. Beardsley, D. (1982). The ethics of mandatory sentencing. In *Ethics, public policy, and criminal justice,* ed. F. Elliston and N. Bowie. Cambridge, MA.: Oelgeschlager, Gunn and Hain.

Bentham, J. (1950). *The theory of legislation.* London: Routledge and Kegan Paul.

Bodenheimer, E. (1979). Compromise in the realization of ideas and values. In *Compromise in ethics, law, and politics,* ed. J. Pennock and J. Chapman. New York: New York University Press.

Bonnicksen, A. (1982). *Civil rights and liberties.* Palo Alto, CA: Mayfield Publishing Co.

Brody, B. (1983). *Ethics and its applications.* New York: Harcourt Brace Javanovich, Inc.

Cardozo, B. (1921). *The nature of the judicial process.* New Haven: Yale University Press.

———— (1928). The paradoxes of legal science. Westport, CT: Greenwood Press.

Coser, L. (1956). *The functions of social conflict.* New York: Free Press.

———— (1967). *Continuities in the study of social conflict.* New York: Free Press.

Crump, D. (1979). Determinate sentencing: The promises and perils of sentence guidelines. *KY Law J.* 68:1-100.

Deutsch, M. (1969). Conflicts: Productive and destructive. *Intergroup Rel* 25:7-41.

———— (1973). *The resolution of conflict: Constructive and destructive processes.* New Haven, CT: Yale University Press.

Dewey, J. (1930). *Human nature and conduct.* New York: The Modern Library.

Dobson, D. (1960). The creative role of conflict examined. *Intergroup Rel* 6:5-32.

Dworkin R. (1978). *Taking rights seriously.* Cambridge, MA: Harvard University Press.

Ely, J. (1978). On discovering fundamental values. *Harv Law R* 92:5-55.

———— (1980). *Democracy and distrust.* Cambridge: Harvard University Press.

Feeley, M. (1983). *Court reform on trial: Why simple solutions fail.* New York: Basic Books.

Feinberg, J. (1970). The nature and value of rights. *The Value Inq* 4:243-57.

Fletcher, G. (1972). Fairness and utility in tort theory. *Harv Law R* 85:537-73.

_____ (1978). *Rethinking criminal law*. Boston: Little, Brown and Company.

Fogel, D. (1975). *"We are the living proof": The justice model for corrections*. Cincinnati: Anderson Publishing Co.

Fogel, D., and Hudson, J., eds. (1981). *Justice as fairness: Perspectives on the justice model*. Cincinnati: Anderson Publishing Co.

_____ (1968). *On law and justice*. Cambridge, MA: Harvard University Press.

Fried, C. (1978). *Right and wrong*. Cambridge, MA: Harvard University Press.

Gross, H. (1979). *A theory of criminal justice*. New York: Oxford University Press.

Harris, M. (1975). Disquisition on the need for a new model for criminal sanctioning systems. *W Va Law R* 77:283-325.

Hart, H.L.A. (1979). Between utility and rights. In *The idea of freedom*, ed. A. Ryan. Oxford: Oxford University Press.

_____ (1980). Positivism and the separation of law and morals. In *Philosophy of Law*, ed. J. Feinberg and M. Gross. Belmont, CA: Wadsworth.

Holmes, O.W. (1881). *The common law*. Boston: Little, Brown and Co.

Horton, J. (1966). Order and conflict theories of social problems as competing ideologies. *Am J Sociol* 71:701-13.

Jenkins, I. (1980). *Social order and the limits of the law*. Princeton, NJ: Princeton University Press.

Kant, I. (1959). *Foundations of the metaphysics of morals*. Trans. L. W. Beck. Indianapolis: Bobbs-Merrill.

_____ (1965). *The metaphysical elements of justice*. Trans. J. Ladd. Indianapolis: Bobbs-Merrill.

Kelly, J. (1970). Make conflict work for you. *Harv Bus Rev* (July) 103-13.

Kerr, C. (1954). Industrial conflict and its resolution. *Am J Sociol* 60:230-45.

Klockars, C. (1983). *Thinking about police: Contemporary readings*. New York: McGraw-Hill.

Kuhn, T. (1970). *The structure of scientific revolutions*. (2nd ed.) New York: Basic Books.

May, R. (1975). *The courage to create*. New York: Bantam Books.

Meador, P. (1980). Some yins and yangs of our judicial system. *Am Bar Assn J* 66:122.

Mill, J.S. (1959). On the connection between justice and utility. In *Great books of the western world*, ed. R. Hutchins. (vol. 43) Chicago: Encyclopedia Britannica.

_____ (1966). On liberty. In *John Stuart Mill: A selection of his works*, ed. J. Robson. New York: Odyssey Press.

Murphy, J. (1979). *Retribution, justice, and therapy.* Hingham, MA; Reidel Publishing Co.

Narvesan, J. (1967). *Morality and utility.* Baltimore: Johns Hopkins Press.

Nozick, R. (1974). *Anarchy, state, and utopia.* New York: Basic Books.

Packer, H. (1968). *The limits of the criminal sanction.* Stanford: Stanford University Press.

Palmer, J. (1977). *Constitutional rights of prisoners.* Cincinnati: Anderson Publishing Co.

Peters, T., and Waterman, R. (1982). *In search of excellence.* New York: Warner Books.

Pittman, R. (1960). Equality versus liberty: The eternal conflict. *Am Bar Assn J* 46:873-90.

Rawls, J. (1971). *A theory of justice.* Cambridge: Harvard University Press.

—— (1955). Two concepts of rules. *Philos Rev* 64:3-13. Richards, D. (1981a). Moral philosophy and the search for fundamental values in constitutional law. *Ohio State Law J* 42:319- 33.

—— (1981b). Rights, utility, and crime. In *Crime and justice: An annual review of research* (Vol. 3), ed. M. Tonry and N. Morris. Chicago: University of Chicago.

Rothman, D. (1980). *Conscience and convenience: The asylum and its alternatives in progressive America.* Boston: Brown and Co. Saltzburg, S. (1980). Foreword: The ebb and flow of constitutional criminal procedure in the Warren and Berger courts. *Georgetown Law J* 69:151-209.

Schumacher, E. (1977). *A guide for the perplexed.* New York: Harper and Row.

Sidgwick, H. (1907). *The methods of ethics.* London: MacMillan.

Sherman, L. (1982). *Ethics in criminal justice education.* Hastings-on-Hudson, NY: The Hastings Center, Institute of Society, Ethics, and Life Sciences.

Silver, M. (1976). *Values education.* Washington, DC: National Education Association.

Simmel, G. (1955). *Conflict and the web of group affiliation.* Glenco, IL: Free Press.

Singer, R.G. (1979). *Just deserts: Sentencing based on equality and deserts.* Cambridge, MA: Ballinger Publishing Co.

Smart, J.J.C., and Williams, B. (1973). *Utilitarianism, for and against.* Cambridge: Cambridge University Press.

Spader, D. (1982). Criminal sentencing and punishment: The search for the golden zigzag. *S D L Rev* 28:1-52.

_____ (1984). Rule of law vs. rule of man: The search for the golden zigzag between conflicting fundamental values. *J Crim Just* 12:379-94.

Stein, P., and Shand, J. (1974). *Legal values in western society.* Chicago: Aldine Publishing Co.

Storr, A. (1968). *Human aggression.* New York Bantam Books.

Summers, R. (1982). *Instrumentalism and American legal theory.* Ithaca, NY: Cornell University Press.

Tapp, J., and Levine, F. (1977). *Law, justice and the individual in society.* New York: Holt Rinehart and Winston.

von Hirsch, A. (1976). *Doing justice: The choice of punishments.* New York: Hill and Wang.

Walzer, M. (1983). *Spheres of justice: A defense of pluralism and equality.* New York: Basic Books.

Walker, N. (1980). *Punishment, danger and stigma: The morality of criminal justice.* Totowa, NJ: Barnes and Noble Books.

Way, H. (1980). *Criminal justice and the American constitution.* Belmont, CA: Wadsworth Publishing Co.

Wertheimer, A. (1976). Deterrence and retributism. *Ethics: An International Journal of Social, Political, and Legal Philosophy* 86:181-99.

Williams, B. (1979). Conflict of values. In *The idea of freedom,* ed. A. Ryan. Oxford: Oxford University Press.

Zalman, M. (1977). The rise and fall of the indeterminate sentence. *Wayne L. Rev* 24:45-95.

NOTES

1. The more dynamic terms "zig and zag" or "zigzag" are used rather than "the golden mean." The term "zigzag" is closely synonymous with other such terms as "ebb and flow" (Saltzburg, 1980:161), "rise and fall" (Zalman, 1977:45), "yin and yang" (Meador, 1980), "promises and perils" (Crump, 1979), "seesaw" (Jenkins, 1980:253), "wavy line" (Bonnicksen, 1982:55-6), all of which point out the dynamic, shifting, oscillating movement between polarities.

2. Utility has been deliberately qualified with the adjective "social" in order to avoid the inclusion of individual utilitarianism, which in its most pejorative sense is a form of hedonistic egoism (Brody, 1983:15) and in its most praise-worthy sense is a form of heroic altruism. John Stuart Mill detested the former, calling it "a doctrine worthy only of swine" (1959:448) and advocated the latter, believing it was epitomized in "the golden rule of Jesus of Nazareth" and urging "in human beings the power of sacrificing their own greatest good for the good of others" (p.453-4). Social utility, on the other hand, focuses on the collective of individuals, and in its earliest reformist stages favored a strict form of equal treatment, "Each to count as one and only one." Throughout this article, the term "utility" refers to social utilitarianism, not individual utilitarianism.

3. It should be noted that the rights/utility conflict has many overlapping similarities with the law/discretion conflict (Spader, 1984). The most obvious is the movement in the United States to protect rights, whether they are natural rights, religious rights, human rights, personal rights, civil rights, political rights, women's rights, prisoner's rights, and so on, by making them legal rights, which backs them with the force of law. In other words, the rights perspective and "justice model" find their counterpart in the rule of law, and the utilitarian perspective tends to favor rule of man or discretion to accomplish the future good of society. In criminal justice, the latter usually seeks the discretionary flexibility to stop and frisk, interrogate, preventively detain, use diversion or rehabilitative methods, and so on (Spader, 1982, 1984).

4. In their development and their meaning, rule-based moralities and rights-based theories are not synonymous. Theorists who believe there are no natural or moral rights limit the use of the word "rights" to legal rights. There is not space in this article to discuss the debate between the natural law advocates of moral rights and the positivists' attempt to limit rights to the legal realm. Also, the concept of rights is rather recent, but it finds many of its origins and justifications in the rule-based moralities. In short, rights-based theories may be rule-based, but not all rule-based moralities are rights-based, because many rule-based moralities preceded the concept of rights. The former is ageless, not the latter.

5. For an extensive bibliography, see Nichol, J. (1982) Bibliographical Update/The Nature and Foundations of Rights. *Criminal Justice Ethics* 1:64-69.

I.
INTRODUCTION—
QUESTIONS AND SCENARIOS

CHAPTER ONE

1. Gold's description of the ethics of caring and the principles of Taoism indicate that once we have begun arguing about moral issues, we have already lost touch with our natural caring selves. How do you feel about the relationship between reasoning and morality? Is is possible to reason what is right or must a sense of "right" come from within?

2. If a sense of right comes naturally from within, does this mean that man/woman is basically good?

3. What types of factors would make a person (or a society) lose touch with the caring that Taoists view as natural? Which of these factors are especially relevant to criminal justice decision-making?

4. Bo Lozoff indicates that if a person has lost touch with natural caring, this ability can be restored through meditation. What is your assessment of this approach to rehabilitation? What kind of evidence would you want to see to assess the program's effectiveness?

5. How could the principles of connectedness influence decision-making in criminal justice, in areas such as arrest and detention and the development of alternative sentencing programs?

CHAPTER TWO

1. Spader writes that all decisions are decisions carrying value choices. On the whole, do the values underlying decision-making in the criminal justice system tend to reflect more of a concern for rights or utility?

2. Consider the issue of pretrial release, that is, the release of arrested persons prior to trial. Describe the rights/utility conflict that surrounds decision-making in this area. Spader indicates that such conflicts can be productive and creative. Identify the potentially positive outcomes of a debate on the issue of pretrial release.

3. Do you think individuals have a tendency to make decisions based primarily on one set of values or the other (e.g., rights/utility) or do people pick and choose their ethical foundations to suit particular arguments? Is consistency something to be valued in this regard?

4. Do most people try to reason right from wrong in their efforts to make difficult decisions, or do other issues play a greater role? Is this process any different today than it was 50 or 100 years ago?

5. What is the value of reading about and discussing ethical issues? to change values? to clarify values? Do people with a clearer set of values make different decisions than those with "muddled" values? Can you give an example from your own life that illustrates your view on this matter?

SCENARIOS

1. The United States is currently confronting a drug crisis. While drug use in the general population seems to be declining, drug use and sales among criminals is continuing to increase. Some citizens are calling for stiffer penalties for illegal drug use while others are calling for decriminalization, even legislation of certain drugs. Suppose you were a staff assistant to a congressman whose committee was investigating the ethics of drug control policy. What issues would be relevant to this assessment? How could a morally correct approach to drug-crime policy be developed? Whose rights would have to be protected? What societal benefits and deficits would you consider? How could this policy be developed in a way that promoted caring and concern for all in society?

2. You are the Police Chief in a very large city. Your investigators have been trying to track down a serial killer who has been on a rampage for about three months. To date, the total dead is 15 young women. Your officers have a man in custody who fits the bill. He has several non-violent crimes to his credit and fits the description of the killer you have received from what few witnesses you have. The media is pushing hard for his conviction. The public wants somebody behind bars. Your gut tells you the guy is guilty but not of this crime. He just isn't the type. You feel certain that he would be convicted if prosecuted. The public, your superiors, and the media are breathing down your neck. What do you do?

3. You have just been convicted of a crime you didn't commit. You know who did commit the crime and you also know that person framed you. You have been sentenced to 20 years in a maximum security prison with a chance of parole after having served seven of those years. Of course, there are appeals, but with the way your luck has been running you can't count on them being successful. You have heard of situations like this happening, but you never thought it would happen to you. What are your options from a legal and personal standpoint?

II. ETHICAL ISSUES IN POLICING

Police work has been called a "morally dangerous" endeavor, and with good reason. Not only are the temptations faced by the average patrol officer much greater than those confronted in other occupations, but the nature of the work itself requires activities that can easily cross over the line from acceptable to unethical conduct.

Police corruption is a broad area of concern. For some observers it includes everything from the simple acceptance of a free meal from a small business owner, to the receipt of kickbacks from attorneys and tow truck drivers, to police-organized theft.

Many of the problems of police corruption are linked to the tremendous amount of discretion possessed by the patrol officer. Most of us would agree that it is sometimes acceptable to use this discretion to avoid giving a ticket or making an arrest. When good judgment determines that no action is necessary or there are other means of addressing the problem, discretion is clearly being put to good use. But, when these decisions are influenced by offers of money, drugs or sexual favors, the use of discretion becomes tainted, and the actions corrupt.

Situations confronting police officers offer temptations of their own. The money found on a drunk, the cash and drugs found at the scene of a crime—

these can tempt officers who are on their honor to report what they find. In the area of narcotics control, such temptations are always present.

There are still other dilemmas confronting the police officer who does not give in to the temptations of corruption. In many ways, crime control efforts foster an "ends justifies the means" mentality. To the extent that due process guarantees are seen as somehow interfering with crime control efforts, attempts to work around these "technicalities" come to be viewed as justified. This is especially true in regard to the control of vice and narcotics activities, where proactive and deceptive methods, such as "sting" operations and undercover work, are routine.

In many ways, police officers must walk a fine line. Overzealousness and the use of unnecessary force is undesirable, but so is a reluctance to intervene or back up another officer when the situation requires it. When officers use patrol time to avoid their responsibilities rather than to execute them, the professional image of the entire department suffers.

To avoid corruption, police departments must attempt to recruit and hire honorable men and women. These persons must be educated and trained to deal with whatever problems they confront. There is also a need for the police organization to take steps to keep standards high. These efforts include the development of explicit policy covering the variety of potentially corrupting situations and the implementation of active internal affairs units. Perhaps more important, however, is the creation of an organizational climate that fosters candid and open public examination of police practices, and a responsiveness to line officers and the dilemmas they confront.

DECEPTION BY POLICE   3

Jerome H. Skolnick

The ideal of legality implies that those convicted of crimes will not only be factually but legally guilty. A political commitment to legality is, after all, what distinguishes democratic governments from totalitarian ones. Yet, for every ideal there seems to be a practical challenge. The ideal of right to bail is challenged by the reality of the criminal's dangerousness, the presumption of innocence by the reality of factual guilt, the right to counsel by the triviality of certain offenses or the difficulties of providing counsel to those who have just been informed of their privilege against self-incrimination. Hard and fast rules limiting police conduct may challenge common sense, while the absence of such rules may invite arbitrary and abusive conduct. This paper discusses one of the most troubling and difficult questions pertaining to the ideal of legality: To what extent, if at all, is it proper for law enforcement officials to employ trickery and deceit as part of their law enforcement practices?[1]

Whatever the answer to that question—if indeed an answer can be formulated—it has to be measured against a hard reality of the criminal justice system. That reality is: Deception is considered by police—and courts

57

as well—to be as natural to detecting as pouncing is to a cat. As we shall see, that is why it is so difficult both to control deceptive practices of detectives and to prescribe long-term measures to guarantee control.

A seminal, thought-provoking attempt has been made in Sissela Bok's important book on lying.[2] Bok does not deal explicitly with deception by detectives as she does with deception by social scientists. But, she does refer to certain police practices in what must be regarded as the central chapter of her book—that on justification of deception, where she introduces standards for backing away from the Kantian categorical imperative.[3] Essentially, she argues for combining two standards for justifiable deception, insisting, first, on a public offering of justification for a lie and, second, on having the justification offered to an audience of reasonable persons. The chapter goes on to develop these notions in creative and original ways, but does not fully develop the implications of her guidelines for the detecting process. I would like to offer some observations which have been stimulated by her analysis about the detecting process itself.

THE NORMATIVE CONTEXT OF DETECTING

Detecting occurs in the context of fluid moral constraints that are circumscribed by a tradition of due process of law, by ever-changing and not altogether clear interpretations of individual rights offered by the courts, and by the social organization of policing that develops its own moral norms and constraints. Finally, this amalgam of normative prescription is set within the context of an adversary system of justice.

If all that sounds complicated and confusing, it is. It suggests that, because of the multiple contexts of police action, there are unstable, even contradictory, norms. Is detecting to be considered akin to a poker game, where the players understand that deception is part of the game? It surely is not like the doctor-client, or even the social scientist-subject relationship. The detective is not treating the subject, nor is the detective merely observing.

The detective deceives to establish grounds for convicting and punishing. The detecting process is informed and controlled by notions of fairness and dignity, but these notions, as embodied by law, are often unclear both in outcome and justification. The law often, but not always, supports police deception. The law permits the detective to pose as a consumer or purveyor of vice[4] but does not allow the policeman to employ certain ruses to gain entry without a search warrant[5] or to obtain a search warrant with a false affidavit.[6] The police subculture—the workaday normative order of police—permits, and sometimes demands, deception of courts, prosecutors, defense attorneys, and defendants but rarely, if ever, allows for deception of fellow policemen.[7] Police thus work within a severe but often agonizingly contradictory moral order which demands certain kinds of fidelities and insists upon other kinds of betrayals. The police milieu is normatively contradictory, almost to the point of being schizophrenogenic. Norms regarding deception, written and implied, abound in this moral order.

THE STAGES OF DETECTING

Deception occurs at three stages of the detecting process: investigation, interrogation, and testimony. If we place these three stages within the framework of a broad portrait of the moral cognition of the policeman, we observe that the acceptability of deception varies inversely with the level of the criminal process. Thus, deception is most acceptable to police—as it is to the courts—at the investigation stage, less acceptable during interrogation, and least acceptable in the courtroom.

If we inquire as to why that should be, the answer seems fairly obvious. Each stage is related to a set of increasingly stringent normative constraints. Courtroom testimony is given under oath and is supposed to be the truth, the whole truth, and nothing but the truth. Nobody is supposed to lie in a courtroom. When a policeman lies in court, he may be able to justify his deception on the basis of an alternative set of normative judgments (assuming that he is acting as a prosecution witness and is not himself the defendant), but he is still aware that courtroom lying violates the basic norms of the system he is sworn to uphold. Nevertheless, police do lie in the courtroom, particularly when they believe that judicial interpretations of constitutional limits on police practices are ill conceived or overly constraining in that they interfere with the policeman's ability to do his or her job as the police subculture defines it.

I shall argue in this paper that courtroom lying is justified within the police culture by the same sort of necessity rationale that courts have permitted police to employ at the investigative stage: The end justifies the means. Within an adversary system of criminal justice, governed by due process rules for obtaining evidence, the policeman will thus lie to get at the truth. The contradiction may be surprising, but it may be inevitable in an adversary system of justice where police perceive procedural due process norms and legal requirements as inconsistent obstacles to truth and the meting out of just deserts for the commission of crime.

TESTIMONIAL DECEPTION

As I have indicated, it is difficult to prove a causal relationship between permissible investigative and interrogatory deception and testimonial deception. Police freely admit to deceiving suspects and defendants.[8] They do not admit to perjury, much less to the rationalization of perjury. There is evidence, however, of the acceptability of perjury as a means to the end of conviction. The evidence is limited and fragmentary and is certainly not dispositive. However, the evidence does suggest not only that a policeman will perjure himself—no surprise that—but that perjury, like corruption, does not lend itself to "rotten apple" explanations.[9] Perjury, I would suggest, like corruption, is systematic, and for much the same sort of reason—police know that other police are on the take, and police know that other police are perjuring themselves. The following two items of evidence suggest that perjury represents a subcultural norm rather than an individual aberration.

Table 3.1

New York City Police Officers' Allegations Regarding Discovery of Evidence in Misdemeanor Narcotics Offenses, 1960-62			
	Percent of Arrests		
	Six-month period		
How Evidence Found	Before Mapp	After Mapp	Difference
I. Narcotics Bureau			
(a) Hidden on person	35	3	−32
(b) Dropped or thrown to ground	17	43	+26
II. Uniform			
(a) Hidden on person	31	9	−22
(b) Dropped or thrown to ground	14	21	+ 7
III. Plainclothes			
(a) Hidden on person	24	4	−20
(b) Dropped or thrown to ground	11	17	+ 6

Original source: Comment, "Effect of *Mapp v. Ohio* on Police Search and Seizure Practices in Narcotics Cases," *Col. J. Law & Social Problems* 4 (1968): 94.

Scholarly evidence of testimonial lying was revealed in a study conducted by Columbia law students in which they analyzed the effect of *Mapp v. Ohio*[10] on police practices in New York City. In *Mapp*, the Supreme Court held that the federal exclusionary rule in search and seizure cases was binding on the states. New York was the only large state that had not previously adopted the exclusionary rule as a matter of state law. (The exclusionary rule, of course, suppresses at trial evidence that was illegally obtained—usually in violation of the Fourth Amendment.) The students analyzed the evidentiary grounds for arrest and subsequent disposition of misdemeanor narcotics cases before and after the *Mapp* decision. Based on officers' accounts of the evidence for the arrest (see Table 3.1) the student authors concluded that

> uniform police have been fabricating grounds of arrest in narcotics cases in order to circumvent the requirements of *Mapp*. Without knowledge of the results of this study, the two Criminal Courts judges and the two Assistant District Attorneys interviewed doubted that a substantial reform of police practices had occurred since *Mapp*. Rather, they believe that police officers are fabricating evidence to avoid *Mapp*.[11]

Such lies came to be known as "dropsy" testimony since the police testified that those charged with drug possession were now dropping illicit drugs on the ground rather than keeping them where they were. Prior to *Mapp*, evidence obtained from unlawful searches of the person was admissible, even when illegally obtained. New York State was governed by the famous 1926 dictum of Judge Cardozo, who, while he was on the bench of the New York Court of Appeals, had dismissed the federal rule with the observation that under it "the criminal is to go free because the constable had blundered."[12] Obviously, the New York police had not been blundering prior to *Mapp*. Instead, they simply and routinely ignored the requirements of the Fourth Amendment.

In a more popular account, Robert Daley's fascinating *Prince of the City*, the former New York Deputy Police Commissioner writes of a surveillance showing that, on the one hand, defendants were guilty of hijacking television sets and that, on the other, cops were stealing some of the hijacked sets. The evidence was obtained through a legal wiretap. The detectives erased that part of the tape proving that the precinct cops had stolen some of the sets. Daley writes, "Tomorrow they would deny the erasure under oath....It was the type of perjury that detectives...committed all the time in the interest of putting bad people in jail."[13]

The point here is not whether to deplore the police violations of the

Fourth Amendment or the lying of police in the testimonial context; rather, it is to understand how police who engage in it themselves come to justify it, so that moral prescriptions might be given a better chance of being persuasive to police who do not find them compelling in practice.

The policeman lies because lying becomes a routine way of managing legal impediments—whether to protect fellow officers or to compensate for what he views as limitations the courts have placed on his capacity to deal with criminals. He lies because he is skeptical of a system that suppresses truth in the interest of the criminal. Moreover, the law permits the policeman to lie at the investigative stage, when he is not entirely convinced that the suspect is a criminal, but forbids lying about procedures at the testimonial stage, when the policeman is certain of the guilt of the accused. Thus, the policeman characteristically measures the short-term disutility of the act of suppressing evidence, not the long-term utility of due process of law for protecting and enhancing the dignity of the citizen who is being investigated by the state.

I quote at this point from a passage in *Justice without Trial* which recent discussions with police persuade me is still essentially valid:

> The policeman...operates as one whose aim is to legitimize the evidence pertaining to the case, rather than as a jurist whose goal is to analyze the sufficiency of the evidence based on case law....
> The policeman respects the necessity for "complying" with the arrest laws. His "compliance," however, may take the form of post hoc manipulation of the facts rather than before-the-fact behavior. Again, this generalization does not apply in all cases. Where the policeman feels capable of literal compliance (as in the conditions provided by the "big case"), he does comply. But when he sees the case law as a hindrance to his primary task of apprehending criminals, he usually attempts to construct the appearance of compliance, rather than allow the offender to escape apprehension.[14]

As I stated earlier, I am not aware of an ethical theory that would condone perjured testimony. Bok's standards for justifying deception would provide a useful guideline here, because the lying policeman would be required to justify courtroom perjury before a relevant public. This is precisely the sort of test I think Bok had in mind. Although police might justify perjury to each other over drinks after work or in the corridors of the locker room, I can scarcely imagine any policeman willing to justify such conduct in a public setting—unless he was perhaps on a television talk show, wearing a mask and wig. But any hesitation on the part of an officer to testify could be caused by fear of a perjury charge, not by moral scruples about lying in courtroom situations where criminals might go free.

INVESTIGATIVE DECEPTION

Let us examine more closely the rationale for lying at the investigative stage. Here, police are permitted by the courts to engage in trickery and deception and are trained to do so by the police organization. One might properly conclude, from examining police practices that have been subjected to the highest appellate review, that the police are authoritatively encouraged to lie.[15] Detectives, for example, are trained to use informers or to act themselves as informers or agents provocateurs when the criminal activity under investigation involves possession or sale of contraband. The contraband itself does not much matter. From an enforcement perspective, the problems involved in apprehending those who sell counterfeit money are almost identical to those involved in trapping dealers of illegal drugs. Years ago, when I studied a vice squad intensively, the squad was asked to help the United States Secret Service in apprehending a counterfeiting ring. They were asked because vice squads are especially experienced in law enforcement practices involving use of informants, deception, security of information, and, most generally, the apprehension of offenders whose criminality is proven by the possession for sale of illegal materials. A similar point can be made with respect to burglary enforcement. Victims (or police) rarely observe burglars in action. In fact, burglars are usually apprehended when detectives are able to employ a decoy or an informer who tells them that so-and-so is in possession of stolen goods.

The line between acceptable and unacceptable deception in such enforcement patterns is the line between so-called entrapment and acceptable police conduct. How does the law presently define entrapment? From my reading, the definition is hazy, murky, unclear. Two approaches are employed in legal writing about entrapment. One, the subjective approach, focuses upon the background, character, and intention of the defendant. Was he or she the sort of person who would have been predisposed to have committed the crime, even without the participation of the government official or agent? The objective test, by contrast, sets its sights on the nature of governmental participation. Justice Frankfurter, concurring in *Sherman v. United States,* presented the objective test as follows: "The crucial question, not easy to answer, to which the court must direct itself is whether the police conduct revealed in the particular case falls below standards to which common feelings respond, for the proper use of governmental power."[16] More recently, in *United States v. Russell*, Justice Rehnquist wrote the majority opinion affirming the prevailing rule—the subjective test—in a case where an undercover agent for the Federal Bureau of Narcotics and Dangerous Drugs told the suspect that he represented an organization that was interested in controlling the manufacture and distribution of methamphetamine.[17] The narcotics agent offered to supply Russell with a chemical that was an essential, hard-to-find ingredient in the manufacture of methamphetamine in return for half the drug produced. The agent told Russell that he had to be shown a sample of the drug in the laboratory where it was being produced before he would go through with the deal.

Russell showed him the laboratory and told the agent he and others had been making the drug for quite some time. The agent left and returned to the laboratory with the necessary chemical and watched while the suspects produced the drug. The narcotics agent did not actively participate in the manufacturing of the drug, but he was courteous and helpful to those who did. When a suspect dropped some aluminum foil on the floor, it was testified, the narcotics agent picked it up and put it into the cooker.

The majority of the court held that Russell was not "entrapped" because he had been an active participant in an illegal drug manufacturing enterprise that began before the government agent appeared on the scene and continued after the government agent left the scene. Russell was not an "unwary innocent," but an "unwary criminal." The subjective test, in short, permits police to engage in deceptive practices provided that the deception catches a wolf rather than a lamb.[18]

The objective test, focusing on the activities of the government, seems to suggest a more high-minded vision of the limits of police deception. By a high-minded vision, I mean to suggest one which conceives of significant limitations on police conduct in the interest of maintaining a civilized or moral constabulary. For example, a civilized police should not be permitted to torture a suspect in order to obtain a confession, even if it should turn out that the tortured party was an unwary criminal, that is, even if torture should produce the truth.[19] Nor, to cite a real case, would a civilized police be permitted to pump the stomach of a suspected narcotics dealer to show that pills that he had just swallowed contained morphine, even if that is exactly what the pills did contain.[20]

But the objective test may lose its objectivity when it relies on such concepts as "common feelings" or the "conscience of the community."[21] Although these concepts seem to imply enduring qualities or values, one could also argue that such concepts are variables. "Common feelings" might allow for far more latitude in police practices in a "high fear of crime" period than in a "low fear" period. Some might argue that values should be tested in the crucible of experience, and that flexibility is itself a virtue. The trouble is that one person's flexibility may be interpreted as another's lack of principle.

Moreover, "common feelings" may not be informative when we consider particular examples. I am reminded of a passage in Arthur Schlesinger's biography of Robert Kennedy, where Schlesinger tries to resolve the issue of whether Kennedy really knew about FBI wiretapping when he was Attorney General. Schlesinger relates a conversation between J. Edgar Hoover and Kennedy, where Hoover tells Kennedy that he had the situation "covered."[22] According to Schlesinger, Hoover felt that he had thus informed Kennedy of the wiretap, while Kennedy took the term "cover" to mean that a secret government informant had worked his way into the suspect's entourage.

Assuming for the purposes of argument that Kennedy did not know about the wiretapping, by what principle is a wiretap or bug to be considered less morally acceptable than a secret informant?[23] A wiretap or bug clearly invades expectations of privacy. But wiretaps and bugs enjoy two advantages over secret informants. First, the evidence they report as to what the defendant did or did not say is trustworthy. Second, and perhaps more important, a bug cannot encourage lawbreaking: It can neither advocate nor condone such conduct. It is not clear to me how an objective standard would distinguish between the two, and I find myself genuinely puzzled as to why informants are usually thought to be morally acceptable, while bugs are not. Indeed, an argument could be made that when the government attempts to modify dispositions (by employing secret informants who worm their way into the confidence of suspects, for example), that this is more violative of human dignity than the involuntary extraction of evidence from the body, even through stomach pumping. At least one whose stomach is being pumped can identify his adversary, while the secret informant "messes with the mind," as it were.

In any event, for the purpose of my more general argument it is enough to acknowledge that both legal tests of entrapment—objective and subjective—permit police to employ an enormous amount of routine deception, although the prevailing subjective test permits even more. Even in the dissenting opinion in Russell, Justice Stewart, supporting the objective test, writes that "the government's use of undercover activity, strategy, or deception is [not] necessarily unlawful. Indeed, many crimes, especially so-called victimless crimes, could not otherwise be detected."[24] In short, police are routinely permitted and advised to employ deceptive techniques and strategies in the investigative process. The police may occasionally trap a lamb, but the courts tacitly acknowledge that in the real world police deal mostly with wolves—and in the eyes of the courts a wolf might be wearing the clothing of either a congressman or a cocaine dealer.

Judicial permissiveness regarding investigative deception suggests how difficult it would be to defend a Kantian imperative against lying even in the abstract and how impossible it would be for any such defense to be accepted by courts, police, and the public. I shall conclude this discussion of investigative deception by suggesting a hypothesis: Judicial acceptance of deception in the investigation process enhances moral acceptance of deception by detectives in the interrogatory and testimonial stages of criminal investigation, and thus increases the probability of its occurrence.

This hypothesis does not suggest that every detective who deceives also perjures himself. It does suggest that deception in one context increases the probability of deception in the other. This hypothesis cannot be tested and therefore may not hold. It cannot be tested, because a true test would require an experimental design where we could manipulate the independent variable (authoritative permission to employ investigative trickery) and measure the dependent variable (courtroom perjury by police). Since we can neither manipulate the former nor measure the latter, the hypothesis, however plausible, must remain speculative.

INTERROGATORY DECEPTION

In the remainder of this paper, I shall assume that the previously mentioned hypothesis is plausible and organize discussion around it. Thus, let us turn our attention to deception and interrogation—and here I shall confine my remarks to in-custody interrogation, although I recognize that the line between *custody* and *precustody* is unclear, and that the one between *conversation* and *interrogation* is also unclear. For the present, I simply want to make a historical reference to the in-custody interrogation problem which *Miranda v. Arizona*, decided in 1966, sought to resolve.[25] The holding of *Miranda* has now become so familiar as to be part of American folklore. The case held that the arrested person must be informed of his or her right to remain silent, must be warned that any statement he or she does make may be used as evidence, and must be told that he or she has the right to the presence of an attorney. The accused should also be informed that an attorney will be provided if he or she cannot afford one. The court also held that the government has a "heavy burden" to prove that a waiver of such rights was made voluntarily, knowingly, and intelligently.[26]

The *Miranda* decision was the evolutionary outcome of the Supreme Court's response to the admission, in state and federal courts, of confessions which, in the early part of the century, were based on overt torture, later on covert torture (the third degree), and later still on deception and psychological intimidation. Overt torture is exemplified by the facts in *Brown v. Mississippi,* where black defendants were beaten and whipped until they confessed. By 1936, the Supreme Court could no longer overlook the glaring fact that a confession so elicited was deemed admissible by the Supreme Court of the State of Mississippi.

But punitive in-custody interrogation was, of course, not confined to the South. The 1931 Wickersham Commission reported numerous instances of covert torture in many cities between 1920 and 1930.[27] The chief distinction between covert and overt torture is not in the severity of pain induced, but in its deniability. The Mississippi sheriffs did not deny whipping their black suspects. They were brutal but truthful. By contrast, the third degree classically involved deniable coercion: starving suspects, keeping them awake day and night, confining them in pitch-black, airless rooms, or administering beatings with instruments which left few, if any, marks. For example, a suspect might be hit over the head with a blackjack (though a telephone book would be placed between the blackjack and the head) or he might be hit with a rubber hose.[28]

Other types of in-custody interrogation might evoke forms of torture even more terrifying but also more deniable. Detectives in one police department reportedly hung suspects from their heels outside windows in tall buildings to induce confessions. Others simply required that defendants stand erect and be forbidden use of bathroom facilities. The dramatic impact of the sadism of the third degree[29] has tended to obscure the fact that, in using it, the police necessarily condoned systematic deception of the courts as well as torture of suspects. Thus, not only did the police subculture's norms of the period permit station house physical punishment of those whom the police might have felt deserved it, these norms also condoned wholesale perjury—disregard of the moral authority of the courts and of the oaths taken in them.[30]

Miranda overruled *Crooker v. California,*[31] and *Cicenia v. LaGay,*[32] both of which were cases where the accused asked to see a lawyer after he agreed to be interrogated. In Cicenia's case, not only did he ask to see a lawyer, but his lawyer, who had arrived at the police station, had asked to see his client. *Miranda* might well be interpreted as a case where the Supreme Court was concerned not only with whether a confession was coerced—that had long been a concern of the courts—but whether the right of the accused not to be coerced was being effectuated properly in the context of the adversary system. The dissenters in *Crooker*—Douglas, Warren, Black, and Brennan— took a strong position on the right to counsel at the pretrial stage, arguing:

> The right to have counsel at the pre-trial stage is often necessary to give meaning and protection to the right to be heard at the trial itself. It may also be necessary as a restraint on the coercive power of the police[33]....No matter how well educated, and how well trained in the law an accused may be, he is surely in need of legal advice once he is arrested for an offense that may exact his life[34]....The demands of our civilization expressed in the due process clause require that the accused who wants a counsel should have one at any time after the moment of arrest.[35]

The dissent also wrote that "the third degree flourishes only in secrecy."[36] It is quite clear, I think, that Justices Warren, Douglas, Black, and Brennan (and later Fortas, with whom they were to form a majority in *Miranda*) simply did not trust police to behave noncoercively when they had a suspect in custody; only counsel, they believed, would constrain police.

Ironically, compelling evidence for the view that police custody is inherently coercive was elicited from a 1962 book by professional police interrogators Fred E. Inbau and John E. Reid, entitled *Criminal Interrogation and Confessions*.[37] This book was a revision and enlargement of the second half of Inbau and Reid's earlier book, *Lie Detection and Criminal Investigation*.[38] The book is replete with suggestions for coercive and deceptive methods of interrogation, which the authors clearly considered necessary and proper for police conducting an investigation. Inbau and Reid were not advocates of the third degree. On the contrary, their book, seen in historical context, was a reformist document, representing a kind of dialectical synthesis between the polarities of third degree violence and civil liberties for protection of human dignity. Such a synthesis would have been progressive in the 1930s.

The benchmark test employed by Inbau and Reid was: "Although both 'fair' and 'unfair' interrogation practices are permissible, nothing shall be done or said to the subject that will be apt to make an innocent person confess."[39] A more philosophically based and sophisticated version of the Inbau and Reid position (and a more modern one) is Joseph Grano's "mental freedom" test of voluntariness. It is an objective test, asking "whether a person of ordinary firmness, innocent or guilty, having the defendant's age, physical condition, and relevant mental abnormalities (but not otherwise having the defendant's personality traits, temperament, intelligence, or social background), and strongly preferring not to confess, would find the interrogation pressures overbearing."[40] What might these pressures be?

It is worthwhile, I think, to quote substantially from the *Miranda* decision itself, partly to understand the impact Inbau and Reid's books had on the courts, and partly to understand what sorts of police trickery might or might not be regarded as coercive. Justice Warren wrote:

> The officers are told by the manuals that the principal psycho-logical factor contributing to a successful interrogation is privacy—being alone with the person under interrogation." The efficacy of this tactic has been explained as follows:
>
>> If at all practicable, the interrogation should take place in the investigator's office or at least in a room of his own choice. The subject should be deprived of every psychologi-cal advantage. In his own home he may be confident, indig-nant, or recalcitrant. He is more keenly aware of his rights and more reluctant to tell of his indiscretions or criminal behavior within the walls of his home. Moreover his family and other friends are nearby, their presence lending moral support. In his office, the investigator possesses all the advantages. The atmosphere suggests the invincibility of the forces of the law.
>
> To highlight the isolation and unfamiliar surroundings, the manuals instruct the police to display an air of confidence in the suspect's guilt and from outward appearance to maintain only an interest in confirming certain details. The guilt of the subject is to be posted as a fact. The interrogator should direct his comments toward the reasons why the subject committed the act, rather than court failure by asking the subject whether he did it. Like other men, perhaps the subject has had a bad family life, had an unhappy childhood, had too much to drink, had an unrequited desire for women. The officers are instructed to minimize the moral seriousness of the offense, to cast blame on the victim or on society. These tactics are designed to put the subject in a psychological state where his story is but an elaboration of what the police purport to know already—that he is guilty. Explanations to the contrary are dismissed and discouraged.
>
> The texts thus stress that the major qualities an interrogator should possess are patience and perseverance.[41]

The manuals also suggest that suspects be offered legal excuses for their actions, says the *Miranda* Court. The interrogator is instructed to tell the suspect something like:

Joe, you probably didn't go out looking for this fellow with the purpose of shooting him. My guess is, however, that you expected something from him and that's why you carried a gun—for your own protection. You knew him for what he was, no good. Then when you met him he probably started using foul, abusing language and he gave some indication that he was about to pull a gun on you, and that's when you had to act to save your own life. That's about it, isn't it, Joe?[42]

If the suspect does not respond to the understanding interrogator, notes the Court, another investigator is brought in—Mutt, the tough guy who plays against Jeff's nice guy role.

In this technique, two agents are employed. Mutt, the relentless investigator, who knows the subject is guilty and is not going to waste any time. He's sent a dozen men away for this crime and he's going to send the subject away for the full term. Jeff, on the other hand, is obviously a kindhearted man. He has a family himself. He has a brother who was involved in a little scrape like this. He disapproves of Mutt and his tactics and will arrange to get him off the case if the subject will cooperate. He can't hold Mutt off for very long. The subject would be wise to make a quick decision. The technique is applied by having both investigators present while Mutt acts out his role. Jeff may stand by quietly and demur at some of Mutt's tactics. When Jeff makes his plea for cooperation, Mutt is not present.[43]

Although *Miranda* is generally interpreted as focusing on the inherently coercive aspects of custodial interrogation, it should be noted that interrogatory tactics employ both deception and coercion. It is questionable whether custodial interrogation would be effective without deception. Indeed, deception appears to serve as custodial interrogation's functional alternative to physical coercion. Hence, deception and the inherent coercion of custody are inescapably related in modern interrogation.

Miranda generated enormous controversy. Studies were conducted by scholars and law reviews to try to demonstrate the impact of *Miranda*.[44] (It would be interesting to conduct a new round of studies to see if the findings of the older ones still hold.) Basically, the studies came to much the same conclusion: The *Miranda* warning did not appreciably reduce the amount of talking that a suspect would do, nor did *Miranda* significantly help suspects in making free and informed choices about whether to talk. A nice statement of how Miranda warnings could be rendered ineffectual, written by an author of the *Yale Law Journal's* study of *Miranda's* impact, appeared in the *Yale Alumni Magazine* in 1968.

Even when detectives informed suspects of their rights without undercutting devices, the advice was often defused by implying that the suspect had better not exercise his rights, or by delivering the statement in a formalized, bureaucratic tone to indicate that the remarks were simply a routine, meaningless legalism. Instinctively, perhaps, detectives tended to create a sense of unreality about the *Miranda* warnings by bringing the flow of conversation to a halt with the statement, "...and now I am going to inform you of your rights." Afterwards, they would solemnly intone: "Now you have been warned of your rights," then immediately shift into a conversational tone to ask, "Now would you like to tell me what happened?" By and large the detectives regarded advising the suspect of his rights as an artificial imposition on the natural flow of the interrogation.[45]

Miranda also generated a substantial law review literature— some might say an industry—because the United States Supreme Court has been unwilling to set the only standard that would eliminate practically all the *Miranda* problems. That standard would be: Once the *Miranda* warnings are given, the accused is also given a lawyer who explains the implications of the warning.[46]

The privilege against self-incrimination existed before *Miranda*. The *Miranda* ruling essentially argues that, as part of due process, the government should not be permitted to make its case on the basis of the defendant's ignorance. Defendants must be informed of their rights. If we accept *Miranda* and take it seriously, we also must acknowledge that suspects do not—across the board—possess the legal acumen to waive their *Miranda* rights. In the late 1960s, at least, persons of "ordinary firmness" interpreted—or misinterpreted—their *Miranda* rights in such a way so as not to exercise them. From the perspective of those who would like to see *Miranda* overturned, that might not be a problem. But it also suggests that the average suspect, however "ordinarily firm," is not legally competent.

Those who are legally competent (lawyers) will routinely advise suspects to maintain silence. The continuing debate over *Miranda* reflects an ambivalence over enforcing the rule that the values expressed by the *Miranda* majority seem to call for: There can be no confession without a genuinely voluntary and knowledgeable waiver, exercised after consultation with a lawyer. The Crooker minority was unquestionably correct in its assessment that people cannot fully understand the implications of legal warnings—offered, after all, in the rather coercive situation of arrest—without legal consultation. We apparently still prefer to offer the government an edge based on the defendant's ignorance. Knowledgeable defendants will remain silent. The ignorant will talk.

Grano's "ordinary firmness" test necessarily implies overruling *Miranda*. His test, which is oriented to crime control, would surely result in far more admissible evidence than a genuinely voluntary, lawyer-advised, waiver would. The present *Miranda* rule lies somewhere in between. Perhaps we tolerate *Miranda* because, on the whole, we have learned that it does not matter very much. Pressures of in-custody interrogation are such that, apparently, most suspects will talk despite the *Miranda* warning. In any event, most confessions are elicited in cases where there is a victim, where the confession is not the only evidence, and where the suspect is willing to plead guilty to a lesser offense.

Besides, once the suspect begins to talk, the very techniques the court sought to avoid are probably permissible. When a policeman says, in the kindliest of tones, "Look Joe, it will be better for you to confess," he is of course essentially deceiving the suspect into believing that he is the suspect's friend rather than his adversary.

In a recent article, Welsh S. White has argued that certain interrogation tactics are, nevertheless, likely to risk depriving the suspect of his constitutional rights.[47] Accordingly, White believes that the court should prohibit, via per se exclusions, "police conduct that is likely to render a resulting confession involuntary or to undermine the effect of required *Miranda* warnings or a suspect's independent right to an attorney."[48] What would some of these prohibitions be? One would be against deceiving a suspect about whether an interrogation was taking place, as in *Massiah v. United States*.[49] There, after indictment, one confederate, Colson, agreed to cooperate with the government, and deceptively interrogated his accomplice, Massiah. The resulting incriminatory statements were held inadmissible as a violation of the Sixth Amendment right to counsel. White argues that this right should be triggered at the point of arrest.

He also argues that statements elicited from "jail plants" should be prohibited, on grounds that someone who is experiencing the pressures of confinement is more likely to confide in a police agent.[50] Slightly different forms of trickery, which White also advocates prohibiting, are police misrepresentations of the seriousness of the offense or police use of threats or promises for confessing.

Finally, White argues for prohibition of "father figure" trickery, wherein a police officer falsely acts like a friend or counselor rather than an adversary. White offers as one example the famous Connecticut murder case, *State v. Reilly*, where the principal interrogating officer manipulated an eighteen-year-old into falsely confessing that he murdered his mother.[51] White treats the case primarily as an example of the officer pretending to be a father figure. White's discussion, however, omits entirely what two books about the case point to as the real culprit—the use of the polygraph during the interrogation of Reilly, who confessed after being told by the "father figure" that a machine, which could read his mind, had indicated that he actually was the murderer.[52]

THE POLYGRAPH AS A DECEPTIVE DEVICE

Recall that Inbau and Reid were not only advocates of deceptive interrogation. They were also proponents and developers of polygraph examination techniques. The polygraph is an instrument which measures changes in blood pressure, pulse, respiration, and perspiration. Detection of lies via the examination of physical change is actually a throwback to early forms of trial by ordeal. There are reports of a deception test used by Hindus based on the observation that fear may inhibit the secretion of saliva.[53] To test credibility, an accused as given rice to chew. If he could spit it out, he was considered innocent; but if it stuck to his gums, he was judged guilty. Until 1895, however, nobody had ever used a measuring device to detect deception. In that year, the Italian criminologist Cesare Lombroso used a combination of blood pressure and pulse readings to investigate crime. Before the First World War, others experimented with blood pressure and respiratory recordings. John A. Larson, perhaps the most scholarly of the Chicago-Berkeley group which sought to advance the "science" of lie detection, built an instrument in 1921 which he called a "polygraph;" It combined all three measures—blood pressure, pulse, and respiration. His junior collaborator, Leonard Keeler, added galvanic skin response to the list. Contemporary lie detector machines basically employ all these measures, although there are some other technical improvements as well. For example, integrated circuits and other components reduce the margin of error in measurement.

According to a survey conducted by the *New York Times* in 1980, the lie detector is widely used by law enforcement groups:

The Federal Bureau of Investigation conducted 1900 polygraph examinations in 1979, an increase of about 800 from 1978. The number of polygraph examinations administered by the Army, Navy, Marines and Air Force increased by 18 percent in two years, from 5710 to 6751. Polygraphs are finding a steadily growing market among state and local law enforcement agencies, litigants in civil cases and private retailers, who use the device to screen job applicants and combat pilferage.[54]

It is understandable but distressing that the use of the polygraph should be increasing. It is distressing because the validity of polygraph results is flawed by fundamental theoretical problems, not by technical ones. The increase in use is understandable, because even though the polygraph is not a dispositive truth-finding device, it is nevertheless an effective instrument of social control.

In the past, one problem of polygraph examination was imprecision of measurement. Thus, the machine recorded blood pressure, but there was a question as to whether it recorded blood pressure accurately. There is no doubt that imprecision of measurement was a problem in the past, but the problems with the lie detection process itself were far more fundamental and serious. These problems stem from the inadequacy of the theory behind lie detection. That theory involves the following premises: The act of lying leads to conscious conflict; conflict induces fear or anxiety; and these emotions are accompanied by measurable and interpretable physiological changes.[55]

But the assumptions of the theory are questionable. The act of lying does not always lead to conscious conflict. Some witnesses believe their own stories, even when they are false. Even when witnesses know they are lying, they may not experience much fear. Or, innocent witnesses may experience fear and anxiety just by being asked threatening questions. All this depends on witnesses' individual personalities, social backgrounds, what they are testifying to, and to whom they are testifying. Polygraph examiners acknowledge that subjects must "believe in" the lie detector.

Even if witnesses do experience fear and anxiety, these emotions may not consistently be expressed as changes in bodily response. If all bodily response rose and fell exactly with emotional states, the responses would have a precise relationship to each other. But that is not the case. Bodily responses do not vary regularly, either with each other or with emotional states. If they did, only a unigraph, not a polygraph, would be required. Four imprecise measures are not more accurate than one precise measure.

Since the relations among lying, conflict, emotion, and bodily responses are so fuzzy, the accuracy of the lie detector is not comparable to that of, say, blood tests or X rays. It is unlikely that a dozen lie detector examiners would consistently reach the same conclusions regarding truth or falsity if they depended only on the squiggles produced by a polygraph.

So why is the use of lie detectors sharply increasing? The fact that the polygraph is not reliable does not mean it is ineffective as a social control instrument. Crime suspects may confess when questioned by a skilled interrogator. When a suspect is strapped into what he or she would view as a technologically foolproof "lie detector," the coercive power of the interrogator is heightened. The interrogator is not an adversary, but an objective scientific observer. Even those suspicious of father figures may embrace the trappings of science.

Job applicants, in particular, are effectively "screened" with a lie detector. Consider the following lines of questioning. First, softballs: Is your name John Jones? Are you thirty-six years old? Were you born in New York City? Then, hardballs: Have you ever done anything you are ashamed of? Have you ever stolen anything? Have you ever known anyone who has stolen anything? Who? Have you ever engaged in homosexual acts? And so forth. This sort of questioning may well produce results.

There are thus two quite different empirical issues regarding the polygraph. Is it highly accurate, like X rays and blood tests? The answer is no. Is it effective in eliciting information from subjects who believe in it? The answer is yes. Whether the lie detector ought to be used by police—or by employers—is ultimately an ethical question. Should we allow deceptive, intrusive, yet nonviolent methods of interrogation in various institutions of a free society? Different people will have different answers to that question. But at least we should ask the right questions when considering the role of the so-called lie detector in American society.

The ethical problem is even more complicated because some who employ the lie detector actually believe that it detects lies, while others use it primarily as a technique of psychological intimidation. The police sergeant who told Peter Reilly that "this machine will read your mind" and then falsely persuaded Reilly that he had killed his own mother, thus eliciting from Reilly a critical but untrue confession, may himself have believed that the polygraph detects lies. Did the sergeant also believe that the lie detector reads the mind?

The lie detector is symbolically scientific, and its technologically sophisticated trappings commend it to the most thoughtful and professional segments of the policing community. Thus, police use the polygraph because they believe in it. Yet the technique's results can convict innocent people, where old-fashioned techniques of deception would not. An instance of this, the case of F.B. Fay, is reported by psychophysiologist David T. Lykken.[56] Fay was asked by a police polygraphist in Toledo in 1978, "Did you kill Fred?" and "Before age twenty-four did you ever think about doing anyone bodily harm to get revenge?" It was assumed that, if Fay were innocent of Fred's murder, the second or "control" question would frighten Fay more, and that this would, in turn, "dampen" his autonomic reaction to the first or "relevant" question. Unfortunately for Fay, he responded more strongly to the "relevant" questions. The examiner, therefore, testified that Fay's denials were deceptive, and he was found guilty of murder and sentenced to prison for life. In October 1980, the actual killers were identified, and Fay was released after serving two and a half years.

In sum, then, we have to educate the law enforcement community as to the realistic limits of the polygraph. This will be difficult, partly because there is, as I have noted here, considerable controversy over use of the polygraph, and partly because, for the reasons I have already suggested, it is a uniquely valuable tool of interrogation. I myself have no hesitancy in stating where I stand on use of the instrument. I would argue against its use—first, because the false claims for its accuracy permit the highest degree of nonviolent coercion, and second, because cool nonreactors (sociopaths, skilled con men, the mildly self-drugged) can beat the test. Finally, if one of the important reasons for the *Miranda* rule is the inherent coerciveness of police interroga-tion, then how much more coercive is an interrogation by a questioner who is armed with a deceptively scientific instrument that can "read the mind?"

CONCLUSION

I have tried in this article to offer several observations about deception in the detecting process. First, I have suggested that detecting is a process mov-ing from investigation, often through interrogation, to testimony. Police are offered considerable latitude by the courts during the investigation stage. This latitude to deceive, I have argued, carries over into the interrogation and testimonial stages as a subculturally supported norm. I have suggested that there is an underlying reason for this. When detectives deceive suspects in the course of criminal investigations or interrogations, they typically are not seeking to promote their own self-interest (as a detective would if he had lied about accepting bribes). On the contrary, the sort of deception employed to trap a narcotics dealer or dealer in stolen goods, or to elicit a confession from a murderer or rapist, is used for the public interest. The detective—and here I am speaking of the professional detective who explicitly condemns the use of physical violence but accepts employing psychological intimidation during interrogation—is also interested in eliciting truth. This results, I have sug-gested, in a paradox. The end of truth justifies for the modern detective the means of lying. Deception usually occurs in the interest of obtaining truth.

Both the detective and the civil libertarian, I have suggested, employ a utilitarian calculus. In so doing, each reveals the obvious limitations of such a calculus for resolving major issues of public policy. The detective measures the costs of the act of lying against the benefits to the crime victim and the general public. The civil libertarian is also concerned with the public interest but measures it in terms of rules protecting the long-range interests of all citizens in a system of governance, as opposed to the shorter range interests of punishing perpetrators.

The law reflects the tension between due process and crime control imperatives by establishing different—and inconsistent— standards for investigation and interrogation. At the investigative stage, the law's subjective test of entrapment comes perilously close to tests like Inbau and Reid's "innocent person" or Grano's more sophisticated "mental freedom" test: Both permit deceptive and coercive interrogation against wolves but not lambs.

Is there a moral justification for distinguishing between governmental deception at the investigative stage and at the interrogation stage? One could approach this issue by asking: What would be the rule of law regarding police deception in a moral society? It seems clear that in a moral society, authorities such as police would not be permitted to employ tactics that are generally regarded as immoral against those suspected, or accused, of a crime.

Indeed, we already have such rules: Police are not permitted to coerce a suspect physically. The police may, however, subject suspects to psychological coercion provided they consent to be interrogated. Unreliability is one reason we prohibit the admission of evidence obtained from physically coerced confessions. But we could have a rule distinguishing between a pure mea culpa confession and one which produces material evidence, such as a gun or a body. We do not have such rules partly because we deplore physically coercive tactics even when used against the guilty; we also do not have them because we fear that physical coercion would become a routine aspect of police interrogation. Physical coercion is clearly indistinguishable from deceit and trickery, and few of us would, really, I suspect, choose to be smashed in the face with a rifle butt, or hung from a high window, rather than be betrayed by a friend who is actually and secretly a police informant gathering incriminating evidence.

The more difficult question is whether deception—which we accept at the investigative stage—is as morally offensive as psychological coercion. Recall that earlier I discussed the distinction between gathering information by a secret informant and gathering it by electronic eavesdropping. I suggested there that I could not see any principle by which one was, on balance, worse than the other, even though we can perceive different sorts of objections to each. The wiretap or bug clearly invades privacy, while the secret informant invades both privacy—in some ways more, in some ways less, than electronic eavesdropping—and personality. Not only is the secret informant privy to actions and conversations one would never consent to have had overheard; the secret informant also modifies personality by deliberately attempting to impair judgment. The wiretap is, in social science jargon, an "unobtrusive measurer." By contrast, the informant necessarily produces a reaction—speech, behavior—on the part of the observed, and may prove influential in determining that reaction.

If there is a distinction between investigative and interrogatory trickery and deceit, it has to be based on situational ethics, the morality of practical necessity. Practically speaking, it is impossible to enforce consensual crime statutes—bribery, drug dealing, prostitution—without employing deception. This need for deception may not be as clear at the interrogation stage. Often, evidence can be produced independently of confessions, and occasionally, false confessions are elicited.

But confessions may also be a practical necessity in many cases, particularly when dealing with the most serious sorts of criminals, such as murderers, rapists, and kidnappers. Miranda himself, it may be recalled, had confessed to the forcible kidnapping and rape of a nineteen-year-old woman. Why should situational ethics permit lying to a drug dealer but forbid in-custody conversational questioning of a forcible rapist? That question can be answered on historical and constitutional grounds, but it is hard to see how to make consistent common sense out of it.

I cannot here reconcile such inconsistencies, nor am I writing to lobby the Supreme Court. But I would like to conclude by suggesting that apparent inconsistency makes law look more like a game than a rational system for enforcing justice. Because of this appearance of inconsistency, police are not likely to take the stated rules of the game seriously and are encouraged to operate by their own codes, including those which affirm the necessity for lying wherever it seems justified by the ends.

NOTES

1. See generally, Welsh S. White, "Police Trickery in Inducing Confessions," *U. Pa L. Rev.* 127 (1979):581-629; Welsh S. White, "Interrogation without Questions: Rhode Island v. Innis and United States v. Henry," *Mich. L. Rev.* 78 (1980):1209-51.

2. Sissela Bok, *Lying: Moral Choice in Public and Private Life* (New York: Pantheon, 1978).

3. See, for example, the discussion in Chapter VII, "Justification," of the group decision to deceive the public. Bok says it is based on the shared belief that the group's norms are good and that any means used to achieve group ends would also therefore be good (Bok, *Lying,* p. 97). See also the discussion of unmarked police cars as justifiable deception because the practice is publicized, while entrapment is not deemed justifiable unless the public agrees this is proper police behavior (Bok, *Lying,* pp. 98-99).

4. See, generally, Cory Marx, "Undercover Cops: Creative Policing or Constitutional Threat?" *Civ. Libs. Rev.* 4 (July/August 1977):34-44.

5. United States v. Ressler, 536 F. 2d 208 (1976), and list of cases cited in the body of that opinion.

6. Franks v. Delaware, 98 S. Ct. 2674 (1979).

7. As to "code of honor" regarding deception, see Lawrence W. Sherman, *Scandal and Reform: Controlling Police Corruption* (Berkeley and Los Angeles: University of California, 1978), pp. 46-67. As to existence of police subculture, see Ellwyn R. Stoddard, "A Group Approach to Blue-Coat Crime," in *Police Corruption: A Sociological Perspective,* ed. Lawrence W. Sherman (Garden City, N.J.: Doubleday, Anchor Books, 1974), pp. 277-304.

8. Jerome Skolnick, *Justice without Trial,* 2nd ed. (New York: Wiley & Sons, 1975), p. 177.

9. *The Knapp Commission Report,* City of New York Commission to Investigate Allegations of Police Corruption and the City's Anti-Corruption Procedures (New York, 1972), discussed in Sherman, *Scandal and Reform,* p. 160.

10. Mapp v. Ohio, 367 U.S. 643 (1961).

11. Quoted and discussed in Dallin Oaks, "Studying the Exclusionary Rule in Search and Seizure," *U. Chi. L. Rev.* 37 (1970):665-757.

12. People v. Defore, 242 N.Y. 13 (1926).

13. Robert Daley, *Prince of the City: The True Story of a Cop Who Knew Too Much* (Boston: Houghton Mifflin Co., 1978), p. 73.

14. Skolnick, *Justice,* pp. 214-15.

15.   For a discussion of institutional support for trying to cover up misuse of force charges, see Paul Chevigny, *Police Power* (New York: Pantheon, 1969), p. 139. For case law and discussion of trickery and deception at the investigative stage, see Yale Kamisar, *Police Interrogation and Confessions* (Ann Arbor: University of Michigan Press, 1980).

16.   Sherman v. United States, 356 U.S. 369 (1958).

17.   United States v. Russell, 411 U.S. 423 (1973).

18.   Welsh S. White, "Police Trickery."

19.   Brown v. Mississippi, 297 U.S. 278 (1936).

20.   Rochin v. California, 342 U.S. 165 (1952).

21.   Ralph A. Rossum, "Entrapment Defense and the Teaching of Political Responsibility: The Supreme Court as Republican Schoolmaster," *Amer. J. Crim. L.* (1978):287-306.

22.   Arthur M. Schlesinger, Jr., *Robert Kennedy and His Times* (Boston: Houghton Mifflin, 1978), p. 285.

23.   Provisions for issuing a warrant to wiretap are stringent. The rule is that wiretaps may be conducted only after a warrant has been issued. Title III of 18 U.S.C. 2510-20 prescribes a careful procedure for obtaining a warrant to use electronic surveillance, and the federal law preempts state law on this subject. By contrast, an informant paid by the D.E.A., for example, may freely roam about southwestern Florida, working his way into any corner of the drug subculture, without specific judicial authorization. See Stuart Penn, "The Informer," *Wall Street Journal*, 10 May 1982.

24.   United States v. Russell, 411 U.S. 423 (1973).

25.   Miranda v. Arizona, 384 U.S. 486 (1966).

26.   Lego v. Twomey, 404 U.S. 477 (1972) (Voluntariness must be proven by a preponderance of evidence).

27.   *Report on Lawlessness in Law Enforcement*, National Commission on Law Observance and Enforcement (Washington, D.C.: United States Government Printing Office, 1931).

28.   Ernest J. Hopkins, *Our Lawless Police: A Study of the Unlawful Enforcement of the Law* (1931; reprint ed., New York: Da Capo Press, 1972), pp. 236-63.

29.   A list of such tactics is found in the Wickersham Report; see note 27.

30.   Modern commentators claim that the most outrageous examples of the third degree tactics are no longer employed in American police departments. See Robert M. Fogelson, *Big City Police* (Cambridge, Mass.: Harvard University Press, 1977), p. 302.

31. Crooker v. California, 357 U.S. 433 (1958).

32. Cicenia v. LaGay, 357 U.S. 504 (1958).

33. Crooker v. California, 357 U.S. 433, 443 (1958).

34. Ibid., p. 446.

35. Ibid., p. 448.

36. Ibid., p. 443.

37. Fred E. Inbau and John E. Reid, *Criminal Interrogation and Confessions* (Baltimore: Williams and Wilkins Co., 1962).

38. Fred E. Inbau and John E. Reid, *Lie Detection and Criminal Interrogation*, 3rd ed. (Baltimore: Williams and Wilkins Co., 1953).

39. Inbau and Reid, *Criminal Interrogations and Confessions*, p. 208.

40. Joseph Grano, "*Voluntariness, Free Will, and the Law of Confessions*," *Va. L. Rev.* 65 (1979):906.

41. Miranda v. Arizona, 384 U.S. 436, 449-50 (1966), citing Charles O'Hara *Fundamentals of Criminal Investigation* (Springfield, Ill.: Charles Thomas Publishing Co., 1956), p. 99.

42. Ibid, pp. 451-52, citing Inbau and Reid, *Criminal Interrogation and Confessions*, p. 40.

43. Ibid, p. 452, citing O'Hara, *Fundamentals*, p. 104, and Inbau and Reid, *Criminal Interrogation*, pp. 58-59.

44. Project, "Interrogations in New Haven: The Impact of Miranda," *Yale L.J.* 76 (1967): 1519-1648; Richard H. Seeburger and R. Stanton Wettick, Jr., "Miranda in Pittsburgh— A Statistical Study," *U. Pitt. L. Rev.* 29 (1967): 1-26; Cyril D. Robinson, "Police and Prosecutor Practices and Attitudes Relating to Interrogation," *Duke L.J.* 1968:425-524.

45. Richard E. Ayers, "Confessions and the Court," *Yale Alumni Magazine* (December, 1968): 18, 20. Cited in Yale Kamisar, Wayne R. LaFave, and Jerold H. Israel, *Modern Criminal Procedure: Cases, Comments, Questions*, 5th ed. (St. Paul, Minn.: West Publishing Co., 1980), p. 632.

46. John Baldwin and Michael McConville, "Police Interrogation and the Right to See a Solicitor," *Crim. L. Rev.* 1979: 145-52; Welsh S. White, "Police Trickery."

47. Welsh S. White, "Police Trickery," p. 586.

48. Ibid., pp. 599-600.

49. Massiah v. United States, 377 U.S. 201 (1964).

50. United States v. Henry, 100 S.Ct. 2183 (1980).

51. State v. Reilly, No. 5285 (Conn. Super. Ct. Apr. 12, 1974), vacated 32 Conn. Supp. 349, 355 A.2d 324 (Super. Ct. 1976).

52. Donald S. Connery, *Guilty Until Proven Innocent* (New York: G.P. Putnam's Sons, 1977); Joan Barthel, *A Death in Canaan* (New York: E.P. Dutton, 1976).

53. David T. Lykken, *A Tremor in the Blood: Uses and Abuses of the Lie Detector* (New York: McGraw-Hill Book Co., 1981), p. 26.

54. Robert Pear, "As Use of the Polygraph Grows, Suspects and Lawyers Sweat," *New York Times*, 13 July 1980.

55. Jerome Skolnick, "Scientific Theory and Scientific Evidence: An Analysis of Lie Detection," *Yale L.J.* 70 (1961):699.

56. David T. Lykken, "Review: The Art and Science of the Polygraph Technique," *Contemporary Psychology* 26 (1981):480.

OVERSTEPPING POLICE AUTHORITY   4

Howard Cohen

Police authority can be at once highly specific and exceedingly vague. It is specific insofar as it is conferred by statute with respect to law enforcement and, then, amplified or refined by departmental policy and procedures. It is vague in the areas of peace-keeping and public safety where the variety of activities expected of the police is, typically, not legislated, but rather left for departments and officers to define for themselves—within limits of community acceptability.[1] This combination of specific and vague authority might not be particularly troublesome if the areas of law enforcement, peace-keeping, and public safety were distinct spheres of police work. However, police operate in a world that is not nicely packaged and clearly labeled.[2] They regularly step into situations in which neither their objectives nor their functions are particularly obvious. Indeed, in many police encounters there are laws that may have been broken, disputes that might yet erupt or dissolve, and persons who are potentially dangerous or in danger. If anything is reliable in police work, it is that circumstances are likely to change when an officer enters the picture; such change will, in part, determine whether law enforcement, peace-keeping, or public safety should be accorded highest priority.

The consequences of this fluidity of police functions for police authority are troublesome. A situation that the officer interprets as calling for law enforcement may require that he use his authority in very specific ways. The same situation, seen in terms of peace-keeping or public safety, may permit him less restricted disposition of a problem. That these forms of exercising authority can be at odds is clearly illustrated in the following example.

In his account of his own police training, George Kirkham, a former university instructor in criminal justice, describes an encounter he and his field training officer had with two suspicious characters.

Case 1: At ten o'clock another unit began covering Beat Ninety-four and we returned to patrolling the ghetto. It was just before midnight when we made a right turn onto Washington Street, and D'Angelo abruptly braked the cruiser. He put the car in reverse and backed up several yards, then sat motionless, staring at the darkness.

I looked around. I couldn't see anything. "What's the matter?" I whispered.

"Okay, come outta there," he ordered in a loud voice. He unsnapped his gun, resting one hand on its grip as he got out and stood behind the open car door.

I still couldn't see anything.

"Watch yourself," he said without turning to look at me. I was out of the car on my side now, still wondering what he was talking about. He beamed a shaft of light from the cruiser's spotlight into an alley and brought it to rest on a pile of wooden fruit crates. I saw movement as two black figures stepped slowly from behind the crates and stood in the spotlight's glare. They began walking toward us.

"Watch the one on your right," D'Angelo instructed. I could see them both clearly now for the first time—two black youths in their late teens. "What did they do?" I asked as I watched the pair approach us.

"Don't know," he said, still without taking his eyes off them. "They was walking along being real cool back there. Then they seen us coming and ducked into that alley." "On the car," he said simply to the man on the left as he walked up.

The man quickly assumed what is often referred to as "the position"— feet wide apart, palms flat on the car. I guessed it was not the first time he had been stopped by the police. "Shake the other one down," D'Angelo instructed as he began running his hands across the first man's shirt and trousers.

I stepped from behind the door and called out to the second man. "Excuse me, but I'm going to have to ask you to put your hands on the car." I was a little embarrassed at having made such a request without really knowing quite why.

"Say what, man?" The figure came toward me with both hands in the pockets of a wind-breaker jacket.

"I said—"

"He said to get your ass on the car! Now move!"

I turned and saw that D'Angelo's revolver was out of its holster, pointed directly at the man. The man's eyes grew wide as he saw the gun.

"And take them hands outta your pockets nice and easy! That's it. Now get on the car like that officer told you."

I started frisking the second man.

"Well, well. What we got here?" D'Angelo said. He reached deep in the first man's groin area and emerged with a small nickel-plated revolver. "How about the other one?" he asked as I finished running both hands down a pantleg. He began handcuffing the first man.

I stopped as I felt something soft and spongy in the man's left sock. "There's something in his sock," I said as I stood up, "but it's too soft to be a weapon of any kind. I think it's a plastic bag of some sort. Do you want me to run a record check on him before we let him go?"

D'Angelo looked at me with a puzzled expression on his face. "What the hell you mean, 'let him go'?" he exclaimed. "Find out what's in that sock."

"We can't do that," I protested.

I was familiar with legal restrictions placed on the police. Under the Supreme Court decision in *Terry v. Ohio*, it had been legal for me to frisk the man's outer clothing for weapons in order to protect myself in light of the pair's suspicious conduct, but it would be illegal for me to go beyond that extremely limited "Search" and examine the man's sock without first having actual grounds to make an arrest. D'Angelo's recovery of a gun from the other man had been legal only because he had first felt an object which any police officer would have good reason to believe might be a weapon. That had justified a search of the man's crotch. But a soft object beneath a sock? Surely D'Angelo must know the law, I thought.

"Here, keep an eye on this one," he said. He walked over to where the second man was still spread-eagled against the patrol car. He reached inside the sock and withdrew a plastic bag filled with small, tightly folded aluminum foil packets. "Smack," he said as he opened one of them and examined its contents. "Four, five, six decks. You're under arrest, too, friend. Gimme your handcuffs, Doc."

I handed them to him as my mind connected the white powder and the street label for heroin.

We transported both men to the city jail and booked them. Once were we back inside the car D'Angelo looked at me and said, "Don't ever hesitate to draw down on assholes like them two if they don't move when you tell 'em to. It's something they understand."

D'ANGELO'S BEHAVIOR VS. KIRKHAM'S

Kirkham, I would say, understood this encounter primarily, if not exclusively, in terms of law enforcement. In those terms his authority was explicitly circumscribed by the law of search and seizure, particularly at that time by *Terry v. Ohio*. He was concerned to establish probable cause for arrest, and where he could not, to end his involvement with the suspects. He was well aware of the limits of his authority and was unwilling to act beyond those limits.

D'Angelo, on the other hand, showed disregard and perhaps contempt for the law of search and seizure. He was not, however, acting from ignorance of the law. Rather, he seemed to be treating this encounter as a matter of public safety. D'Angelo saw two dangerous people, one of whom turned out to be armed. All of his street sense told him they were probably drug users and dealers. The last thing he wanted to do was give them the message that they were safe from him. He intimidated, threatened, searched one of them illegally, and arrested them. But his concern here was less with law enforcement than it was with public safety. Two addicts (and, in all probability, thieves) knew they were being watched. A gun and a small quantity of heroin were removed from the street. If D'Angelo did not reduce drug use and related crime, he at least made a contribution to controlling or containing it within his jurisdiction. He was exercising his authority as a peace-keeper in the name of public safety.

If D'Angelo intended that his arrest would lead to a conviction, then he had overstepped his authority as a law enforcement officer. His search was illegal, and conviction on the drug offense would require perjury by two officers. To take this case forward would be to expose bad police work—an improper exercise of legal authority. There remains, however, the question of whether D'Angelo's actions would be defended on other grounds. May he give public safety a higher priority than law enforcement in this case? Or has he overstepped his authority in any form by trying to do something other than enforce the law here? In short, a defense of D'Angelo's actions assumes that the objectives he hoped to achieve might to some extent be determined by him: he might set priorities by putting public safety ahead of law enforcement and sacrificing a potential conviction in order to contain (or at least harass) junkies and dealers. However, if D'Angelo was wrong about this, then he overstepped his authority as surely as if his goal had been law enforcement.

Actually, there are two ways to conceptualize this problem. On the one hand, we may suppose that police officers have an area of authority that is broader than law enforcement. Then the question is: may officers ever exercise that authority when it conflicts with their authority to enforce the law? Alternatively, we may suppose that any police action beyond law enforcement constitutes overstepping authority. The question then is: Are there conditions under which officers are justified in overstepping their authority? My own preference is for the former conceptualization of the problem.

Before scrutinizing a defense of D'Angelo's actions more carefully, it is useful to remind ourselves that criticism of D'Angelo's behavior does not imply an endorsement of Kirkham's. As a trainee, Kirkham is timid and naive about the reality of street life. His deference to the suspects is probably dangerous, since it conveys uncertainty about his willingness to exercise his authority. Moreover, Kirkham seems to be unaware of the possibility that he has responsibilities other than law enforcement when he is on the street. Even if D'Angelo has ultimately made a wrong decision about his priorities, at least he understands the options. Kirkham does not seem to realize that there is anything more at stake in this encounter than a weapons or narcotics arrest. So, although Kirkham has not overstepped his authority in this case, it does not follow that he has handled it properly.

At this point in our investigation it is clear that D'Angelo has overstepped his authority as a law enforcer but not clear whether he has, as a reasonable alternative, properly exercised his authority as a public safety officer. The defense of the position that he has done so (or at least that he is justified in overstepping his authority) is developed from the assumptions (a) that it is the job of the police to suppress or control drug use, and (b) that confiscation of drugs is at least as effective as conviction of drug users in achieving this control. In short, the defense of D'Angelo is a classic case of invoking ends (a) to justify means (b).

THE ENDS-MEANS TEST

Under what circumstances can ends be used to justify the means involved in carrying them out? Despite connotations of Machiavellianism in this pattern of reasoning, there are conditions under which appeal to ends if an appropriate defense of the means to achieve them. These conditions are most usefully conceived as a "test" to which ends-means reasoning must be put in order to satisfy the demands of justification. There are four conditions:

1. The end must itself be good.
2. The means must be a plausible way to achieve the end.
3. There must be no alternative, better, means to achieve the same end.
4. The means must not undermine some other equal or greater end.

It is, perhaps, obvious that if the end is to stand as justification for the means, its own goodness must not be open to question. If one's end is to increase the misery of the weak and the helpless, then the means to achieve this end cannot be justified, whether they meet conditions (2) through (4) or not. In fact, there is no point in going on to explore whether the means meet these further conditions if the end does not meet the first one. To the extent that the end is not clearly evil but only morally questionable, this form of justification of means will accordingly be problematic. In short, this test for justification of a course of action as a means can be applied only in circumstances where the value of the end is not seriously in dispute.

Given the value of the end, the means must also be established as a plausible way to achieve it. This test cannot be used to justify any action whatever simply by invoking the good intention of trying to achieve a good end. If my end is to feed the hungry, investing the money I have raised in lottery tickets is not justifiable because it does not meet the second condition. The chances of increasing my resources by gambling in the lottery are simply too remote. As the connection between means and end becomes more plausible, the possibility of justification grows. I might, for example, use the money I raised to start a food cooperative in a poor neighborhood. Even if this course of action does not ultimately achieve my end (any one of a number of things might go wrong and destroy my plan), so long as the means are plausibly connected to the end, they satisfy the second condition.

The third condition requires that we compare our chosen means to possible alternatives that might well achieve the same end. If my end is to convince a local merchant to refund my money for defective merchandise, a letter from my lawyer is one means and a visit from a hired enforcer is another. The former is better than the latter, since it is a legally permissible form of coercion. Consequently, as long as the legal course of action is plausible (that is, as long as it meets the second condition), resorting to an enforcer will not meet the third condition. Thus, even if the end is good and the means are a plausible way to achieve it, the test for justification is not yet met.

Finally, the means to achieve a given end cannot be justified if at the same time they are undermining of other ends that may be of equal or greater importance than the end of immediate concern. In addition to the fact that hiring an enforcer in the example above fails to meet the third condition, it also fails to meet the fourth. I may receive my refund only to be convicted of extortion and sentenced to jail. My freedom is a higher end than the restitution of a few dollars. Similarly, I might consider whether I am justified in telling a lie (means) to protect a friend (end). Even if I am convinced that loyalty to one's friends is a good thing (1), that the lie will, in fact, work

(2), and that there is no way short of lying that I can succeed in protecting my friend (3), my action may still not meet the fourth condition. If through my lie others are harmed to a greater extent than my friend would be had I not lied, then I cannot say that my means has not undermined a more important end. The fourth condition requires that I balance the good of achieving my end against the possible damage that achieving that end might also do. If the damage is greater than the good, then the end cannot stand as justification for the means.

D'ANGELO AND THE FIRST THREE CONDITIONS

This ends-means test is a very useful way to explore D'Angelo's effort to remove some heroin and a user from the street. It will help us to understand whether he overstepped his peace-keeping authority or, if he did, the extent to which that action might be justified nevertheless. For, if D'Angelo's actions can meet these four conditions, the charge that he is overstepping his authority would either be false or would lose its gravity.

It is hard to quarrel with containment or control of heroin as a good end of police work. In our society, heroin is physically and psychologically destructive to its users, a major source of income for organized crime, and the stimulus for unmeasured amounts of prostitution and theft to support users' addiction. There are, of course, those who argue that drug use, per se, is a victimless crime and should not be regulated by the state. Whatever may be said for that position in the abstract, there is no reason to suppose that police containment and control of heroin users under existing circumstances is less than a good end, assuming here that this really is D'Angelo's end, and that he is not, for example, planning to take the heroin in order to sell it. In other words, given current social realities, police action in this area does aim at increasing public safety and providing a social service that is widely regarded as beneficial. D'Angelo's defense meets the first condition. D'Angelo's means are also plausible ways to bring about his desired end. Despite its illegality, searching people in ghetto alleys is likely to turn up a sufficient quantity of heroin to make it "worth" the time and effort. I am not now considering the disregard of the conditions of probable cause or the violence done to individual rights. Condition (2) demands only that there be a link of likely effectiveness between means and end. If the means could not possibly bring about an end, then they cannot be justified by invoking it. Indeed, if the means are even very unlikely to achieve the end, justification would be problematic. In this case, however, the means are quite likely to be fairly effective a high percentage of time. D'Angelo no doubt "knows who to look for" when he is trying to root out heroin users. He might be wrong in a given instance, but this condition does not require the perception of hindsight. Rousting suspicious characters who fit the description of drug users is a plausible way to find heroin. D'Angelo knows this, and he is not alone in this knowledge. The objections to this means of conducting police business has never been that it doesn't work.

The third condition that must be satisfied to justify D'Angelo's actions is somewhat more difficult to meet. This condition requires that there be no better means that could (plausibly) achieve the same end. I think it is incontestable that a means that did not involve an illegal search would be better than D'Angelo's. The qualification, however, must be that the alternative could achieve the same end. D'Angelo must be able to argue that proceeding within the limits of search and seizure rules would not result in confining and controlling heroin users.

Police officers who are inclined to defend D'Angelo in this example generally take one of two positions. First, they point out that to follow the rules in this case is to leave the suspects with the drugs—as Kirkham would have done. There was no legally defensible probable cause for a search beyond the weapon search. Since there is no legal basis for arrest, there is no alternative means to get the heroin off the street. The choice is to accomplish the end or not; accomplishing it some other way is not an option here.

A second, more aggressive defense of D'Angelo's actions takes the position that arrest and conviction of drug users is not itself a very potent means for controlling or containing heroin use. Arrest and even conviction does not get the drug user off the streets; bail, suspended sentences, and probation all have the effect of making the legal system a minor, acceptable risk for the addict and small dealer. In drug cases, the argument goes, the legal system does not effectively deter from criminal behavior either the addicts who are caught or those who should be sobered by the experiences of those who are caught. Vigorous surveillance, however, and the certainty that police will confiscate their drugs on the street is a threat that addicts understand. It is a more pervasive threat and one that can lead addicts to watch their step or, at best, curtail their activities.

If one accepts this description of first, the consequences of D'Angelo's means and second, the legal alternative, then at this stage of our analysis, police strategy in dealing with suspected heroin addicts should pay no attention to questions of proper arrest procedures. Even is legal arrest and conviction are sometimes possible (probable cause is, after all, not an impossible standard), nonlegal means of dealing with addicts are actually preferable in the sense that they will more effectively lead to the desired goal. While I would not argue that D'Angelo's actions (compared to the legal alternatives) would be effective in all jurisdictions, this argument may be plausible in some. Let us assume at this juncture and for the sake of the argument that D'Angelo's actions meet the third condition of justification.

D'Angelo and the Fourth Condition

The most serious issues of overstepping authority arise in a consideration of the fourth condition: that the means do not undermine some other equal or greater end. Here we must try to put the containment and control of heroin into a more general context and face the question of priorities in the multiplicity of police functions. Are there ends as important as or more important than controlling heroin use that are undermined by D'Angelo's methods? There are at least two candidates for such ends: first, the enforcement of law, including the law of search and seizure and narcotics laws, and, second, police adherence to and respect for due process of law.

Narcotics law enforcement, to the extent that it is an activity police ought to pursue for its own sake—and not merely because it accomplishes some higher purpose—is surely undermined by D'Angelo's approach to policing in this case. If his goal was to gain a conviction for possession of narcotics, the illegal search precluded that possibility, assuming that perjury to gain conviction would not further the end of law enforcement as a goal, since it would violate condition (4) as well. Prior to the illegal search, D'Angelo had the option of running a warrants check on the suspect or perhaps identifying him as a candidate for future arrest. By going for the immediate result of intimidation and confiscation, D'Angelo gave up the possibility of a conviction for this crime.

Adherence to and respect for due process of law are also quite obviously undermined by D'Angelo's actions in this case. The illegal search directly violates the legal rights of the suspect, and D'Angelo's conscious willingness to do so demonstrates a lack of respect for his own legal obligations. There may, of course, be times when a violation of legal process does not indicate a general disrespect for it, but such occasions require at least an appeal to extenuating circumstances. D'Angelo has no grounds for such an appeal. His methods have the ring of routine operating procedure for him.

Given that these two ends are undermined by D'Angelo's actions, the question remains: Are they as important as or more important than the containment and control of heroin addicts? If either or both are of such importance, then D'Angelo's actions cannot ultimately be justified by an appeal to ends—no matter how effective they might be.

Although law enforcement and adherence to and respect for the law are highly valued as ends in our society, it will not do simply to assert that they are of greater value than more particular ends, such as control of narcotics. To take this position would be to lose sight of the fact that the law is also a tool and that we expect the police to regard a number of more particular ends as taking precedence in their work. For example, in a fairly common type of police activity, responding to fights in barrooms, giving precedence to law enforcement for its own sake or for the sake of adherence to legal process would lead to unacceptable results.

Consider the following case:

> *Case 2.* An officer is called to a barroom by the bartender to intervene in a fight between two patrons. There has been no property damage to the bar, and the bartender only wants these patrons ejected. When the officer arrives, the fighters are no longer hitting one another, but they are still speaking angrily. The officer tells both patrons to leave the bar. One is ready to comply, but the second says he will not leave until the first is arrested for assault and battery. He claims that the other man struck him first and that he merely defended himself. Furthermore, he offers to produce witnesses to that effect.

There is little doubt that from a legal standpoint a crime has been committed, and there is a correct legal process to follow in such cases. Typically, the first patron agrees to file a complaint and the second is arrested and ultimately arraigned. In most cases like this, however, police officers would refuse to permit the use of the legal machinery. Rather, they would most likely send both patrons on their separate ways with a warning that a repeat call will mean jail for both of them. Officers tend to believe that barroom fights are the shared responsibility of the parties involved. They are skeptical of the accounts of blame they hear and skeptical of the possibility of learning the truth. Moreover, the kind of people who become involved in such fights are just the people police do not regard as reliable complainants. Unless the fight erupts again in the presence of the police, the demands of the first patron will be ignored. If this incident can be resolved in a way that avoids law enforcement and the legal process, the officers will count it as a success—and they will be right to do so. The adverse consequences of an unprosecuted assault and battery case pale in comparison to the social and economic costs of using the criminal justice system to extend a fight from the barroom into the courtroom that would have been over at the scene. Furthermore, the legal solution runs the risk of making these disputants' relationship worse than it is. Clearly, then, in this case we would not want to assign either the end of law enforcement or the end of adherence to legal process a higher status than the end of neighborhood peace.

This is a case in which there is general agreement among police officers and, I think, among the public at large that ending the fight is more important than law enforcement or the adherence to the respect for legal process, per se. Because this is such a clear case, we can say with some confidence that a simple assertion that law enforcement and legal process must always take precedence over more immediate social goals is not satisfactory. If it is sometimes more important to put neighborhood peace over the enforcement of law, then it is at least possible that the same might be said of control of narcotics and addicts. However, because the narcotics case—at least in the D'Angelo incarnation of it—engenders less general agreement about the appropriateness of police use of their authority, we can not say simply that it is analogous to the case of the barroom fight.

To gauge the extent to which D'Angelo's actions may or may not meet the fourth condition of the "ends-means" test (that the means do not undermine some end of equal or greater importance), we need to look at another case in which there would be general agreement that the resolution of an immediate social problem was not more important than the enforcement of law or the adherence to legal process.

> *Case 3.* A citizen has been robbed of personal property: televisions, jewelry, appliances, and the like. The citizen reports the theft to the police and several days later an officer appears at the door. The officer, a detective who has been assigned the case, says that he knows who the thief is and that he believes he can negotiate the return of the lost items before they are fenced in exchange for a promise from the citizen not to press charges. The officer is quite sure that without such a promise the items will not be recoverable. He says that he could get a warrant and arrest the thief, but to do so would take time and risk the loss of the possessions. The promise that no charges would be pressed would permit the return of the possessions and would allow the detective to have the thief in his debt as a possible future informant.

Despite the attraction of recovered property in this third case, there is strong reason to suppose that the means that sidestep law enforcement and legal process here would carry too great a price. These circumstances are ripe with the possibility of police corruption. In the worst case, this extralegal method of recovering property might induce the officer to extract a percentage of the recovered goods from the victim. Or, should extorting the victim prove too risky, the officer could extort the thief, perhaps forcing the thief to steal even more in order to support his "protector." Even if we assume, however implausibly, that the officer in Case 3 is well-meaning and honest, his methods are likely to make thieves feel relatively safer from arrest than they would otherwise. Thus, the officer's means of recovering property, however effective in this instance, could put property in the neighborhood at greater risk in the long run. In short, the extralegal means of recovering property in Case 3 are likely to undermine the end of police honesty. Indeed, they are likely to undermine the end of security of property in the neighborhood in the long run as well.

The value of law enforcement and legal process in Case 3 is greater than the value of recovering one citizen's property, because laws and procedures tend to hold police officers accountable for their actions, discourage opportunities for corruption, and maintain an adversarial relationship between officers and thieves. These consequences of enforcement of property law are not merely more important than the protection or recovery of property, they are crucial foundations of a system in which property can ultimately be protected from theft.

Case 3 is significantly different from Case 2, the barroom fight, because extralegal processes in the latter do not contain the seeds of a larger threat to either police honesty or the protection of society. Case 2 presents no opportunity for extortion; neither patron is able to use the police for personal advantage, nor have the police anything personal to gain from resolving the incident. Furthermore, barroom patrons, in general, are not put in greater jeopardy by this informal resolution. It is not likely that the fight will recur just because one party was not arrested.

What can the contrast between these cases tell us about the relative value of the ends of law enforcement in the heroin confiscation case? We began our investigation of the possibility that D'Angelo's actions met the fourth condition of the ends-means test by noting that law enforcement and adherence to legal process per se were not obviously greater ends than the control of heroin. What Case 3, by contrast to Case 2, shows us is that extralegal means of maintaining social order need also be evaluated in terms of their potential to support corruption and thereby to undermine the very order that purportedly justifies them.

Even if we assume that D'Angelo is a completely honest officer, his method of controlling narcotics and addicts tends to isolate police activity behind a wall of secrecy. D'Angelo may be able to explain his illegal search to his sergeant, but he will thereby have put his sergeant in the position of turning the addict loose or of requiring a false arrest report. The false report, if pursued, could lead to perjury and complicity that would drive these officers to a conspiracy of secrecy. This imperative of secrecy is, at best, debilitating of relationships among police and prosecutors and so contributes to the very conditions that incline some to make the aggressive defense of these methods.

If we assume that D'Angelo will not involve his sergeant as a co-

conspirator, then the wall of secrecy will be built at the street level. D'Angelo will have to lie to his sergeant about the circumstances of the arrest, or he may simply dispose of the heroin and turn his suspect loose. In either event, only the most naive sergeant would take reports on such cases at face value. If the sergeant permitted D'Angelo his means, he would be encouraging his squad members to act on their own—outside the realm of accountability.

It seems to me that whatever one may wish to believe about the honesty of individual officers in making extralegal narcotics arrests, the probability that some officers will be corrupted by this arrangement is quite high. The opportunity to take drugs for personal use or resale is pervasive, and the sergeant's nonsupervision makes the risk of discovery relatively low.

If my line of reasoning is at least plausible here, then we may say that the defense of D'Angelo's actions fails the fourth condition of the ends-means test: his actions tend to undermine ends of equal or greater importance than the confiscation of heroin.

By undermining the legal processes of administration of the law of search and seizure and narcotics laws, D'Angelo contributes to the conditions of secrecy and police isolation that foster corruption in narcotics enforcement and, presumably, further entrench the use of heroin. Even if D'Angelo is an honest and well-intentioned officer, his methods, if permitted to flourish, undermine his own goals. I conclude that D'Angelo has overstepped his peace-keeping authority and is not justified in doing so.

The larger lesson, of course, is that although the ends sometimes do justify the means, as they appear to in Case 2, we cannot presume that they will. However, the process of subjecting our means to the test of justification is a valuable exercise that can shed much light on the moral consequences of police practices. It requires that police articulate and rank their priorities, and that they evaluate their actions within that larger moral framework.

NOTES

1. Cohen, *Authority: The Limits of Discretion*, MORAL ISSUES IN POLICE WORK (F. Elliston & M. Feldberg eds. 1985); see also Cohen, *A Dilemma for Discretion*, POLICE ETHICS: HARD CHOICES IN LAW ENFORCEMENT (W. Heffernan & T. Stroup eds. 1985).

2. There are a number of recent works on the variety and ambiguity of the police role. They include: Bittner, *The Capacity to Use Force as the Core of the Police Role*, MORAL ISSUES IN POLICE WORK, *supra* note 1; C. KLOCKARS, IDEA OF POLICE (1985); J. COOPER, YOU CAN HERE THEM KNOCKING—A STUDY IN THE POLICING OF AMERICA (1981); J. SKOLNICK, JUSTICE WITHOUT TRIAL (1966); P. Davis, Working Role of the Police Officer—Unofficial Policework and Order Maintenance (Doctoral Dissertation, UCLA, 1979); Rumbout & Bittner, *Changing Conceptions of the Police Role—A Sociological Review*, CRIME AND JUSTICE—AN ANNUAL REVIEW OF RESEARCH (N. Morris & M. Tonry eds. 1979).

LEARNING POLICE ETHICS 5

Lawrence Sherman

There are two ways to learn police ethics. One way is to learn on the job, to make your moral decision in haste under the time pressures of police work. This is by far the most common method of learning police ethics, the way virtually all of the half million police officers in the United States decide what ethical principles they will follow in their work. These decisions are strongly influenced by peer group pressures, by personal self-interest, by passions and emotions in the heat of difficult situations.

The other way may be a better way. One can learn police ethics in a setting removed from the heat of battle, from the opinions of co-workers, and from the pressures of supervisors. He can think things through with a more objective perspective on the issues. He should be able to make up his mind about many difficult choices before he actually has to make them. And he can take the time to weigh all sides of an issue carefully, rather than make a snap judgment.

The purpose of this article is to provide a basis for this other, less common way of learning police ethics, by making the alternative—the usual way of learning police ethics—as clear as possible. This portrait of the on-the-job method is not attractive, but it would be no more attractive if we were to paint the same picture for doctors, lawyers, judges, or college professors. The generalizations we make are not true of all police officers, but they do reflect a common pattern, just as similar patterns are found in all occupations.

LEARNING NEW JOBS

Every occupation has a learning process (usually called "socialization") to which its new members are subjected. The socialization process functions to make most "rookies" in the occupation adopt the prevailing rules, values, and attitudes of their senior colleagues in the occupation. Very often, some of the existing informal rules and attitudes are at odds with the formal rules and attitudes society as a whole expects members of the occupation to follow This puts rookies in a moral dilemma: Should the rookies follow the formal rules of society or the informal rules of their senior colleagues?

These dilemmas vary in their seriousness from one occupation and one organization to the next. Young college professors may find that older professors expect them to devote most of their time to research and writing, while the general public (and their students) expects them to devote most of their time to teaching. With some luck and a lot of work they can do both.

Police officers usually face much tougher dilemmas. Like waiters, longshoremen, and retail clerks, they may be taught very early how to steal—at the scene of a burglary, from the body of a dead person, or in other opportunities police confront. They may be taught how to commit perjury in court to insure that their arrests lead to conviction or how to lie in disciplinary investigations to protect their colleagues. They may be taught how to shake people down, or how to beat people up. Or they may be fortunate enough to go to work in an agency, or with a group of older officers, in which none of these violations of official rules is ever suggested to them.

Whether or not rookie police officers decide to act in ways the wider society might view as unethical, they are all subjected to a similar process of being taught certain standards of behavior. Their reactions to that learning, as the years pass by, can be described as their *moral careers:* the changes in the morality and ethics of their behavior. But the moral career is closely connected to the *occupational career:* the stages of growth and development in becoming a police officer.

This article examines the process of learning a new job as the context for learning police ethics. It then describes the content of the ethical and moral values in many police department "cultures" that are conveyed to new police officers, as well as the rising conflict within police agencies over what those values should be. Finally, it describes the moral career of police officers, including many of the major ethical choices officers make.

BECOMING A POLICE OFFICER

There are four major stages in the career of anyone joining a new occupation.[1]

- the *choice* of occupation
- the *introduction* to the occupation
- the first *encounter* with doing the occupation's work
- the *metamorphosis* to a full-fledged member of the occupation

Police officers go through these stages, just as doctors and bankers do. But the transformation of the police officer's identity and self-image may be more radical than in many other fields. The process can be overwhelming, changing even the strongest of personalities.

CHOICE

There are three aspects of the choice to become a police officer. One is the *kind of person* who makes that choice. Another is the *reason* the choice is made, the motivations for doing police work. The third is the *methods* people must use as police officers. None of these aspects of choice appears to predispose police officers to be more or less likely to perform their work ethically.

Many people toy with the idea of doing police work, and in the past decade the applicants for policing have become increasingly diverse. Once a predominately white male occupation, policing has accepted many more minority group members and attracted many more women. More college-educated people have sought out police work, but this may merely reflect the higher rate of college graduates in the total population.

What has not changed, apparently, is the socioeconomic background of people who become police. The limited evidence suggests police work attracts the sons and daughters of successful tradespeople, foremen, and civil servants—especially police. For many of them, the good salary (relative to the educational requirements), job security, and prestige of police work represent a good step up in the world, an improvement on their parents' position in life.

The motivation to become a police officer flows naturally from the social position of the people who choose policing. People do not seem to choose policing out of an irrational lust for power or because they have an "authoritarian personality." The best study on this question showed that New York City police recruits even had a lower level of authoritarian attitudes than the general public (although their attitudes become more authoritarian as they become adapted to police work, rising to the general public's level of authoritarian attitudes).[2] Police applicants tend to see police work as an adventure, as a chance to do work out-of-doors, without being cooped up in an office, as a chance to do work that is important for the good of society, and not as a chance to be the "toughest guy on the block." Nothing in the motivation to apply for a police position seems to predispose police officers towards unethical behavior.

Nor do the methods of selecting police officers seem to affect their long-term moral careers. There was a time when getting on the force was a matter of bribery or political favors for local politicians, or at least a matter of knowing the right people involved in grading the entrance examinations and sitting on the selection committees. But in the 1980s the selection process appears to be highly bureaucratic, wherein impersonal multiple-choice tests scored by computers play the most important role in the process.

To be sure, there are still subjective background investigations, personal interviews, and other methods that allow biases to intrude upon the selection process. But these biases, if anything, work in the direction of selecting people who have backgrounds of unquestioned integrity. Combined with the high failure rate among all applicants—sometimes less than one in twenty is hired, which makes some police departments more selective in quantitative terms than the Harvard Law School—the selection process probably makes successful applicants feel that they have been welcomed into an elite group of highly qualified people of very high integrity.

INTRODUCTION

But this sense of high ideas about police work may not last for long. The introduction to policing provided by most police academies begins to convey folklore that shows the impossibility of doing things "by the book" and the frequent necessity of "bending the rules."

Police recruit training has changed substantially over the past 30 years. Once highly militaristic, it has recently taken on more the atmosphere of the college classroom. The endurance test-stress environment approach, in which trainees may be punished for yawning or looking out the window, may still be found in some cities, but it seems to be dying out. Dull lectures on the technical aspects of police work (such as how to fill out arrest reports) and the rules and regulations of the department are now often supplemented by guest lectures on theories of crime and the cultures of various ethnic groups.

But the central method of *moral* instruction does not appear to have changed. The "war story" still remains the most effective device for communicating the history and values of the department. When the instructor tells a "war story," or an anecdote about police work, the class discipline is relaxed somewhat, the interest and attention of the class increase, and an atmosphere of camaraderie between the class and the instructor is established. The content of the war story makes a deep impression on the trainees.

The war stories not only introduce police work as it is experienced by police officers—rather than as an abstract ideal— they also introduce the ethics of police work as something different from what the public, or at least the law and the press, might expect. Van Maanen recounts one excerpt from a police academy criminal law lecture that, while not a "story," indicates the way in which the hidden values of police work are conveyed:

> I suppose you guys have heard of Lucky Baldwin? If not, you sure will when you hit the street. Baldwin happens to be the biggest burglar still operating in this town. Every guy in this department from patrolman to chief would love to get him and make it stick. We've busted him about ten times so far, but he's got an asshole lawyer and money so he always beats the rap.... If I ever get a chance to pinch the SOB, I'll do it my way with my thirty-eight and spare the city the cost of a trial.[3]

Whether the instructor would actually shoot the burglary suspect is open to question, although he could do so legally in most states if the suspect attempted to flee from being arrested. More important is the fact that the rookies spend many hours outside the classroom debating and analyzing the implications of the war stories. These discussions do help them decide how they would act in similar circumstances. But the decisions they reach in these informal bull sessions are probably more attributable to peer pressure and the desire to "fit in" to the culture of the department than to careful reflection on moral principle.

ENCOUNTER

After they leave the academy, the rookies are usually handed over to Field Training Officers (FTOs). In the classic version of the first day on patrol with the rookie, the FTO says, "Forget everything they taught you in the academy, kid; I'll show you how police work is really done." And show they do. The rookie becomes an observer of the FTO as he or she actually does police work. Suddenly the war stories come alive, and all the questions about how to handle tough situations get answered very quickly and clearly, as one police veteran recalls:

> On this job, your first partner is everything. He tells you how to survive on the job...how to walk, how to stand, and how to speak and how to think and what to say and see.[4]

The encounter with the FTO is only part of the rookie's "reality shock" about police work. Perhaps even more important are the rookie's encounters with the public. By putting on the uniform, the rookie becomes part of a visible minority group. The self-consciousness about the new appearance is heightened by the nasty taunts and comments the uniform attracts from teenagers and others.[5] The uniform and gun, as symbols of power, attract challenges to that power simply because they are there.[6] Other people seek out the uniform to manipulate the rookie to see the power on behalf of their personal interests. Caught frequently in the cross fire of equally unreasonable citizen demands, the rookie naturally reacts by blaming the public. The spontaneous reaction is reinforced by one of the central values of the police culture: the public as enemy.[7]

This is not different from the way many doctors view their patients, particularly patients with a penchant for malpractice suits. Nor is it different from the view many professors have of their students as unreasonable and thick-headed, particularly those who argue about grades. Like police officers, doctors and professors wield power that affects other people's lives, and that power is always subject to counterattack. Once again, Van Maanen captures the experience of the rookie:

> [My FTO] was always telling me to be forceful, to not back down and to never try to explain the law or what we are doing to a civilian. I really didn't know what he was talking about until I tried to tell some kid why we have laws about speeding. Well, the more I tried to tell him about traffic safety, the angrier he got. I was lucky

just to get his John Hancock on the citation. When I came back to the patrol car, [the FTO] explains to me just where I'd gone wrong. You really can't talk to those people out there; they just won't listen to reason.[8]

It is the public that transforms the rookie's self-conception, teaching him or her the pains of exercising power. The FTO then helps to interpret the encounters with the public in the light of the values of the police culture, perhaps leading the rookie even further away from the values of family or friends about how police should act.

The FTO often gives "tests" as he or she teaches. In many departments, the tests are as minor as seeing if the rookie will wait patiently outside while the FTO visits a friend. In other departments, the test may include getting the rookie involved in drinking or having sex on duty, a seriously brutal slugfest against an arrestee, or taking bribes for nonenforcement. The seriousness of the violations may vary, but the central purpose of the test does not: seeing if the rookie can keep his or her mouth shut and not report the violations to the supervisors. A rookie who is found to be untrustworthy can be, literally, hounded and harassed from the department.

Finally, in the encounter stage, the rookie gets the major reality shock in the entire process of becoming a police officer. The rookie discovers that police work is more social work than crime fighting, more arbitration of minor disputes than investigations of major crimes, more patching of holes in the social fabric than weaving of webs to catch the big-time crooks. The rookie's usual response is to define most of the assignments received as "garbage calls," not *real* police work. Not quite sure whom to blame for the fact that he or she was hired to do police work but was assigned everything else, the rookie blames the police executive, the mayor and city council, and even previous U.S. presidents (for raising public expectations). But most of all the rookie blames the public, especially the poor, for being so stupid as to have all these problems, or so smart as to take advantage of welfare and other social programs.

METAMORPHOSIS

The result of those encounters is usually a complete change, a total adaptation of the new role and self-conception as a "cop." And with that transformation comes a stark awareness of the interdependence cops share with all other cops. For all the independence police have in making decisions about how to deal with citizens, they are totally and utterly dependent on other police to save their lives, to respond to a call of an officer in trouble or in need of assistance, and to lie on their behalf to supervisors to cover up minor infractions of the many rules the department has. This total change in perspective usually means that police accept several new assumptions about the nature of the world:

- Loyalty to colleagues is essential for survival.
- The public, or most of it, is the enemy.
- Police administrators are also the enemy.
- Any discrepancy between these views and the views of family and friends is due simply to the ignorance of those who have not actually done police work themselves.

These are their new assumptions about the *facts* of life in police work, the realities which limit their options for many things, including the kinds of moral principles they can afford to have and still "survive," to keep the job, pay the mortgage, raise the kids, and vest the pension. This conception of the facts opens new police officers to learning and accepting what may be a new set of values and ethical principles. By the time the metamorphosis has been accomplished, in fact, most of these new values have been learned.

CONTENT OF POLICE VALUES TEACHING

Through the war stories of the academy instructor, the actions and stories of the FTO, the bull sessions with other rookies and veterans, and the new officer's encounters with the public, a fairly consistent set of values emerges. Whether the officer accepts these values is another question. Most students of police work seem to agree that these are the values (or some of them) that are taught:

1. Discretion A: *Decisions about whether to enforce the law, in any but the most serious cases, should be guided by both what the law says and who the suspect is.* Attitude, demeanor, cooperativeness, and even race, age, and social class are all important considerations in deciding how to treat people generally and whether or not to arrest suspects in particular.

2. Discretion B: *Disrespect for police authority is a serious offense that should always be punished with an arrest or the use of*

force. The "offense" known as "contempt of cop" or P.O.P.O. (pissing off a police officer) cannot be ignored. Even when the party has committed no violation of the law, a police officer should find a safe way to impose punishment, including an arrest on fake charges.

3. Force: *Police officers should never hesitate to use physical or deadly force against people who "deserve it" or where it can be an effective way of solving a crime.* Only the potential punishments by superior officers, civil litigation, citizen complaints, and so forth should limit the use of force when the situation calls for it. When you can get away with it, use all the force that society should use on people like that—force and punishment which bleeding-heart judges are too soft to impose.

4. Due Process: *Due process is only a means of protecting criminals at the expense of the law-abiding and should be ignored whenever it is safe to do so.* Illegal searches and wiretaps, interrogation without advising suspects of their Miranda rights, and if need be (as in the much-admired movie, *Dirty Harry*), even physical pain to coerce a confession are all acceptable methods for accomplishing the goal the public wants the police to accomplish: fighting crime. The rules against doing those things merely handcuff the police, making it more difficult for them to do their job.

5. Truth: *Lying and deception are an essential part of the police job, and even perjury should be used if it is necessary to protect yourself or get a conviction on a "bad guy."* Violations of due process cannot be admitted to prosecutors or in court, so perjury (in the serious five percent of cases that ever go to trial) is necessary and therefore proper. Lying to drug pushers about wanting to buy drugs, to prostitutes about wanting to buy sex, or to congressmen about wanting to buy influence is the only way, and therefore a proper way, to investigate these crimes without victims. Deceiving muggers into thinking you are an easy mark and deceiving burglars into thinking you are a fence are proper because there are not many other ways of catching predatory criminals in the act.

6. Time: *You cannot go fast enough to chase a car thief or traffic violator nor slow enough to get to a "garbage" call; and when there are no calls for service, your time is your own.* Hot pursuits are necessary because anyone who tries to escape from the police is challenging police authority, no matter how trivial the

initial offense. But calls to nonserious or social-work problems, like domestic disputes or kids making noise, are unimportant, so you can stop to get coffee on the way or even stop at the cleaner's if you like. And when there are no calls, you can sleep, visit friends, study, or do anything else you can get away with, especially on the midnight shift, when you can get away with a lot.

7. Rewards: *Police do very dangerous work for low wages, so it is proper to take any extra rewards the public wants to give them, like free meals, Christmas gifts, or even regular monthly payments (in some cities) for special treatment.* The general rule is: take any reward that doesn't change what you would do anyway, such as eating a meal, but don't take money that would affect your job, like not giving traffic tickets. In many cities, however, especially in the recent past, the rule has been to take even those awards that do affect your decisions, as long as they are related only to minor offenses—traffic, gambling, prostitution, but not murder.

8. Loyalty: *The paramount duty is to protect your fellow officers at all costs, as they would protect you, even though you may have to risk your own career or your own life to do it.* If your colleagues make a mistake, take a bribe, seriously hurt somebody illegally, or get into other kinds of trouble, you should do everything you can to protect them in the ensuing investigation. If your colleagues are routinely breaking the rules, you should never tell supervisors, reporters, or outside investigators about it. If you don't like it, quit—or get transferred to the police academy. But never, ever, blow the whistle.

THE RISING VALUE CONFLICTS

None of these values is as strongly or widely held as in the past. Several factors may account for the breakdown in traditional police values that has paralleled the breakdown of traditional values in the wider society. One is the increasing diversity of the kinds of people who join police departments: more women, minorities, and college graduates. Another is the rising power of the police unions which defend individual officers who get into trouble—sometimes even those who challenge the traditional values. A third factor is the rise of investigative journalism and the romantic aura given to "bucking the system" by such movies as *Serpico*. Watergate and other recent exposés of corruption in high places—especially the attitude of being "above the law"—have probably made all public officials more conscious of the ethics of their behavior. Last but not least, police administrators have increasingly taken a very stern disciplinary posture towards some of these traditional police values and gone to extraordinary lengths to try to counteract them.

Consider the paramount value of loyalty. Police reformer August Vollmer described it in 1931 as the "blue curtain of secrecy" that descends whenever a police officer does something wrong, making it impossible to investigate misconduct. Yet in the past decade, police officers in Cincinnati, Indianapolis, New York, and elsewhere have given reporters and grand juries evidence about widespread police misconduct. In New York, police officers have even given evidence against their colleagues for homicide, leading to the first conviction there (that anyone call recall) of a police officer for murder in the line of duty. The code of silence may be far from breaking down, but it certainly has a few cracks in it.

The ethics of rewards have certainly changed in many departments over the past decade. In the wake of corruption scandals, some police executives have taken advantage of the breakdown in loyalty to assign spies, or "field associates," to corruption-prone units to detect bribe-taking. These officers are often recruited for this work at the police academy, where they are identified only to one or two contacts and are generally treated like any other police officer. These spies are universally hated by other officers, but they are very hard to identify. The result of this approach, along with other anti-corruption strategies, has been an apparent decline in organized corruption.[9]

The ethics of force are also changing. In the wake of well-publicized federal prosecutions of police beatings, community outrage over police shootings, and an explosion in civil litigation that has threatened to bankrupt some cities, the behavior and possibly the attitude of the police in their use of force have generally become more restrained. In Los Angeles, Kansas City, Atlanta, New York, Chicago, and elsewhere, the number of killings of citizens by police has declined sharply.[10] Some officers now claim that they risk their lives by hesitating to use force out of fear of being punished for using it. Even if excessive use of force has not been entirely eliminated, the days of unrestrained shooting or use of the "third degree" are clearly gone in many cities.

The increasing external pressures to conform to legal and societal values, rather than to traditional police values, have generated increasing conflict among police officers themselves. The divide-and-conquer effect may be seen in police officers' unwillingness to bear the risks of covering up for their colleagues now that the risks are much greater than they have been. Racial conflicts among police officers often center on these values. At that national level, for example, the National Organization of Black Law Enforcement Executives (NOBLE) has been battling with the International Association of Chiefs of Police (IACP) since at least 1979 over the question of how restrictive police department firearms policies should be.

These conflicts should not be overemphasized, however. The learning of police ethics still takes place in the context of very strong communication of traditional police values. The rising conflicts are still only a minor force. But they are at least one more contingency affecting the moral choices police officers face as they progress through their careers, deciding which values to adopt and which ethical standards to live by.

THE POLICE OFFICER'S MORAL CAREER

There are four major aspects of moral careers in general that are directly relevant to police officers.[11] One is the *contingencies* the officer confronts. Another is the *moral experiences* undergone in confronting these contingencies. A third is the *apologia*, the explanation officers develop for changing the ethical principles they live by. The fourth and most visible aspect of the moral careers of police officers is the *stages* of moral change they go through.

CONTINGENCIES

The contingencies shaping police moral careers include all the social pressures officers face to behave one way rather than another. Police departments vary, for example, in the frequency and seriousness of the rule-breaking that goes on. They also vary in the openness of such rule-breaking, and in the degree of teaching of the *skills* of such rule-breaking. It is no small art, for example, to coax a bribe offer out of a traffic violator without directly asking for it. Even in a department in which such bribes are regularly accepted, a new officer may be unlikely to adopt the practice if an older officer does not teach him or her how. In a department in which older officers explicitly teach the techniques, the same officer might be more likely to adopt the practice. The difference in the officer's career is thus shaped by the difference in the contingencies he or she confronts.

The list of all possible contingencies is obviously endless, but these are some of the more commonly reported ones:

- the values the FTO teaches
- the values the first sergeant teaches
- the kind of citizens confronted in the first patrol assignment
- the level of danger on patrol
- whether officers work in a one-officer or two-officer car (after the training period)
- whether officers are assigned to undercover or vice work
- whether there are conflicts among police officers over ethical issues in the department
- the ethical "messages" sent out by the police executive
- the power of the police union to protect officers from being punished
- the general climate of civic integrity (or lack of it)
- the level of public pressure to control police behavior

Contingencies alone, of course, do not shape our behavior. If we were entirely the products of our environment, with no freedom of moral choice, there would be little point in writing (or reading) books on ethics. What contingencies like these do is push us in one direction or another, much like the waves in the ocean. Whether we choose to swim against the tide or flow with the waves is up to each of us.

MORAL EXPERIENCES

The moral experience is a major turning point in a moral career. It can be an agonizing decision about which principles to follow, or it can be a shock of recognition as you finally understand the moral principles implicit in how other people are behaving. Like the person asleep on a raft drifting out to sea, the police officer who has a moral experience suddenly discovers where he or she is and what the choices are.

Some officers have had moral experiences when they found out the system they worked for was corrupt: when the judge dismissed the charges against the son of a powerful business executive, or when a sergeant ordered the officer not to make arrests at an illegal after-hours bar. One leading police executive apparently went through a moral experience when he was first assigned to the vice squad and saw all the money that his colleagues were taking from gamblers. Shocked and disgusted, he sought and obtained a transfer to a less corrupt unit within a few weeks.

Other officers have had moral experiences in reaction to particular incidents. One Houston police rookie was out of the academy for only several weeks when he witnessed a group of his senior colleagues beat up a Mexican-American, Joe Campos Torres, after he resisted arrest in a bar. Torres drowned after jumping or being pushed from a great height into a bayou, and no one knew how he had died when his body was found floating nearby. The officer discussed the incident with his father, also a Houston police officer, and the father marched the young officer right into the Internal Affairs Division to give a statement. His testimony became the basis of a federal prosecution of the other officers.

Other officers may have a moral experience when they see their ethics presented in public, outside of the police culture. New York City police captain Max Schmittberger, for example, who had been a bagman collecting graft for his superiors in New York's Tenderloin district, was greatly moved by the testimony of prostitutes he heard at the hearings of the Lexow Committee investigating police corruption in 1893. He told muckraking reporter Lincoln Steffens that the parade of witnesses opened his eyes to the reality of the corruption, so he decided to get on the witness stand himself to reveal even more details of the corruption.

No matter what contingencies occur to prompt a moral experience, the police officer faces relatively few choices about how to react. One option is to drift with the tide, letting things go on as they have been. Another option is to seek an escape route, such as a transfer, that removes the moral dilemma that may prompt the moral experience. A third option is to leave police work altogether, although the financial resources of police officers are not usually great enough to allow the luxury of resigning on principle. The fourth and most difficult option is to fight back somehow, either by blowing the whistle to the public or initiating a behind-the-scenes counterattack.

Not all moral experiences are prompted by criminal acts or even by violations of rules and regulations. Racist jokes or language, ethnic favoritism by commanders, or other issues can also prompt moral experiences. With some officers, though, nothing may ever prompt a moral experience; they may drift out to sea, or back to shore, sound asleep and unaware of what is happening to them.

APOLOGIA

For those officers with enough moral consciousness to suffer a moral experience, a failure to "do the right thing" could be quite painful to live with. "Even a bent policeman has a conscience," as a British police official who resigned on principle (inadequate police corruption investigations in London) once observed.[12] In order to resolve the conflict between what they think they should have done and what they actually did, officers often invent or adopt an acceptable explanation for their conduct. The explanation negates the principle they may have wished they actually had followed, or somehow makes their behavior consistent with that principle.

Perhaps the most famous apologia is the concept of "clean graft:" bribes paid to avoid enforcement of laws against crimes that don't hurt people. Gambling and prostitution bribes were traditionally labeled as "clean graft," while bribes from narcotics pushers were labeled "dirty graft." (As narcotics traffic grew more lucrative, however, narcotics bribes were more often labeled "clean.")

The apologia for beating a handicapped prisoner in a moment of anger may draw on the police value system of maintaining respect for authority and meting out punishment because the courts will not. The apologia for stopping black suspects more often than white suspects may be the assumption that blacks are more likely to be guilty. No matter what a police officer does, he or she is apt to find *situationally justified* reasons for doing it. The reasons are things only the officer can understand, because only the officer knows the full story, all the facts of the *situation*. The claim of situational expertise, of course, conveniently avoids any attempt to apply a general moral principle to conduct. The avoidance is just as effective in the officer's own mind as it would be if the apologia were discussed with the officer's spouse, clergyman, or parents.

Perhaps the most important effect of the apologia is that it allows the officer to live with a certain moral standard of behavior, to become comfortable with it. This creates the potential for further apologias about further changes in moral standards. The process can clearly become habit-forming, and it does. The progression from one apologia to the next makes up the stages of moral change.

STAGES

The stages of moral change are points on a moral continuum, the different levels of moral improvement or of the "slippery slope" of moral degeneration. Such descriptions sound trite and old-fashioned, but they are commonly used by officers who get into serious trouble—such as being convicted for burglary—to account for their behavior.

The officers caught in the Denver police burglary ring in 1961, for example, appear to have progressed through many stages in their moral careers before forming an organized burglary ring:

1. First they suffered moral experience that showed them that the laws were not impartially enforced and that judges were corrupt.
2. Then they learned that other police officers were dishonest, including those who engaged in "shopping," i.e., stealing goods at the scene of a nighttime commercial burglary, with the goods stolen by the police thus indistinguishable from the goods stolen by others.
3. They joined in the shopping themselves and constructed an apologia for it ("the insurance pays for it all anyway").
4. The apologia provided a rationale for a planned burglary in which they were burglars ("the insurance still pays for it").
5. The final stage was to commit planned burglaries on a regular basis.

These stages are logically available to all police officers. Many, perhaps most officers progress to Stage 3 and go no further, just as most professors steal paper clips and photocopying from their universities but not books or furniture. Why some people move into the further stages and others do not is a problem for the sociology of deviance, not ethics. The fact is that some officers do move into the more serious stages of unethical conduct after most officers have established the custom in the less serious, but still unethical, stages.

Each aspect of police ethics, from force to time to due process, has different sets of stages. Taken together, the officer's movement across all the stages on all the ethical issues makes up his or her moral career in police work. The process is not just one way; officers can move back closer to legal principles as well as away from them. But the process is probably quite connected across different issues. Your moral stage on stealing may parallel your moral stage on force.

LEARNING ETHICS DIFFERENTLY

This article has treated morality as if it were black and white, i.e., as if it consisted of clear-cut principles to be obeyed or disobeyed. Many issues in police ethics are in fact clear-cut and hold little room for serious philosophical analysis. One would have a hard time making a rational defense of police officers stealing, for example.

But what may be wrong with the way police ethics is now taught and learned is just that assumption: that all police ethical issues are as clear-cut as stealing. They are not. The issues of force, time, discretion, loyalty, and others are all very complex, with many shades of gray. To deny this complexity, as the formal approaches of police academies and police rule books often do, may simply encourage unethical behavior. A list of "dos" and "don'ts" that officers must follow because they are ordered to is a virtual challenge to their ingenuity: catch me if you can. And in the face of a police culture that has already established values quite contrary to many of the ethical rules, the black-and-white approach to ethics may be naive.

As indicated above, an alternative approach may be preferred. This would consider both clear-cut and complex ethical issues in the same fashion: examining police problems in the light of basic moral principles and from the moral point of view. While there may be weaknesses in this alternative approach, it may well be the more sound road to ethical sensitivity in the context of individual responsibility.

NOTES

1.   See John Van Maanen, "On Becoming a Policeman," in *Policing: A View from the Street,* eds. Peter Manning and John Van Maanen (Santa Monica, Calif.: Goodyear, 1978).

2.   See John McNamara, "Uncertainties in Police Work: The Relevance of Recruits' Backgrounds and Training," in *The Police: Six Sociological Studies,* ed. David J. Bordua (New York: Wiley, 1967).

3.   Van Maanen, "On Becoming a Policeman," p. 298.

4.   Ibid., p. 301.

5.   See William Westley, *Violence and the Police* (Cambridge, Mass.: M.I.T. Press, 1970), pp. 159-60.

6.   See William Ker Muir, Jr., *Police: Streetcorner Politicians* (Chicago: University of Chicago Press, 1977).

7.   See Westley, *Violence,* pp. 48-108.

8.   Van Maanen, "On Becoming a Policeman," p. 302.

9.   See Lawrence Sherman, "Reducing Police Gun Use" (Paper presented at the International Conference on the Management and Control of Police Organizations, Breukelen, the Netherlands, 1980).

10.   Ibid.

11.   Cf. Erving Goffman, "The Moral Career of the Mental Patient," in *Asylum: Essays on the Social Situation of Mental Patients and Other Inmates* (Garden City, N.Y.: Anchor Books, 1961), pp. 127-69.

12.   See Sherman, "Reducing Police Gun Use."

II.
Ethical Issues
In Policing—
Questions and Scenarios

Chapter Three

1. Skolnick views police work as sanctioning lying, particularly at early stages of police work. Here, the end is considered to justify the means. According to your own view, how pervasive is the problem of police lying? How serious a problem is it? Based on what we have learned about rights and utility, how do you assess the morality of these actions?

2. Do you think deception can be practiced at one stage of police work (undercover work), but strictly avoided at another stage (testimony)?

3. Should the police use deceptive means to catch offenders? Will honest people ever be caught by such efforts? What about honest but morally weak individuals? Can an honest person be tempted into criminal activity?

4. Should a sliding scale be used, justifying greater deception when there is more evidence that a suspect is guilty? Would this scale justify lying under oath if it were the best means of convicting a person strongly believed to be guilty?

5. What is the likelihood of making an innocent person confess? Do all defendants have the kind of trials and defense attorney assistance that would eventually uncover a false confession?

6. Skolnick asks "why should situational ethics permit lying to a drug dealer, but forbid in-custody conversation questioning of a forcible rapist?" Do such inconsistencies make the law look more like a "a game than a rational system for enforcing justice?"

CHAPTER FOUR

1. Is Cohen's ends-means test an attempt to reconcile concerns with both rights and utility?

2. According to Cohen, actions taken by police oficers must be evaluated in terms of their immediate effect and their long-term effect on the role of law enforcement in a free society. Who should make such decisions? the individual officer? the officer's immediate supervisor? the police chief? Who should be responsible for monitoring police decisions in this regard?

3. What is the best way to insure that individual officers make good decisions regarding ends and means when they are out on the street?

4. Cohen's means-end test requires an effort to prioritize police objectives so that it can be determined whether a particular act undermines a greater goal. How would you prioritize police objectives? What are the highest goals of police work? ends than cannot be compromised?

CHAPTER FIVE

1. According to Sherman, the moral dilemmas confronting police officers are extremely complex, and the instruction in how to confront these dilemmas is either overly simplistic or otherwise inadequate. What type of instruction would be of greatest value? Is it possible, for example, to influence the actions of police officers through classroom study?

2. Why is it difficult for police officers to make moral judgments that are not in line with those of their peers?

3. Police work has been described as "morally dangerous" work, that is, work that is difficult to accomplish in an ethical fashion while maintaining a clear standard of ethics. How do you evaluate this description?

4. How significant are the value conflicts between citizens and police officers? In what areas might disagreement be the greatest?

Scenarios

1. You are a police chief of a small town. One of your recent recruits has been discovered taking kickbacks from a tow truck business for accident referrals. In every other regard the officer seems to be an excellent employee. The complaint was brought to you by a rival tow truck business but has now become common knowledge in the department. What ethical issues are involved in this case? What should you do as police chief?

2. You are the mayor of a major city. The police chief has been quoted as saying that honesty in law enforcement is almost impossible to achieve in today's corrupt environment. The media and others are highly critical of his statement, but he says he was just being truthful and realistic. What is your opinion on the matter? What actions, if any, would you take?

3. You are a police officer. You have just apprehended a drug pusher that you have been after for quite some time. It has been a long and arduous case. This pusher is only one step down from the drug distributor, and you know if you can just get him to talk, you will have the distributor, too. You know the rules, but you also know of countless lives that have been lost or ruined because of this man and his boss. You and your partner have been interrogating him for hours with nothing to show for it. You are not supposed to be left alone with him, but your partner steps out for coffee. Do you take it upon yourself to see that he has an incentive to talk. What do you do? What are your reasons?

III. ETHICS AND THE COURTS

It has been argued that while our criminal justice system is not perfect, it does yield a kind of "rough justice." No one is guilty of exactly the crime for which they are convicted, and no one receives exactly the penalty they deserve, but the majority of people do receive a disposition that approximates justice.

This view is probably accurate, but it is also somewhat troubling. While it is an eminently pragmatic approach, one may question the extent to which justice can be "approximated." One can also question the process by which this approximation is achieved. When defense attorneys and prosecutors struggle against each other in the adversary process, is truth the likely outcome, or just a lucky possibility? Is the process any more agreeable when there is little real argument, just a negotiation over charge and sentence recommendation?

This is hardly the process one would design to find the right punishment to fit the crime or the criminal. But in whose hands should such decisions be placed? The legislature can attempt to ensure greater consistency through determinate sentencing, but such efforts often result in higher penalties than judicial discretion would yield. And in this period of prison overcrowding, what is the correct use of incarceration? One is forced to juxtapose a moral obligation to minimize prison costs that serve to shortchange state health, education and welfare programs, with an equally important obligation to protect the community from crime.

119

The decisions that defense attorneys, prosecutors, judges and legislators must make are difficult ones, requiring a balancing of sound ethical judgments with the pragmatic realities of their positions. To assist their students in dealing with these problems, law schools provide instruction in professional ethics. This is normally achieved by requiring students to complete a course that addresses the practicing attorney's obligations to the client, to the bar, and to the court. Questions have been raised, however, about the utility of requiring a single isolated ethics course, as opposed to integrating a concern with ethics into the general curriculum. While the former provides more intense and focused study, the latter encourages the incorporation of ethical concerns into every aspect of law. This latter course may be a more effective means of instilling high standards, because many ethical dilemmas seem to be a direct result of the conflicting obligations inherent in the practice of law.

ETHICS AND THE COURTS—
THE PRACTICE OF LAW

Pure Legal Advocates and Moral Agents: Two Concepts of a Lawyer in an Adversary System

6

Elliot D. Cohen

It is sometimes asked if a good lawyer in an adversary system also can be a good person. We must first notice that there are two different senses of the term *good* employed in this question. In its first occurrence, good may be taken in its instrumental sense to mean, roughly, *effective*. In its second occurrence, *good* may be taken in its moral sense to mean *morally good*. Thus the question is whether an effective lawyer also can be a morally good person. And the latter question, it is clear, can be answered only if we have some idea of what we mean by a morally good person, and by an effective lawyer.

Accordingly, in this paper I shall first outline what we take to be salient marks of a morally good person. Second, I shall examine one sense of a lawyer, what we call the *pure legal advocate concept*, in which a good lawyer does *not* satisfy our criteria of a morally good person. Third, I shall examine a further concept of a lawyer, what might be called the *moral agent concept*, according to which a good lawyer is, *ipso facto*, a morally good person. Fourth, I shall show how the moral agent concept of a lawyer may be brought to bear on the American Bar Association's *Code of Professional Responsibility*. Fifth, in the light of my analysis of the Code, I shall examine the ABA's current code of ethics, the *Model Rules of Professional Conduct*. Sixth, I shall answer some possible objections to applying the moral agent concept.

MORALLY GOOD PERSONS

Following one tradition, let us say that a morally good person is a person who, through exercise and training, has cultivated certain morally desirable traits of character, the latter traits being constituted by dispositions to act, think, and feel in certain ways, under certain conditions, which are *themselves* morally desirable.[1] What traits of character in particular are morally desirable and to what extent and in what combinations they must be cultivated for a person to be morally good are admittedly no settled matters. Still, there are some traits which at least most of us would countenance as being important, if not essential, ingredients of the morally good personality. It is such traits of character with which I shall be concerned, particularly those among them which seem to be the most relevant to legal practice.

What then are some such characteristic marks of a morally good person?

1. We would not ordinarily countenance a person as being morally good if we believed that he was not a *just* person, that is, if we thought that he was not disposed to treat others justly. There are, however, two senses of *just* and *unjust* in which a person may be said to treat others justly or unjustly.

   First, a person may be said to treat others justly when, in distributing some good or service among them, she observes the principle of treating relevantly similar cases in a similar fashion; and she may be said to treat others *unjustly*, in this sense, when she violates this principle. For example, a physician who consistently distributes medical service among the ill on the basis of medical need would, *ceteris paribus*, be acting justly in this sense; whereas one who distributes such service without regard to medical needs, but instead with regard to race or religion, would, in this sense, be acting unjustly. This is so because we typically regard medical need as the controlling factor in distributing health care; whereas race and religion appear to be quite irrelevant in such a context.

   We may, however, be said to treat others justly when we are

respectful of their legal and moral rights, or when we give to
them what they rightfully deserve; and we may be said to treat
others unjustly when we intrude upon their legal or moral rights
or when we treat them in ways in which they do not deserve to be
treated. For example, one acts justly, in this sense, when he keeps
an agreement with an individual who has the right to insist upon
its being kept; or a judge acts justly, in this sense, when he hands
down a well-deserved punishment to a legal offender; whereas a
person perpetrates an injustice upon another, in this sense, when
he fails to uphold a binding agreement or when he inflicts injury
upon an innocent party.[2]

Let us say, then, that the just person is one who is disposed
to treat others justly in *both* of the above senses. That is, she
tends to be consistent in her treatment of others—she does not
normally make biased or arbitrary exceptions. But she is also the
sort of person who respects individual rights and can usually be
counted upon to make good her obligations to others.

2. Being morally good also would appear to require being *truthful*.
A *truthful person* is one who is in the habit of asserting only
things he *believes* to be true. Thus, he is in the habit of asserting
things with the intention of *informing* his hearers and not deceiving them about the truth. An *untruthful* person, on the other
hand, is in the habit of asserting things which she *disbelieves*;
and this she does with the intention of deceiving her hearers
about the truth.[3] Moreover, the untruthful person may deceive
not merely through her spoken word but also by other means.
She may, for example, leave false clues or simply remain silent
where such measures are calculated to mislead.[4] This is not to
suggest that such tactics are never justified; it is rather to say
that, when they constitute the rule instead of the exception, the
person in question has fallen below that level of truthfulness
which we should normally require of a morally good person.

3. Being a morally good person also would seem to demand at least
some measure of *moral courage*. Indeed, it would appear that a
person could not be just or truthful if he did not have any such
measure; for it often takes courage to be honest or to do what is
just. By a *morally* courageous person, we mean a person who is
disposed to do what he thinks is morally right even when he
believes that his doing so means, or is likely to mean, his suffering some substantial hardship. As Aristotle suggests, it is "the

mark of a brave man to face things that are, and seem, terrible for a man, because it is noble to do so and disgraceful not to do so."[5]

And, therefore, we can say, along with Aristotle, that a person who endures hardship just for the sake of some reward—such as fame or fortune—or for the sake of avoiding some punishment—such as public disfavor or legal sanctions—is not acting truly courageously in this sense, for he acts not because it is morally right to do so but to gain a reward or avoid a punishment.[6]

4. The moral quality of a person is often revealed through her monetary habits. Indeed, for some individuals, the making of money constitutes an end in itself for which they willfully transgress the bounds of morally permissible conduct—for example, the pimp, the drug dealer, the thief, and the hit man. And some—those whom we characterize as stingy, miserly, tight—cling to their money with such tenacity that they would sooner allow great inequities to occur than surrender a dollar.

The morally good person, on the other hand, would appear to be one who has developed _morally respectable_ monetary habits. Such a person Aristotle calls a _liberal_ person, one who, he states, "will both give and spend the right amounts and on the right objects, alike in small things and in great, and that with pleasure; he will also take the right amounts and from the right sources."[7] Following Aristotle, let us say then that a morally good person must also be, to some degree, a _liberal_ person.

5. We also should expect a morally good person to be _benevolent_. By this we mean that she is disposed to do good for others when she is reasonably situated and to do no harm. And the concern she has for the well-being of others does not arise from some ulterior motive but rather _for its own sake_. Furthermore, she is disposed to feel certain ways under certain conditions—for example, feeling sorrow over another's misfortune or taking pleasure in another's good fortune or in helping another.[8]

It is not supposed, however, that to be a morally good person one must be disposed to benefit others at great sacrifice to oneself; nor is it supposed that such a person must go very far to benefit or feel sympathetic toward those who do not stand in any concrete personal relation, such as friendship or kinship. Still, a person who does not go an inch to benefit _anyone_—unless justice demands it—and who sympathizes with no one is perhaps at most a minimally good person. But one who intentionally harms others, as a matter of course, with pleasure or without regret, cannot normally be regarded as being benevolent. Indeed, such is a mark of a malevolent or morally base person.

6. So too would we expect to find _trustworthiness_ in a morally good person. That is, we should expect such a person to be in a habit of keeping the confidences and agreements which he freely accepts or enters upon. Indeed, the person who breaks faith for no good reason is not just being dishonest; he is also being a "traitor" or a "double-crosser."

This, however, is not to suppose that an individual must _never_ breach a trust if he is to be a morally good person. There are undoubtedly some extenuating circumstances in which breaking a trust would be the morally right thing to do—as when keeping it involves working some greater injustice upon someone than that involved in breaking it.[9] Nor is it to be supposed that trustworthiness is a sufficient condition of being morally good. There may be loyalty among thieves, for instance, but we should not for that reason alone take their lot to be morally good.

7. A morally good person, I would suggest, is one who is regularly disposed to do her _own_ moral thinking—that is, to come to her own decisions about moral issues on the basis of her own moral principles and then, in turn, act upon her considered judgment. Kant expressed this fact by saying that the will of a morally good person (that is, a morally good will) is one which is determined "autonomously."[10] Following his usage, let us say then that a morally good person is a person who possesses _moral autonomy_.

Being such a person is undoubtedly no easy matter, for moral decisions are frequently difficult ones to make. For instance, in cases of conflict between one's moral principles, one must weigh one principle against another and then "strike a moral balance"—as, for instance, in a case where keeping a promise involves inflicting harm upon another or when, in determining the value of the consequences of an act, one must balance the good consequences against the bad ones. And clearly such determinations are not mere matters of logical deduction. All that one reasonably can be expected to do in such cases is to try one's level best. But it is a mark of a morally autonomous person, and thus of a morally good person, that he actually _makes_ such an earnest effort.

Keeping the foregoing criteria of a morally good person in mind, let us now turn to an analysis of lawyers.

THE PURE LEGAL ADVOCATE CONCEPT

Following one traditional usage, we can say that the concept of a lawyer is a *functional* concept—that is, it may be defined in terms of the function or role which a lawyer *qua* lawyer is supposed to perform, in an analogous manner, in which a watchdog may be defined in terms of its function of guarding property or in which a carpenter's hammer may be defined in its function of driving nails. Hence, just as a good (effective) watchdog may be defined as a dog that performs well the function of guarding property, so too may a good (effective) lawyer be defined as a person who performs well the function or role of a lawyer.[11] What, then, we may ask, is the function or role of a lawyer?

One sense of *lawyer* is that in which his role as lawyer is restricted to that of his client's legal advocate, and in which sense a good lawyer is thus conceived as being *simply* an effective legal advocate. This sense, which we shall hereafter call the *pure legal advocate concept,* is exemplified in the classic statement made by Lord Brougham when he defended Queen Caroline against George IV in their divorce case before the House of Lords. He states:

> An advocate, in discharge of his duty, knows but one person in all the world, and that person is his client. To save that client by all means and expedients, and at all hazards and costs to other persons, and, amongst them, to himself, is his first and only duty.[12]

The pure legal advocate concept is also more recently suggested by Canon 15 of the ABA *Canons of Professional Ethics,* which states:

> the lawyer owes 'entire devotion to the interest of the client, warm zeal in the maintenance and defense of his rights and the exertion of his utmost learning and ability,' to the end that nothing be taken or be withheld from him, save by the rules of law, legally applied.[13]

This concept is also suggested, among other places, in *The Ethics of Advocacy* by Charles P. Curtis.[14]

Given the pure legal advocate concept, it is easy for one to conclude that the necessary and sufficient mark of a good lawyer is her tendency to win cases by all legal means. For, as was said, this concept supposes that a good lawyer is simply an effective legal advocate; and it is easy to suppose that the necessary and sufficient mark of an effective legal advocate is her tendency to win cases legally. A good lawyer hence emerges as a legal technician skillful in manipulating legal rules for the advancement of her clients' legal interests; in this sense, the good lawyer is no different than a skillful chess player able to manipulate the rules of chess to win *his* game.

Furthermore, given this concept, a lawyer may, and indeed is required to, do certain kinds of things on behalf of his client which would ordinarily be regarded as being morally objectionable. In such instances all that matters, so far as lawyering is concerned, is that such acts are legal means of advancing the client's legal interests. For instance, a defense attorney in a rape case may cross-examine the prosecutrix, whom he knows to be telling the truth, about her chastity for purposes of casting doubt upon her truthful testimony. Or, he may permit his client to take the stand knowing well that the client will perjure himself. Or, a lawyer in a civil case may invoke a legal technicality (for example, the statute of limitations) on behalf of his client to defeat a just cause against him. Or, a corporate lawyer on a continuing retainer may represent a client who seeks to keep a factory in operation which creates a public health hazard emitting harmful pollutants into the air.[15]

However, some who countenance the pure legal advocate concept— namely, those sometimes referred to as *rule utilitarians*—hold that such immoralities as the above-mentioned are the necessary evils of maintaining an adversary system which itself does the greatest good. The working assumption here is that the adversarial form of legal administration, wherein two zealous advocates are pitted against each other before an impartial judge, constitutes the best-known way of maximizing truth and justice; and that furthermore this system works best when lawyers disregard their personal moral convictions and thereby restrict their professional activities to the zealous legal representation of their clients.[16]

If the rule utilitarian is correct, then lawyering so conceived can be said to be a morally justified function, notwithstanding that, on that view, a lawyer may be required to engage in conduct which by common standards is morally objectionable. Thus, when seen in this light, the lawyer emerges as a promoter of the highly prized ends of justice and truth, and as an individual who, because of her service to society, is worthy of praise and admiration. Indeed, she begins to seem like a morally good person.

Nevertheless, I want to suggest that the appearance is deceiving, that, on the contrary, the lawyer so conceived will inevitably fall short of our marks of a morally good person. Moreover, I want to suggest that, as a result of such shortcomings, there is substantial disutility in the pure legal advocate concept of lawyering which its utilitarian exponents rarely take into account in their utilitarian justification of it.

Let me emphasize that I am supposing, along with Aristotle, that it takes exercise and training to cultivate the character traits of a morally good person; one is not simply born with them.[17] My claim is, accordingly, that the legal function as construed under the pure legal advocate concept, with its emphasis on suppression of the individual lawyer's personal moral convictions, does not allow for the cultivation of these traits and is, in fact, quite conducive to their corresponding vices.

Furthermore, I am supposing that a lawyer cannot easily detach his professional life from his private life and thereby cannot easily be one sort of person with one set of values in the one life and a quite different sort with quite different values in the other life.[18]

The latter supposition is justified by the substantial amount of empirical evidence that exists correlating the personality traits of individuals with their specific vocations.[19] One ambiguity, however, is whether individual vocations influence personality traits[20] or personality traits influence choice of vocation, or some combination of both; for any one of these hypotheses would explain the correlation.

Some studies have supported the hypothesis that personality traits influence choice of profession—that is, that people with certain personalities are attracted to certain professions to satisfy their individual needs.[21] But even if this hypothesis is true, and the other above-mentioned hypotheses are false, it is clear that the kind of person found in a profession will remain a function of the way the profession itself is conceived. Specifically, on the hypothesis in question: We would expect the personalities of those choosing careers in law to depend upon their conception of a lawyer. But, if I am correct, then legal practice as construed on the pure legal advocate model could seem attractive only to those individuals who would feel comfortable in a professional climate which discourages, rather than promotes, the personality traits of a morally good person as here understood.

MORAL SHORTCOMINGS OF THE PURE LEGAL ADVOCATE

1. It appears that a lawyer, on the pure legal advocate concept, inevitably will fall short of being a *just* person. For, although she does not violate the principle of treating relevantly similar cases similarly when she gives special preference to her client—

inasmuch as being a client would appear to be a *relevant* dissimilarity for the purposes of an adversary system—she does, indeed, work injustices through the violation of the *moral rights* of individuals, for on this concept, the lawyer's fundamental professional obligation is to do whatever she can, within legal limits, to advance the legal interests of her clients. But from this basic obligation there derives a more specific one which, contra Kant, may be expressed thus: "Whenever legally possible, treat others not as ends but as means toward winning your case." For example, the criminal defense lawyer is thereby authorized to knowingly destroy the testimony of an innocent rape victim to get an acquittal for his client; and a civil lawyer is authorized to knowingly deprive another of what he rightfully deserves by invoking the statute of limitations for the purpose of furthering his client's interests. But we shall concur with Kant that lawyers, like anyone else, have a duty to treat others with the respect which they, as persons, have a right to insist upon.

2. Nor will the pure legal advocate meet the mark of *truthfulness*. For, from her cardinal obligation there derives the secondary obligation of being *un*truthful where doing so can legally contribute toward winning the case. An example of a lawyer who complies with this obligation is one who remains silent when she knows that her client has, under oath, lied to the court. The lawyer, by wittingly saying nothing, engages in deceptive behavior—she contributes to the court's being deceived as to the truth— and is on that count *herself* guilty of being untruthful. Indeed, scrupulous adherence to this obligation could hardly support anything but an untruthful habit.

3. Nor does the concept in question support *moral courage*. For, according to it, the personal moral convictions of a lawyer are irrelevant to his function and should not serve as reasons for zealous representation of clients, or for any sacrifices—of time, money, reputation, and the like—which he may make on their behalf. Indeed, if he is to do his job well, then he must get into the habit of *not* being influenced by his moral outlook. Rather, any sacrifice he may make should be for the sake of obtaining a legal victory, be it a moral one or not. It is plausible to suppose, however, that where morality takes a back seat, ulterior motives such as the self-aggrandizement obtained through winning will serve as the primary motivation.

4. Nor does the pure legal advocate concept support _liberality_. For, the pure legal advocate, through her unconcern with the moral character of her clients and the purposes for which they hire her, acquires the habit of taking money from dishonorable individuals for unsavory purposes. She thus emerges as a professional who can be hired, for a good sum, to do the dirty work of a villain or a scoundrel. Indeed, she then begins to seem more like a hired assassin than like the liberal person whom Aristotle had in view. The high-priced corporate lawyer who wittingly helps her corporate client to market a dangerous product provides us with one example of such a lawyer; and the high-priced criminal lawyer who specializes in defending mass murderers is another.

5. Furthermore, the pure legal advocate concept does not appear to satisfy the minimum condition of _benevolence_—that is, the non-malevolence expected of a morally good person. For, from his primary obligation there derives the secondary obligation to employ even such means to forward a client's interests as are injurious to others, so long, of course, as they are legal. But this also means that a lawyer must learn to put off sympathetic feelings which a benevolent person would normally have. In particular, he must get used to working injury upon others without having any strong feelings of guilt, sorrow, or regret, for, to be sure, such feelings could serve only to interfere with the execution of his basic obligation to his client. The result is thus a callous attitude in his dealings with others. As Charles Curtis puts it, the lawyer "is required to treat others as if they were barbarians and enemies."[22] And, notwithstanding the benefits the lawyer may confer upon his clients, we should not want to call such a person benevolent.

6. Prima facie, it appears that the morally desirable character trait of _trustworthiness_ derives strong support from the pure legal advocate concept. For, indeed, it appears that a lawyer cannot put on the most effective representation of her client's interests unless she is also prepared to hold in confidence the secrets entrusted to her by her client. A problem with this view, however, arises in the case in which there is a conflict between a lawyer's obligation to keep her client's confidence and some other _moral_ obligation—for instance, that of not harming thereby innocent persons. In such a case, the restricted lawyer is required to keep her client's confidence so long as it is legally possible and in her client's best interest to do so. Her judgment

as to what is under the circumstances morally best is then quite irrelevant. But, it is a mark of a morally good person to choose what she thinks is, all things considered, the *morally right* thing to do in such a situation. Hence, whereas a morally good person sees his obligation to keep confidences as one among several moral principles which may at times override one another, the pure legal advocate sees *her* professional obligation to keep her clients' confidences as binding upon her independent of the moral propriety of doing so in any particular case.

In any event, even if it is admitted that the pure legal advocate concept reinforces trustworthiness, which *in itself* is a morally good trait, this still does not show that the good lawyer, on this conception, can be a morally good person. For, as we have seen, there are *further* requisites of a morally good life.

7. I have suggested that an important quality of a morally good person is that he has *moral autonomy*. However, the pure legal advocate concept offers no stimulus to the cultivation of this trait for, as we have seen, the pure legal advocate inhabits a world in which his moral judgment is quite beside the point. If morality is relevant, it is so at the level of the judge or the legislator, but it is quite outside the purview of the lawyer's function. The lawyer must know the law and must know that he owes his undivided allegiance to his client. Given the latter, he can easily accommodate himself to the requirements of the law. His decisions are, in effect, made for *him* by the system he serves. He is more like a cog in a machine and less like a person. But the moral world is inhabited by *persons*—that is, individuals who autonomously confront their moral responsibilities; so that, for a lawyer who has grown comfortable with passing the buck of moral responsibility there is little hope he will aspire to the morally good life.

THE MORAL AGENT CONCEPT

If I am correct, then it appears that the pure legal advocate who scrupulously adheres to her restricted role, far from being a morally good person, will be given ample opportunity to become—if she is not already—quite the opposite. For, she will thereby be placed in a professional climate conducive to her being unjust rather than just; untruthful rather than truthful; unmotivated by a moral outlook rather than morally courageous; illiberal rather than liberal; callous rather than benevolent; morally irresponsible rather than morally autonomous. In short, she will fall well below the minimum standards of a morally good person.

But if all this is true, then there will, it seems, be a good deal of *disutility* in the pure legal advocate concept which, indeed, any utilitarian exponent of it ought to consider in computing its overall balance of utility. For, it appears that such personality traits as those mentioned above, when associated with our concept of a lawyer, can serve only to bring disrespect upon the legal profession and, by association, upon the legal system as a whole. And this low regard may well lead to a commonplace view of the adversary system as a haven for the guilty and the wicked and as something of which the innocent and the morally good ought to steer clear. It can very well serve to discourage persons of strong moral character from entering the legal profession.[23] It is also quite plausible that pure legal advocates who by virtue of their knowledge of and relation to the law are uniquely situated to contribute to needed changes in unjust laws will disconcern themselves with such moral reformation. Moreover, add to these the disutility involved in the unsavory acts performed by pure legal advocates on behalf of their clients in the normal course of discharging their professional obligations—the injuries thereby done to individual litigants as well as to others—and there is at least a strong prima facie case for abandoning the adversary system entirely for a different model (an inquisitorial model for instance) or for adopting a lawyer in an adversary system which avoids these disutilities.

Fortunately, there is a further concept of a lawyer which, while not abandoning the adversarial approach, serves to avoid much of the disutility mentioned above.

This further sense, hereafter called the *moral agent concept,* is exemplified, for example, in the remarks on advocacy made by Lord Chief Justice Cockburn, in the presence of Lord Brougham, at a dinner given in honor of M. Berryer on November 8, 1864. He stated:

> My noble and learned friend, Lord Brougham, whose words are the words of wisdom, said that an advocate should be fearless in carrying out the interests of his client: but I couple that with this qualification and this restriction—that the arms which he wields are to be the arms of the warrior and not of the assassin. It is his duty to strive to accomplish the interest of his clients *per fas,* but not *per nefas;* it is his duty, to the utmost of his power, to seek to reconcile the interests he is bound to maintain, and the duty it is incumbent upon him to discharge, with the eternal and immutable interests of truth and justice.[24]

The moral agent concept was also expressed, more recently, by John Noonan when he remarked that:

a lawyer should not impose his conscience on his client; neither can he accept his client's decision and remain entirely free from all moral responsibility, subject only to the restraints of the criminal law. The framework of the adversary system provides only the first set of guidelines for a lawyer's conduct. He is also a human being and cannot submerge his humanity by playing a technician's role.[25]

And this concept is suggested elsewhere by Richard Wasserstrom, Jeremy Bentham, and *The Report of the Joint Conference on Professional Responsibility*.[26]

Given the moral agent concept, we may no longer say that the good lawyer is simply the effective legal advocate; he is, rather, one who is effective in *morally as well as legally* advocating his client's cause. Hence, one cannot infer from this concept that the good lawyer is one who tends to win his cases. For, on this concept, he is not merely a good legal technician; he is also one who conducts himself in the manner of a *morally good person*—that is, as a person with morally desirable character traits.

It is evident, however, that a lawyer cannot so conduct herself unless she also subscribes to the *moral principles* to which a morally good person would subscribe were she to participate in an adversarial process. If our analysis of a morally good person is supposed, then such principles would need to be ones supportive of the personality traits set forth in that analysis. To wit, from these character traits we may derive a corresponding set of moral principles which are adjusted to an adversarial context. I suggest the following formulations, although other similar formulations are possible:

- Treat others as ends in themselves and not as mere means to winning cases. (Principles of Individual Justice)
- Treat clients and other professional relations who are relatively similar in a similar fashion. (Principle of Distributive Justice)
- Do not deliberately engage in behavior apt to deceive the court as to the truth. (Principle of Truthfulness)
- Be willing, if necessary, to make reasonable personal sacrifices — of time, money, popularity and so on—for what you justifiably believe to be a morally good cause. (Principle of Moral Courage)
- Do not give money to, or accept money from, clients for wrongful purposes or in wrongful amounts. (Principle of Liberality)

- Avoid harming others in the process of representing your client. (Principle of Nonmalevolence)
- Be loyal to your client and do not betray his confidences. (Principle of Trustworthiness)
- Make your *own* moral decisions to the best of your ability and act consistently upon them. (Principle of Moral Autonomy)

We can say that the above principles, or ones like them, at least in part *constitute or define* the moral agent concept of a lawyer; for they are principles to which a lawyer's conduct must to some extent conform if he is to function not simply as a legal advocate but also as a morally good person.

I am not suggesting that these principles are unconditional ones. Indeed, to say so would be unrealistic since they will inevitably come into conflict with one another when applied to specific contexts, thereby making it impossible for the lawyer to satisfy all principles at once. (That is, in order to be truthful, a lawyer may need to betray a client's trust, and conversely.) Rather, what I am suggesting is that such principles impose upon a lawyer conditional—or prima facie—obligations which, in cases of conflict, must be weighed, one against the other, by the lawyer in question in the context in question.

Let me offer an example which will illustrate the difference between applying, in conflict situations, the above multi-principle model and the pure legal advocate model. In *Lawyers' Ethics in an Adversary System,* Monroe Freedman cites the following:

In a recent case in Lake Pleasant, New York, a defendant in a murder case told his lawyers about two other people he had killed and where their bodies had been hidden. The lawyers went there, observed the bodies, and took photographs of them. They did not, however, inform the authorities about the bodies until several months later, when their clients had confessed to those crimes. In addition to withholding the information from police and prosecutors, one of the attorneys denied information to one of the victim's parents, who came to him in the course of seeking his missing daughter.[27]

According to Freedman, the lawyers in the above-cited case were simply discharging their *unconditional* professional obligation to represent their clients' legal interests. However, if the moral agent concept is supposed, then it is clear that the above lawyers could have revealed where the bodies were buried. Admittedly, according to the Principle of Trustworthiness, a lawyer has a (prima facie) obligation to keep his client's confidences. But, he also has

But who can you trust??

further (prima facie) obligations such as those of Truthfulness, Individual Justice, and Nonmalevolence. I think that a plausible case can be made that the latter principles were sacrificed to some extent by the lawyers in the Lake Pleasant case at least insofar as their treatment of the relatives of the deceased was concerned. And it is plausible, I believe, to argue that the moral weight of the latter principles, taken collectively, outweighed that of the Principle of Trustworthiness taken by itself in the situation in question. This need not have been what the lawyers in the cited case should have finally decided to be the correct balancing of principles. The point I want to make is rather that the lawyers did have in the first place, on the conception in question, the *moral autonomy* (as legitimized by our Principle of Moral Autonomy) to make such a judgment on the matter. It is just such moral autonomy—with its weighing of competing moral principles, one against the other—that the pure legal advocate concept disallows.

Of course, if lawyers are allowed such autonomy, there arises the difficulty of providing *criteria* for arbitrating between conflicting principles. This difficulty, we have seen, does not arise on the pure legal advocate model since the pure legal advocate is, in effect, insulated from making moral trade-offs by her unconditional allegiance to her client's legal interests.

One normative view regarding how a lawyer, in accordance with the moral agent concept, might go about solving moral dilemmas takes the form of a "pure" utilitarianism. According to such an ethic, all eight of our principles are to be understood as receiving their ultimate justification from the principle of utility. Hence, in case of conflict the final court of appeal will be the principle of utility itself.

I do not think, however, that such a basis for solving lawyers' moral dilemmas would be adequate. My objection is that which has traditionally been made against utilitarian ethics which are not tempered by justice considerations. Suppose, for example, a criminal lawyer is defending an influential politician accused of rape. Suppose also that the politician admits his guilt to his attorney but nevertheless informs her of his intention to testify under oath (to that which is false) that the defendant first made sexual advances toward him. Now suppose that the politician in question is in the process of bringing about a change in taxation which would mean substantial tax reductions for millions of Americans, and that, furthermore, these efforts would most likely be defeated if the politician in question were convicted of rape. On the pure utilitarian criterion, it would appear that the attorney in question would be committed to allow the politician to perjure himself notwithstanding the defeat of the true rape claim; for the greatest good would (*ex hypothesi*) be served by allowing the politician to escape the charge of rape through his perjured testimony. But, in such a case it would seem unjust (by the Principle of Individual Justice) to sacrifice the well-being of the truthful rape victim for the tax reduction. Indeed, in doing so, the lawyer would arguably commit a grossly immoral act. But, if so, the principle of utility untempered by some principle(s) of justice—such as the Principle of Individual Justice or the Principle of Distributive Justice—would be an inadequate criterion for settling lawyers' moral dilemmas.

A modified utilitarian approach would be to construct a meta-level rule telling lawyers which principle is to receive priority in cases of conflict. The meta-level rule is then to be justified on the basis of the utility of having such a rule. For example, it could be held that the greatest good is ultimately served by requiring lawyers, as a matter of course, to give priority to truthfulness over nonmalevolence.

I do not think, however, that such a position would be tenable. First, like rule utilitarianism in general, it leads to a kind of rule worship where lawyers are asked to abide by a rule even in contexts where the greatest good would not be served by subscribing to it or in which justice considerations would seem to proscribe acting in accordance with it. Furthermore, the view in question is inconsistent with the Principle of Moral Autonomy, which legitimizes a lawyer's acting according to his own considered moral judgments. Indeed, in one of its forms—the one in which the Principle of Trustworthiness is unconditionally ranked above all other principles—this view would seem to be extensionally equivalent to the pure legal advocate model according to which a lawyer is asked to ignore his personal moral convictions.

How then is a lawyer, on the moral agent concept, to resolve antimonies arising between these principles? Although I do not see any formula for doing so, this is not to suggest that one resolution is as respectable as any other. For one thing, there is a difference between the ethical judgment of a lawyer who is *factually enlightened* and one who is not. For example, the judgment of a lawyer who allows trustworthiness to override harm in a particular case without adequate knowledge of the nature and extent of the harm is less respectable than the judgment of a lawyer who takes account of such facts.

Still, once the facts are known, a decision must be made in their light; and I think it would be intellectually dishonest to suggest that there is some principle(s) from which we may logically deduce our decision. Principles take us just so far, leaving the final verdict in our hands.

It is the lack of clear, noncontroversial criteria for resolving moral dilemmas and the ensuing feeling that ethics is, in the end, a matter of "fiat" or "personal preference" that may make some feel uncomfortable about giving lawyers moral autonomy. However, it should be kept in mind by those who worry about the "gray" areas of ethics that the making of ethical decisions is already an accepted and unavoidable part of the role of *some* officials in our legal system. For example, given the "open-textured" quality of legal rules and precedents themselves, judges often need to rely upon their own *moral* evaluations in deciding whether a given set of facts falls under a given legal rule or precedent.[28] But, if judges can handle their moral problems—and I believe that in general they do handle them—then there appears to be less reason to fear that lawyers cannot or will not handle *their* moral problems.

THE MORAL AGENT CONCEPT AND THE ABA CODE OF PROFESSIONAL RESPONSIBILITY

In his classical formulation of a natural law jurisprudence, St. Thomas Aquinas distinguishes between certain basic moral principles, those which he calls *general* principles of natural law and certain *secondary* ones, the latter being more specific deductions from the former. For example, he tells us that "One must not kill" is a secondary principle deducible from "One should do harm to no man." Moreover, such secondary principles, he maintains, assume the status of *human laws* provided they are enforced by the state.[29]

I think Aquinas' distinction between general and secondary principles of natural law is instructive for our purposes; for, if we construe the legal profession on the moral agent concept, then we might say that our eight principles constitute certain general "natural laws" of legal practice—*natural* in the sense that they are at least in part definitive of the lawyer's role—from which more specific moral principles can be deduced.[30] Moreover, an examination of the *ABA Code of Professional Responsibility* reveals that some such deductions have indeed assumed the force of law.

What follows is a listing of some, although not all, corollaries of our general principles as they occur in the Code.[31] In the light of this list, I shall suggest certain revisions required in the Code if it is to support adequately the moral agent concept of a lawyer. I shall then, in the next part of this paper, use these revisions as a basis for criticizing the ABA's current code of ethics, the *Model Rules of Professional Responsibility*.

It will be noted that some of the principles listed below are prefixed by "EC" (*ethical consideration*), whereas others are prefixed by "DR" (disciplinary rule). The former are "aspirational in character" and are "intended to provide guidance, but their violation is not intended to result in disciplinary action." The disciplinary rules, on the other hand, state the "minimum level of conduct below which no lawyer can fall without being subject to disciplinary action." I think, however, that it would be unsound to infer, from the fact that violations of DRs are subject to disciplinary action whereas violations of ECs are not, that the CRs are somehow more important to legal practice. At least this inference would be unsound from the point of view of the moral agent conception which stresses aspirational aspects of morality as well as ground-floor duties. Moreover, it should be noted that some states actually consider the ECs to be obligatory in character.[32]

INDIVIDUAL JUSTICE

DR 7-105(A) A lawyer shall not present, participate in presenting, or threaten to present criminal charges solely to obtain an advantage in a civil matter.

DR 4-101(B)(3) Except when permitted under DR 4-101(C),[33] a lawyer shall not knowingly use a confidence or secret of his client for the advantage of himself or of a third person, unless the client consents after full disclosure.

DISTRIBUTIVE JUSTICE

DR 8-101(A)(2) A lawyer who holds a public office shall not use his public position to influence, or attempt to influence, a tribunal to act in favor of himself or of a client.

DR 5-105(A) A lawyer shall decline proffered employment if the exercise of his independent professional judgment in behalf of a client will be or is likely to be adversely affected by the acceptance of the proffered employment, except to the extent permitted under DR 5-105(C).[34]

DR 5-105(B) A lawyer shall not continue multiple employment if the exercise of his independent professional judgment in behalf of a client will be or is likely to be adversely affected by his representation of another client, except to the extent permitted under DR 5-105(C).

TRUTHFULNESS

DR 7-102(A)(3)-(7) In his representation of a client a lawyer shall not (3) conceal or knowingly fail to disclose that which he is required by law to reveal; (4) knowingly use perjured testimony or false evidence; (5) knowingly make a false statement of law or fact; (6) participate in the creation or preservation of evidence when he knows or it is obvious that the evidence is false; (7) counsel or assist his client in conduct that the lawyer knows to be illegal or fraudulent.

DR 7-102(B)(1) A lawyer who receives information clearly establishing that his client has, in the course of the representation, perpetrated a fraud upon a person or tribunal shall promptly call upon his client to rectify the same, and *if his client refuses or is unable to do so, he shall reveal the fraud to the affected person or tribunal.*[35]

MORAL COURAGE

EC 2-27 Regardless of his personal feelings, a lawyer should not decline representation because a client or a cause is unpopular or community reaction is adverse.

EC 2-25 Every lawyer, regardless of professional prominence or professional workload, should find time to participate in serving the disadvantaged. The rendition of free legal services to those unable to pay reasonable fees continues to be an obligation of each lawyer....

LIBERALITY

DR 2-106(A) A lawyer shall not enter into an agreement for, charge, or collect an illegal or clearly excessive fee.

DR 7-109(C) A lawyer shall not pay, offer to pay, or acquiesce in the payment of compensation to a witness contingent upon the content of his testimony or the outcome of the case....

NONMALEVOLENCE

DR 7-102(A)(1) In his representation of a client, a lawyer shall not file a suit, assert a position, conduct a defense, delay a trial, or take other action on behalf of his client when he knows or when it is obvious that such action would serve *merely* to harass or maliciously injure another.[36]

EC 7-10 The duty of a lawyer to represent his client with zeal does not militate against his concurrent obligation to treat with consideration all persons involved in the process and to avoid the infliction of *needless* harm.[37]

TRUSTWORTHINESS

DR 4-101(B)(1)-(2) Except when permitted under DR 4-101(C),[38] a lawyer shall not knowingly (1) reveal a confidence or secret of his client; (2) use a confidence or secret of his client to the disadvantage of the client.

DR 7-101(A)(1) A lawyer shall not intentionally fail to seek the lawful objectives of his client through reasonably available means permitted by law and the disciplinary rules, except as provided by DR7-101(B).

DR 7-101(B) A lawyer does not violate this disciplinary rule, however, by acceding to reasonable requests of opposing counsel which do not prejudice the rights of his client, by being punctual in fulfilling all professional commitments, by avoiding offensive tactics, or by treating with courtesy and consideration all persons involved in the legal process.

It may appear, from a brief study of the above rules and considerations, that the moral agent concept is well entrenched in the Code. I do not believe, however, that this is quite right; for, although secondary precepts drawn from our general principles can be found in significant numbers, the principle of moral autonomy, which legitimizes trade-offs between principles where conflicts arise, is not unequivocally visible.

Consider DR 7-102(B)(1), cited above under Truthfulness. The italicized portion suggests that the lawyer's allegiance to this client is not so unconditional after all. However, this clause was amended as of March 1, 1974, by the ABA to include the further proviso "except when the information is protected as a privileged communication."[39] Thus amended, the lawyer is disallowed the autonomy to reveal such frauds even when, in a given context, he considers the obligation of truthfulness to override that of confidentiality.

In recognition of such autonomy, the rule in question might be revised along the following lines:

DR 7-102(B)(1) (REVISED) A lawyer who receives information clearly establishing that his client has, in the course of representation, perpetrated a fraud upon a person or tribunal shall promptly call upon his client to rectify the same, and if his client refuses or is unable to do so, he shall reveal the fraud to the affected person or tribunal *except* when the information is protected as a privileged communication *and* the lawyer sincerely believes, after careful consideration of the relevant facts, that, notwithstanding the perpetration of the fraud, the disclosure of such privileged information in such cases would be morally wrong.

The above revision seems to me to present a compromise between the version of the rule as amended in 1974 and the earlier formulation. For, like the 1974 rule, it recognizes a lawyer's obligation of confidentiality; and, like the earlier versions, it recognizes an obligation of truthfulness. But, unlike both versions, it gives a lawyer the autonomy to make trade-offs between these two obligations when conflicts arise. In short, this revision recognizes that neither truthfulness nor confidentiality is absolute; that one can, on occasion, give way to the other.

For example, if a complainant in a rape case confidentially informed her lawyer that she had falsely denied under oath her former unchastity in order to protect her reputation as well as the prospects of winning her case, the lawyer might be hard put to disclose such privileged information to the court. On the other hand, if a defendant in a rape case confidentially informed his lawyer of his having falsely denied under oath that he even saw the prosecutrix on the night of the alleged rape, then the lawyer might be hard put *not* to reveal the information *even* if privileged. In the former case, the fraudulent testimony would not completely destroy the prospects of an informed verdict; in the latter case, though, the fraudulent testimony would greatly impede the search for truth if not corrected. As such, a lawyer might allow confidentiality to be overridden by truthfulness in the latter case although not in the former case. My proposed formulation of DR 7-102(B)(1) at least has the virtue of recognizing such possibilities.

Consider EC 7-10, cited above under Nonmalevolence. It asserts two "concurrent" duties—namely, the duty of a lawyer to represent her client with zeal and her duty to treat others with consideration and to avoid the infliction of "needless harm." But what harm is to be termed "needless" for purposes of this consideration?

One response is that "needless" harms are those which are not necessary for the purpose of advancing the client's legal concerns. This understanding would, it seems to me, be consistent with the Code's use of "merely" in DR 7-102(A)(1); for actions which serve "*merely* to harass or maliciously injure another" do not serve also to advance legal interests. When so under-

stood, however, EC 7-10 is tantamount to saying that lawyers should not harm others *if* this is not in the client's legal interest. But what if it *is* in the client's legal interest to harm another? On the present understanding, and in the absence of any further proviso, the lawyer would apparently be bound by her obligation to her client.

If EC 7-10 is to unequivocally recognize two "concurrent" obligations— one proscribing harming others and the other prescribing zealous advocacy—it will need to be reformulated. But, clearly, once two such obligations are recognized, the possibility of conflict between them arises—a possibility which does not occur when the proscription is only against "needless" harms as above understood and not against harms in general. Moreover, the resolution of such conflicts calls for lawyers' moral autonomy—that is, a lawyer must then attempt to make reasonable trade-offs between these obligations when they conflict. In short, the lawyer becomes a moral agent confronted with moral dilemmas.

To bring EC 7-10 into line with the moral agent concept, I would accordingly suggest something like the following reformulation:

> EC 7-10 (REVISED) In his representation of a client, a lawyer should not engage in conduct, even if in his client's best legal interest, when, upon careful consideration of relevant facts and likelihoods, he sincerely believes that, notwithstanding his obligation to his client, the seriousness of the harm which would thereby ensue to others would render his so acting morally untenable.

The above formulation, unlike the former one, recognizes two concurrent obligations which can at times conflict; furthermore, it gives the individual lawyer the *moral autonomy* to rationally resolve such dilemmas.

Once EC 7-10 is so revised, I would have no objection to DR 7-102(A)(1). This could then be understood as an unconditional proscription of harmful acts serving no legal interest—which is as it should be on the present conception. It would obviously be untenable, however, to set forth a DR which *un*conditionally proscribed *all* harmful acts!

Consider, too, secondary precepts of trustworthiness—in particular, DR 7-101(A)(1). It states that the exceptions to a lawyer's zealous advocacy for her client's lawful objectives are provided for by DR 7-101(B), which runs as follows:

> DR 7-101(B) In his representation of a client, a lawyer may (1) where permissible, exercise his professional judgment to waive or fail to assert a right or position of his client; (2) refuse to aid or

participate in conduct that he believes to be unlawful, even though there is some support for an argument that the conduct is legal.

The first clause of the above rule gives the lawyer the personal autonomy to refuse to assert a position opted for by her client. However, it is not clear that this autonomy extends to *moral* disputes, for EC 7-9 states the following:

> **EC 7-9** In the exercise of his professional judgment on those decisions which are for his determination in the handling of a legal matter, a lawyer should always act in a manner consistent with the best interests of his client. However, when an action in the best interest of his client seems to him to be unjust, he may ask his client for permission to forego such action.

Presumably, DR 7-101(B)(1) must refer to matters concerning the best interest of the client, although not to moral ones; for, according to EC 7-9, a lawyer caught up in a moral dilemma may *ask* the client to forego the course of action in question; but this is other than to actually "waive or fail to assert a right or position of his client."

It appears, then, that to bring the code into line with the moral agent concept, a further "morals" proviso is needed for DR 7-101(B). I suggest something like the following:

> **DR 7-101(B)(3)** In his representation of a client, a lawyer may refuse to aid or participate in conduct that he sincerely believes, after careful reflection on the relevant facts, to be unjust or otherwise morally wrong notwithstanding his obligation to seek the lawful objectives of his client.

Similarly, revisions along the following lines are needed in EC 7-9:

> **EC 7-9 (Revised)** In the exercise of his professional judgment on those issues which are for his determination in the handling of a legal matter, a lawyer should typically act in a manner consistent with the best interests of his client. However, in those cases where he sincerely believes, after careful reflection on the relevant facts, that an action in the best interest of his client is unjust or otherwise immoral, he should inform his client of the same and forego such action.[40]

Finally, to bring the moral agent concept into clear focus, I would suggest adding to the Code a general ethical consideration regarding lawyers' moral autonomy. It may, perhaps, read as follows:

A cardinal duty of a lawyer is to zealously represent his clients' interests within the bounds of the law; but it must also be kept in view that a lawyer, as a servant of such values as truth and justice, is also a moral agent with a duty to *morally* uphold the legal interests of his clients. A lawyer should never allow his role as advocate to blind him to his own sense of property.

The foregoing suggestions are not intended to cover all the changes in the Code which would need to be made *if* it were to adequately support the moral agent concept. They are, however, ones which seem to me to be necessary ones. In general, these changes would aim at increasing lawyers' moral autonomy within the parameters of an adversarial process. Without such autonomy, the other moral principles reflected in the Code—other than that of Trustworthiness—would be without force. Where the obligation to zealously pursue the client's legal interests conflicts with other principles— such as Nonmalevolence and Truthfulness, as well as the secondary principles thereof—the lawyer, on the unrevised formulation of the Code, is entitled to pay only lip service to them.

One issue, however, is whether such lawyer autonomy *ought*, in the first place, to be codified—that is, built into a code of legal ethics. After all, it might be argued, a code of legal ethics needs to be enforceable if it is to be efficacious in controlling lawyers' conduct; and the discretionary approach would tend to make such enforceability either difficult or impossible.

There are several responses to the above argument. First, codifying lawyer autonomy in the manner here suggested is not tantamount to giving a lawyer a license to do *whatever* she thinks (rightly or wrongly) is morally indicated. A lawyer's increased moral autonomy will still be circumscribed around *other* legal realities. For example, it would not be permissible for a lawyer who has moral autonomy to counsel a client to commit perjury or to intentionally present false testimony to a tribunal *even* if she thought, with all sincerity, that there were overriding moral reasons—say, utilitarian ones—for doing so. Indeed, such a lawyer who failed to recognize the limits of her authority would still find herself subject to disciplinary action.

Second, it would be an oversimplification of the situation to suppose that the *specific* disciplinary rules which incorporate moral autonomy would be rendered totally unenforceable. Although it is true that a lawyer who exercises his moral discretion, where permitted by a disciplinary rule, could not be subject to disciplinary action for doing so, it is false to suppose that disciplinary action could not be taken against him on other grounds. For example, my revised version of DR 7-102(B)(1) permits a lawyer moral discretion about revealing frauds perpetrated upon a person or tribunal by his client. But this does not mean that a lawyer can, for example, accept additional fees from a client in return for withholding information about his perjurious testimony. Indeed, such conduct would still constitute a violation of DR 7-102(B)(1), as revised, and it would be subject to disciplinary action. To this extent DR 7-102(B)(1) would retain some measure of enforceability. And the same thing could be said, *mutatis mutandis,* about the discretionary authority conferred upon a lawyer by my DR 7-101(B)(3).

Third, not all the suggested revisions I have made pertain to disciplinary rules. Some—such as those of EC 7-10, EC 7-9, and my suggestion for a general ethical consideration about lawyers' moral autonomy—have instead been concerned with ethical considerations. And, strictly speaking, ethical considerations are not always supposed to be *enforceable;* yet they still do provide important guidelines of lawyers' professional conduct no less than the disciplinary rules, which are always supposed to be enforceable.

Fourth, the latter consideration raises a question about the primary purpose of a code of professional ethics. Even if a significant measure of enforceability is lost by codifying lawyers' moral autonomy, I do not believe that the raison d'etre of the Code will be sacrificed. It is plausible to argue that the *primary* purpose of a code of professional ethics is to *guide* professionals' actions. It is only when this primary function breaks down that issues of enforcement even arise.[41] To be sure, the imposition of sanctions for noncompliance may serve to strengthen the motive of conformity to the rules as announced. But this is not the only way to encourage such conformity. The cultivation of an *internalized* sense of professional responsibility is still another.[42]

A further objection to codifying the moral agent concept might be put as follows. Lawyers, like anyone else, are fallible in their moral judgments. Hence, instead of placing the burden of moral decisionmaking in their hands, it would seem more of a solution to protect the rights of litigants and other affected parties by instituting appropriate laws, thereby providing new legal boundaries to which the lawyer must conform her advocacy. In this way, a lawyer may be free to concentrate her efforts on the zealous defense of her client's interests *within the bounds of the law* without the added headache of moral decisionmaking.

The above argument, in my estimation, makes a valid point. Our laws *should* strive as much as possible to protect the rights of litigants and other affected parties. But it errs when it supposes that the expansion of law in this direction will serve to eliminate moral dilemmas in legal practice. A similar fallacy has, it seems to me, occurred in reasoning concerning the role of a judge. I have in mind here what has sometimes been called "formalism," "conceptualism," or "mechanical jurisprudence"—that is, the belief that by formulating general rules, the need to exercise discretion when applying them to particular cases may be eliminated. But, as I have suggested earlier,[43] the "open-textured" nature of such rules makes unavoidable the exercise of discretion when subsuming particular cases under them; and, indeed, such discretion can be, and frequently is, of a *moral* character. Similarly, it would be mistaken to suppose that by formulating general rules concerning the rights of litigants and affected others the lawyer may be relieved of the need to exercise moral discretion in the course of complying with those rules. For *their* "open-textured" character will still leave space for moral dilemmas. In short, moral problems are inevitable in legal practice; hence a lawyer might as well be given the autonomy to intelligently address them, rather than ignore them, transfer them to other lawyers by withdrawing from morally perplexing cases, or otherwise attempt to avoid them. As shall be suggested in the following discussion, the ABA in its recent move to revise the Code has explicitly acknowledged the limited capacity of general rules to dictate moral outcomes and therewith the need for moral discretion on the part of lawyers.

The Moral Agent Concept and the ABA Model Rules of Professional Conduct

The ABA has recently adopted its *Model Rules of Professional Conduct*.[44] This document constitutes an attempt at a comprehensive revamping of the 1969 Code.

One salient change is in its format. The Model Rules, unlike the Code, do not distinguish between ethical considerations and disciplinary rules. Rather, all the new rules are taken to be obligatory and much of what appears in the ECs of the Code is incorporated into the rules themselves or into *comments* on the rules which contain explanations of, and rationales behind, the rules.[45]

The Model Rules, I believe, represent an important step in the direction of the moral agent concept. Indeed, the Preamble provides a clear suggestion of this concept:

> Virtually all difficult ethical problems arise from conflicts between a lawyer's responsibilities to clients, to the legal system and to the lawyer's own interest in remaining an upright person while earning

a satisfactory living. The Rules of Professional Conduct prescribe terms for resolving such conflicts. Within the framework of these Rules many difficult issues of professional discretion can arise. Such issues must be resolved through the exercise of sensitive professional and moral judgment guided by the basic principles underlying the Rules.

And, again, the late Robert J. Kutak, Chairman of the ABA Commission on Evaluation of Professional Standards, in commenting on the discussion draft of the Rules, asserted that

an implicit theme running through the draft is the recognition that a certain measure of professional discretion is required on the part of a lawyer confronted with ethical choices among competing values. No rules that honestly attempt to grapple with the dilemmas of ethical choice can dictate in every case what the proper choice must be. But codes and rules can—and, we believe, the discussion draft does—compel the reasoned exercise of that choice.[46]

However, notwithstanding such recognition of lawyers' moral autonomy, I believe that much of what I have said about the 1969 Code can be said, *mutatis mutandis,* about the current Model Rules. For example, Rule 3.3(a)(2), regarding "Candor toward the Tribunal," makes it obligatory for a lawyer to disclose a client's perjury to the court should the client himself refuse to do so.[47]

Now Rule 3.3(a)(2) has, I think, the virtue of recognizing unequivocally that the bond of lawyer-client confidentiality is not an absolute. In this respect, it represents a significant advance beyond DR 7-102(B)(1) as amended by the ABA in 1974 (although the amended form was only adopted by some, not all, states).[48] However, it seems to me that 3.3(a)(2) does not go quite far enough when it supposes that candor toward the tribunal must, in *all* cases of perjury (or at best in all such cases not falling under a constitutional requirement),[49] override lawyer-client confidentiality. And, in this regard, I believe that my revised version of DR 7-102(B)(1), suggested earlier,[50] is instructive, for, as there noted, it provides the lawyer with the *autonomy* to balance truthfulness against trustworthiness in the *context* in *which the conflict arises.* Rule 3.3(a)(2) does not allow the lawyer any such discretion. But, as Kutak himself admitted, "no rules that honestly attempt to grapple with the dilemmas of ethical choice can dictate in every case what the proper choice must be."

Rule 1.2 of the Model Rules addresses the scope of the lawyer's authority in handling his client's case. According to this rule, "The client has ultimate authority to determine the purposes to be served by legal representation, within the limits imposed by law and the lawyer's professional obligations."[51]

But what is a lawyer to do if a client insists upon pursuing objectives or means which, although legal, are morally undesirable? What if, for instance, the client's unscrupulous tactics will have "material adverse effect" upon a third party? Apparently, the lawyer will be unauthorized by the rule in question to follow her own moral conscience, for a lawyer "should defer to a client regarding such questions as...concern for third persons who might be adversely affected."[52] I submit that my reformulations of DR 7-101(B) and EC 7-9, suggested earlier,[53] at least have her virtue of allowing a lawyer, in such cases, to follow her own moral conscience.

Rule 4.4, concerning "Respect for Rights of Third Persons," says that

> In representing a client a lawyer shall not use means that have no substantial purpose other than to embarrass, delay, or burden a third person....

However, in this rule, "no other substantial purpose" appears to be functioning in a similar way in which "merely" and "needless" function, respectively, in DR 7-102(A)(1) and EC 7-10.[54] For, presumably, a means employed by a lawyer which served to advance a client's legal interests but which also served to cause significant harm to a third person *would* have a substantial purpose other than the harm incurred; and, as such, the conduct in question would be permissible under Rule 4.4 and perhaps mandated by Rule 1.2—should the client insist upon such a course of action. But I believe that a rule which adequately reflects the moral agent concept would proscribe such conduct if the lawyer considered the resulting harm to be of such seriousness as to render the course of action morally untenable. In this regard, my earlier reformulation of EC 7-10[55] is instructive.

There has been much controversy generated in the ABA House of Delegates surrounding the correct formulation of Rule 1.6 of the Model Rules, which pertains to "Confidentiality of Information." The earlier 1981 draft of this rule proposed by the Kutak Commission allowed lawyers a good deal of discretion in revealing confidential information. For instance, it permitted— but did not require—a lawyer to reveal confidential information "to prevent the client from committing a criminal or fraudulent act that the lawyer believes is likely to result in death or substantial bodily harm, or substantial injury to financial interest or property of another;" as well as "to rectify the consequences of a client's criminal or fraudulent act in the commission of which the lawyer's services had been used."[56]

Now, this formulation of Rule 1.6, as proposed by the Kutak Commission, clearly recognizes the prima facie character of Trustworthiness as well as the importance of the Principle of Autonomy, which gives lawyers authority to balance competing moral claims in the specific contexts in which they arise—other things being equal. In this regard, the rule in question goes a considerable distance toward exemplifying the moral agent concept of a lawyer.

However, the Kutak Commission's formulation of Rule 1.6 did not survive intact; and the amended version of Rule l.6 which was finally approved by the ABA House of Delegates in August, 1983, "eliminated much of the discretion to reveal client confidences that the proposed rule would have given."[57] The approved version of Rule 1.6 permits a lawyer to reveal confidential information which the lawyer reasonably believes necessary to "prevent the client from committing a criminal act that the lawyer believes is likely to result in imminent death or substantial bodily harm." Therein, the earlier reference to "fraudulent acts"—in addition to criminal ones—is dropped; the autonomy to reveal confidential information for purposes of preventing "substantial injury to financial interest or property of another" is no longer recognized; and such autonomy for purposes of "rectifying the consequences of a client's criminal or fraudulent act in the commission of which the lawyer's services had been used" is not recognized.

Nor does the approved version of Rule 1.6 represent any significant advance upon the 1969 Code, so far as the moral agent concept is concerned.[58] In fact, Rule 1.6 as amended would seem to be *inconsistent* with Rule 3.3, which makes it obligatory for a lawyer to reveal to a tribunal information pointing to a client's perjury; for, given the confidential nature of any such information, Rule 1.6, as amended, would seem to require that such information *not* be revealed.[59]

One way of resolving this apparent inconsistency would be to *dis*allow a lawyer to reveal a client's perjured testimony. But another way to resolve it would be to unequivocally acknowledge the prima facie or conditional status of confidentiality. And this would be tantamount to granting lawyers the autonomy to balance, in context, confidentiality against other competing values—namely, truthfulness as well as other principles constitutive of the moral agent concept. The Kutak Commission's formulation of Rule l.6 has, in my estimation, cast its vote in the latter direction; and it at least has the virtue of being consistent with Rule 3.3

Rule 6.1 on "Pro Bono Publico Service" holds that a lawyer has a responsibility to "render public interest legal service." This responsibility, it states, may be discharged by:

providing professional service at no fee or a reduced fee to persons of limited means or to public service or charitable groups or organizations, by service in activities for improving the law, the legal system or the legal profession, and by financial support for organizations that provide legal services to persons of limited means.

Prima facie, the above rule appears to have made an advance toward the moral agent concept, especially insofar as it supports the principles of Moral Courage and Liberality. However, in the Comment on this rule, it is stated explicitly that the responsibility in question "is not intended to be enforced through disciplinary process." The upshot of this has been to render the new rule equivalent in effect to EC 2-25 of the 1969 Code, which also recognized such a responsibility. (In fact, EC 2-25 has been incorporated directly into the Comment provided for Rule 6.1.) This is so because the only possible practical difference between Rule 6.1 and EC 2-25 could be in terms of enforceability. But Rule 6.1 is intended to be no more enforced than the old EC—which, of course, was not enforced. Therefore, it does not truly constitute an advance toward the moral agent concept.

It should be remarked, however, that the earlier draft of the Model Rules proposed by the Kutak Commission did *not*, in its Comment on Rule 6.1, state that the responsibility it creates "is not intended to be enforced by disciplinary process." Had this version of 6.1 survived intact—which it did not—it would have constituted a significant move in the direction of the moral agent concept.

The foregoing remarks on the Model Rules, as well as those on the Code, have not been intended as a thoroughgoing critique. They do, however, point to some key places in the Model Rules where more attention should be focused *if* such rules are to more adequately reflect the moral agent concept. A crucial question, obviously, is whether such a concept, as here characterized, is the appropriate route to travel.

I have already argued that the alternative to the moral agent concept—that is, the pure legal advocate concept—can have unwelcome effects upon the moral character of lawyers and that this, in turn, can have a significant measure of social disutility which *any* utilitarian calculus (whether this calculus be "pure" or mixed with deontological considerations) should consider. Yet there are also arguments *against* this conception. I will now discuss what seem to be to be two very common ones.

THE MORAL AGENT CONCEPT:
SOME ARGUMENTS AGAINST IT ANSWERED

According to one argument, if lawyers are given the autonomy to break confidences with clients in those situations in which they judge further serious moral principles to be overriding, then the obligation lawyers have to keep their clients' confidences will be destroyed. As a result, clients will cease to confide in their lawyers and thus will withhold information necessary for an adequate defense of their legal interests. The final result will then be the demise of the adversary system itself and its accompanying benefits. For example, according to Monroe Freedman,

> the adversary system, within which the lawyer functions, con-
> templates that the lawyer frequently will learn from the client infor-
> mation that is highly incriminating and may even learn, as in the
> Lake Pleasant case, that the client has in fact committed serious
> crimes. In such a case, if the attorney were required to divulge that
> information, the obligation of confidentiality would be destroyed,
> and with it, the adversary system itself.[60]

First, the argument in question rests upon the unfounded assumption that the obligation of confidentiality will be destroyed if lawyers are allowed to take exception to it in serious moral conflicts. That is, because lawyers in general are allowed to make such exceptions does not mean that they will no longer see themselves as being under an obligation to keep their clients' confidences. To argue thus is like arguing that if certain exceptions to the proscription against killing are permitted—such as self-defense—then people will no longer see themselves as having a duty not to kill others. The fall down the slippery slope does not necessarily occur.

Second, those who advance the argument in question do not provide adequate evidence to support the claim that clients in general will cease to confide in their lawyers if they are not given an unconditional guarantee by their lawyers that all information conveyed, no matter what, will be taken confidentially. Indeed, even such intimate bonds as friendship, to which the lawyer-client relation has sometimes been compared,[61] have their moral limits. We do not typically expect our friends to surrender their moral integrity for our security. Yet that fact does not serve to destroy the bond of trust existing in such a relation. The claim that the bond of trust existing between lawyer and client will be destroyed if lawyers are given their moral autonomy appears to be equally as unfounded.

Third, even if it is admitted that according lawyers such moral autonomy will cause *some* clients, even some innocent ones, to omit information necessary for their adequate defense, this fact does not entail that the problem will be so widespread and serious as to lead to the destruction of the adversary system. It must also be kept in mind that an unconditional bond of confidentiality also generates difficulties. (Consider, for example, those resulting from the lawyers' actions in the Lake Pleasant case.) Moreover, there are favorable consequences of according lawyers moral autonomy which must also be taken into account. Thus, for example, Bentham suggests that one such consequence would be "that a guilty person will not in general be able to derive quite so much assistance from his law advisor, in the way of concerting a false defense, as he may do at present.[62]

In short, there is simply no clear proof that the effects of according lawyers the autonomy to take moral exception to the confidentiality principle would be so dramatic as to destroy the adversary system.

It is sometimes argued that, if lawyers were permitted the power of accepting or refusing employment or of retaining or withdrawing from cases, according to their personal moral judgments as to the guilt of a party or as to the goodness of a cause, then the role of the judge would be usurped; the lawyer, in effect, would become the judge. And this could, in turn, present serious moral difficulties, particularly for defendants in criminal cases. For there it may be argued that, if an individual defendant seems guilty enough, then no criminal lawyer will take his case, and, as such, he will be deprived of his constitutional right to counsel and to his day in court. Moreover, it is often difficult for a criminal lawyer to withdraw from a case he has already undertaken without leaving the impression that his ex-client is guilty. And, of course, it is always possible that a person who seems guilty is not *actually* guilty.[63]

I do think, however, that the above argument succeeds in destroying the moral agent concept. For one thing, it depends upon the untenable assumption that if the moral agent concept is generally accepted, then *no* criminal lawyer will defend seemingly guilty individuals. It is more realistic to suppose that, no matter *what* concept is adopted, there will always be *someone* to take up such a cause.

But more importantly, the argument appears to be attacking a straw man. For there is no inconsistency between a criminal lawyer's defending an apparently guilty client and her accepting the moral agent concept. None of our eight moral principles constituting that concept would, in fact, militate against her doing so. Indeed, it appears that an adequate understanding of our principle of distributive justice would demand that criminal lawyers *not* allow individuals, no matter how guilty they might *seem* to be, to be deprived of their constitutional right to counsel. Moreover, it often takes *moral courage* to represent clients who have come under public disfavor (see EC 2-27). Hence, the moral agent concept appears to support criminal lawyers' defense of the guilty rather than to proscribe it.

Nor do I think that there is any solid support for the claim that, if lawyers accept the moral agent concept with its insistence upon lawyers' moral autonomy, the role of the judge will be usurped by the lawyer. For such autonomy is not tantamount to license. The autonomous lawyer is still his client's advocate; it is his job to defend his client's legal interests and to present them in the clearest and most forceful light. But he must accomplish this task within the parameters of morality—that is, without forfeiting his moral integrity. It is not at all clear, therefore, why such a conception must lead to usurpation of the judge's role by the lawyer.

CONCLUDING REMARKS

Again we return to the question whether a good lawyer, in an adversary system, can be a morally good person. In answering this, a great deal depends upon our concept of a lawyer. For it is our full conception of the role of a professional which sets the parameters on the kind of personality compatible with that role and which serves to shape the personalities of its participants accordingly, or to invite those sorts who would fit it. I do not mean to suggest by this that there are not currently practicing lawyers who fit our criteria of morally good persons. This would be an absurd suggestion. Yet it is, I think, probable that most of these individuals have adopted the moral agent concept in some form or other.

If the legal profession is to move further in the direction of the moral agent concept, some changes must be made in its understanding. I have suggested, for example, some ways in which the *Code of Professional Responsibility* could be revamped in this direction. Indeed, the *Model Rules of Professional Conduct* now embraced by the A.B.A. seems to me to be, in some respects, an initial step in this direction.

But it will, I submit, take more than the revamping of the Code in order to fully institute the moral agent concept. The spirit of this concept will need to be *internalized,* as well, through the appropriate education. Above all, law schools and prelaw curricula will need to provide prospective lawyers with the facilities for cultivating an understanding of, and sensitivity to, moral problems. For the lawyer's ability to deal sensibly with such moral problems is an essential part of his professional function. It is beyond the scope of this paper to outline in detail what such curricula would consist of, but they would, undoubtedly, include diverse courses in applied ethics and legal philosophy.[64]

Presently, the legal profession is, I think, on a course toward the moral agent concept. Conceptual shifts of this magnitude, however, do not spring up full-blown overnight; they take time and occur in stages. But, to be sure, it is a process worth nurturing, not just for the good of the legal profession itself, but for the good of all of us whom the profession so vitally serves.[65]

(1) Don't you want your Lawyer to Be A Pure Leg. Adv.

NOTES

1. See ARISTOTLE, NICOMACHEAN ETHICS, Bk. II. All quotations in this paper from ARISTOTLE'S ETHICS are from 9 The Works of Aristotle (W.D. Ross ed. 1963).

2. Compare Joel Feinberg's distinction between "comparative" and "noncomparative" senses of justice in his SOCIAL PHILOSOPHY 98-99 (1973). Compare also John Stuart Mill's discussion of justice in his UTILITARIANISM ch. 5.

3. See Chisholm & Feehan, *The Intent to Deceive*, 74 J. of Phil. 143-59 (1977).

4. Compare C. FRIED, RIGHT AND WRONG 57-58 (1978).

5. ARISTOTLE, *supra* note 1, at 1117a16.

6. Id. at 1116a15-b3.

7. Id. at 1120b29-31.

8. Compare H. Sidgwick, THE METHODS OF ETHICS 238-39 (1962); compare also A. Smith, THE THEORY OF MORAL SENTIMENTS 345 (1966).

9. Compare, e.g., the discussion of justified violations to the rule fo confidentiality between a physician and his patient in T.L. Beauchamp & J.F. Childress, PRINCIPLES OF BIOMEDICAL ETHICS 214-17 (1979).

10. I. Kant, GROUNDWORK OF THE METAPHYSIC OF MORALS 98-99 (H.J. Paton Trans. 1964).

11. A person can admittedly perform the function of a lawyer without actually *being* a lawyer, in an analogous manner in which a rock can serve the function of a hammer without actually being a hammer. Further conditions must also be satisfied—for example, a lawyer must have gone to law school and passed the bar. For this complication in the analysis of functional concepts—which is here ignored for the sake of simplicity—see G.H. von Wright, THE VARIETIES OF GOODNESS 20-22 (1968).

12. M.H. Freedman, LAWYERS' ETHICS IN AN ADVERSARY SYSTEM 9 (1975).

13. American Bar Association, CANONS OF PROFESSIONAL ETHICS (1908).

14. See Curtis, *The Ethics of Advocacy*, 4 Stan. L. Rev. 3-23 (1951).

15. The cited examples appear, respectively, in Freedman, *supra* note 12 at ch. 4, esp. 48-49; Freedman, *Professional Responsibility of the Criminal Defense Lawyer: The Three Hardest Questions*, 64 Mich. L. Rev. 1474-78 (1966) Fried, *The Lawyer as Friend: The Moral Foundations of the Lawyer-Client Relations*, 85 Yale L.J. 1064 (1976); Wasserstrom, *Lawyers as Professionals: Some Moral Issues*, 5 Hum. Rts. 8 (1975).

16. "Are there no limits (short of violating criminal laws and rules of court) to the partisan zeal that an attorney should exert on behalf of a client who may be a murderer, a rapist, a drug pusher, or a despoiler of the environment? Is the lawyer never to make a conscientious judgment about the impact of the client's conduct on the public interest and to temper the zealousness of his or her representation accordingly? I believe that the adversary system is itself in the highest public interest...and that it is, therefore, inconsistent with the public interest to direct lawyers to be less than zealous in their roles as partisan advocates in an adversary system." Freedman, *Are Three Public Interest Limits on Lawyers' Advocacy:*, 2 J. of the Legal Prof. 47 (1977).

17. ARISTOTLE, *Supra* note 1 at 1103a15-b1.

18. Compare Richard Wasserstrom's suggestion that the behavior engaged in by the Watergate lawyers on behalf of Richard Nixon—lying to the public, dissembling, stonewalling, tape-recording conversations, playing dirty tricks, etc.—was "the likely if not inevitable consequence of their legal acculturation," *supra* note 15 at 15.

19. For example, *see generally, Factors and Theories of Career Development*, in B. Shertzer & S. Stone, FUNDAMENTALS OF GUIDANCE ch. 12 (1981).

20. See, e.g., the discussions of studies on the influence of vocations upon personality traits in Komarovsky & Sargent, Research into Subcultural Influences upon Personality, in CULTURE AND PERSONALITY 145-48 (S.S. Sargent and M.W. Smith eds. 1949).

21. See, e.g., Teevan, *Personality Correlates of Undergraduate Fields of Specialization*, 18 J. of Consulting Psychology 212-14 (1954).

22. Curtis, *supra* note 14 at 5.

23. See Teevan, *supra* note 21.

24. Costigan, *The Full Remarks on Advocacy of Lord Brougham and Lord Chief Justice Cockburn at the Dinner to M. Berryer on November 8, 1864*, 19 Calif. L. Rev. 523 (1931).

25. Noonan, *The Purpose of Advocacy and the Limits of Confidentiality*, 64 Mich. L. Rev. 1492 (1966).

26. See, respectively, Wasserstrom, *supra* note 15; J. Bentham, Rationale of Judicial Evidence, bk. 9, ch. 5, in 7 THE WORKS OF JEREMY BENTHAM (J. Bowring ed. 1843); American Bar Association and the Association of American Law Schools, *Professional Responsibility: Report of the Joint Conference*, 44 A.B.A. J. 1161 (1958).

27. M. Freedman, *supra* note 12 at 1.

28. Compare Jones, *Legal Realism and Natural Law*, in THE NATURE OF LAW (M.P. Golding ed. 1966).

29. See St. Thomas Aquinas, Summa Theological, 1. 11., Q. 94, a. 6; Q. 91, a. 3.

30. If we do say this, then we will be countenancing a "natural law" conception of lawyering resembling in its essentials a "natural law" conception of law. For just as the latter conception denies any separation between law and morality, such a conception of lawyering denies any separation between *legal practice* and morality. We could, perhaps, also carry the analogy with jurisprudence further and suggest that the pure legal advocate conception of a lawyer establishes for legal practice a "legal positivist" conception which maintains a separation (conceptually) between legal practice and morality in a similar way in which "legal positivist" conceptions of law maintain a separation (conceptually) between law and morality.

31. All rules listed are from the AMERICAN BAR ASSOCIATION, CODE OF PROFESSIONAL RESPONSIBILITY (1969), hereinafter cited as A.B.A. CODE. Their classification under the eight principles, however, is my own.

32. See the *Preliminary Statement* to the A.B.A. Code.

33. According to Dr 4-101(C)(1)-(4), a lawyer may reveal "(1) confidences or secrets with the consent of the client or clients affected, but only after a full disclosure to them; (2) confidences or secrets when permitted under Disciplinary Rules or required by law or court orders; (3) the intention of his client to commit a crime and the information necessary to prevent the crime; (4) confidences or secrets necessary to establish or collect his fee or to defend himself or his employees or associates against an accusation of wrongful conduct." A.B.A. Code.

34. DR 5-105(C) states: "In the situations covered by DR 5-105 (A) AND (B), a lawyer may represent multiple clients if…he can adequately represent the interests of each and if each consents to the representation after a full disclosure of the posible effects of such representation on the exercise of his independent professional judgment on behalf of each." A.B.A. Code.

35. The italics are mine.

36. The italics are mine.

37. The italics are mine.

38. See A.B.A. Code, *supra* note 33.

39. See M. Freedman, *supra* note 12 at 257-59.

40. The provision that a lawyer should inform his client of his decision to forego the action in question seems to me to follow from our Principle of Individual Justice as well as that of Trustworthiness.

41. Compare H.L.A. Hart's discussion of the criminal law and its sanctions in THE CONCEPT OF LAW 38-39 (1961)

42. This concept is discussed briefly later; see p. 50 of this article.

43. See p. 24 of this paper.

44. American Bar Association, Model Rules of Professional Conduct, reprinted in 52 U.S.L.W. 1-27 (Aug. 16, 1983) (No. 7). Final approval of the Model Rules came at the Annual Meeting of the American Bar Association, Atlanta, July 28, 1983-August 4, 1983.

45. It should be noted that the Ethical Considerations proposed in the preceding part of this paper could well be incorporated into the commentary format followed by the Model Rules. Hence, these proposals continue to be relevant notwithstanding the A.B.A.'s decision to omit Ethical Considerations as such from their ethical code. I owe this point to Professor William Heffernan.

46. R.J. Kutak, 66 AMERICAN BAR ASSOCIATION JOURNAL 48 (1980).

47. It should, however, be noted that although, according to Rule 3.3, the obligation to disclose a client's perjury also applies to criminal defense lawyers, this obligation is "qualified by constitutional provisions for due process and the right to counsel in criminal cases." This means that, in some jurisdictions, such a lawyer may, notwithstanding this obligation, be required to "present an accused as a witness if the accused wishes to testify, even if counsel knows the testimony will be false." See the parts of the Comment accompanying Rule 3.3 which are entitled "Constitutional Requirements," "Refusing to Offer Proof Believed to be False," and "Perjury by a Criminal Defendant."

48. See the discussion of this amendment, at p. 50 of this paper.

49. See note 47 above.

50. See id.

51. Comment, Rule 1.2, Model Rules.

52. Id.

53. See p. 51 of this paper.

54. See *Nonmalevolence,* p. 49 of this paper.

55. See p. 51 of this paper.

56. AMERICAN BAR ASSOCIATION COMMISSION ON EVALUATION OF PROFESSIONAL STANDARDS, FINAL DRAFT OF THE MODEL RULES OF PROFESSIONAL CONDUCT Rule 1.6 (1981).

57. *Midyear Meeting of American Bar Association,* 51 U.S.L.W. 2489 (Feb. 22, 1983).

58. Compare DR 4-101(C) of the Code as cited in note 33 above.

59. See the discussion concerning consistency in the report on the *Midyear Meeting of the American Bar Asociation, supra* note 56 at 2491.

60. M. Freedman, *supra* note 12 at 5.

61. See e.g., Fried *supra* note 15.

62. Compare generally, M. Freedman, *supra* note 12.

63. Compare generally, M. Freedman, *supra* note 12.

64. Investigations of this sort are already in progress. See e.g., The Council for Philosophical Studies, S. Gorovitz & B. Miller, PROFESSIONAL RESPONSIBILITY IN THE LAW: A CURRICULUM REPORT FROM THE INSTITUTE ON LAW & ETHICS (Summer 1977).

   (The Center for Philosophy and Public Policy at the University of Maryland has also recently announced the availability of a model course on "Ethics and the Legal Profession" prepared by Professor David Luban. A copy can be obtained by sending $2.50 for postage and handling to Maryland Courses, Center for Philosophy and Public Policy, Woods 0123, University of Maryland, College Park, MD 20742.).

65. I am thankful to Professor Walter Probert and Judge Charles Smith for their assistance in obtaining important references. I am also thankful to Gale Spieler Cohen and an anonymous referee of *Criminal Justice Ethics* for their contribution to some of the ideas contained herein.

WHY PROSECUTORS MISBEHAVE 7

Bennett L. Gershman

The duties of the prosecuting attorney were well-stated in the classic opinion of Justice Sutherland fifty years ago.[1] The interest of the prosecutor, he wrote, "is not that he shall win a case, but that justice shall be done. As such, he is in a peculiar and very definite sense the servant of the law, the twofold aim of which is that guilt shall not escape or innocence suffer. He may prosecute with earnestness and vigor—indeed, he should do so. But, while he may strike hard blows, he is not at liberty to strike foul ones."[2]

Despite this admonition, prosecutors continue to strike "foul blows," perpetuating a disease which began long before Justice Sutherland's oft-quoted opinion. Indeed, instances of prosecutorial misconduct were reported at least as far back as 1897,[3] and as recently as the latest volume of the *Supreme Court Reporter*.[4] The span between these cases is replete with innumerable instances of improper conduct of the prosecutor, much of which defies belief.

One of the leading examples of outrageous conduct by a prosecutor is *Miller v. Pate*,[5] where the prosecutor concealed from the jury in a murder

163

case the fact that a pair of undershorts with red stains on it, a crucial piece of evidence, were stained not by blood but by paint. Equally startling is *United States v. Perry*,[6] where the prosecutor, in his summation, commented on the fact that the "defendants and their counsel are completely unable to explain away their guilt."[7] Similarly, in *Dubose v. State*,[8] the prosecutor argued to the jury: "Now, not one sentence, not one scintilla of evidence, not one word in any way did this defendant or these attorneys challenge the credibility of the complaining witness."[9] At a time when it should be clear that constitutional and ethical standards prevent prosecutors from behaving this way,[10] we ought to question why prosecutors so frequently engage in such conduct.

Much of the above misconduct occurs in a courtroom. The terms "courtroom" or "forensic misconduct" have never been precisely defined. One commentator describes courtroom misconduct as those "types of misconduct which involve efforts to influence the jury through various sorts of inadmissible evidence."[11] Another commentator suggests that forensic misconduct "may be generally defined as any activity by the prosecutor which tends to divert the jury from making its determination of guilt or innocence by weighing the legally admitted evidence in the manner prescribed by law."[12] For purposes of this analysis, the latter definition applies, as it encompasses a broader array of behavior which can be classed as misconduct. As will be seen, prosecutorial misconduct can occur even without the use of inadmissible evidence.

This article will address two aspects of the problem of courtroom misconduct. First, it will discuss why prosecutors engage in courtroom misconduct, and then why our present system offers little incentive to a prosecutor to change his behavior.

WHY MISCONDUCT OCCURS

Intuition tells us that the reason so much courtroom misconduct by the prosecutor[13] occurs is quite simple: it works. From my ten years of experience as a prosecutor, I would hypothesize that most prosecutors deny that misconduct is helpful in winning a case. Indeed, there is a strong philosophical argument that prosecutorial misconduct corrupts the judicial system, thereby robbing it of its legitimacy. In this regard, one would probably be hard pressed to find a prosecutor who would even mention that he would consider the thought of some form of misconduct.

Nonetheless, all of this talk is merely academic, because, as we know, if only from the thousands of cases in the reports, courtroom misconduct does occur. If the prosecutor did not believe it would be effective to stretch his argument to the ethical limit and then risk going beyond that ethical limit, he would not take the risk.

Intuition aside, however, several studies have shown the importance of oral advocacy in the courtroom, as well as the effect produced by such conduct. For example, the student of trial advocacy often is told of the importance of the opening statement. Prosecutors would undoubtedly agree that the opening statement is indeed crucial. In a University of Kansas study,[14] the importance of the opening statement was confirmed. From this study, the authors concluded that, in the course of any given trial,[15] the jurors were affected most by the first strong presentation which they saw. This finding leads to the conclusion that if a prosecutor were to present a particularly strong opening argument, the jury would favor the prosecution throughout the trial. Alternatively, if the prosecutor were to provide a weak opening statement, followed by a strong opening statement by the defense, then, according to the authors, the jury would favor the defense during the trial. It thus becomes evident that the prosecutor will be best served by making the strongest opening argument possible, and thereby assist the jury in gaining a better insight into what they are about to hear and see. The opportunity for the prosecutor to influence the jury at this point in the trial is considerable, and virtually all prosecutors would probably attempt to use this opportunity to their advantage, even if the circumstances do not call for lengthy or dramatic opening remarks.[16]

An additional aspect of the prosecutor's power over the jury is suggested in a University of North Carolina study.[17] This study found that the more arguments counsel raises with respect to the different substantive arguments offered, the more the jury will believe in that party's case. Moreover, this study found that there is not necessarily a correlation between the amount of objective information in the communication and the persuasiveness of the presentation.

For the trial attorney, then, this study clearly points to the advantage of raising as many issues as possible at trial. For the prosecutor, the two studies taken together would dictate an "action packed" opening statement, containing as many arguments that can be mustered, even those which might be irrelevant or unnecessary to convince the jury of the defendant's guilt. The second study would also dictate the same strategy for the closing argument. Consequently, a prosecutor who, through use of these techniques, attempts to assure that the jury knows his case may, despite violating ethical standards to seek justice,[18] be "rewarded" with a guilty verdict. Thus, one begins to perceive the incentive that leads the prosecutor to misbehave in the courtroom.[19]

Similar incentives can be seen with respect to the complex problem of controlling evidence to which the jury may have access. It is common knowledge that, in the course of any trial, statements frequently are made by the attorneys or witnesses, despite the fact these statements may not be admissible as evidence. Following such a statement, the trial judge may, at the request of opposing counsel, instruct the jury to disregard what they have heard. Most trial lawyers, if they are candid, will agree that it is virtually impossible for jurors realistically to disregard these inadmissible statements. Studies here again demonstrate that our intuition is correct and that this evidence often is considered by jurors in reaching a verdict.

For example, an interesting study conducted at the University of Washington[20] tested the effects of inadmissible evidence on the decisions of jurors. The authors of the test designed a variety of scenarios whereby some jurors heard about an incriminating piece of evidence while other jurors did not. The study found that the effect of the inadmissible evidence was directly correlated to the strength of the prosecutor's case. The authors of the study reported that when the prosecutor presented a weak case, the inadmissible evidence did in fact prejudice the jurors. Furthermore, the judge's admonition to the jurors to disregard certain evidence did not have the same effect as when the evidence had not been mentioned at all. It had a prejudicial impact anyway.

However, the study also indicated that when there was a strong prosecution case, the inadmissible evidence had little, if any, effect.[21] Nonetheless, the most significant conclusion from the study is that inadmissible evidence had its most prejudicial impact when there was little other evidence on which the jury could base a decision. In this situation, "the controversial evidence becomes quite salient in the jurors' minds."[22]

Finally, with respect to inadmissible evidence and stricken testimony, even if one were to reject all of the studies discussed, it is still clear that although "stricken testimony may tend to be rejected in open discussion, it does have an impact, perhaps even an unconscious one, on the individual juror's judgment."[23] As with previously discussed points, this factor—the unconscious effect of stricken testimony or evidence—will generally not be lost on the prosecutor who is in tune with the psychology of the jury.

The applicability of these studies to this analysis, then, is quite clear. Faced with a difficult case in which there may be a problem of proof, a prosecutor might be tempted to sway the jury by adverting to a matter which might be highly prejudicial. In this connection, another study[24] has suggested that the jury will more likely consider inadmissible evidence that favors the defendant rather than inadmissible evidence that favors conviction.[25]

Despite this factor of "defense favoritism," it is again evident that a prosecutor may find it rewarding to misconduct himself in the courtroom. Of course, a prosecutor who adopts the unethical norm and improperly allows jurors to hear inadmissible proof runs the risk of jeopardizing any resulting conviction. In a situation where the prosecutor feels there is a weak case, however, a subsequent reversal is not a particularly effective sanction when a conviction might have been difficult to achieve in the first place. Consequently, an unethical courtroom "trick" can be a very attractive idea to the prosecutor who feels he must win.[26] Additionally, there is always the possibility of another conviction even after an appellate reversal. Indeed, while a large number of cases are dismissed following remand by an appellate court, nearly one half of reversals still result in some type of conviction.[27] Therefore, a prosecutor can still succeed in obtaining a conviction even after his misconduct led to a reversal.

An additional problem in the area of prosecutor-jury interaction is the prosecutor's prestige; since the prosecutor represents the "government," jurors are more likely to believe him.[28] Put simply, prosecutors "are the good guys of the legal system,"[29] and because they have such glamour, they often may be tempted to use this advantage in an unethical manner. This presents a problem for the prosecutor in that the "average citizen may often forgive, yea urge prosecutors on in ethical indiscretions, for the end, convictions of criminals, certainly justifies in the public eye any means necessary."[30] Consequently, unless the prosecutor is a person of high integrity and is able to uphold the highest moral standards, the problem of courtroom misconduct inevitably will be tolerated by the public.

Moreover, when considering the problems facing the prosecutor, one also must consider the tremendous stress under which the prosecutor labors on a daily basis. Besides the stressful conditions faced by the ordinary courtroom litigator,[31] prosecuting attorneys, particularly those in large metropolitan areas, are faced with huge and very demanding case loads. As a result of case volume and time demands, prosecutors may not be able to take advantage of opportunities to relax and recover from the constant onslaught their emotions face every day in the courtroom."[32]

Under these highly stressful conditions, it is understandable that a prosecutor occasionally may find it difficult to face these everyday pressures and to resist temptations to behave unethically. It is not unreasonable to suggest that the conditions under which the prosecutor works can have a profound effect on his attempt to maintain high moral and ethical standards. Having established this hypothesis, one can see yet another reason why courtroom misconduct may occur.

WHY MISCONDUCT CONTINUES

Having demonstrated that courtroom misconduct may in many instances be highly effective, the question arises as to why such practices continue in our judicial system. A number of reasons may account for this phenomenon. Perhaps the most significant reason for the continued presence of prosecutorial misconduct is the harmless error doctrine. Under this doctrine, an appellate court can affirm a conviction despite the presence of serious misconduct during the trial. As Justice Traynor once stated, the "practical objective of tests of harmless error is to conserve judicial resources by enabling appellate courts to cleanse the judicial process of prejudicial error without becoming mired in harmless error."[33]

Although the definition advanced by Justice Traynor portrays the harmless error doctrine as having a more desirable consequence, this desirability is undermined when the prosecutor is able to misconduct himself without fear of sanction. Additionally, since every case is different, what constitutes harmless error in one case may be reversible error in another. Consequently, harmless error determinations do not offer any significant precedents by which prosecutors can judge the status of their behavior.

By way of illustration, consider two cases in which the prosecutor implicitly told the jury of his personal belief in the defendant's guilt. In one case, the prosecutor stated, "I have never tried a case where the evidence was so clear and convincing."[34] In the other case, the prosecutor told the jury that he did not try cases unless he was sure of them.[35] In the first case the conviction was affirmed, while in the second case the conviction was reversed. Interestingly, the court in the first case affirmed the conviction despite its belief that the "prosecutor's remarks were totally out of order,"[36] Accordingly, despite making comments which were "totally out of order," the prosecutor did not suffer any penalty.

Contrasting these two cases presents clear evidence of what is perhaps the worst derivative effect of the harmless error rule. The problem is that the stronger the prosecutor's case, the more misconduct he can commit without being reversed. Indeed, in the *Shields* case, the court stated that "the guilt of the defendant was clearly established not only beyond a reasonable doubt, but well beyond any conceivable doubt."[37] For purposes of our analysis, it is clear that by deciding as they do, courts often provide little discouragement to a prosecutor who believes, and rightly so, that he does not have to be as careful about his conduct when he has a strong case. The relation of this factor to the amount of courtroom misconduct cannot be ignored.

Neither can one ignore the essential absurdity of a harmless error determination. To apply the harmless error rule, appellate judges attempt to evaluate how various evidentiary items or instances or prosecutorial misconduct may have affected the jury's verdict. Although it may be relatively simple in some cases to determine whether improper conduct during a trial was harmless, there are many instances when such an analysis cannot properly be made but nevertheless is made. For example, consider the situation when an appellate court is divided on whether or not a given error was harmless. In *United States v. Antonelli Fireworks Co.*,[38] two judges (including Judge Learned Hand) believed that the prosecutor's error was harmless. Yet, Judge Frank, the third judge sitting in the case, completely disagreed, writing a scathing dissent nearly three times the length of the majority opinion. One wonders how harmless error can be fairly applied when there is such a significant difference of opinion among highly respected members of a court as to the extent of harmfulness of trial errors. Perhaps even more interesting is the Supreme Court's reversal of the Court of Appeals for the Second Circuit's unanimous finding of harmless error in *United States v. Berger*.[39] As noted, *Berger* now represents the classic statement of the scope of the prosecutor's duties. Yet, in his majority opinion for the Second Circuit, Judge Learned Hand found the prosecutor's misconduct harmless.

The implications of these contradictory decisions are significant, for they demonstrate the utter failure of appellate courts to provide incentives for the prosecutor to control his behavior. If misconduct can be excused even when reasonable judges differ as to the extent of harm caused by such misbehavior, then very little guidance is given to a prosecutor to assist him in determining the propriety of his actions. Clearly, without such guidance, the potential for misconduct significantly increases.

The *Shields* case presents yet another factor which suggests why the prosecutor has only a limited incentive to avoid misconduct. In *Shields*, the court refused to review certain "potentially inflammatory statements" made by the prosecutor because of the failure of the defense to object.[40] Although this approach has not been uniformly applied by all courts, the implications of this technique to reject a defendant's claim are considerable. Most important, it encourages prosecutors to make remarks that they know are objectionable in the hope that defense counsel will not object. This situation recalls the previous discussion, which dealt with the effect of inadmissible evidence on jurors. Defense counsel here is in a difficult predicament. If he does not object, he ordinarily waives any appealable issue in the event of conviction. If he does object, he highlights to the jury the fact that the prosecutor has just done something which some jurors may feel is so damaging to the defendant that the defense does not want it brought out.

The dilemma of the defense attorney in this situation is confirmed by a Duke University study.[41] In that study, jurors learned of various pieces of evidence which were ruled inadmissible. The study found that when the judge admonished the jury to disregard the evidence, the bias created by that evidence was not significantly reduced.[42] Consequently, when a prejudicial remark is made by the prosecutor, defense counsel must act carefully to avoid damaging his client's case. In short, the prosecutor has yet another weapon, in this instance an arguably unfair aspect of the appellate process, which requires preservation of an appealable issue.[43]

A final point when analyzing why prosecutorial misconduct persists is the unavailability or inadequacy of penalties visited upon the prosecutor personally in the event of misconduct. Punishment in our legal system comes in varying degrees. An appellate court can punish a prosecutor by simply cautioning him not to act in the same manner again, reversing his case, or, in some cases, identifying by name the prosecutor who misconducted himself.[44] Even these punishments, however, may not be sufficient to dissuade prosecutors from acting improperly. One noteworthy case[45] describes a prosecutor who appeared before the appellate court on a misconduct issue for the third time, each instance in a different case.

Perhaps the ultimate reason for the ineffectiveness of the judicial system in curbing prosecutorial misconduct is that prosecutors are not personally liable for their misconduct. In *Imbler v. Pachtman*,[46] the Supreme Court held that "in initiating a prosecution and in presenting the state's case, the prosecutor is immune from a civil suit for damages under Section 1983."[47] Furthermore, prosecutors have absolute rather than a more limited, qualified, immunity. Thus, during the course of a trial, the prosecutor is absolutely shielded from any civil liability which might arise due to his misconduct, even if that misconduct was performed with malice.

There is clearly a need for some level of immunity to be accorded all government officials. Without such immunity, much of what is normally done by officials in authority might not be performed out of fear that their practices are later deemed harmful or improper. Granting prosecutors a certain level of immunity is reasonable. Allowing prosecutors to be completely shielded from civil liability in the event of misconduct, however, provides no deterrent to courtroom misconduct.

CONCLUSION

This analysis was undertaken to determine why the issue of misconduct seems so prevalent in the criminal trial. For the prosecutor, the temptation to cross over the allowable ethical limit must often be irresistible because of the distinct advantages that such misconduct creates in assisting the prosecutor to win his case by effectively influencing the jury. Most prosecutors must inevitably be subject to this temptation. It takes a constant effort on the part of every prosecutor to maintain the high moral standards which are necessary to avoid such temptations.

Despite the frequent occurrences of courtroom misconduct, appellate courts have not provided significant incentives to the prosecutor to avoid misconduct. It is not until the courts decide to take a stricter, more consistent approach to this problem that inroads will be made in the effort to end it. One solution might be to impose civil liability on the prosecutor who misconducts himself with malice. Although this will not solve the problem, it might be a step in the right direction.

NOTES

1. Berger v. United States, 295 U.S. 78 (1935).

2. Id. at 88.

3. See Dunlop v. United States, 165 U.S. 486 (1897), where the prosecutor, in an obscenity case, argued to the jury "I do not believe that there are twelve men that could be gathered by the venire of this court..., except where they were bought and perjured in advance, whose verdict I would not be willing to take...." Id. at 498. Following this remark defense counsel objected, and the court held that statement to be improper.

4. See Caldwell v. Mississippi, 105 S. Ct. 2633 (1985) (improper argument to capital sentencing jury): United States v. Young, 105 S. Ct. 1038 (1985) (improper argument but not plain error).

5. 386 U.S. 1 (1967). In this case, the Supreme Court overturned the defendant's conviction after the Court of Appeals for the Seventh Circuit had upheld it. The Court noted that the prosecutor "deliberately misrepresented the truth" and that such behavior would not be tolerated under the Fourteenth Amendment. Id. at 67.

6. 643 F.2d 38 (2d Cir. 1981).

7. Id. at 51.

8. 531 S.W.2d 330 (Texas 1975)

9. Id. at 331. The court noted that the argument was clearly a comment on the failure of the defendant to testify at trial.

10. See Griffin v. California, 380 U.S. 609 (1965), where the Supreme Court applied the Fifth Amendment to the states under the Fourteenth Amendment.

11. Alschuler, "Courtroom Misconduct by Prosecutors and Trial Judges," 50 Tex. L. Rev. 627, 633 (1972).

12. Note, "The Nature and Function of Forensic Misconduct in the Prosecution of a Criminal Case," 54 Col. L. Rev. 946, 949 (1954).

13. Of course, there is also a significant amount of defense misconduct which takes place. In this respect, for an interesting article which takes a different approach than this article, see Kamm. "The Case for the Prosecutor," 13 U. Tol. L. Rev. 331 (1982), where the author notes that "courts carefully nurture the defendant's rights while cavalierly ignoring the rights of the people."

14. Pyszczynski, "The Effects of Opening Statement on Mock Jurors' Verdicts in a Simulated Criminal Trial," II J. Applied Soc. Psychology 301 (1981).

15. All of the cited studies include within the report a caveat about the value of the study when applied to a "real world" case. Nonetheless, they are still worthwhile for the purpose of this analysis.

16. In some jurisdictions, attorneys may often use the voir dire to accomplish the goal of early influence of the jury.

17. Calder, "The Relation of Cognitive and Memorial Processes to Persuasion in a Simulated Jury Trial," 4 J. Applied Soc. Psychology 62 (1974).

18. See Model Code of Professional Responsibility EC 7-13 (1980) ("The duty of the prosecutor is to seek justice.").

19. Of course, this may apply to other attorneys as well.

20. Sue, S., R.E. Smith, and C. Caldwell, "The Effects of Inadmissible Evidence on the Decisions of Simulated Jurors–A Moral Dilemma," 3 J. Applied Soc. Psychology 345 (1973).

21. Perhaps lending validity to application of the harmless error doctrine, which will be discussed later in this article.

22. Sue, note 20 *supra* at 351.

23. Hastie, *Inside the Jury* 232 (1983).

24. Thompson, "Inadmissible Evidence and Jury Verdicts," 40 J. Personality & Soc. Psychology 453 (1981).

25. The author did note that the defendant in the test case was very sympathetic and that the results may have been different with a less sympathetic defendant.

26. Of course, this begs the question: "Is there a prosecutor who would take a case to trial and then feel that he didn't have to win?" It is hoped that, in such a situation, trial would never be an option. Rather, one would hope for an early dismissal of the charges.

27. Roper, "Does Procedural Due Process Make a Difference?" 65 Judicature 136 (1981). This article suggests that the rate of nearly 50 percent of acquittals following reversal is proof that due process is a viable means for legitimizing the judiciary. While this is true, the fact remains that there is still a 50 percent conviction rate after reversal, thereby giving many prosecutors a second chance to convict after their original misconduct.

28. See People v. McCoy, 220 N.W. 2d 456 (Mich. 1974), where the prosecutor, in attempt to bolster his case, told the jury that "the Detroit Police Department, the detectives in the Homicide Bureau, these detectives you see in court today, and myself from the prosecutor's office, we don't bring cases unless we're sure, unless we're positive." Id. at 460.

29. Emmons, "Morality and Ethics–A Prosecutor's View," Advanced Criminal Trial Tactics 393-407 (P.L.I. 1977).

30. Id.

31. For an interesting article on the topic, see Zimmerman, "Stress and the Trial Lawyer," 9 Litigation 4, 37-42 (1983).

32. For example, the Zimmerman article suggests time off from work and "celebration" with family and friends to effectively induce relaxation.

33. R. Traynor, *The Riddle of Harmless Error* 81 (1970).

34. People v. Shields, 58 A.D.2d 94, 96 (N.Y.), aff'd. 46 N.Y.2d 764 (1977).

35. People v. McCoy, 220 N.W.2d 456 (Mich. 1974).

36. Shields, 58 A.D.2d at 97.

37. Id. at 99.

38. 155 F.2d 631 (2d Cir. 1946).

39. 73 F.2d 278 (1934), rev'd, 295 U.S. 78 (1935).

40. Shields, 58 A.D.2d at 97.

41. Wolf, "Effects of Inadmissible Evidence and Level of Judicial Admonishment to Disregard on the Judgments of Mock Jurors," 7 J. Applied Soc. Psychology 205 (1977).

42. Additionally of note is the fact that if the judge rules the evidence and did not admonish the jury, then the biasing effect of the evidence was eliminated. The authors of the study concluded that by being told not to consider certain evidence, the jurors felt a loss of freedom and that to retain their freedom, they considered it anyway. The psychological term for this effect is called reactance.

43. Of course, this does not mean that appeals should always be allowed, even in the absence of an appealable issue. Rather, one should confine the availability of these appeals to the narrow circumstances discussed.

44. See United States v. Burse, 531 F.2d 1151 (2d Cir. 1976), where the court named the prosecutor in the body of its opinion.

45. United States v. Drummond, 481 F.2d 62 (2d Cir. 1973).

46. 424 U.S. 409 (1976).

47. Id. at 431, 42 U.S.C. 1983 authorizes civil actions against state officials who violate civil rights "under color of state law."

ETHICS AND THE COURTS—
SENTENCING

ETHICAL ISSUES IN SENTENCING 8

Lawrence F. Travis, III

Sentencing is the decision of what to do with the person convicted of a criminal offense. Traditionally, we have responded to criminality by imposing a punishment on the criminal. Von Hirsch (1976:34) defined criminal punishment as, "the infliction by the state of consequences normally considered unpleasant, on a person in response to his having been convicted of a crime." Graeme Newman (1983:6) simply states, "Punishment must, above all else, be painful." For our purposes then, criminal punishment is the purposeful infliction of pain on a person as a result of a criminal conviction.

There is an element of reflex in punishment. That is, when we are harmed by someone or something, we tend to strike back in reaction. Mackie (1982) traced the origins of criminal punishments to such reflex responses. Criminal punishment is, at least partly, a return of harm for harm, or wrong for wrong. Yet, there is an old saying that two wrongs do not make a right.

If ethics is the study of morality and what is right or wrong, it is likely that no aspect of the criminal justice process is more amenable to ethical examination than sentencing. By committing a crime, the offender has wronged society. By punishing, society arguably "wrongs" the offender. The purpose of this paper is to examine the question, how can punishment be justified? While we do not normally apply the saying about two wrongs to the question of criminal punishment, it seems apropos. How can we justify the purposeful infliction of pain, even on those convicted of crimes? What factors make punishment right or whether we should punish are inter-related questions. The answers to these questions depend upon how sentencing is defined.

THE PURPOSE OF CRIMINAL PUNISHMENT

Should we punish? This question is so basic that it is often unasked and unanswered. Yet, when, whom and how we punish are contingent on why we punish. We tend to believe that criminals should be punished. The wrong they do by committing crimes demands a punitive response. We often disagree, however, on why crime requires punishment. Traditionally, four reasons for punishment have been advanced: deterrence, incapacitation, treatment, and desert.

DETERRENCE

Deterrence supports punishment as an example of what awaits law breakers. This example is expected to convince would-be offenders to avoid criminal behavior. Deterrence is based on a conception of human beings as rational and guided by a pleasure principle. That is, humans do things that please them and avoid things that hurt them. Further, they weigh the likely consequences of their behavior and choose activities accordingly (Paternoster, 1987).

In order for a punishment to deter, two conditions must be met. First, the penalty must be severe enough so that the pain of the punishment outweighs the pleasure of the crime. For example, a fifty-dollar fine for theft of one hundred dollars would not deter because the criminal would still realize a profit. Second, the penalty must be imposed. If the criminal is very unlikely to be caught and/or punished, the threat of the penalty is not likely to be "real." The lower the chance of punishment, the greater the chance of crime.

Deterrence works on two levels. General deterrence applies when the offender is punished so that others will learn not to commit a crime. Thus the purpose of the punishment is to deter the general public from crime. Specific deterrence occurs when the penalty is designed to convince the particular offender not to commit another crime in the future.

As a justification for punishment, deterrence emphasizes the needs of the collective over those of the individual. The purpose of punishment is to control future crime. A deterrence rationale would allow the imposition of a severe penalty for a minor offense if that penalty would prevent a large enough number of future offenses. For example, a ten-thousand-dollar fine for a ten-dollar theft could be justified under deterrence if it would prevent at least one thousand such thefts.

INCAPACITATION

Like deterrence, incapacitation is a justification for criminal punishment based on the promise of reducing future crime. In contrast to deterrence, however, incapacitation supports penalties that prevent offenders from having the chance to commit new crimes. While deterrence seeks to convince offenders that crime will not benefit them, incapacitative penalties seek to limit the offender's being able to commit a new crime.

One reason to incarcerate a convicted offender is that, at least while in prison, that person is not able to harm society by committing more crimes. The primary problem with incapacitation as a justification for punishment is our liability to accurately predict who is likely to commit future crimes (Visher, 1987). Research to date seems to indicate that incapacitative penalties entail a significant increase in prison population (Van Dine, Conrad & Dinitz, 1979; Greenwood, 1982). To be sure that dangerous offenders are "locked up," we must also incarcerate relatively large numbers of non-dangerous offenders.

TREATMENT

Another justification for punishment is to allow for the treatment of rehabilitation of criminal offenders. This philosophy assumes that crime is caused by a variety of reasons, such as poverty, discrimination, or individual pathology. Punishments are designed to change the offender's need or desire to commit crime. Like deterrence and incapacitation, the ultimate goal of treatment is a reduction in future crime. Unlike those other two rationales, treatment emphasizes the individual offender (Cullen & Gilbert, 1982).

Studies of the effects of treatment suggest that most programs currently available are not very effective (Martinson, 1974; Bailey, 1966). Yet, efforts to treat criminal offenders continue, and many programs show promise of effectiveness for the future (Gendreau & Ross, 1987). As with the prediction problems of incapacitation, treatment attempts are limited by our inability to design and implement effective programs.

DESERT

A final rationale for criminal punishment is desert, also sometimes called "retribution." This justification for punishment is the only one of the four that is "backward looking." Unlike deterrence, incapacitation or treatment, a desert rationale does not seek reductions in future crime. Rather, desert is based on the idea that the offender deserves to be punished as a result of committing a crime.

As a justification for punishment, desert places limits on both who may be punished, and the degree to which someone may be punished. Desert requires that penalties only be imposed on those who have committed a crime. Further, a desert rationale requires that the punishment be commensurate (proportional to) with the severity of the crime committed. In these ways, desert may be considered to emphasize the interests of the individual offender over those of the collective.

UTILITARIANISM VERSUS FAIRNESS

These four rationales and their varying emphases on the individual or collective interests in punishment highlight the ethical dilemma identified by Packer. The core issue involves the role of utility in punishment. Utility means benefit, or the "good" expected as a result of punishment. Those who support punishment on the basis of the good it will produce emphasize a utilitarian rationale. Those who support punishment regardless of its effects are non-utilitarian.

In brief, we can say that deterrence, incapacitation and treatment are utilitarian purposes of punishment. Desert is a non-utilitarian justification. Only the desert rationale supports the imposition of punishments regardless of their effects. The other rationales depend upon some good resulting from the penalty.

If someone is convicted of a crime, should they be punished? If no one else will know that a crime went unpunished and the offender will not commit another crime in the future, there is no reason to punish under a deterrence rationale; no one will be deterred by the penalty. Similarly, given that the offender will not commit another crime, there is no need to incapacitate or treat the offender. Thus, utilitarian purposes cannot support the imposition of a penalty in this instance.

Yet, most of us will be uncomfortable with allowing a criminal to escape punishment. At base, most of us support a desert rationale for punishment. Those who commit crimes deserve to be punished, regardless of the effects of punishment on future levels of crime.

Mackie (1981) refers to this as the "paradox of retribution." By this he meant that it is not possible to explain or develop a desert rationale within a reasonable system of moral thought, yet it is also not possible to eliminate desert from our moral thinking. In short, retribution (desert) does not make sense. Desert suggests that wrongful acts should be punished but offers no reason for punishment. Mackie resolves the paradox by saying that punishment is essentially a reflex based on emotions. We react to things and people who hurt us by hurting them in return.

Given this emotional need to harm those who harm us, we will punish criminals without regard for possible beneficial effects of punishment. As punishment became institutionalized in society, jurists and philosophers developed more rational justifications for punishment based on utilitarian notions. These notions may explain particular punishments and the selection of specific offenders for punishment, but they do not fully explain why we punish.

If Mackie's assessment is correct, it means that we will punish criminals routinely without regard to the effects of punishment. However, most penalties will also reflect some utilitarian purposes in terms of deterrence, incapacitation or treatment. In practice, this is what usually occurs.

It is not uncommon for those convicted of crime to be sentenced for a variety of reasons. The judge may "throw the book" at the defendant to deter others. Correctional officials may attempt to treat the offender while executing the punishment. A paroling authority may deny release to a prisoner based on the belief that the inmate should be incapacitated. Thus, the use of a punishment is based on desert, but the precise nature and extent of punishment is affected by considerations of a utilitarian nature.

It is these utilitarian purposes of punishment that raise the ethical dilemma of sentencing as a balance between the needs of the collective and those of the individual. During the 1970s, desert or retribution experienced a renaissance (Cullen & Gilbert, 1982). This renaissance defined retribution as a limiting factor in punishment (Frankel, 1972; Fogel, 1975; Von Hirsch,

1976; Twentieth Century Fund, 1976).

As a limit, desert requires that offenders be punished. It also requires that punishments not be excessive in relation to the seriousness of the offense. Von Hirsch and Hanrahan (1979) proposed a "modified just deserts" sentencing rationale. They argued that desert sets outer limits on punishment, but that utilitarian considerations could be used to allow different penalties being imposed on offenders convicted of the same crime within those limits. Thus, burglary may deserve imprisonment of between one and three years. The sentencing judge would be able to impose a three-year term for incapacitation or deterrence but would not be allowed to impose more than the upper limit of three years. Similarly, the judge would be required in deterrence, incapacitation, or treatment, because burglary deserves punishment of at least one year.

The resurgence of desert was directed at fairness in criminal punishments. Proponents of desert based sentencing were concerned with what they perceived as unfair disparities in criminal punishments. Under the laws of most states, it was possible for offenders convicted of the same offense to receive widely divergent penalties. One person convicted of burglary might be placed on probation while another might serve several years in prison. Reliance on a desert rationale would narrow this range of penalties, thereby insuring that similar offenders convicted of similar crimes would experience more similar punishments.

To these observers, desert would lead to a more equitable distribution of punishment than had occurred under utilitarian models. In general, they believed the offender had a right to be protected from severe penalties based on considerations of future crime. It would be unjust to punish someone very harshly in order to deter others, or to deter that individual. Penalties based on specific deterrence, incapacitation, and treatment were considered to be unjust because they punish the offender for crimes not yet committed. General deterrence could also be unjust if someone was severely punished based on a belief that others might commit crimes. Desert requires that the offender being punished be guilty of the offense for which punishment was administered.

This discussion indicates the importance of prediction to an understanding of the ethics of punishment. All three of the utilitarian rationales for punishment depend upon a prediction of future criminality by either the offender or others in the general population. The prediction problem is a thorny issue in sentencing. Judges, parole authorities and others are expected to protect society through their sentencing decisions, yet they must also be concerned with the rights of the individual offender. Desert was viewed as a means of limiting the effect of predictions on the severity of punishments imposed. In this way, predictions could still be considered, but the interests of offenders could also be protected.

The ethical issue surrounding prediction comes down to a question of fairness. Some people say that it is unfair to punish an offender for crimes that have not yet been committed or to punish an offender because of a fear that others will commit crimes. Others argue that it is unfair to society not to punish offenders when such punishment might protect society from further crime.

At the level of fairness to the individual offender, general deterrence and collective incapacitation (Visher, 1987), whereby convicted offenders are similarly sentenced in hopes of reducing general levels of future crime, are less troublesome than individual predictions. If everyone convicted of an offense receives a similar punishment, whether for general deterrent or incapacitative purposes, individual fairness in terms of equivalent penalties is achieved. The question of whether it is ethical to punish these people for expected future crimes remains, but at the level of comparable penalties they are treated "fairly." When the penalty is based on predictions of future criminality by the specific offender, however, not even this gross definition of "fairness" can be assured.

When penalties are assigned on the basis of assessments of the risk of future crime posed by the individual offender, sentences are individualized and fairness is more difficult to achieve. Rather than treat categories of offenders equally by imposing sentences on all offenders in the category which are designed to meet general deterrence or incapacitation goals, individualized prediction is designed to identify certain offenders who will receive more or less severe penalties. The application of differential punishment based on prediction in specific cases raises questions of accuracy and discrimination which affect our judgment of the ethics of these punishment strategies.

PREDICTION FOR PUNISHMENT

Clear & O'Leary (1983:35-38) recognized the central role of prediction in all aspects of criminal justice. Society expects its criminal justice apparatus to protect it from crime, and part of this protection involves the identification of risk and taking steps to minimize the chance of future crimes. The assignment of criminal penalties involves the prediction of future criminality at some level. Sentence decisionmakers do consider the likelihood of future crime in choosing penalties. In doing so, they make distinctions among convicted offenders about which offenders will receive what levels of penalty.

In any attempt to predict "dangerousness" among a population of criminal offenders, two types of error are possible. An offender who does not pose a risk of future crime may be erroneously predicted to be dangerous. This type of error is called a "false positive" because the offender was falsely (erroneously) predicted to be positive on danger. Conversely, an offender who actually poses a danger of future crime may be erroneously predicted to be "safe." This type of error is called a "false negative" because the offender was falsely (erroneously) predicted to be negative on danger.

False positives are subjected to greater levels of punishment than they need or deserve based on their actual dangerousness. Because they are predicted to be dangerous, we will incapacitate them or subject them to more severe sanctions to insure specific deterrence or treatment. False negatives are punished less than they need or deserve based on their actual dangerousness. Because they are predicted to be safe, we return them to society quickly and allow them to commit additional crimes.

If we accept prediction as an appropriate consideration in sentencing, the use of differential sanctions is ethically justifiable based on the need to protect society. Yet, it remains wrong to subject a non-dangerous offender to more severe punishment. Similarly, it would be wrong not to punish more severely an offender who is actually dangerous. Not only do false negatives experience less punishment than their accurately identified peers, we also fail to meet our obligation to protect society from future crime.

Both false positives and false negatives are treated unfairly because neither group receives the penalty it deserves. False positives are punished too much and false negatives are punished too little. Barring one hundred percent accuracy, any predictive scheme will make both types of mistakes and create both types of injustice. At present, we do not have total accuracy in prediction. In practice, false positives occur about eight times for every true positive (accurately identified dangerous offender). Further, we currently predict accurately only about half of the truly dangerous offenders, so that our false negative rate is roughly equal to our true negative rate (Wenk, Robison & Smith, 1972). That is, we make many mistakes.

The lack of accuracy in our predictions has led some observers to argue that we should not predict future criminality as part of sentencing. They suggest that prediction leads to unacceptably high levels of error and unfairness. Their position is that it is unethical to base punishment decisions on what we know to be faulty information. Even if we accept prediction as a goal of punishment, they argue that it is wrong to punish even one offender more than is necessary.

This position clearly emphasizes the interests of the individual over those of the collective. To protect the rights of false positives, they argue that we must abandon punishment based on prediction. The result of abandoning prediction would be that all offenders, even those who pose a danger, are subjected to the lesser levels of punishment given to non-dangerous offenders. An alternative solution to this dilemma, of course, is to impose harsher penalties on all offenders, as if they were all dangerous. This might lead to "fair" punishment in that everyone receives a similar penalty as in collective incapacitation strategies, but critics would argue that this is unethical because it imposes disproportionate penalties on everyone.

The purpose of prediction is to discriminate between those offenders who require more punishment and those who can safely be given less punishment. A related ethical concern is how the predictive system achieves this discrimination. It is possible that errors in prediction are not random but that they work against specific groups. Thus, predictive schemes may result in differential punishment for blacks and whites, men and women, the poor and higher economic classes. The possibility of discriminatory punishment raises the question of discrimination in punishment as an ethical concern.

Available data indicate that our more severe punishments of incarceration and the death penalty are disproportionately applied to certain groups of people. Petersilia (1983) noted that the justice system differentially selects youth, blacks, the poor and urban residents for harsher punishments. Blacks are more likely to be arrested, convicted and imprisoned than their numbers in the general population would indicate. In 1981, for example, blacks comprised 12% of the population but 47% of prison inmates. Females comprised 51% of the total population, but only about 5% of the incarcerated population. These figures indicate the possibility that blacks and women experience discrimination in criminal justice processing. Visher (1983) argues that women are subjected to paternalism, for example.

More detailed analyses of the data indicate that these differential rates of imprisonment for various groups reflect differences in the frequency and severity of crimes committed. Klein, Turner and Petersilia (1988) reported that criminal sentences in California were based more on the seriousness of offense, prior criminal record, and justice process variables than on race. They suggested that the California Determinate Sentencing Act contributed to racial equity in sentencing by defining the factors on which sentences should be based.

Generally, the best predictor of future crime is past crime. That is, those offenders who have previously committed crimes are more likely to do so again than are those who have not. The California sentences examined by Klein, et al. (1988) indicated that prior record explained differences in sentences more than did race. A simple conclusion then might be that prediction does not lead to discrimination.

The fact remains, however, that the ethically acceptable factors that predict future crime—prior record, criminal justice history, and offense seriousness, appear to be related to race, sex, and social class. The conclusion that these factors are more determinative of punishment than race does not necessarily mean that sentencing decisionmakers do not discriminate.

A closer look at prediction in sentencing reveals that discrimination may be a latent effect (Petersilia & Turner, 1985). Stecher and Sparks (1982) noted that those who develop prediction indices may err when they exclude race from consideration. The heart of their observation is that predictive factors are associated with race, and ignoring race in any analyses allows researchers to ignore the effect of prediction on racial or other minorities.

For example, defendants who make bail may be less likely to be imprisoned. Blacks may be less likely to make bail because they are more often unemployed or otherwise lack "ties to the community." Blacks then are more likely to be imprisoned. Failing to consider the effect of race on making bail may result in a predictive device that institutionalizes a practice of incarcerating greater percentages of blacks than whites. Stecher and Sparks urge the inclusion of race in the development of sentencing guidelines so that it is possible to see the relationships between certain predictive factors and race.

Similar arguments can be applied to the treatment of the poor, women, or other groups. Simply identifying a set of factors that are ethically acceptable considerations in punishment does not mean that discrimination will not occur. If blacks are more likely to commit crimes than whites, they are more likely to receive harsh punishments than whites. If women are less likely to commit serious "street crimes" than men, they are less likely to receive harsh punishments.

The problem is that the relationships between race, sex, socioeconomic status and predictor variables are complex. Race, for example, may be related to unemployment because of societal discrimination. In turn, unemployment may be related to involvement in crime and criminal justice processing decisions (bail, probation and parole supervision, and the like), which in turn are related to future criminality. Punishments based on the likelihood of future criminality as predicted from prior record or criminal justice history will reflect the effects of race. However, because the sentence decision relies only on prior criminal record and criminal justice history, the effect of race may be hidden from those making the punishment decision.

In practice, all black offenders may suffer more severe criminal penalties because some blacks are more likely to commit future crimes than most whites. If this occurs, many black offenders receive unfair punishments because they are treated as being more dangerous than they are. The situation is analogous to automobile insurance premiums for young male drivers. All young male drivers pay high premiums because, as a group, young males are most likely to be involved in traffic accidents. Nonetheless, many young males are excellent, safe drivers.

The problem for society is akin to that faced by automobile insurance companies. Punishments based on predictions of future crime treat some individual offenders unfairly, just as blanket assignment of certain groups of drivers to "high risk" classes for insurance. At what point, if ever, does this unfair treatment of individual offenders (or drivers) render the prediction effort ethically unjustifiable?

CONCLUSIONS

An examination of the ethics of sentencing raises many questions, but provides few answers. As previously mentioned, the answers are judgment calls that depend upon the individual doing the judging. A central determinant of how one may resolve these ethical issues is the resolution of the conflict between the needs of the collective and those of the individual offender. If the interests of the individual predominate, one is likely to support a desert or treatment justification for punishment and oppose most predictive efforts. On the other hand, if one emphasizes societal protection, it is likely that they will support a deterrence incapacitative rationale and the use of prediction in sentencing.

This difference in perspective is reflected in how one views errors of prediction. If false positive errors are more troubling than false negative errors, there is a greater concern for unfairness in the punishment of individuals. If false negative errors are more troublesome, it evidences a greater concern for public safety. Those who emphasize community protection are usually willing to accept false positive errors, arguing that it is not unjust to punish them more severely than their actual risk would warrant.

The two positions make different assumptions about punishment. Crime control (emphasis on collective needs) assumes that all offenders should receive the harshest penalties allowed by law, and thus those predicted to be safe are "getting a break." It does not recognize an ethical dilemma arising from the fact that some offenders are punished more severely than others. Due process (emphasis on individual interests) assumes that all offenders would receive the least severe penalties, and the state must justify more severe penalties for those predicted to be dangerous.

In addition to these divergent views on whether prediction results in some offenders receiving leniency (crime control) or harsher penalties (due process) there are those who oppose prediction at all. Some argue that it is simply wrong to punish someone for what they might do in the future. If it is acceptable to increase the penalty for someone who appears dangerous, why not incapacitate or otherwise punish those who have not yet committed a crime but who are likely to do so in the future? These persons argue that only conviction of a crime can justify the imposition of a sanction, and that predicted offenses can not ethically justify punishment.

To continue this argument, what do we do with someone who was given a greater penalty based on predicted danger who then commits a future crime? Suppose an offender was convicted of burglary and given a prison term twice as long as the average burglar because they were predicted to be dangerous. If that person commits another burglary after release, have they already been punished, or should we punish them again? If we punish them for the new crime, haven't they been punished twice for the same offense, once when it was predicted and again when it occurred?

If one supports a deterrent rationale for punishment, are there any limits on sentencing? If it is possible to deter crime by simply saying someone broke the law and punishing them, do we need to require a conviction before the imposition of sentence? Similarly, if more severe punishments are more effective deterrents, can we not use the death penalty for minor offenses? If torture would deter crime, should we resort to torturing offenders?

Each of us may very well answer these and other questions related to sentencing differently. In essence, these are all ethical questions which are asking about what is right or wrong with sentencing and criminal punishment. The ethics of sentencing can be stated as a question of justice. We need to determine what are just punishments, and how can sentences be imposed justly. As Von Hirsch (1976:5) stated it, "While people will disagree about what justice requires, our assumption of the primacy of justice is vital because it alters the terms of the debate. One cannot, on this assumption, defend any scheme for dealing with convicted criminals solely by pointing to its usefulness in controlling crime: one is compelled to inquire whether that scheme is a just one and why."

REFERENCES

Bailey, W. (1966) "Correctional outcome: An evaluation of 100 reports," *Journal of Criminal Law, Criminology & Police Science* 57:153-60.

Clear, T.R. and V. O'Leary (1983) *Controlling the offender in the community* (Lexington, MA: Lexington Books).

Cullen, F.T. & K.E. Gilbert (1982) *Reaffirming rehabilitation.* (Cincinnati, OH: Anderson).

Fogel, D. (1975) *"We are the living proof..."* (Cincinnati, OH: Anderson).

Frankel, M.E. (1972) *Criminal sentences: Law without order.* (New York: Hill & Wang).

Gendreau, P. & R. Ross (1987) "Revivification of rehabilitation: Evidence from the 1980s," *Justice Quarterly* 4(3):349-407.

Greenwood, P. (1972) *Selective incapacitation.* (Santa Monica, CA: Rand).

Klein, S.P., S. Turner & J. Petersilia (1988) *Racial equity in sentencing.* (Santa Monica, CA: Rand).

Lundman, R. (1980) *Police and policing: An introduction.* (New York: Holt, Rinehart & Winston).

Mackie, J.L. (1982) "Morality and the retributive emotions," *Criminal Justice Ethics* 1(1):3-10.

Martinson, R.M. (1974) "What works?," *The Public Interest* (Spring): 22.

Newman, G.R. (1983) *Just and painful.* (New York: MacMillan).

Packer, H. (1966) *The limits of the criminal sanction.* (Stanford: Stanford University Press).

Paternoster, R. (1987) "The deterrent effect of the perceived certainty and severity of punishment: A review of the evidence and issues," *Justice Quarterly* 4(2):173-217.

O'Leary, V. & D. Duffee (1971) "Correctional policy: A classification of goals designed for change." *Crime & Delinquency* 18(3):379.

Petersilia, J. (1983) *Racial disparities in the criminal justice system.* (Santa Monica, CA; Rand).

_____. and S. Turner (1985) *Guideline-based justice: The implications for racial minorities.* (Santa Monica, CA: Rand).

Stecher, B.A. & R.F. Sparks (1982) "Removing the effects of discrimination in sentencing guidelines," in M. Forst (ed.) *Sentencing reform.* (Beverly Hills, CA: Sage):113-129.

Twentieth Century Fund Task Force on Criminal Sentencing (1976) *Fair and certain punishment.* (New York: McGraw-Hill).

Van Dine, S., J.P. Conrad & S. Dinitz (1979) "The incapacitation of the chronic thug," *Journal of Criminal Law & Criminology* 65:535.

Visher, C. (1987) "Incapacitation and crime control: Does a 'lock 'em up' strategy reduce crime?" *Justice Quarterly* 4(4):513-43.

———. (1983) "Gender, police arrest decisions and notions of chivalry," *Criminology* 21(1):5-28.

Von Hirsch, A. (1976) *Doing justice.* (New York: Hill & Wang).

———. & K.J. Hanrahan (1979) *The question of parole.* (Cambridge, MA: Ballinger).

Wenk, E.A., J.O. Robison & G.W. Smith (1972) "Can violence be predicted?" *Crime & Delinquency* 18(3)393-402.

MYTH THAT PUNISHMENT CAN FIT THE CRIME

9

Harold E. Pepinsky & Paul Jesilow

The class was a graduate seminar in "Philosophical Issues of Law and Social Control" The teacher had just finished the introductory lecture, filling three blackboards with a proof in symbolic logic that there is no adequate justification for punishment.

A student asked, "What would you do if a man raped your daughter?"

"I'd try to reason with him."

"What if you couldn't reason with him?"

"I'd kill the sonuvabitch."

—State University of New York at Albany, 1976

You may recall how Shylock lost his case in Shakespeare's *Merchant of Venice*. He had contracted to receive a pound of flesh if a borrower defaulted on a loan, and the court ruled in favor of Shylock's claim to the flesh after the borrower's default. Portia ordered a final judgment: yes, Shylock was entitled to his pound of flesh, but no more. If he cut out the slightest fraction more

191

than a pound, or if so much as a single drop of blood fell out of the wound, Shylock would be in breach of the agreement and hence criminally liable for harm done. The court agreed, and Shylock was forced to abandon his quest for justice in favor of mercy.

During the past decade, many in the American-criminological community have been driven to Shylock's position. On one hand, they accept as fact that taking pounds of flesh from offenders neither rehabilitates them nor reduces crime. On the other hand, they figure a social contract has to be upheld, and that anyone who breaches the contract by breaking the law must be made to suffer in due measure by a just society. Lawyer/criminologist Andrew Von Hirsch has coined the term "just deserts" to refer to this ultimate rationale for punishment of offenders. The punishment should fit the crime—no more, no less.

The classical notion of retribution is known as *lex talionis*, or "an eye for an eye." If I blind someone in one eye and am blinded in turn, that is justice. But, the equation will not precisely fit. If, for instance, I blind my victim without warning, then the victim suffers after the event, but not before. If I am then sentenced to be blinded in return, I suffer anticipation of the event as well. It is like taking a drop of blood along with the pound of flesh. Harm under one set of circumstances is bound to include elements that harm under other circumstances lacks. One reason some theologians postulate that vengeance must be left in God's hands and not given over to mere mortals is that, in the final analysis, we are incapable of constructing an equation that takes all circumstances and types of harm into account.

Punishment for crime is generally far less straightforward even than taking an eye for an eye. The most common form of punishment we use today is length of incarceration, but few of our prisoners are punished for confining others. Most are there for taking others' property without the owners' permission. French historian Michel Foucault has pointed out what a remarkable achievement it has been for Americans to decide that harm can be measured in days, months, and years. The human obsession for rationality drives people to think lives are interchangeable with machine parts whose cost and productive value can be quantified. So now the cost of a burglary can be measured against the length of time we deny a person's freedom. But when clearly thought about "How many years of a person's liberty equals the value of a lost television set?" has to be seen as an absurd question. The same applies to laying offenses along a scale of punishment. If you send your daughter to her room for 10 minutes for breaking a fifty-cent tumbler in a fit of anger, would you send her to her room for 13 days, 21 hours, and 20 minutes to uphold moral principle and teach her a lesson if she broke a $1,000 antique vase? You might well show your anger and demand that she help mend the vase as well as possible, but that bid for accountability and responsibility would scarcely be retributive—would hardly be punitive at all. British criminologist Leslie Wilkins has carried the problem a step further by noting that crimes are not punished; offenders are. Attribution theorists like psychologist Joanne Joseph Moore have been studying how people assess the culpability of defendants. They find, for example, that jurors weigh a number of characteristics of victims and offenders. In the theft of a television, it would matter whether the jurors thought that the victim was an unattractive character who might have angered the offender, or whether the offender was thought to be a basically respectable person who came under an accomplice's evil influence, or whether the defendant seemed to smile rather than show remorse when the victim testified. Our criminal law recognizes some of this complexity, beginning with the requirement for most offenses not only that the defendant be found to have committed a wrongful act, but be found to have intended it. The law also allows other grounds for finding defendants not guilty, or for aggravating or mitigating offenses. Going further, sociologists Victoria Swigert and Ronald Farrell find that defendants charged with criminal homicide in an Eastern city were most likely to be convicted of first-degree murder rather than of lesser offenses if their physical appearance corresponded to the local psychiatric category, "normal primitive." Try as they might, human beings seem to be incapable of judging people by judging their acts alone, and their predispositions affect their decisions of how much harm a defendant has done and how long they should suffer for it.

Twenty years ago, sociologists Thorsten Sellin and Marvin Wolfgang put together a scale of seriousness of offenses from rankings that judges, police, and students gave to a set of crimes. Other researchers have since found that different categories of people produce much the same scale, both in the United States and in Canada. The problem is that real criminal cases entail real defendants and real complainants, so that in practice, those who assess offenses have room to feel considerable justification for concluding that one theft of $100 worth of property from a dwelling is more serious than another. Had Shylock been a surgeon trying to excise a one-pound tumor from a patient who objected on religious grounds, Portia might even have argued Shylock's case.

It is one thing to say that offenders ought to be given their just deserts. It is quite another to figure out what "just deserts" are.

Guidelines used by sentencing judges in various jurisdictions take several variables into account, including legal seriousness of offense charged, prior record, employment status, and bail status of the defendant. These guidelines have been found to predict whether defendants will be sent to jail with about 80 percent accuracy. It is harder to predict how long a jail sentence will be imposed or what form or length of community supervision will be given. Meanwhile, experienced defendants report bewilderment over getting off when they have done something serious and being severely sentenced when their guilt is questionable or their offense trivial. Cases are legion of co-defendants receiving widely disparate sentences.

A common exercise among those who teach criminal justice courses is to give students hypothetical cases and ask them to decide which sentence should be imposed. The sentences asked for not only vary widely among students both for each case and across cases, but many times exceed the limits the law allows.

Consensus about punishment offenders deserve is limited in our society. This is not too surprising. The variety of offenses covered by penal codes is staggering; and the variety of circumstances of defendants' cases are greater still. Consensus would require that crime witnesses react with equal horror. It would require that witnesses readily cooperate in giving full information. More to the point, it would require substantial acknowledgment from about two million Americans currently serving sentences behind bars or in the community that they got their due, and all these views would have to coincide with penalties provided by law if the state were to embody retributive justice.

The problem goes further. Since, as we have seen, crime is so common among Americans, there is often dissensus as to whether punishment is deserved at all. For example, it is well documented that most middle-aged Americans have at least experimented with marijuana, and that a substantial number of otherwise respectable Americans use it regularly. Possession of small amounts of the drug is completely legal only in Alaska, finable in some states, and remains a major felony punishable by years in prison in others. Cultivation of the plant for sale is a crime in all American jurisdictions, and yet a large and growing number of farmers—who would never use the drug themselves—have turned to cultivating this profitable cash crop. Some honest, hard-working growers are quite upset about criminals who try to steal from them, although of course they are in no position to ask for police protection or to take out insurance. Some people think those who are involved in the sale and distribution of marijuana ought to be lined up against a wall and shot. How on earth is consensus to be achieved?

A number of writers propose that so-called crimes without victims, like those involving marijuana, ought to be decriminalized or even legalized. That in itself, however, would not solve the problem for other crimes. How many people can candidly say they, or their nearest-and-dearest, never stole (perhaps equipment or food from work) or vandalized (perhaps kicked a vending machine or "toilet papered" a house), or assaulted (perhaps got in a minor scuffle) or trespassed, or lied for personal gain? These are the kinds of offenses that dominate criminal court dockets. How severely would we punish ourselves for our own crimes?

Consensus on punishment requires that criminals be truly extraordinary. They must do that which people generally find intolerable, practically unimaginable. We have little trouble agreeing that the crimes of John Wayne Gacy, or Steven Judy, or Charles Manson are outrageous, and although we may differ over the death penalty, we agree that their transgressions call for an extreme sanction. There is a consensus that burying young men in one's garden, or raping and strangling a strange woman and her children, or hanging and stabbing a pregnant woman in a ritual, is beyond our wildest fantasies. If a major city were to reserve punishment for something like the worst offender of the month, popular consensus might be achieved that a punishment constituted just deserts.

Controlling Punishment

To fit the crime, punishment not only needs to have a certain level, but needs to be swift and sure. If punishment is long delayed, the connection between it and the offense becomes strained. Retribution is an expression of moral outrage, of the passion of the moment over wrong done. It makes little sense to punish someone who has long been behaving properly for a transgression long past. That is the reason that statutes of limitation cut off prosecution for all but the most serious crimes after some time has elapsed.

Criminal justice officials cannot help but be guided by conscience and are inclined to believe in the justice of what they have done. If suddenly called upon to punish offenders more severely, they will do so more selectively and with greater deliberation. If called upon to punish more often, they will temper their severity. If called upon to speed up punishment, they will show more leniency and discharge more suspects or punish without taking evidence of innocence into account.

These patterns are well documented. In the eighteenth century, for example, the British Parliament made a number of offenses punishable by death. As the courts faced imposing death sentences in more kinds of crimes, informal settlement of cases rose to prominence, and most of those sentenced to death were reprieved. In the early 1970s, Governor Nelson Rockefeller sponsored legislation in New York State that mandated life sentences for those selling illicit drugs. Under the law, charges could not be reduced once defendants had been indicted. So, police were less inclined to charge suspects with sale of drugs, prosecutors were more likely to charge defendants with a lesser offense like simple possession of drugs, defendants had little incentive to refrain from requesting jury trials which added to the judicial backlog, and conviction rates among those going to trial dropped as juries proved reluctant to convict on such serious charges. On the other hand, when penalties have been substantially reduced, as in Nebraska for possession of marijuana in the early 1970s, arrests and convictions have surged before settling down at a new plateau.

Since the 1950s, the Dutch have concentrated on increasing the likelihood that defendants brought to trial would get convicted. Convictions have increased, but, in the process, delays in getting to trial are at the point at which many defendants seem to drop out of the system, and the severity of sentence has dropped to the point where it can be measured in days rather than months or years. The average daily convict population has remained roughly constant, at about 20 or 22 per 100,000 Dutch, the lowest known rate in the world.

In a study of experimental programs to reduce trial delay, political scientist Mary Lee Luskin found that punishment decreased by six days for every ten days' shortening of the time between the initial charging and the final court disposition. And as those who have been to traffic court—where "justice" is swift—can attest, penalties are not only light, but pleas of innocence are likely to be ignored in the rush of business; the innocent are nearly as subject to punishment as the guilty.

Suppose we want to make punishment both swift and sure while closely controlling its severity. The problem of making these three elements of punishment coincide is similar to trying to hold the south poles of three electromagnets together. If you increase the electrical energy going through any of the magnets, it will tend to push the other magnets away. If you clamp down hard, you may be able to hold the magnets together awhile, but as your hand tires they are likely to slip. In criminal justice, increasing the energy and attention devoted to any of the three elements of punishment will make the other two slip out of control.

As the current is turned down toward zero, holding the magnets together becomes relatively effortless. Similarly, a small criminal justice force with practically no crime to respond to will be in a good position to respond swiftly, surely, and with measured severity to crimes that it handles. They will be able to devote singular attention to each offense. As rare and peculiar events, offenses will meet popular consensus that they are intolerable. Hence, citizens will more readily collaborate with law enforcement forces to put evidence together and to identify offenders. When the offender is brought to trial, the likelihood of conviction will be high, and concensus will be forthcoming on the punishment the clear and distinctive deviant deserves. If criminal justice officials are to make punishment swiftly and surely fit crimes, criminal justice must be a small and largely superfluous force in a practically crime-free society. If more resources are put into the criminal justice system of a society with a high crime rate, the system will further break down and fail even more dismally to provide a just response to crime. This is exactly what has happened in the United States. As we have added personnel and money to an already large criminal justice force, we have been confronted with a system that fills prisons with too severely punished minor offenders, manifestly fails to respond to most offenses, prolongs trial and punishment in cluttered courts, and is capricious about whom is punished and for how long.

IMPLICATIONS FOR CRIME CONTROL

Some advocates of retribution do not care whether punishment prevents crime. They argue that a citizenry deserves to have offenders punished regardless of whether punishment offers more than the satisfaction of moral indignation. If current attempts to build up law enforcement are only made to satisfy moral indignation, they are unjustified. Public dissatisfaction with delays, uncertainty, and improper severity will more than offset the desire for revenge.

Retribution can be thought to prevent crime, however. The state that shows itself capable of making punishments fit crimes can be assumed to earn public respect for its authority, and by extension, to earn public respect for its laws. A people who respect the state and its law can be expected to behave lawfully.

From another perspective, swift, sure punishment of controlled severity can be expected to deter people—both from committing a first offense and from committing additional crimes. It is important to recognize a key distinction between punishing for retribution and punishing for deterrence. For retribution, punishment is to be proportional to harm done by offenders; for deterrence, punishment is to cost offenders just more than they gain by committing offenses. At extremes, offenders who killed simply to take ten cents from their victims might be executed for the sake of retribution, and fined eleven cents to achieve deterrence. As Italian nobleman Cesare Beccaria wrote in the eighteenth century, a system designed to deter crime will generally impose far less severe punishments than one designed to achieve retribution. Since heavier punishments delay and reduce certainty of punishment, they impair its power to deter.

Still, consensus on light punishment is no easier to achieve with a massive criminal justice system; and, a system that deters through punishment should have hardly any crime left to punish. From the perspective of deterrence, it is a sign of failure that a system that already punishes plentifully should be called upon to punish still more in order to prevent crime.

If anything, American criminal justice seems to play a role in promoting disrespect for law and order. Various independent estimates reach a common conclusion: Imprisoning growing numbers of offenders has at best a marginal effect on crime rates, since so many people fill the void by starting lives of crime. It may be that repressive criminal justice systems here and elsewhere (as in Argentina, Chile, the Soviet Union, and South Africa) reflect or cause popular brutality. The fact remains that societies in which punishment is extensive have large and intractable problems of crime and violence. Societies that generate punishment generate crime, while relatively peaceful societies (the Netherlands and Japan, for example) find less pressure to punish.

There are more fundamental forces than criminal justice that enable people to live together peacefully. If we can slow down people's response to disputes so that they have time to act with greater deliberation and accommodation to needs of offenders and victims alike, there will be more of a chance that the punishment will fit the crime.

A Life for a Life?
Opinion and Debate   10

Robert Johnson

Most Americans support the death penalty for the crime of murder. The threat of execution, they believe, scares potential killers straight and hence saves the innocent lives they would have taken. At a deeper, more visceral level, however, most people simply want murderers to be paid back for their crimes. Deterrence is gravy. The main course is retributive justice, leavened with revenge: A life for a life.

Few murderers have been executed recently, but that is changing. Legal appeals are running out for hundreds of condemned prisoners. At least one jurist has greeted this trend with impatient approval. "Enough is enough on these appeals," said Texas Judge Michael McSpadden. "It's time to enforce the laws." Speaking of one notorious resident of Texas' death row, McSpadden vowed: "We will do it as soon as possible. I'm not going to give him one day longer." His brethren on the Supreme Court appear to be of similar mind, demanding, with a hint of irony, "a presumption of finality" in these cases. The message from the High Court, says editorialist Colman McCarthy, is that the Justices are "tired of capital punishment cases, that it is time for the states to get on with them."

Should the states indeed decide to "go for it," to quote McCarthy, the result will be an avalanche of executions. Justice Department calculations suggest that executions could occur at a rate as high as three per week. Even death penalty foes like Henry Schwarzschild, who, as head of the ACLU death penalty task force, is prone to underestimate in these matters, fears an execution a week. Whichever estimate you believe, a morbid pace of executions would be maintained for years—there are more than 1400 prisoners awaiting execution. Nothing remotely similar to this has happened since the Great Depression, an era that is notable for its harsh justice.

Admittedly, an execution or so a week pales in comparison to the thousands of executions which have recently taken place in countries like China and Iran, where the rate of state killings of criminals may reach as high as 1,000 a month. But in these countries the issue is terror, not justice. Law is a cover for rule by brute force and even, on occasion, mob violence. Life, even innocent life, is considered cheap and is further cheapened by executions. In contrast, our concern is for justice under law and our preeminent value is humaneness, emphasizing the value of human life, including the lives of those guilty of atrocious crimes. Our humanitarian values thus compel us to re-examine our commitment to the death penalty and to consider less drastic ways of punishing our worst criminals.

Murderers Are People, Too

An execution is always a tragic ending to human life. The belief that the person put to death has committed a terrible crime and in some abstract sense may deserve to die does not change this fact. Yet many people ignore the tragic side of the death penalty. They have no empathy or fellow feeling for those who kill. Some, for instance, see murderers as so many anonymous crime statistics. For others, murderers are monsters, animals, or some species of psychopath. These jaundiced views, moreover, are not restricted to an uninformed and vindictive segment of the populace. Walter Berns, a scholar and advocate of the death penalty, openly mocked Supreme Court Justice Brennan for contending that "Even the vilest criminal remains a human being possessed of human dignity." It was only a few years back that the Chief Justice of Georgia's Supreme Court likened murderers to mad dogs. That must still unsettle the 100 or so condemned prisoners (kennelled?) on Georgia's death row and subject to his rulings on their appeals. An editorialist in Alabama sounded a similar theme when he described execution as "an act approaching judicial euthanasia," a merciful gesture putting brutish criminals out of their (our?) misery. William Raspberry, a syndicated columnist, summed up this point of view when he observed that "It is possible for a criminal to commit acts so heinous as to place himself outside the category of human, to render him subject to extermination as one might exterminate a mad dog, without consideration of how the animal came to contract rabies in the first place."

For most people, then, executing murderers is not seen as killing fellow human beings. By executing murderers we disown them, wash our hands of them, punish them as only monsters should be punished: violently, with utter disregard for their humanity. We seek a life for a life because there is no middle ground with monsters, no extenuation, mitigation, or mercy. Their lives do not reflect error, foible, or fate; they embody evil and malevolence. With them, fire must be met with fire, violence must beget violence, all accounts must be closed, irrevocably.

These sentiments are widely and even fervently held today, but they are wrong nonetheless. Murderers are dangerously flawed human beings—they are not creatures beyond comprehension or control. Their violence is not a specter or disease that afflicts them without rhyme or reason, nor is it merely a convenient vehicle for ugly passions. Rather, their violence is an adaptation to bleak and often brutal lives. "There is nothing as internal as pain," states convicted killer Jack Abbott, who speaks from experience, "especially human pain. The catalog of suffering it would take to record the intricacies of pain that led to the manifestation of an act of...murder would be very melancholy to relate." Abbott's violence and that of most violent men is ultimately spawned by the hostility and abuse of others, and it feeds on low self-confidence and fractured self-esteem. Paradoxically, their violence is a twisted form of self-defense that serves only to confirm the feelings of weakness and vulnerability that provoke it in the first place. When their violence claims innocent victims, it signals not a triumph of nerve but a loss of control. Violence is thus a human failing, and it must be punished accordingly.

Why not simply execute murderers and be done with them? Granted they are human beings, but they are still dangerous. Besides, a hard life may make violence understandable, but it doesn't give anyone the right to harm or kill another person. Nobody put a gun to their heads and forced them to kill; they chose to kill their victims, and they deserve a punishment that fits their crime.

A KILLING BY ANY OTHER NAME

How do we decide what punishment fits the crime of murder, particularly the premeditated and often heinous murders that people think of when they call for the death penalty? Lex talionis—retaliation in kind, an eye for an eye—is perhaps the most cogent moral principle that can be invoked, in the abstract, to support the death penalty for the crime of murder. This principle is, according to philosopher Jeffrey Reiman, "the law enforcement arm of the golden rule." People should be treated the way they treat others. "Treating others as you would have them treat you," explains Reiman, "means treating others as equal in worth to you.... Treating people as they have actually treated others enforces the golden rule," but only up to a point, at least in an imperfect world in which access to the human and material resources which promote the development of personhood is decidedly unequal. As psychiatrist Willard Gaylin tells us, the impoverished lives of violent men typically place them beyond the golden rule.

> To be totally unaccepted, to be totally unloved— indeed, to be almost totally disapproved—either requires the rejection of one's self (an intolerable situation) or a total dissociation from the judging individual. Such total dissociation is dangerous, however, when we are required to live in a social community. Surely the kind of...brutality that is evidenced in the newspapers every day, in which a streetmugger hits a random woman over the head with a lead pipe as a convenient means of gaining the $6 in her purse, implies more than just the need for $6. It suggests that the concept of identity has been destroyed, or never developed; that the person now feels so 'other' that he is no longer within the framework of identification necessary for introjection of a value system. Such behavior is beyond the golden rule, for that implies the identity of personhood between the other and you. Obviously, it is more analogous to the squashing of a bug approaching your picnic table. To give up on one's self is to give up on one's own personal value, and ultimately to give up on a sense of values.

Does enforcing the equal worth of persons hold out the prospect of justice for these offenders? Does it take account of the forces that shape their lives? Is it not disingenuous to claim that violent men in effect choose to be subjected to violence in return, a claim that pays tribute to a personhood we violate or ignore until the juncture of punishment, at which point we "honor" them with yet another indignity? Paradoxically, violent men live by a golden rule of sorts, with others cast as agents and targets of violence. For them, the golden rule boils down to "might makes right," and it is on the basis of this primitive retributive notion that they will understand the death penalty.

Moreover, even if the golden rule does apply to these offenders, it has a different meaning when invoked by individuals and institutions. When person A hits person B in a fit of anger, person B, now angry, responds in kind. It may not be advisable for B to do so, but it is understandable, given his anger, and just, given what has been done to him. Person A deserves a taste of his own medicine and person B, who is not obligated to be a saint, can justifiably give it to him. But the equation is different when the state enters the picture. The state redresses harms long after they have occurred; passions have subsided and cooler heads are meant to prevail. (Person B might also act dispassionately and long after the offense, but this, as criminologist Graeme Newman's analysis of the history of punishment makes painfully clear, is not the typical instance of person-to-person retribution). The dynamics of the offense must be considered and weighed in assessing a just penalty, and a panoply of sanctions can be used to achieve this end. Objectivity and compassion are expected to operate. So is the generous side of the golden rule— the notion that one can be a model of correct conduct not by matching harm with harm but by showing both the offender and society that there is a better way to solve problems.

Delegating the administration of justice to the state was meant to make us more civilized, to end blood feuds and raise our punishments to a level of mature, compassionate discourse. Surely neither "eye for an eye" justice nor the golden rule requires that we, through the state, replicate crimes under color of law. One would hope that we are not enjoined by any notion of justice to compete with criminals to see who can mete out the worst harms. And surely "retributive justice," as it is called in academe, does not condone violence when there are equitable and humane alternatives to punish the offender and protect the society.

Thus, while it is true that murderers must be paid back for what they have done to their victims, this must be done in a way that is just and proper and not simply an imitation of their violence. This point is obvious as it applies to other crimes, including other violent crimes. No one seriously entertains the notion of robbing robbers, mugging muggers, or raping rapists, even if this is, strictly speaking, what these offenders deserve. Instead, these criminals are imprisoned for periods of time that are believed to produce suffering equivalent to, or commensurate with, the suffering wrought by their crimes.[1] We settle for something on the order of "eye for an eye" justice in the hope that the penalty, which balances such values as justice and mercy, won't be worse than the crime it punishes. We also hope that the penalty of imprisonment might at least on occasion prove constructively painful—that criminals might come out of prison better persons than when they went in. By using prison we aim to administer a civilized and potentially civilizing punishment in line with Plato's dictum: "Judgment by sentence of law is never inflicted for harm's sake. Its normal effect is one of two; it makes him that suffers it a better man, or, failing that, less of a wretch...."[2]

The idea that we should kill killers has always had a fairly wide following, however. Indeed, support for the death penalty goes far beyond the laws presently on our books. It is a sad fact, for instance, that public opinion supports the death penalty for all manner of murders, including some that lack premeditation. Why this retributive passion?

One reason why it may be easy to contemplate executing murderers is simply that a killing can be imitated literally and discreetly by agents of the state. Justice can be rendered with decorum. This is certainly not the case with other serious crimes such as rapes, robberies, or even burglaries. State-sponsored sodomy of rapists, for instance, is hard to envision, and presumably even harder to carry out. One imagines—and hopes—there would be fewer volunteers to carry out this punishment than is presently the case for executions. Volunteer executioners speak about "doing one's duty," however onerous and thankless the task, in the name of law and justice. They even appear on television talk shows and are well received by audiences! One is tempted to think of them as admirable citizens, working as they do without recompense in the war against crime. This temptation can be easily resisted in the case of other punishments ostensibly warranted by retributive justice—rape for the rapist being an excellent example—where the punishment's affinity with criminal violence is easier to see.

Another reason we execute murderers with few qualms, and occasionally with enthusiasm, is that these offenders are readily seen as monsters, and of course one can't equivocate with monsters. If ever violence warranted counterviolence, it would be with these creatures! But it is vital to recognize that killing killers is really no different from visiting any other crime upon its author. The fact that lesser offenders, including rapists, robbers, and even burglars, have been executed in the past doesn't change this point. It simply indicates that we were less discriminating in our use of the term 'monster,' and allowed murderers to define justice for the whole melange of entities that came under that label.

Put bluntly, an execution is a premeditated killing, no more and no less. Fittingly, it is often preceded by trials in which, according to criminologist Stephen Gettinger, an inadequate defense is "the single outstanding characteristic" of capital defendants who, as a result, appear in court as "creatures beyond comprehension, virtually gagged and masked in preparation for the execution chamber." Death row confinement culminates the preparatory process. Here, in Camus' analysis and in my own research, we learn that the condemned suffer a "living death." They are literally dehumanized—alive as bodies but, in varying degrees, dead as persons—and curiously reminiscent of the dehumanized monsters that haunt our imagination. Their executioners experience a parallel though less extreme fate; they suffer a limited and essentially symbolic form of dehumanization in which they relinquish their personhood and become instruments of the death penalty's violence. "It is a paradox of bureaucratically administered violence," as I have observed elsewhere, "that men must be dehumanized—dead as persons—to play their roles as killers and victims." The executions themselves bear this out. As any witness to one will attest, an execution is a methodical and chilling affair, as much a violation of a person's humanity as a murder. In fact, among the most shocking murders are those characterized as "execution-style slayings," a comparison that highlights the cold-blooded and dehumanizing character of executions for everyone involved. It is irrelevant that an execution is carried out in antiseptic surroundings and after extended legal appeals. Society may convert a killing into a bureaucratic event or procedure, but it cannot thereby change its nature.

A LIFE FOR A LIFE

Murderers treat their victims like objects to be violated and discarded, but we as a society must not fashion our punishments after their acts. (Indeed, at the heart of the Eighth Amendment ban against "cruel and unusual punishments" is the prohibition of punishments which "deny the dignity of man.") Instead, murderers, like other criminals, must be punished as human beings who deserve to suffer in a way that is commensurate with the harm they have caused. Thus, their punishment must approximate death and yet respect their humanity by treating them as full-blooded persons and not as mere physical objects.

This means lengthy prison terms for murderers. When we sentence criminals to prison we demand a painful suspension of their lives—a temporary death, if you will—until they are deemed worthy of return to the society of the living.[3] But how long is enough? At what point does a prison term inflict enough pain to pay back the murderer for his crime?

The answer varies. The context in which the crime occurs, for example, is a critical factor in assessing punishment. Sentences presently take account of some specific contextual factors, such as duress or the presence or absence of explicit prior intent. But more general and often crucial contextual factors (such as those raised by Gaylin, above, relating to the brutalization of the human spirit) are rarely, if ever, considered in any systematic way. Sensibilities also come into play. Pain is a subjective experience, and what constitutes sufficient pain will depend on the capacity of the person who inflicts or authorizes punishment to empathize with the criminal. This presents a serious problem in the case of murder, since few of us are able to empathize with murders. Yet, if we are unable to put ourselves in their shoes, unable to feel for them, we are unable to develop a sense of their suffering and hence unable to determine when they have suffered enough.

In fact, in the absence of empathy, there is no limit to the pain one can inflict, since by definition the pain affects someone for whom one feels nothing and whom one naturally assumes feels nothing himself. This means that we imagine we are dealing with cold-blooded felons, the extreme case of which is the monster, who are impervious to pain and hence must be punished according to a scale of suffering far in excess of what we would apply to ourselves or others like us. We may even believe that there is no really adequate punishment. It is perhaps for this reason that we can bandy about prison terms of 5, 10, 20, 40 or (in states like Texas) literally thousands of years as though they were civilized, even "soft," penalties.

Perhaps a way out of this dilemma is to relate prison sentences to our own life experiences. A four-year sentence for instance, sounds like a snap, a travesty of justice in the case of murder. But imagine spending the whole of one's high school years, including summers, separated from loved ones and confined for the greater part of each day to a cage. A ten-year sentence would take up one's entire grade school term (including summers), plus two full years for good measure. For the average American, who is middle aged, a 30- or 40-year sentence comes close to obliterating any life at all. Though a true life sentence falls short of execution, surely no criminal deserves a harsher fate than this!

The majority of murderers can point to a host of mitigating circum- stances in their lives and in their crimes (though, as noted above, only some of them are presently recognized in law). One must hope that, for them, serving sentences of no more than ten years would be sufficient punishment. Some are more culpable and would no doubt deserve longer sentences; a few might marshall an impressive array of exonerating conditions and warrant shorter terms of confinement. Our worst murderers, those "monsters" we presently consign to the death chamber because their actions seem to place them beyond the bounds of human decency, would of course be eligible for lengthy prison terms, including a natural or true life sentence.

True life sentences are only rarely meted out in our courts, and never with explicit recognition that this sentence—in which the offender is slated to spend his entire remaining life in prison—is in fact a kind of death penalty. True life prisoners remain physically alive and in the company of other convicts and guards; they are treated as human beings and remain members, however marginal, of the human community. They can forge a life of sorts behind bars, but one organized on existential lines and etched in suffering, for, at a profoundly human level they experience a civil death, the death of freedom. The prison is their cemetery, a 6' by 9' cell their tomb. Their freedom is interred in the name of justice. They are consigned to mark the passage of their lives in the prison's peculiar dead time, which serves no larger human purpose and confers few rewards. In effect, they give their civil lives in return for the natural lives they have taken. A true life sentence, then, can and should be used as a practical moral alternative to the death penalty, a civilized and potentially even civilizing application of the golden rule in the extreme case of cold-blooded and unmitigated murder.

Perhaps the primary objection to this proposal during these hard economic times is the price tag. We've all heard about the cost of new prison construction, which can run in the neighborhood of $60,000 per cell, and about per capita confinement costs of anywhere from $5,000 to $25,000 a year. True life sentences would presumably cost a fortune in new cell construction and in bills incurred to keep men confined for 40 or more years at a time, depending upon average prisoner longevity. One can readily envision, for example, a tab of some $600,000 per prisoner sentenced to a life term. One is likely to think that, if nothing else, executions are humane for taxpayers.

But the actual cost of true life sentences would fall considerably short of these estimates and would roughly parallel the cost of executions. We won't have to build new cells for true life prisoners. These prisoners would be confined under any sentencing scheme, whether on death rows or in standard maximum security prisons. When crowding is a problem, less serious offenders can be released to make room for murderers, a policy that seems eminently sensible. Moreover, "The actual out-of-pocket costs to keep a man alive in any prison," as criminologist John Conrad as observed, "is less than $5,000 per year."[4] In states like Texas, where confinement costs are low, it is much cheaper still. A true life term, calculated as a forty year sentence of imprisonment, would cost taxpayers no more than $200,000 per prisoner in states like New York and California, and would cost considerably less in other states. While these costs are quite high, they compare favorable with the cost of death sentences, which require complicated trials, lengthy appeals, years of special custodial housing for the condemned, and elaborate ritual killings. There are, in other words, no bargain punishments for murder. Neither executions nor life sentences come cheap.

Beyond the matter of cost, some people will balk at the idea of a true life sentence because they don't believe prison is punishment. They refuse to subsidize the lives of luxury to which country club prisons are presumed to accustom the convicts. This cynical but widely held view is seriously misleading. A prison joke has it that the country club prison is much like the Loch Ness monster: There are sporadic citizen sightings but no scientific confirmations. Prisons are costly to operate, but little of this money is spent on convict sustenance, let alone the amenities of life. For instance, in New York, a state noted for a progressive penal system, a prisoner's meal bill comes to under two dollars a day! Some country club! In point of fact, prisons are spartan environments. A lifetime in prison is a lifetime of suffering and privation.

Other objections to this proposal relate to public safety. After all, dead prisoners pose no threats, whereas life prisoners appear to be at least potential dangers to the community. For all intents and purposes, however, true life prisoners are punished and incapacitated for life. Maximum security prison walls (as distinct from the notoriously permeable fences that enclose medium and minimum security prisons) virtually assure that society has nothing more to fear from these prisoners.[5] Nor are they a special threat to other prisoners or guards. Most lifers, in fact, are compliant prisoners; those who are more troublesome can be segregated from the main prison population. Finally, the presence of life prisoners may indirectly promote public safety by discouraging at least some other prisoners from their criminal ways, if for no other reason than that lifers stand as flesh-and-blood testaments to the wages of violent crime.

A true life sentence is an awesome judgment, but unlike a death sentence it need not destroy the prisoner or impart a legacy of irreversible mistakes. A life sentence is a painful punishment but it can be borne with dignity. It can also be changed. New evidence may alter a verdict or indicate a lesser sentence; substantial and enduring changes of character may, in extraordinary cases, permit the resurrection of a few of these prisoners, for example by means of special pardons. New evidence is only rarely discovered, of course, and pardons are even harder to come by, but at least avenues of mercy and redress remain open to us in our search for justice.

A true life sentence should replace execution as our most severe penalty. A civil life for a natural life is punishment enough—for our worst murderers, who must pay dearly for their crimes, and for the society which must take cold comfort in the administration of that punishment.

NOTES

1. Imprisonment bears a superficial resemblance to the kidnapping situation, but there are intrinsic and important differences. There are always some programs and ameliorative resources in prison, as well as activities such as work, which can have reformative value. More fundamentally, there is the longstanding belief that the "pains of imprisonment" can be constructive in the same sense that the "pains" of monastic life can be constructive and result in an improvement of the inmate's character.

2. No civilizing consequences even remotely attach to killings or executions, at least in the modern mind. Ironically, Plato did envision executions in his Republic. He saw crime as a kind of disease which contaminated and tortured its host; the serious and incurable criminal would be released from his earthly bondage by execution, a punishment which was presumed to make him "less of a wretch." Philippe Aries tells us that other notions of death prevalent before the 20th century, particularly those associated with a forgiving God and a congenial afterlife, made a foreseen death a "tame" and desirable arrangement. Here, too, execution might be conceived as a blessing of sorts, allowing the criminal to come to terms with his Maker. In our secular age, where men are neither believed possessed by criminal demons of one sort or another nor the confident beneficiaries of a guaranteed afterlife, the benefits of death cannot be invoked to defend the death penalty.

3. Interestingly, prisoners until fairly recently were viewed as the legal equivalent of dead men. They were "civilities mortuus," and their estates, if they had any, were "administered like that of dead men."

4. Higher estimates of confinement costs incorrectly attribute overhead expenses–that is, the fixed costs of running prisons independent of who is in them and how many people are in them–to individual prisoners. They also discount one unique economic aspect of life sentence prisoners' confinement, noted by Conrad: "Most lifers tend to be employed, sooner or later, on productive jobs, which may eliminate the cost of keeping them altogether.

5. To be sure, convicts sometimes escape from maximum security prisons. The rate of such escapes is, however, quite low. Even less common are escapes from prison that are accompanied by violent crimes against the public. We are reminded by van den Haag that prisons are costly, in the main, "because they are too secure."

A LIFE FOR A LIFE?
REPLY—

OPINION & DEBATE

Ernest van den Haag

A *Life for a Life* often asserts what it asserts vaguely and without evidence, or argument, so as to leave me rather baffled. Nonetheless, I shall confine myself to replying to the points against the death penalty made therein, since I have presented my arguments for the death penalty elsewhere.[1]

Professor Johnson complains about the "morbid pace of executions"—three a week—which he predicts on the basis of reports from anonymous Justice Department informants. He does not say what a healthy pace of executions would be. At the current (non-morbid?) pace most persons sentenced to death will die of old age.

"In the absence of empathy" Professor Johnson writes, "there is no limit to the pain one can inflict, since, by definition the pain affects someone for whom one feels nothing and whom [sic] one naturally assumes feels nothing himself." I know of no evidence indicating that in the "absence of empathy there is no limit to the pain one can inflict," nor do I know how that absence is established. There is no evidence for Professor Johnson's view, that those who favor the death penalty typically have no empathy with murderers. Couldn't it be that execution is thought necessary, despite empathy? Or because of it? Does Professor Johnson confuse empathy with sympathy? Even so, did Melville's Captain Vere lack sympathy for Billy Budd, whom he had executed for what amounted, at most, to negligent manslaughter?

The suggestion that empathy sets limits to the infliction of pain is plainly wrong. Sadists like to inflict pain because they feel empathy, not because they don't—that is, after all, why they inflict pain on people, and not on furniture. Further, why does one "naturally" assume that anyone for whom one feels no empathy would "feel nothing himself?" One would have to be quite confused to confuse one's lack of empathy with someone else's pain with the other person's not feeling pain. I have never known anyone who lacks empathy with the pain of others to deny that others feel pain. No evidence is offered. Incidentally, Professor Johnson's view, that those who favor the death penalty believe that murderers to be executed feel no pain, contradicts his prior assertion, that those who favor the death penalty want murderers to be executed because of vindictiveness. If they "naturally" assume that murderers do not suffer, how are they vindictive?

It is difficult to cope with this style of argument. Nevertheless let me try to extract what specifics I can find and consider them *seriatim*.

"Murderers are people, too" Professor Johnson writes, but the death penalty dehumanizes them by showing "utter disregard for their humanity." We are not told why execution is inconsistent with regard to humanity. By definition? such as: "to execute someone is to disregard his humanity?:" If so, the definition strikes me as circular and impossible to confuse with an argument.

Philosophers, such as Immanuel Kant, G.F.W. Hegel and many others, have argued that their humanity, their human dignity, not only permits, but actually demands, that murders be executed and that not to do so would deny the human dignity, the humanity, of murderers. Kant may be wrong. I believe he is. But he offered an argument. Professor Johnson does not. He merely asserts that execution shows "utter disregard" for the murderer's "humanity" and does not tell us why, as though assertion were argument.[2] This is reiterated throughout. We are told that "men must be dehumanized to execute or be executed," but we are not told wherein this means anything other than that Professor Johnson disapproves of executions. He complains that they are "methodical and chilling." Would he want them to be spontaneous and warm? or to be public festivals, as in the past?

According to Professor Johnson, advocates of the death penalty believe that "murderers are beyond comprehension or control." He does not tell what proportion of retentionists hold this silly belief or how he found out. I favor the death penalty and believe that murderers can be comprehended. But I do not believe that "tout comprendre c'est tout pardonner," Mme. de Stael (and Professor Johnson?) notwithstanding. I can also believe that most would-be murderers can be controlled, best by the threat of the death penalty. Finally, I believe that knocking down strawmen is not a helpful way of arguing the cause of abolition, or any other.

Professor Johnson has Jack Abbott, a convicted killer, "who speaks from experience," testify that "violence…is ultimately spawned by the hostility and abuse of others…." I suspect that Abbott's testimony is a mite self-serving. Professor Johnson apparently does not. Anyway, he endorses Abbott's view, with psychological speculations suggesting that murderers murder because they have not been loved enough and suffer from "fractured self-esteem." This should mitigate their punishment. Surely, some well-loved people do murder (or is murdering itself the evidence for "fractured self-esteem?") and some unloved people do not. How does Professor Johnson's explanation apply to Mafiosi, leading a close and rich family life? Or to murderers who murdered because they love someone not otherwise attainable? Professor Johnson's explanation hardly explains much. But even if explanatory, as it probably is for some murders, how would it mitigate, or reduce, the murderer's responsibility for his crime? Causation is not compulsion. If a court finds that the murderer could, but did not choose to, control his act—else he could not be found guilty—why does Professor Johnson think that "fractured self-esteem"—if it were the cause—is the same as lack of control? How does a cause become an excuse?

Professor Johnson writes that "delegating…justice to the state was meant to raise our punishments to a level of mature compassionate discourse" ("discourse" leaves me confounded, but let that go) which would exclude the death penalty. The premise is wrong, and the conclusion does not follow. The history of punishment does not suggest that delegation to the state was meant to reduce them. Nor did it. Reductions did occur in the last 200 years, for reasons independent of delegation to the state.

At any rate it is a *petitio principii* to argue that the death penalty should be abolished because we were meant to be "mature and compassionate." What Professor Johnson has to show is that maturity, or compassion, require abolition of the death penalty. He merely asserts it.

Further on, Professor Johnson argues that, since the *lex talionis* cannot determine punishment for many crimes, such as rape, or fraud, it should not determine the punishment for murder. Why not? If we can't feed everybody, does it follow that we should not feed anybody? There are arguments against the *lex talionis*. This is not one.

Professor Johnson calls an execution a "premeditated killing." It is. But he neglects to mention that it differs from premeditated murder by being a lawful punishment for a crime. That, indeed, is the difference between crimes, including premeditated murder, and punishments, including executions. The physical characteristics of crimes and punishments may well be identical. Crimes differ from punishments in their social characteristics. Professor Johnson writes in a footnote that imprisonment differs from kidnapping because of the "ameliorative resources" of prisons. These are contingent. The essential difference is that kidnapping is a crime—unlawful imprisonment—and lawful imprisonment is the punishment for it, regardless of "ameliorative resources."

Professor Johnson suggests that some term of imprisonment is enough or, anyway, nicer, as a punishment for murder. I have dealt with this matter elsewhere.[3] He also tries to persuade us that even life imprisonment would be cheaper than the death penalty. His comparison is based on two common errors. First, he compares the marginal cost of imprisonment with the average cost of the death penalty. (See his footnote 4.) A correct comparison is of the two marginal costs or of the two average costs. Second, he assumes that there will be more trial costs for death penalty cases than for life imprisonment cases, because the death penalty leads to more appeals. Since life prisoners spend their time on *habeas corpus* appeals, I doubt this.

Finally, Professor Johnson argues that "life prisoners may indirectly promote public safety...[since they] stand as flesh and blood testaments to the wages of violent crime." I agree. Life imprisonment may have deterrent effects. Why wouldn't the death penalty? "A life sentence" Professor Johnson goes on "...can be borne with dignity." Sure, and why can a death sentence not be borne with dignity? We are not told.

Rereading Professor Johnson, I gather that he opposes the death penalty and suppose that he has good reasons. Someday I hope to learn what they are.

NOTES

1.   E. van den Haag and John P. Conrad *The Death Penalty: A Debate*, Plenum Publishing Corp., N.Y. (1983).

2.   Professor Johnson also suggests that murders are unlikely to appreciate that they are executed for the sake of their human dignity. This is often true. But Kant thought so too, and Professor Johnson does not address his argument.

3.   E. van den Haag, *loc. cit.*

III.
Ethics and the Courts—
Questions and Scenarios

Chapter Six

1. How would you expect the general public to react to a lawyer who adopted the moral agent concept? Would his/her practice be identifiably different from those of his/her peers?

2. The adversarial process provides the foundation for our system of justice, but it has some limitations as a means to determine the truth. What are some of these limitations? How could they be overcome?

3. Some people might agree that the moral agent concept of an attorney is best for others but personally might prefer the pure legal advocate when they get into legal difficulties. How would you characterize the ethics of this position?

4. Do lawyers have an ethical responsibility to the public and society as a whole, or is their only obligation to their client? Should they have an obligation to society as a whole?

5. How can the moral behavior of an attorney be monitored?

6. Do the rules regarding attorney-client privilege protect only the guilty, or do they play a larger role in our system of laws and government?

CHAPTER SEVEN

1. It appears that the reason prosecutors (and everybody else) misbehave is that it works. How important is it that prosecutors behave in an ethical fashion? It is more important to obtain every possible conviction or to achieve convictions in a morally acceptable fashion? How can limits be placed on unethical conduct?

2. Referring back to Gold and his discussion on connectedness, every unethical act reflects back on the actor. How does this process affect prosecutors?

3. Would you expect prosecutors to have moral careers like police officers? What would be the similarities and differences in ethical careers between these two groups of criminal justice officials?

4. Gershman discussed unethical conduct among prosecutors during the trial process. But, most criminal cases do not go to trial. Does this mean that ethical problems are avoided when plea agreements are arranged between prosecutor and defense attorney? What new ethical dilemmas might confront lawyers engaged in these plea-bargaining efforts?

CHAPTER EIGHT

1. What are the four traditional purposes of criminal punishment?

2. Should criminal punishments be based on predictions of future crime? If so, what types of errors would we probably expect to make with such predictions?

3. In what ways do the needs of the community for protection from crime conflict with the interests of the individual offender in avoiding state intervention at the point of sentencing?

4. Mackie suggests that punishment is a reflex at base. Why does he come to this conclusion, and do you agree with him?

5. Why do sentencing decisions discriminate against certain groups, and what should be done to minimize discrimination?

CHAPTER NINE

1. Pepinsky and Jesilow argue that there is too much punishment in the United States. How would you evaluate their position regarding this issue?

2. According to Pepinsky and Jesilow, it is impossible to fit the punishment to the crime in a large, heterogenous population. If this is an accurate assessment, what options for sentencing rationales remain?

3. What would be the requirements of a sentencing system that promoted respect for law and the criminal justice system?

CHAPTER TEN

1. For many murderers, violence is an adaptation to bleak and brutal lives. Given this reality, how do the ethics of utility, rights, and connectedness and caring frame the issues surrounding the death penalty?

2. Is the death penalty an act of violence? If it is an act of violence, how can its use influence levels of violence in society? If it is not an act of violence, what makes it "non-violent?"

3. Death penalty advocates and opponents often point to the costs of incarceration and of lengthy appeals. How should economics influence decisions regarding the use of the death penalty? Are these issues irrelevant, or must they be considered as a practical matter?

4. How concerned should we be about the dignity with which a murderer can meet his or her sentence?

5. Is it necessary for murderers to be monsters to justify their execution? What are the characteristics of a homicide that could justify execution?

Scenarios

1. You are a female defense attorney. Your client has been charged with rape and has admitted that technically he may have raped the woman, but on that night, he contends, he and the victim had both had too much to drink to think clearly. He's not sure how much force he used. He has provided you with names of three of his friends who have also been sexually intimate with the woman in question. When you prepare your case, what factors will influence your development of legal strategy? What will your strategy be? Should you suggest another attorney?

2. You are a deputy district attorney prosecuting a difficult case of child molestation. The evidence against the defendant is rather strong, but he says he was with a casual friend in another part of the city at the time of the crime. The friend is believed to have been hiking cross-country and has not been located; the defendant has no funds to track him down. What should you do?

3. You are a member of a sentencing commission whose task is to make the sentencing process more equitable for rich and poor alike. What would be some of your specific recommendations? What types of problematic issues should you expect to encounter?

4. You are a successful private attorney. You have been defending a young man accused of rape and first degree murder whom you believe is innocent. He has no previous record. All available evidence is circumstantial, and you believe him when he tells you he is innocent. You feel you have successfully defended him until the last day of the trial, when you discover evidence that positively identifies your client as the murderer. You confront him, and he admits to the crime to you but refuses to admit it to anyone else. What action, if any, do you take? What are your reasons?

IV. ETHICAL ISSUES
IN CORRECTIONS

Can offenders be corrected by encouraging them to behave more ethically?; By teaching them how to recognize and analyze moral dilemmas? While few would argue that this practice alone will dissuade many people from crime, it is equally clear that an ability to assess the harmfulness of one's acts and to anticipate consequences may be a prerequisite to moral and law-abiding conduct. Given that ability, one can then specify the skills and contexts likely to encourage ethical conduct.

Correctional staffs inside and outside institutional boundaries also need to know how to assess moral dilemmas and how to behave in an ethical fashion. Too often, situational factors work against this objective as well.

Many correctional institutions are plagued by high staff turnover, which means that a high percentage of guards are rookies. These individuals must confront a population of offenders housed in crowded circumstances, inmates whose chief objective is to do their time with as little discomfort as possible. Prison inmates are generally quite interested in paying off guards to improve their living circumstances, turn a blind eye to various institutional infractions and/or bring illicit substances or weapons into the institution. Because these inmates may know as much about running the institution as some of the guards, it is often very easy for correctional officers to become dependent on inmates for assistance in doing their jobs, only to find that inmates expect something in return.

Probation and parole officers face different but related problems. The "burned out" probation or parole officer may be as reluctant to supervise his clients as the "burned out" police officer is to answer calls. Misuse of authority can mean that a probationer or parolee is harassed by his supervisor. Discrimination is the result when the conditions of release are differentially enforced against certain offenders.

The ultimate power of the probation or parole officer is the ability to initiate revocation proceedings that can send the offender to prison. The challenge is to use this authority in the same manner as the ethical police officer employs his coercive power—with an understanding of humanity but with a willingness to intervene for the greater good.

While probation and parole officers have worked hard to establish themselves as professionals, correctional officers have had greater difficulty in this regard, largely because the positions often require little in the way of education and offer very low pay. For many persons, working as a correctional officer is only an interim job.

The Federal Bureau of Prisons offers a notable exception to this pattern. There, the correctional officer's position is viewed as the entry point on a career ladder. This practice, employed in conjunction with the conscientious screening of new employees and the use of a management scheme that serves to discourage corruption, works to make the federal prison system an environment more likely to promote high ethical standards.

MORAL DEVELOPMENT
AND CORRECTIONS

11

Joycelyn M. Pollock-Byrne

Corrections has remained relatively untouched by the ongoing research on moral development. The interest in the development of a "moral person" and moral reasoning is obviously relevant to the field of corrections, especially since it has implications for the ultimate questions of how to change the morality of an individual offender. In the following analysis of the possible applications, the reader should keep in mind that "bad" and "good" are simplistic categorizations and the definition of "morality" is somewhat controversial. Also, certain "moral issues," such as the immorality of abortion or capital punishment, are not applicable to the concerns of corrections. However, there is a great deal of behavior which is considered immoral by the majority of people, and this behavior is often illegal. While not completely overlapping, i.e., it may be morally acceptable to steal in order to feed your starving children if that was the only way to save their lives, even though the act would still be illegal. More often than not a "bad" act is both immoral and illegal, such as murder and burglary.

The field of corrections attempts to change that behavior which is considered criminal and deviant. Methods of changing behavior have to have some rationale. This rationale is found in the criminological assumptions or the beliefs regarding what makes the individual criminal. Criminology is a social science that asks the question: why do individuals commit crime? Although radical criminologists might ask why some behaviors become defined as crime while others do not; ordinarily there is no controversy in what is considered crime. We have no difficulty recognizing the *mala in se* behavior that has been deviant in most cultures throughout time. Robbing, stealing, and physically injuring or killing another for emotional or financial satisfaction are universally regarded as criminal behavior. Other types of behavior that are also harmful to people, such as toxic waste dumping, are different but no less criminal behavior, although perhaps the criminality of such behavior has only recently been recognized.

The concept of "evil" has been prevalent in human societies. Some assign "evil" to a separate source (the devil or demons), while others believe that evil is an inherent part of humanity that must be constantly suppressed and civilized. Modern thought may be prone to regard evil as a sickness that can be cured. However one comes to grips with the concept, it is clearly an issue in crime and corrections. Regardless of how academic and sanitized the discussion in criminology becomes, the essential question is: How can we explain the terrible things one person or a group of persons does to another, whether it be burglary, assault, rape or murder? Criminologists are only the latest in a long line of philosophers, theologians, writers and others who have asked the same question.

Usually one can identify what criminological assumptions are made by the type of corrections/punishment advocated. For instance, today's punitive "lock them up" mentality, which advocates swift and long sentences with decreasing interest in constitutional rights, must assume that the harsh punishment advocated will deter the offenders who are subjected to it. This presupposes that they are rational and have the ability to make choices regarding their behavior. Similar to the principles of Bentham long ago, this latter day classical school must assume that the criminal is basically like you or me, that because we would fear and detest long prison sentences in harsh prisons and are frightened into obeying the law because of that fear, so too should criminals. This may indeed be true, but there are competing explanations for crime and competing correctional alternatives to strict and severe punishment. One criticism of this approach is that if one prison sentence won't work, the solution must be to make it longer; and if that doesn't work make the sentence harder and longer, and if that doesn't work, the prison sentence should be even longer or capital punishment used to "solve" the problem of crime.

The positivist tradition looks for causes of crime beyond the "bad impulse" and lack of deterrence. Historically and currently researchers are looking into genetic causes, sociological causes and psychological causes that affect criminal behavior. Each of these has implications for correctional treatment. Genetic factors are now being explored again since evidence exists which indicates that although the older simplistic theories are without credence, there may be a complicated relationship between genetics and criminality. For instance, an individual may inherit traits which have to do with how that person physically responds to stimuli, which in turn may affect a propensity for thrill-seeking, which in turn may affect delinquency. Sociological "causes" include income, lack of skills and opportunity, racism, subcultural influences and so on. The correctional approach to these would be to address the environment of the individual. If the subculture is criminogenic, the individual should be removed from it or other influences should be introduced to counteract the subcultural influence. If larger societal issues, such as poverty, are believed to be part of the problem, large scale intervention (such as Johnson's War on Poverty) is attempted. Sociological interventions are criticized as "excusing" the offender by blaming society or the family or the environment for the individual's misdeeds.

Psychological theories of criminality are usually based on maladjustment and inadequate ego development. Psychological intervention comes in the form of psychotherapy, behavioral conditioning, and cognitive approaches. Various correctional treatment programs have a rationale behind them grounded in psychological theory. For instance, behavior modification programs, especially token economies, were popular in prisons and halfway houses for a time. These programs are based on the concepts of behaviorism. Group therapy, employing various hybrid therapies such as Transactional Analysis or Reality therapy, also enjoyed popularity in corrections. These therapeutic interventions were based on a belief that a trained counselor, sometimes in conjunction with a peer group, could affect the ego development of an adult.

In all of the interventions and the criminological assumptions mentioned above, there is little emphasis on evil or good. The idea of immorality seems to be out of place in corrections, and instead we talk of maladaptive behavior or deviance or criminality. The first of these is a psychological term, the second is a sociological one and the third is a legal definition of behavior which could also be called immoral. Only psychology comes close to using the concept of morality in its attempts to explain criminality or deviant behavior. All three orientations—psychotherapy, behavioral conditioning and cognitive approaches— have developed theoretical perspectives that describe and/or attempt to explain moral development. What makes a "good" person may be a controversial subject for philosophers, but psychologists tend to agree that good moral character includes:

(1) the promotion of honesty and integrity;
(2) conformity to group standards;
(3) service to others;
(4) the development of self-control;
(5) consideration for the needs of others over self; and
(6) the demonstration of consistency, initiative, and persistence in tasks and related aspects (Bigner, 1983:269).

The basic source of disagreement between the various approaches to moral development centers on the processes that shape morality. Psychoanalytic theory was the first theory to formally specify an internal mechanism, the super ego's conscience, responsible for the regulation of one's behavior. Freud believed that the development of one's conscience was associated with identification with the like-sexed parent. Today, it is believed that the child can identify with and receive moral instruction from any adult authority (Harris, 1985:389). Freud's theory emphasizes that children initially behave in appropriate ways because of fear that they will lose their parents' love. After the development of a conscience, they feel guilt or shame when they violate (or think about violating) social norms. Thus, the process of internalizing society's rules, for Freud, involved externally controlled rewards and punishment (e.g., learning) coupled with the ego's instinctual forces and defense mechanisms such as identification and introjection.

The behavioral approaches to moral development have concentrated on external processes more than any of the other paradigms. Behaviorists, collectively, usually focus only on external behavior and use the concepts of setting events, reinforcement, punishment and schedules of reinforcement to explain or change behavior. Neo-behaviorists, such as Bandura (1969), have incorporated cognitive concepts such as observational learning in addition to strictly external mechanisms. The basic assumption of all behavioral approaches is that the internalization of morals is achieved by a consistent pattern of rewarding desired behaviors and beliefs.

The cognitive approach is dominated by Piaget. Jean Piaget (1948), a French psychologist, developed descriptive theories of cognitive and moral development. His theories involve stages characterized by what the child can do and understand at various ages. Piaget felt that children progress through the stages of moral development parallel to their progress through the stages of cognitive/intellectual development. The stages within each theory are sequential, hierarchically cumulative, and age-driven (though progress through them can be accelerated somewhat).

Piaget's stages of moral development are as follows. The premoral stage (to age 7) has two substages or phases. The first phase's cognitive counterpart is the sensory-motor stage, and both phases reflect an extremely egocentric self. Very little moral reasoning occurs in the first phase because the intellectual requirements (language) are not yet available. Instead, the child is learning about himself and his world through sensations, impulses and feelings generated by his experiences. The second phase of the premoral stage is marked by a focus on the caretaker/parent (rather than on the self) as an authority figure. This phase corresponds with the preoperational stage of cognitive development (age 2-7).

Piaget's second stage of moral development is referred to as the intermediate and/or concrete stage; and corresponds to the third stage of cognitive development which is also the concrete operations stage. In this stage, the child (8-11) focuses on "the mental relationships between peers and on an equal, give-and-take basis in a concrete situation" (Schiamberg and Smith, 1982:398). The child, during this stage, tends to classify alternatives dichotomously (such as right or wrong) which can result in an inflexibility in their judgment.

Once an individual, usually during adolescence, enters the final stage of cognitive development (formal operations), they are capable of making moral judgments based on realistic appraisals of situational variables and consider both short- and long-term consequences of their behavior. This is the final stage of moral development according to Piaget's theory.

Piaget's theory of morality served as a starting point for Lawrence Kohlberg's (1970) cognitive theory of moral development. Kohlberg's theory lead to a wealth of moral development research. Basically, Kohlberg hypothesized that an individual would go through integrated stages, similar to Piaget's above. The stages are sequential and hierarchial, that is, one does not jump stages to reach a higher level. Also, very few people may reach the highest stage and most tend to cluster in the conventional stages. Development occurs fairly early in adolescence although there may be some growth after that if certain conditions are present. The three levels of sequential moral reasoning, and the two stages making up each level are as follows.

In the *premoral* level (stage one), children first learn conduct as a result of punishment and their innate obedience orientation. In the second stage, the child learns to behave in a particular way to both obtain material rewards and to avoid punishment for inappropriate behavior. In the *conventional* level, the second level of moral development, social relations determine behavior (stage 3), so the individual does what will result in approval (social rewards) by significant others. In stage 4, the individual is concerned with conformity to society; and societal rules are important. At the final *post-conventional* level, morality is seen in terms of self-accepted principles. In stage 5, individual rights are the basis of ideals and principles that have value apart from societal approval. In the final sixth stage, principles of right and wrong become universal and bridge relativistic gaps of time and place (Kohlberg, 1970; Kohlberg, 1976).

While Kohlberg's theory of moral development has generated much theoretical and applied interest in both moral development and the measurement of moral reasoning, it has also been the subject of substantial criticism. Harris (1985) has summarized the criticism directed towards Kohlberg's theory into six areas:

(a) The theory does not identify one's level of moral reasoning with a high degree of accuracy (it is accurate about 75% of the time; the margin of error may be attributed to the possibility that people do not make all moral judgments at one level);

(b) there may be a weaker relationship between the reasoning processes involved and the behavior/conduct exhibited than originally expected;

(c) the theory may discriminate against females since most early samples were all male;

(d) it reflects a liberal political hierarchy and makes it most difficult for conservatives to attain what the theory describes as the highest levels of moral reasoning;

(e) the theory is culturally biased against non-English speaking individuals; and

(f) the theory does not discriminate between social proscription and prescriptions.

Despite this criticism, Kohlberg's theory of moral development is currently considered to be the most comprehensive descriptive theory of moral development. Kohlberg also has developed a method of assessing moral development. The Moral Judgment Interview (MJI) is a series of hypothetical factual situations which provide difficult moral dilemmas to solve. The subject responds to these hypotheticals by telling the examiner what he/she would do and why. Through a series of probes, the examiner explores the reasons for the subjects' choices. These are then rated through a complicated rating structure to arrive at the subject's moral development stage.

The MJI has been used extensively in studies on moral development and moral reasoning but suffers form several significant limitations. Among these are the following. First, administration and scoring of the MJI requires fairly extensive formal training. Second, the MJI is an individual rather than group instrument. Thus, it is difficult to use, because of cost in time and money, for large samples. Third, the data obtained from the MJI is subjective since the MJI is not standardized. This, in turn, makes it both difficult to replicate the findings of studies using the MJI and raises questions about its validity. Finally, the MJI is only designed to identify an individual's level of moral reasoning development. The relationship between an individual's attitudes and behavior is not highly correlated, and the same may be true of one's level of moral reasoning and behavior (Hartshone and May, 1928; Lickona, 1976).

Because of the structural problems inherent in the MJI and practical considerations (i.e., the need for group administration and machine scoring when using large samples), several simpler and/or more objective measures of moral reasoning have been developed based on Kohlberg's stage typology. The Sociomoral Reflection Measure (SRM) was developed specifically as an instrument that could be administered to groups and did not require the intense training necessary to administer and score the MJI (Gibbs, Widaman, & Colby, 1982). Field tests of the SRM demonstrate that the instrument has high reliability and construct validity (the extent to which an instrument measures a specific attribute; in this case, reasoning used to solve a moral problem associated with a specific level of Kohlberg's stages) and high concurrent validity with the MJI. Additionally, the MJI's original construct and external validity were suspect since Kohlberg's original data were obtained from a longitudinal sample of three male cohorts (10, 13, and 16 years of age). The SRM was constructed from data obtained from "relatively large contemporary cross-sectional samples that represented both sexes, and spanned ages 8-66" (Biggs, Widaman, & Colby, 1982:896). Thus, the SRM's norms provide higher external validity (the extent to which results obtained from one group can be generalized to another) and construct validity than does the MJI. Still, use of the SRM requires considerable training in stage-assessment (reliably categorizing an answer as reflecting moral reasoning typical of a specific Kohlbergian stage) and scoring.

In 1984, Gibbs, Arnold, Morgan, Schwartz, Gavaghan, & Tappan, using the SRM as a base, developed and normed an instrument that possesses the strengths of the SRM but can be machine scored and does not require extensive training to administer. This instrument, the Sociomoral Reflection Objective Measure (SROM), has sufficiently high indices of reliability and validity (construct and concurrent) to be of use to researchers and many practitioners.

Rest's (1979) Defining Issues Test (DIT) requires subjects to evaluate or judge the relative importance of considerations or issues (which are keyed to Kohlbergian stages) pertaining to the solution of moral dilemmas (Gibbs,

Widaman, & Colby, 1982:896). The answers are scored, and the results indicate a "p" score which measures the sophistication of the subjects' understanding and application of principles for judging fairness in social dilemmas. The resulting scores are related to age and education, and the DIT is not considered a test of morality per se. Neither is the DIT designed to measure moral reasoning or the ability to produce moral arguments as is the MJI. Not surprisingly, the DIT's concurrent validity (the extent that one instrument accurately predicts performance on another instrument) with the MJI is low.

The SROM and the DIT are recognition measures as opposed to production measures such as the MJI. In recognition measures the subject is not asked to actively select a course of action, rather he/she simply identifies important issues and indicates a solution in a multiple choice format. There are serious questions concerning the validity of recognition measures and whether they measure the same thing that the MJI was designed to measure. Continuing problems exist in all instruments designed to measure moral development or moral reasoning. One issue is the ability of moral development tests to be applied to individuals. It may be that their value lies only in differentiating qualities between groups and that they cannot be used for classification purposes. Related to this issue is the question of predictability. It is unclear whether moral development test results can be correlated with behavior. And while correlations may hold for groups, it is another question whether the tests could predict individual behavior. Finally, because of the continuing questions of the "product" or moral development, i.e., what constitutes morality or moral behavior, tests of the process of moral development may be premature and culturally biased.

Another concern is the construct validity of these tests. Lutwak and Hennessy (1985) point out that validity is affected by the test's reliability, and reliability, in turn, is affected by the internal consistency and temporal stability of the test. The internal consistency reliability coefficients reported for the DIT and MJI are generally between .75 and .84, with the SRM and SROM coefficients generally reported in the mid +.70's (Gibbs, Widaman, & Colby, 1982; Gibbs, et al., 1984). This does not compare favorably to most well developed cognitive abilities measures, which have accepted standards of .90 and above. For the DIT, one problem may be due to the failure to provide an equal number of stage keyed items for each dilemma. Another problem contributing to reliability is temporal stability. Because there is vulnerability in test-retest scores for individuals, any pre/post test differences may not be attributable to intervention efforts but only to measurement error. Thus, it may be impossible to use test scores as measurements of individual change.

Another question of validity is, regardless of the reliability of the testing device, what is being measured? None of the literature reviewed cited long-itudinal and coefficients associated with predictive validity. Even if an instrument accurately predicts the future behavior of a known group, can it validly and reliably be used to make predictions about a single person's future behavior? To date, none of these instruments (DIT, MJI, SRM, or SROM) have been shown to validly predict real behavior outside a testing situation, which is critical to the use of such tests by practitioners.

APPLICATIONS TO CORRECTIONS

Perhaps because of the problems cited above, there have been very few attempts to apply the moral development theories and tests associated with these theories to criminal justice samples. The few studies which do use delinquent or adult groups have found that the tests can differentiate between delinquent and non-delinquent groups. Other studies show promise of individual applications, but up to this point, none have been reported in the literature.

McColgan, Rest and Pruitt (1983) compared an incarcerated adolescent delinquent sample to a non-incarcerated delinquent sample and a control group of non-delinquents, using both the MJI and the DIT. The samples included a group of legally defined and incarcerated delinquents, a group of legally defined but unincarcerated delinquents and a group of non-delinquents who came from similar backgrounds as the delinquents. The research took place in two phases. First the authors interviewed and tested samples of delinquent and non-delinquent youths. Both groups were approximately 15 years of age and from the same geographical area. Both groups were administered the DIT and MJI. The MJI results were sent to Harvard to be scored and the DIT results were computer scored. The DIT showed lower mean moral maturity scores than did the MJI. In the next phase the authors used a group of legally defined but unincarcerated delinquents and matched them with non-delinquents. Twenty-six matched pairs were compared using the DIT and the MJI. The results of the DIT showed a significant difference between the two groups while the MJI did not. They found that while both the DIT and the MJI distinguished the two groups of delinquent and non-delinquent in the first phase, only the DIT achieved statistically significant different scores between the non-incarcerated delinquent sample and the control sample, indicating it was a more sensitive instrument with similar groups. On the other hand, this study was conducted with only 26 matched pairs, and it would be dangerous to assume from this finding that the DIT is a better measurement tool, especially since it is not measuring development per se but the issues or constructs associated with the stages.

In another project 31 male and 29 female adjudicated incarcerated delinquents were compared to 73 high school students from predominantly middle class backgrounds. Each group was administered the SRM and the SROM. The SRM is a production measurement, similar to the MJI. The SROM is a recognition instrument derived from the SRM. The author found that the production measure was more accurate in distinguishing the delinquent sample from the control sample (Gavaghan, et al., 1983).

The debate between the validity of recognition measures versus the drawbacks of production methods continues. While recognition measures may not measure the same thing as the MJI, the MJI and all production measures are costly, non-standardized and need extensive training for evaluators. In the applications thus far, the sample size has been relatively small and the results could be applied only to groups, not individuals. For moral development to be of use to practitioners as a predictive or classification tool, it must be proven to have validity for individuals. Lutwak and Hennessey's criticisms described previously illustrate the potential problems for simple application to an offender problem. Although these tests—both production and recognition measures—have been successful in distinguishing delinquent groups from non-delinquent groups, this is not helpful for predictive purposes. For a test to be useful for corrections, it must be able to accurately evaluate an individual's placement in a stage sequence and also predict behavior from the stage or score. For instance, one would assume that delinquents would cluster in the lower egocentric stages, and this for the most part is true. However, there are different rationales for the same behavior, thus stage placement may not necessarily predict delinquency or conformity completely.

However, there are current applications which illustrate the potential for these moral development measures. For instance, Van Voorhis (1985) details the use of the MJI with a probationer sample in a restitution study. The author and research assistants were trained to use the MJI and performed interviews on 63 probationers in a restitution project. She found that those who scored at a higher stage on Kohlberg's scale responded to different principles of restitution. Specifically, those who had low stage scores responded to the deterrence and instrumental intents of the restitution project, while those whose scores placed them in the higher stages responded to the reparative and rehabilitative intents. The orientations in turn affected the likelihood of competing restitution successfully, those who identified reparative and rehabilitative intents were more likely to be successful. This is one application which illustrates that the reasoning of offenders does affect their future behavior, at least in a correctional program.

Another study, although not conducted with an offender population, shows another possible use for moral development scales or their progeny. Leahy (1981) reports on a research project which sampled 104 white middle class adolescents and their parents. He tested the children using the DIT and various other scales and also surveyed the parents to discover parental child-rearing practices. The results indicated that child-rearing practices were correlated with DIT scores. Those children raised in a home which emphasized unilateral respect or that were non-nurturant were likely to have lower moral judgment scores than those who were raised in a nurturant and/or democratic home environment. Self-image was also related to home environment and in turn related to moral judgment scores. Interestingly there was a difference between boys and girls and their reactions to child-rearing practices. Boys typically had higher moral judgment scores when their mother was less controlling and punitive. Girls had higher scores when the father showed less ambivalence about autonomy and less protectiveness. Acceptance and encouragement by the mother were related to both the son's and the daughter's higher scores. Only the daughter showed higher scores, however, when the father emphasized control and supervision (Leahy, 1981).

This study is important for two reasons. First, it verifies the hypothesis that moral development and judgment are related to upbringing and environment. This is common sense and conforms to other theories of development, such as behaviorism, learning theory, and even Freudian psychoanalysis. Second, it indicates that reaction to upbringing, and therefore moral development itself, may be influenced by sex and possibly other variables. This complicated the whole area of moral development research and its application to corrections.

One use of moral development scales which is extremely applicable to correctional purposes is the use of the scale or scales to measure changes in moral development after an intervention. This would also be important in determining which intervention techniques were most often effective in changing the offender's moral beliefs. Of course, even assuming one was able to measure a change that was not the result of test-retest effect, there would still be correlation necessarily between the change in moral reasoning and actual behavior. However, given the fact that there is some tendency for delinquents to have fairly low scores, it may be possible, with continued research, to follow such a research plan, i.e., test a group of offenders, conduct some intervention technique, retest and discover whether or not change has occurred and then measure subsequent behavior through recidivism figures or other means.

At least one intervention using moral development as the underlying premise and dependent variable has been done. Hickey and Scharf (1980) used the MJI to assess the impact of "moral issue" discussion groups in a prison. They found that after a period of time in these discussion groups, the prisoners showed a small but definite increase in moral development as measured by the MJI. The researchers concluded from this first project that the overwhelming negative effects of prison overshadowed any positive effects on moral development that the discussion groups were able to provide. Consequently, they decided to implement a therapeutic community in prison in which they could control at least some of the negativity associated with the prison environment. In this study, the authors were able to gain the cooperation of prison administrators to establish a "just community" where prisoners had civic responsibilities such as voting on procedures and even punishments for fellow inmates. The discussion groups expanded to include not only hypothetical issues but also real issues that arose in the unit. Pre- and post-test differences after five months of the program averaged an increase of .39 of one moral stage among inmates under 24 years of age. Nearly one-third of the group shifted more than half a moral stage (1980:137). On the other hand, some individuals experienced a regression during this time period and exited the project at a lower moral stage than when they entered. This reinforces the need to be cautious of attributing group changes to individuals when using moral development assessment devices and also illustrates that the reaction to intervention efforts, just as upbringing, is complicated.

While the MJI was used in this particular intervention, it may be possible to conduct other projects with the DIT or some other scale which is easier to apply and score. As Scharf and Hickey found, the intervention which is possibly most beneficial in encouraging movement in a positive direction is one which encourages a free exchange of opinion and exposure to higher levels of thinking. It also helps to have some real application of principles rather than mere discussion groups. These characteristics are really no different than what Kohlberg proposed as an environment for moral growth.

Other correctional interventions which do not use moral development specifically but have relevance to the concepts and application of the scales discussed have been reported in the literature. For instance, the potential use of stage development assessments in classification has been demonstrated by at least one other project. The Community Treatment Project (CTP) in California used Interpersonal Maturity Level scores for classification of delinquents (Beker and Heyman, 1972). The Interpersonal Maturity Level scores are derived from an in-depth interview, much the same way was the MJI. Seven stages represent personality development, with each stage representing increasing maturity in how the individual sees him/herself and the world (Sullivan et al., 1957). Nine delinquent sub-types were identified, all falling into stages two through four. Comparison of Kohlberg's stages of moral development and I levels indicates a great deal of similarity in the constructs between the two tests. In the CTP, I level scores were used to classify delinquents and then to match them to appropriate parole agents. Thus, the subtype which emphasized authority and power issues was matched to a parole agent whose style of supervision matched the needs and maturity level of the individual. Although this project's findings and results have been criticized, it does represent one possible application of development tests to criminal justice samples beyond mere group identification.

Another project, which is ongoing, illustrates the importance of the cognitive approach in understanding and changing delinquent and criminal behavior. Ross, Fabiano and Ewles (1988) report that after exploring a large number of recidivism reduction projects, those which had any degree of success were those which emphasized a cognitive approach. Their findings indicated that the most successful programs were those which had some impact on the offender's thinking. The authors suggest that offenders are developmentally behind non-offenders in a number of cognitive skills that are necessary for social adaptation. For instance, they may have trouble conceptualizing the consequences of their behavior; they may be non-reflective and impulsive. They are likely to be non-empathetic. They are at the egocentric level of cognitive development. They caution that not all offenders would fit this profile; it has relevance primarily to chronic offenders, adolescent offenders, alcohol-abusing offenders, violent offenders and sex offenders. One of the more interesting speculations one might derive from this line of research is that this may explain why so many delinquents drop out of the crime cycle. As individual delinquents mature their cognitive skills also mature, enabling them to absorb the moral judgments which would control their behavior. This is consistent with Piaget and Kohlberg's research, specifically, that those individuals who are at a low cognitive level would be incapable of understanding, much less utilizing, the moral judgment which is found at higher cognitive levels.

Ross and his co-workers believe that cognitive levels and thinking skills can be improved by a number of intervention techniques and have demonstrated the success of such a program with probationer samples (Ross, et al., 1988). The techniques employed included social skills training, creative problem-solving, critical thinking, values education, assertiveness training, negotiation skills training, interpersonal cognitive problem-solving, social perspective-training, role playing and modeling. These learning programs were conducted by trained probation officers and comprised 80 hours. The results showed that those who had the above program had much lower recidivism than those in a control group or a typical life skills training program. The cognitive training group had only an 18% recidivism rate after 9 months, compared with a 70% recidivism rate for the control group and 48% for the life skills group. Unfortunately the sample size of each group was fairly small, making any conclusions cautionary. Each group had only roughly 20 probationers. Still, the results bear notice, and further implementation of the program seems crucial.

It is especially interesting to note the connection between what Ross and his associates are finding and the analysis presented earlier in this paper concerning the possible applications of moral development to corrections. Although the cognitive approach used by Ross is more general than that proposed by the moral development approach, it has basic similarities. In fact, the cognitive deficiencies that Ross describes as being characteristics of problem offenders are precisely those which would block higher moral reasoning ability. Further, Ross and his co-workers have demonstrated that there is some relationship between judgment and behavior.

The other fairly effective correctional technique which is currently used is behavior modification. A comparison of the two approaches illustrates the different assumptions and applications of each. Behavior modifications assumes that by changing the external reward structure, one can achieve change in behavior, and this is successful. Controlled environments using tokens (positive reinforcement) or punishments (aversive conditioning) have been successful in changing behavior while the individual resides in the program. Some of these programs attempt to provide more long-lasting change by introducing discussion groups and training devices designed to help the individual offender control his own reward contingencies to continue positive behavior patterns. However, the long term effects of behavior conditioning is more problematic. If there is no component of the program that enables the individual to understand and manipulate his or her own environmental rewards, the individuals changed behavior lasts only as long as the external rewards are provided. Thus, upon exit the offender is left to deal with the same external environment that provides few, if any, rewards for positive behavior.

Cognitive approaches, on the other hand, concentrate on the internal mechanisms of behavior control. By teaching the individual to think in a different way, i.e., by increasing problem-solving capabilities or by improving empathetic skills, the intervention is designed to change the individual who, in turn, can react to the environment in a different, more mature fashion. Of course, some more sophisticated behavioral programs do that same thing by teaching the individual about external and internal rewards so there is a progression in abstract reasoning ability and impulse control. However, behavior conditioning does not necessarily lead to moral behavior unless there are the features of the higher stage reasoning to support such thoughts. In fact, behaviorism might work best for those who are at the conventional stage, where rewards and punishments are most important. Behavior is determined by whether or not one will be punished or rewarded rather than some higher abstract moral reasoning. The trouble with this stage is that rewards for behaving in a moral manner are sometimes nonexistent and, in fact, often the external rewards and pressures for performing in an unethical or immoral manner are strong.

One thing that seems clear from all the above research is that increasing the punishment meted out to offenders alone will do nothing to improve their moral reasoning and probably thus will have little effect on recidivism. Unless there is a spontaneous or nurtured change in the thinking and reasoning abilities of the offender and a corresponding change in the moral judgments of that offender, it seems clear that behavior would only be subject to change through compliance. That is, the offender may curtail negative behaviors while being watched or while fearing retaliation, but unless that control was present would have no internalized set of principles which would prevent them from continuing to victimize others. Obviously we cannot continue to imprison all delinquents and criminals, nor can we subject all of them to electronic or other means of constant monitoring; thus, it is crucial to continue to search for the most effective intervention which will change their beliefs about what is right and wrong with the assumption that their moral judgments must have some relationship to their behavior.

FUTURE DIRECTIONS

While caution is dictated in applying moral development tests to correctional uses, the potential for useful application is obvious. If more studies can be done to establish the reliability and validity of the objective tests of moral development, such as the SROM and DIT, which are easier to administer, and if the tests themselves can be improved to substantiate their predictive capabilities, then their usefulness would rival anything that is used today in classification. There are several problems which have yet to be resolved. For instance, most of the moral development tests are heavily influenced by education and literacy. Since criminal populations tend to be deficient in these areas, the tests may be misleading or impossible to use. It may be necessary to further refine them for use with non-literate samples, however difficult that might be. The higher stages of moral development, as determined by Kohlberg and his followers, may not necessarily be crucial to support law-abiding behavior (interestingly in some ways, the highest stage might support civil disobedience). There may be more sensitive measures to determine what moral substage is necessary in the prevention or reduction of delinquency. One must first understand, however, how moral reasoning and behavior are related and then be able to show that reasoning ability has some relationship with behavior. The means do not seem to be available at this point to do this.

Moral development research lends theoretical support to moral education and could serve as an evaluative tool for such intervention. The cognitive approach of Ross and his co-workers is one illustration of the type of intervention that might increase development. Scharf and Hickey's intervention is another example. Ultimately, when one looks at the various attempts which have been made to change behavior, including all those discussed in this paper and other sources, moral development may serve as a unifying concept in what an intervention is supposed to accomplish.

REFERENCES

Archer, R.L. (ed.) (1964). *Jean Jacques Rosseau: His Educational Theories Selected From "Emile," "Julie" and Other Writings*. Woodbury, NY: Banon's Educational Series, Inc.

Bear, O. and H. Richards (1981). "Moral reasoning and conduct problems in classrooms," Journal of Educational Psychology 73:664-670.

Beker, J. and D. Heyman (1972). "A critical appraisal of the California Differential Treatment Typology of adolescent offenders," Criminology (May):3-59.

Blasi, A. (1980). "Bridging moral cognition and moral action: A critical review of the literature," Psychological Bulletin 88:1-45.

Bandura. A. (1969). *Principles of Behavior Modification*. New York: Holt, Rinehart and Winston.

Bigner, J. (1983). *Human Development: A Life-Span Approach*. New York: Macmillan.

Gibbs, J.C., K.D. Arnold, R.L. Morgan, E.S. Schwartz, M.P. Gavaghan and M.B. Tappan (1984). "Construction and validation of a multiple-choice measure of moral reasoning," Child Development 55:527-536.

Gibbs, J.C., K.F. Widaman and A. Colby (1982). "Construction and validation of a simplified, group-administrable equivalent to the Moral Judgment Interview," Child Development 53: 895-910.

Hartshone, H. and M.A. May (1928). *Studies in the Nature of Character: I. Studies in Deceit.* New York: Macmillan.

Harris, A.C. (1985). *Child Development*. St. Paul: West Publishing.

Hickey, J. and P. Scharf (1980). *Toward a Just Correctional System*. San Francisco: Jossey-Bass.

Kohlberg, L. (1970). *Moral Development*. New York: Holt, Rinehart and Winston.

Kohlberg, L. (1976). "Moral stages and moralization," in T. Lickona (ed.) *Moral Development and Behavior—Theory, Research and Social Issues*. New York: Holt, Rinehart and Winston.

Kupfersmid, J. and D. Wonderly (1981). "Moral maturity as an avenue to mental health: Another blind alley," Child Study Journal 10:285-296.

Leahy, R. (1981). "Parental practices and the development of moral judgment and self-image disparity during adolescence," Developmental Psychology 17, 5:580-594.

Lickona, T. (ed.) (1976). *Moral Development and Behavior—Theory, Research and Social Issues*. New York: Holt, Rinehart and Winston.

Locke, D. (1983). "Doing what comes morally: The relationship between behavior and stage of moral reasoning," Human Development 26:11-25.

Lutwak, N. and J. Hennessy (1985). "Interpreting measures of moral development to individuals," Measurement and Evaluation in Counseling and Development 18, 1:26-31.

Piaget, J. (1932). The Moral Judgment of the Child. London: Kegan Paul.

Rest, J.R. (1975). "Longitudinal study of the Defining Issues Test of moral judgment: A strategy for analyzing developmental change," Developmental Psychology 11:738-748.

Rest, J. (ed.) (1979). Development in Judging Moral Issues. Minneapolis: University of Minnesota Press.

Ross, R., E. Fabiano, and C. Ewles (1988) "Reasoning and Rehabilitation," International Journal of Offender Therapy and Comparative Criminology 32:29-35.

Sarafino, E.P. and J.W. Armstrong (1986). Child and Adolescent Development. (2d ed.) St. Paul: West Publishing.

Schiamberg, L.B. and K.U. Smith (1982). Human Development. New York: Macmillan.

Skinner, B.F. (1957). Verbal Behavior. New York: Appleton-Century-Crofts.

Sullivan, C.M., Q. Grant and J.D. Grant (1957). "The development of interpersonal maturity: Applications to delinquency," Psychiatry 20:373-385.

van Voorhis, P. (1985). "Restitution outcome and probationers' assessments of restitution: The effects of moral development," Criminal Justice and Behavior 12, 3:259-287.

Keeping an Eye on the Keeper: Prison Corruption and its Control

12

Bernard J. McCarthy

This chapter examines the problem of prison corruption and its control. Prison corruption has been a persistent and troublesome feature of correctional history. Although correctional systems are relatively closed to public scrutiny, periodically, reports of corrupt practices occurring behind prison walls have reached the general public. In recent years, major prison scandals have been reported in Alabama, Arkansas, Delaware, Hawaii, Illinois, New York, and Tennessee. Despite these almost regular occurrences, we know very little regarding the forms, functions, and impact of corrupt practices in corrections. This informational deficiency is related to a larger problem in corrections: the failure to examine the impact of staff behavior on the correctional process (Hawkins, 1976). However, the significance of this problem should not be underestimated. The critical role played by employees in the correctional enterprise has been noted by correctional practitioners and prison reformers.

239

...it is obvious, too, that the best security which society can have, that suitable punishments will be inflicted in a suitable manner, must arise from the character of the men to whom the government of the prison is entrusted (Boston Prison Discipline Society, 1827:18).

In 1870, the Reverend James Woodworth, Secretary of the California Prison Commission, stated:

Until it [prison guard reform] is accomplished, nothing is accomplished. When this work is done, everything will be done, for all the details of a reformed prison discipline are wrapped up in this supreme effort, as oak is in the acorn (Fogel, 1979:69).

Jessica Mitford reported in a critical study of prisons in 1974:

The character and mentality of the keepers may be of more importance in understanding prisons than the character and mentality of the kept (Reid, 1981:211).

Generally, in the area of public service, the integrity of government workers has been viewed as a significant factor in the effective and efficient operation of government. Yet this subject represents one of the least understood areas in corrections. This paper will focus on one dimension of employee behavior in an institutional setting, staff corruption.

Corrupt practices in prison range from simple acts of theft and pilferage to large-scale criminal conspiracies (e.g., drug trafficking, counterfeiting rings, sale of paroles, etc.). These forms of correctional malpractice may be directed at inmates, employees and the general community.

The potential impact of such practices may be great. In terms of its impact on the criminal justice system, corrupt practices undermine and erode respect for the justice system by both offenders and the general public and lead to the selective nullification of the correctional process for certain offenders (e.g., offenders may be able to arrange the purchase of paroles and pardons). Corrupt practices may also lead to a breakdown in the control structure of the organization and to the demoralization of correctional workers. The existence of corrupt practices may also damage the impact of correctional programs designed to change offenders.

Within corrections, the incentives for corrupt behavior are many. From the offenders' perspective, they have everything to gain (i.e., the so-called pains of imprisonment may be neutralized or their release secured) and very little to lose. From the employees' perspective, corrupt practices represent a lucrative albeit illicit way to supplement one's income (usually without significant risk).

This paper examines the problem of staff corruption within a prison system and addresses three basic questions:

(1) What is corruption, and what forms does it take in an institutional setting?
(2) What factors appear to be associated with its relative incidence?
(3) What steps should be taken to control the problem?

DEFINING CORRUPTION IN A CORRECTIONAL ENVIRONMENT

In the correctional literature, the concept of corruption has been used frequently, usually referring to a general adulteration of the formal goals of the correctional process (Sykes, 1956, 1958; Rothman, 1971). For the purposes of this paper, however, corruption is defined more specifically as the intentional violation of organizational norms (i.e., rules and regulations) by public employees for personal material gain.

This definition was formulated on the basis of a review of the corruption literature, particularly the literature on police corruption. As one might expect, there exists varying definitions and corresponding approaches to the study of corruption (Heidenheimer, 1970). In the research on police corruption, most studies appear to use what has been referred to as a public office-centered definition of corruption (Simpson, 1978). The public office-centered definition views corruption as essentially a violation of organizational norms by a public servant for personal gain (Heidenheimer, 1970). Examples of this approach may be found in the writings of Sherman (1974), Meyer (1976), Goldstein (1977), and Barker (1977). This approach has been adopted in this paper. Corruption occurs when a public servant (prison employee) violates organizational rules and regulations for his own personal material gain.

In operationalizing this definition of corruption, certain conditions must be satisfied before an act can be defined as corrupt. First, the action must involve individuals who function as employees. Second, the offense must be in violation of the formal rules of the organization. Third, the offense must involve an employee receiving some personal material gain for the misuse of one's office. These conditions clearly distinguish corrupt behavior from other forms of staff misconduct, such as excessive use of force. The importance of a standard definition of corruption, consistent with the general literature, is

critical in building an information base regarding corrupt practices in corrections and for comparative purposes with the larger criminal justice system.

TYPES OF PRISON CORRUPTION

Unlike the literature on police corruption, very little is known regarding
the types of corrupt practices experienced by correctional agencies. In
addressing this problem, McCarthy (1981) examined the official records of
an internal affairs unit of a state department of corrections.

The internal affairs unit had the responsibility for investigating all allegations of misconduct by staff or inmates. Cases compiled by this unit were
content analyzed to determine the range and types of corrupt practices experienced by this agency. Admittedly this information source provides a limited
view of the problem because it is based on official statistics. However, as
researchers in the field of police corruption have suggested, the records of the
internal affairs unit represent one of the best available sources of information
for examining this topic (Meyer, 1976; Sherman, 1979).

This review of the case files identified several types of corrupt conduct:
theft, trafficking in contraband, embezzlement, misuse of authority, and a
residual or miscellaneous category.

Theft generally involved reports of items reported as stolen from inmates
during frisks and call searches, visitors who were being processed for visiting,
and staff members. This form of misconduct was generally committed by low
level staff, e.g., correctional officers.

Trafficking in contraband involved staff members conspiring with
inmates and civilians to smuggle contraband (drugs, alcohol, money, and
weapons) into or out of correctional facilities for money, drugs, or
services (usually of a sexual nature). The organization of this activity
varied considerably.

Acts of embezzlement were defined as systematically converting state
property to one's own use. This offense was differentiated from theft which
tended to be single events, opportunistic in nature. This offense involved
employees, sometimes with the help of inmates, systematically stealing
money or materials from state accounts (inmate canteens or employee credit
unions) and from warehouses.

Misuse of authority is a general category involving the intentional misuse of discretion for personal material gain. This form of corruption consisted of three basic offenses directed against inmates: the acceptance of
gratuities from inmates for special consideration in obtaining legitimate
prison privileges, e.g., payoffs to receive choice cells or job assignments; the

acceptance of gratuities for special consideration in obtaining or protecting illicit prison activities (allowing illegal drug sales or gambling); and the mistreatment or extortion of inmates by staff for personal material gain (e.g., threatening to punish or otherwise harm an inmate if a payment is not forthcoming).

THE ROLE OF DISCRETION

All forms of corruption involve the misuse of discretion by public employees. The role played by discretion in corrections is significant. Correctional officials are provided with a broad mandate by law to develop and administer correctional agencies. This broad authority extends to devising rules, regulations, and procedures designed to control and otherwise handle offenders under custody. Corruption occurs when officials misuse this discretionary power for personal material gain. At a general level, three forms of discretionary misconduct can be identified: misfeasance, malfeasance, and nonfeasance.

For the purpose of understanding the relationship between corrupt practices and the misuse of authority, the different forms of corruption have been sorted into the three categories of discretionary misconduct. (See Table 12.1).

Misfeasance refers to the improper performance of some act which an official may lawfully do (Black's Law Dictionary, 1968). Offenses in corrections which fall into this category include the acceptance of gratuities for special privileges or preferential treatment (e.g., assignment to honor blocks, access to phone calls), the selective application of formal rewards and punishments to inmates for a fee, the sale of paroles or other forms of releases, and the misuse or misappropriation of state resources for one's own personal gain. All these acts involve an employee misusing the lawful authority vested in his office for personal gain.

Corrupt practices falling into the category of misfeasance are directed at improving the living conditions of inmates, and, as a result, reduce the deprivations associated with imprisonment. The misuse of lawful authority appears to be in an area in which line staff have the greatest opportunities to maximize their personal gain (especially in supplementing their income through the commission of illicit acts), because the nature of their work permits them the greatest influence over routine prisoner conditions.

Table 12.1
Pattern of Corruption by Type of Decision

Corrupt Acts by Discretionary Decisions	Officials Involved
Misfeasance	
Provide Preferential Treatment and Special Privileges	Line Staff
Selective Application of Rewards and Punishments	Line Staff
Forms of Legitimate Release	Administrators
Misappropriation of Resources	Administrators
Malfeasance	
Trafficking	Line Staff
Extortion/Exploitation	Line Staff
Protection Rackets	Line Staff
Embezzlement/Theft	Line Staff & Administrators
Criminal Conspiracies	Line Staff
Nonfeasance	
Failure to Enforce Regulations	Line Staff
Cover Ups	Administrators & Line Staff

Malfeasance refers to direct misconduct or wrongful conduct by a public official or employee, as opposed to the improper use of legitimate power or authority (Black's Law Dictionary, 1968). Corrupt practices which fall in this category involve primarily criminal acts and include theft; embezzlement; trafficking in contraband; extortion; and exploitation of inmates or their families for money, goods and services; protection rackets; assisting escapes (as opposed to arranging paroles or sentence communications); and engaging in criminal conspiracies with inmates for such purposes as forgery, drug sales, and counterfeiting.

Acts of malfeasance appear to represent more aggressive and serious acts by staff to supplement their incomes. This type of offense is similar to the grass eater/meat eater distinction found in studies of police corruption (Knapp Commission, 1973). Meat eaters are viewed as aggressively exploiting every possible situation for personal gain. Grass eaters, on the other hand, take whatever comes their way. For instance, a meat eater might sell drugs in prison, while a grass eater might respond to an inmate's request for drugs.

The last category is nonfeasance. This refers to the failure to act according to one's responsibilities or the omission of an act which an official ought to perform (Black's Law Dictionary, 1968). McKorkle (1970) has suggested that nonfeasance is more responsible for corrupting correctional officers than malfeasance. Two types of corrupt practices appear to be involved in this type of decision: first, selectively ignoring inmate violations of institutional rules, such as looking the other way when marijuana or other drugs are smuggled into the facility by visitors in return for payment; and second, the failure to report or stop other employees involved in misconduct. This second practice might typically consist of a low-level employee not informing on a fellow officer or superior because of an implied or direct promise of personal gain, such as promotion or transfer. In other cases an administrator may fail to stop staff misconduct for fear of public scandal and possible loss of position.

FACTORS ASSOCIATED WITH CORRUPTION

In a U.S. Department of Justice study on municipal corruption (1978), two factors were identified as influencing the degree of corruption experienced by a particular governmental agency: the opportunities for corruption and the incentives to make use of those opportunities (Gardiner and Lyman, 1978). In the following section, these two factors will be examined within the context of a prison environment.

A third factor identified by other studies of public corruption was politics (Gardiner, 1970; Sherman, 1978). Sherman suggests that a leading explanation for police corruption was the capture of the department by the political environment. Corrections is not immune from the power of politics. Correctional programs at the state and local level are influenced by the political process, particularly in terms of the appointment of administrative staff and the allocation of resources.

THE ROLE OF OPPORTUNITIES

The opportunities for corruption arise from the tremendous amounts of discretionary authority allocated by the legislature to correctional officials (Atkins and Pogrebin, 1978). As Costikyan has noted, "Corruption is always where the discretionary power resides" (1967:20). In the prison, employees, particularly low level ones (e.g., correction officers, counselors, and other line workers), are responsible for monitoring and controlling virtually all inmate behavior. These officials constantly make low visibility discretionary decisions which reward positive behavior and penalize negative behavior. These decisions directly affect the day-to-day living conditions experienced by inmates under custody.

In a prison environment, staff members, armed with a limited arsenal of formal rewards and punishments, are given the task of controlling a reluctant, resistant, and sometimes hostile inmate population. Special privileges in the form of extra TV time, phone calls, job assignments, cell changes, conjugal visits, transfers, and furloughs may be used to reward positive behavior. Punishments, in the form of withdrawal of privileges, transfers, or various forms of deprivation (cell restriction to solitary confinement and loss of good time) are used to control inmates.

The way that staff apply these rewards and punishments have both short-term and long-term consequences for inmates and their experience in the correctional system. Accordingly, when one considers the conditions of confinement, the incentives and pressures for inmates to attempt to corrupt staff as one means of improving their living conditions or for staff to exploit their power are apparent. Individuals sentenced to prison are subjected to various levels of deprivations, commonly referred to as pains of imprisonment, which affect both the physical and psychological state of the individuals. Sykes defined these pains of imprisonment as the deprivation of liberty, goods and services, heterosexual relations, autonomy, and security (Sykes, 1958). In dealing with these "pains" associated with confinement, inmates make various adaptations to their immediate environment to help soften its psychological and physical impact. One of the techniques that they may employ is the corruption of correctional employees as a means of neutralizing or improving their conditions of confinement (for example, through the smuggling of drugs, food, radios, money, or the purchase of privileges).

In her journalistic study of an inmate incarcerated in a maximum security prison, Sheehan made the following comment regarding the motivation of inmates in prison:

Most men in the prison are in prison precisely because they were not willing to go without on the street. They are no more willing to go without in prison, so they hustle to afford what they cannot afford to buy (1978:9).

Hustling usually brings the inmates and/or confederates into situations where they need the cooperation of a staff member, either to overlook an infraction, perform a favor, or smuggle in some item. As such, the incentives or pressures for inmates to influence the reward and punishment structure through corruption are enormous. Gardiner and Lyman underscore this point when they state: "Corruption can only occur when officials have an opportunity to exercise their authority in ways which would lead others to want to pay for favorable treatment" (1978:141).

INCENTIVES FOR CORRUPTION

The incentives for employees to take advantage of the power associated with their position in an institutional setting are many. They range from structural or organizational characteristics or prison management to individual factors (e.g., honesty of staff, the financial needs of employees, etc.).

A major incentive for corrupt practices results from defects in the prison organization's control structure. The prison, which is essentially a coercive organization, formally bases its control on the use of coercive power (Etzioni, 1964:59). However, correctional employees, particularly line staff, find that there are limits to the degree of compliance achieved through the use of coercive power (Sykes, 1958; Cloward, 1960). In order to successfully do their job, coercive power must be supplemented with informal exchange relations with inmates. These informal control practices are utilized by staff for control purposes and are responsible for the smooth functioning of the institution and for maintaining an uneasy peace (Sykes, 1958; Cloward, 1960; Irwin, 1980). As Sykes pointed out almost 30 years ago:

> The custodians (guards)...are under strong pressure to compromise with their captives for it is a paradox that they can insure their dominance only by allowing it to be corrupted. Only by tolerating violations of minor rules and regulations can the guard secure compliance in the major areas of the custodial regime (1956:58).

According to Sykes, three factors are responsible for undermining the formal control structure of the prison: friendships with inmates, reciprocal relationships, and defaults. Each of these factors develops at the line staff level as a function of long-term and close working associations between guard and inmate in a closed setting. Irwin (1980), in a contemporary update, cited corrupt favoritism as a significant factor in the day-to-day management of the prison.

Corruption through friendship evolves from the close contact that prisoners and guards share in their daily interaction. In many cases, they get to know one another as individuals, and friendships may develop. These friendships may, in turn, affect how staff members use their authority.

Corruption through reciprocity occurs as an indirect consequence of the exchange relations that develop between inmates and staff: "You do something for me, I'll do something for you."

Corruption through default occurs when staff members (e.g., cell block officers) begin to rely on inmates to assist them with their duties, such as report writing and cell checks. In time, the employee depends on the inmates for their assistance in satisfactorily performing his duties.

Cloward (1960) also pointed out how defects in the prison organization's control apparatus lead staff members to develop informal means of control through the development of various accommodations between the keepers and the kept.

Material accommodations occur when staff provide certain inmates with access to forbidden goods and services that are restricted or contraband in return for their cooperation. Cloward provides an example of this when he quotes an inmate explaining how he makes home brew.

> You go to make arrangements with the mess sergeant. He gets the ingredients and when we're in business.... It's one of those you do this for me and I'll do this for you sort of thing.... The sergeant has to feed 1,500 men. It don't look good if he goofs. He wants the job done right. Now we're the ones who do the work, the cooking and all of that. So the sergeant, he says, okay you can make a little drink. But see to it that you get that food on the lines or the deal's off (1960:37).

Power accommodations occur when selected inmates are provided with access to restricted information as, for example, the date and time of an impending shakedown (search of cells) or access to key correctional personnel. Frequently, these take the form of reciprocal relationships where valuable information is exchanged by both staff and inmates. Inmates inform on one another, and staff in turn may disclose administration plans regarding such activities as the time and place of cell searches.

Status accommodations result when staff provide special deference to certain inmates. According to Cloward:

> The right guy...seems to be left alone (by staff) in spite of conspicuous deviance from official values, and this mark of untouchability results in high status among his peers (1960:40).

Another factor which complicates matters is the type and quality of persons recruited and hired to work in correctional facilities (National Manpower Survey of the Criminal Justice System, 1981). Frequently the quality of manpower is uneven and sometimes substandard because of low pay and poor working conditions. These individuals are placed in situations where they are given considerable discretionary authority (without much training in its use) in a setting where the visibility of their actions is quite low. When this occurs, the probability of corrupt practices increases. Another factor that provides an incentive for corruption is the impact of politics. If the selection and promotion of employees are influenced by politics, decisions may be made by employees that benefit the political party in power.

CONTROLLING CORRUPTION

First of all, it must be recognized that corruption is a regular feature of government processes. The problem of corruption can probably never be eradicated; however, certain steps may be taken to control the problem (Gardiner, 1970:93). In this section, we will examine several strategies that a correctional administrator may adopt to address the problem of corruption within a correctional agency.

A first step in dealing with the problem of corruption is to develop an anti-corruption policy. This policy should define what the agency means by corruption and specify the penalties associated with such practices. (See Ward and McCormack [1978] for an example of developing an anticorruption policy for police departments.) Once this policy has been formulated, it should be disseminated to the employees of the department. Training should also be provided to employees regarding the nature, causes, and impact of corrupt practices.

Second, the correctional agency should develop a proactive mechanism to detect and investigate corrupt practices. This could include the establishment of an internal affairs unit which encourages employees, inmates, and civilians to report charges of staff misconduct. In addition, the use of routine and special audit procedures on a random basis will ensure the proper expenditure of funds.

Third, the correctional administrator should attempt to improve management practices of the prison. This internal reform should be directed at improving the control of the organization. In prior studies of corruption, where leadership and control were weak, the potential for corruption increased (Gardiner, 1970).

Management must take affirmative steps toward reducing the opportunities for corruption. One step in this direction is to structure the use of discretion and make the visibility of low-level decisionmakers more public. Guidelines for the use of discretionary rewards and punishments should be public. For example, specific criteria and a review process should be established to review cell changes, job assignments, and transfers or temporary releases. These decisions should also be periodically reviewed by supervisors to ensure the accountability of decisionmakers. Internal reform should also include screening of employees in order to improve their overall quality. Selection procedures should be upgraded to include psychological testing and formal pre-service training designed to screen our questionable employees. Also, simple police checks of an individual's background could be expanded by requiring in-depth background investigations of prospective employees. In the past, individuals with felony convictions and even escapees have been hired as correctional employees (Governor's Investigative Task Force, Delaware, 1979).

Also, the working conditions of employees should be improved. This could be addressed by improving wage scales, enlarging job responsibilities, and broadening employee participation in decision-making and by increasing efforts toward professionalization by creating opportunities for pre- and in-service training and advancement on the basis of merit.

A fourth and final recommendation addresses the political environment. A correctional administrator has little control over political and community attitudes, but he should take steps to insulate his employees from pressure placed on them from external sources. By requiring merit selection and promotion of employees, a correctional administrator reduces the impact of political interference in the operation of the agency.

In sum, controlling corruption requires a commitment by correctional administrators to improve and upgrade the general correctional environment, particularly the working conditions for staff, to protect employees from political pressures, and to replace a tendency toward complacency, as long as things are quiet, with a concern for accountability.

REFERENCES

Atkins, Burton, and Pogrebin, Mark. *The Invisible Justice System: Discretion and the Law*. 2d ed. Cincinnati, Ohio: Anderson Publishing Co., 1982.

Barker, Thomas. "Social Definitions of Police Corruption." *Criminal Justice Review* 1(Fall 1977):101-110.

Black, Henry Campbell. *Black's Law Dictionary*. St. Paul, Minn.: West Publishing Co., 1968.

Boston Prison Discipline Society (1826-1854). Reprint of 1st-29th Annual Report. Montclair, N.J.: Patterson-Smith, 1972.

Clark, J.P., and Hollinger, Richard C. *Theft by Employees in Work Organizations*. Minneapolis, Minn.: University of Minnesota, 1981. Cited in *Criminal Justice Abstracts* 1(March 1982):19.

Cloward, R. *Theoretical Studies in the Social Organization of the Prison*. Social Science Research Council, 1960.

Costikyan, E. N. "The Locus of Corruption." In *Theft of the City: Readings on Corruption in Urban America*, edited by J.A. Gardiner and D. J. Olsen. Bloomington: Indiana University Press, 1974.

Crouch, Ben, editor. *The Keepers: Prison Guards and Contemporary Corrections*. Springfield, Ill.: Charles C. Thomas, 1980.

Davis, Kenneth C. *Discretionary Justice: A Preliminary Inquiry*. Baton Rouge: Louisiana State University Press, 1960.

Delaware Governor's Investigative Task Force. Interim Report, 9 October 1979. Mimeographed.

Duchaine, N. *The Literature of Police Corruption*. Vol. II. New York: The John Jay Press 1979.

Duffee, D. "The Correction Officer Subculture and Organizational Change." *Journal of Research in Crime and Delinquency* 2(1974):155-172.

Etzioni, Amitai, *Modern Organizations*. Englewood Cliffs, N.J.: Prentice-Hall, 1964.

Fogel, David. *"We Are the Living Proof:" The Justice Model for Corrections*. Cincinnati, Ohio: Anderson Publishing Co., 1979.

Gardiner, J. A. *The Politics of Corruption*, New York: The Russell Sage Foundation, 1970.

Gardiner, J. A., and Lyman, T. R. *Decisions for Sale, Corruption and Reform in Land Use and Building Regulations*. New York: Praeger Publishers, 1978.

Goldstein, H. *Policing in a Free Society*. Cambridge, Mass.: Ballinger Publishing Co., 1977.

Hawkins, Gordon. *The Prison.* Chicago: University of Chicago Press, 1976.

Heidenheimer, Arnold. *Political Corruption: Readings in Comparative Analysis.* New York: Holt, Rinehart and Winston, 1976.

Irwin, John. *Prisons in Turmoil.* Boston: Little, Brown and Co., 1980.

Lombardo, Lucien X. *Guards Imprisoned: Correctional Officers at Work.* New York: Elsevier, 1981.

Lyman, T., Fletcher, T., and Gardiner, J. *Prevention Detection and Correction of Corruption in Local Government.* Washington, D.C.: U.S. Government Printing Office, 1978.

McCarthy, B.J. "Exploratory Study in Corruption in Corrections." Ph.D. dissertation, The Florida State University, 1981.

McKorkle, L. " Guard-Inmate Relationships." In *The Sociology of Punishment and Control,* edited by N. Johnston et al., New York: John Wiley and Sons, 1970.

Meyer, J.D. "Definitional and Etiological Issues in Police Corruption: An Assessment and Synthesis of Competing Perspectives." *Journal of Police Science and Police Administration* 4(1976):46-55.

Mitford, Jessica. *Kind and Usual Punishment.* 1971. Cited in Reid, S. R. *The Correctional System.* New York: Holt, Rinehart and Winston, 1981.

Rothman, D. *The Discovery of the Asylum: Social Order in the New Republic.* Boston: Little, Brown and Co., 1971.

Sheehan, S. *A Prison and a Prisoner.* Boston: Mifflin Co., 1975.

Sherman, L. *Police Corruption: A Sociological Perspective.* New York: Anchor Books, 1974.

———. *Scandal and Reform, Controlling Police Corruption.* Berkeley: University of California Press, 1978.

———. "Obtaining Access to Police Internal Affairs Files." *Criminal Law Bulletin* 15(September-October 1979):449-461.

Simpson, Anthony. *The Literature of Police Corruption.* New York: John Jay Press, 1978.

Sykes, G. "The Corruption of Authority and Rehabilitation." *Social Forces* 34(1956):157-162.

———. *The Society of Captives: A Study of a Maximum Security Prison.* Princeton, N.J.: Princeton University Press, 1958.

U.S. Department of Justice. *The National Manpower Survey of the Criminal Justice System: Corrections.* Washington, D.C.: U.S. Government Printing Office, 1978.

Ward, R., and McCormack, R. *An Anti-Corruption Manual for Administrators in Law Enforcement,* New York: The John Jay Press, 1979.

ETHICAL ISSUES IN
PROBATION AND PAROLE

13

John T. Whitehead

It is no accident that more movies and television shows are made about police officers than about probation and parole officers. Because probation and parole are not as dramatic as policing, the ethical issues in probation and parole are somewhat more ordinary. Probation and parole officers simply do not have the opportunities to become involved in the dramatic matters like corruption that involve some police officers in large cities.

This does not mean that there are no ethical issues in probation and parole. It just means that the issues are usually less dramatic and more subtle. This chapter will discuss some of the problems that can arise in probation and parole work.

Before delving into the ethical issues in probation and parole, it may be helpful to state some assumptions. In this chapter it is assumed that there are certain values to guide ethical choices, such as truth, honesty, fairness, hard work, and consideration for others. For this discussion, it does not matter whether these values are considered moral absolutes or simply mutually agreed upon conventions. Whatever their source, the following discussion assumes such values exist and that most individuals subscribe to them. To give one concrete example that will be discussed more fully below, it is assumed that it is ethical for probation and parole employees to put in a full day's work for a full day's pay. Employees who do less are considered to be acting unethically.

ETHICS AND EFFECTIVENESS

It is not surprising that several authorities have questioned the effectiveness of community supervision. What may surprise some is that the effectiveness of probation or parole can be considered an ethical issue. After reviewing the effectiveness issue, the argument that ethics is involved will be raised.

The most recent and dramatic note in the debate over the effectiveness of probation and parole supervision is the controversy over the Rand Report (Petersilia, Turner, Kahan, & Peterson, 1985). About five years ago, Joan Petersilia of the Rand Corporation authored a report on the effectiveness of probation supervision for felons in California. The report indicated serious problems with felony probation; 65% of the felons studied were rearrested with 40 months and one-third were reincarcerated.

A frequent response to such negative reports is that they are evidence that government bodies are unwilling to spend enough money on probation. Barry Nidrof, Los Angeles Chief Probation Officer summarized this reaction:

> Reduced funding has impacted the ability of probation to carry out its mission. Our clientele is becoming more dangerous at the same time that our resources are diminishing (Petersilia, 1985, p. 340).

Although there is truth in such claims of insufficient funds, there is also more to the problem than spending cutbacks. Part of the problem may be workers—officers and managerial personnel alike—not doing the jobs that they should be doing. This is how alleged lack of effectiveness raises an ethical issue; it may be that individual workers and whole agencies are derelict in their responsibilities. If that is the reason for the ineffectiveness reported in the Rand Study, then ethical irresponsibility on the part of line officers is a primary part of the root problem.

Several reports point to worker malfeasance as contributing to possible ineffectiveness. A General Accounting Office study of Federal probation (1976), for example, noted that about 60% of the court-ordered conditions of sentence were *not* enforced by probation departments. More disturbing was the note that only 38% of the case folders examined had written treatment plans. In other words, in the overwhelming majority of cases, officers were not even taking the trouble to sit down and write out a set of objectives for the offenders they were supervising! This is equivalent to a college professor not bothering to make up a syllabus for a course; there is no plan for action. Likewise, an investigation of juvenile probation in New York City (McFadden, 1982) found that many officers complained of unmanageable caseloads but then sat around doing little or nothing. Richard McCleary (1978) studied parole in one jurisdiction and found that parole officers, "like the rest of us, are interested in doing as little work as possible" (McCleary, 1978, p. 43). He found that parole officers spent much of their time in outside pursuits, such as acquiring a graduate education or running a restaurant. This left little time for direct contact with parolees.

In short, if community supervision is ineffective, part of the reason may be that officers—and the managers who supervise them—are not doing their jobs. Thus workers may not living up to the ethical standard of putting in a full day's work for full day's pay.

The problem with this interpretation is that it can turn into a "blame the victim" phenomenon. What this means is that blaming the problem on lazy officers is too simplistic. Such blaming ignores more important reasons for so-called "laziness."

One such problem is the civil service system in probation and parole. Originally intended to protect employees from the graft-ridden spoils system of former machine politics, the civil service system has created problems of organizational and individual inertia. Since rewards are often tied to longevity (how many years an employee has been on the job) rather than to innovation and effectiveness, employees lose any incentive to be creative or even energetic. The norm becomes CYA (cover your _____) rather than strive for excellence.

Another problem that is often forgotten is that criminology has yet to set forth either an agreed upon theory of why individuals commit crimes or a proven technology to rehabilitate offenders. There are many competing theoretical and intervention claims, but none has resulted in clearcut directions for probation officers in their everyday routines. In fact, current perspectives set forth diametrically opposed intervention principles, ranging from behavior modification with individuals to radical transformation of our capitalist society (see, for example, Vold and Bernard, 1986 for a discussion of criminological theories). Any probation officer who is familiar with criminology knows that the literature breeds confusion as much as clarity.

This does not mean that there is no problem at the individual officer level. Officers still need to do the basics: set up case objectives, monitor offender compliance with court-ordered conditions of supervision, and inform the court when sentence conditions are not followed. These actions may not lead to dramatic cures, but at least officers can feel that they have done their job. When and if criminology comes up with more dramatic cures, officers can implement them.

Before leaving the effectiveness issue, it is important to note that claims of ineffectiveness are only one side of the coin. There are several indications that probation is in fact much more successful than the Rand report suggested. Two studies of felony probation in other states, Kentucky (Vito, 1986) and Missouri (McGaha, Fichter, & Hirschburg, 1987), found that only about 20% of the felons on probation were rearrested within about three years and only about 12% went back to prison. Thus conditions in California may not be representative of conditions in other parts of the country. Some have even cited the Rand study as being unrepresentative of California since it focused on Los Angeles and Alameda counties which may be very different from the rest of that state (National Institute of Justice, 1986). Similarly, recent studies of intensive supervision programs in both Georgia (Erwin, 1987) and New Jersey (Pearson, 1988) revealed satisfactory outcome levels.

THE MISSION OF PROBATION AND PAROLE

Another ethical issue in probation and parole is the mission of community supervision. This refers to the purpose or objective of supervision.

Traditionally the mission of probation and parole supervision has been described as some combination of assistance and control, treatment and security, or service and surveillance (Studt, 1973). In other words, officers are supposed to provide services to offenders while also keeping tabs on them so that the community is protected from new crimes.

In the last few years several authorities have questioned this traditional description of the mission of probation and parole. Patrick McAnany, Doug Thomson, and David Fogel (1984), for example, have argued that probation should strive for justice. In this model, the mission of probation would focus more on the victim than on the offender. Probation officers would become very concerned with the amount of harm done to the victim and seeing to it that the sentencing judge orders restitution to the victim. The primary task of officers would be monitoring the conditions of probation, especially any restitution orders. Assistance would remain part of probation as only a secondary consideration.

Vincent O'Leary and Todd Clear (1984) have argued that probation should reorganize according to a risk control model. By this they mean that sentencing judges and probation officials should attempt to determine what level of risk of new crime each offender poses to the community. Probation conditions should then be tailored to ensure minimal risk. Drunk drivers, for example, might be allowed to drive only to and from work and be ordered to attend both a driver education program and an alcohol counseling program. This would minimize risk to the community. In the risk control model, assistance to the probationer would merit only secondary importance. Assistance would enter the picture only if it related to community safety. A probation officer could not force an offender to undergo a treatment program unless there were a connection between the program and the offender's likelihood of committing a new crime. If a burglar had an alcohol problem but that problem had no relationship to his criminal activity, the probation officer could merely suggest that the offender deal with his alcohol problem.

Other developments in probation and parole imply mission reform but do not necessarily spell out the details. House arrest, electronic monitoring, and intensive supervision (see McCarthy, 1987) are all recent trends which involve greater restraints on probationers. Calls for the abolition of parole release raise the possibility that no special services will be available for prisoners after release beyond the ordinary community resources available to all citizens. Probably the most dramatic of the calls for such innovations is Graeme Newman's (1983) suggestion that the criminal justice system revert to corporal punishment. Newman leaves no room for probation or parole but argues that offenders should be administered electric shock for minor offenses, flogging for slightly more serious infractions, and prison for violent offenses.

Compared with ten years ago, these developments reflect greater concern with offender control and very little concern with assistance. These changes are reflections of public fear of crime and desire for greater punitiveness in the criminal justice system.

An ethical issue in these reconceptualizations of the mission of community supervision is the question of what society owes the offender. The easy answer is that society owes nothing. The criminal has broken the law and he or she must pay his or her debt to society. This view is congruent with the current popularity of neoclassical theories of criminal behavior which emphasize free will and accountability (see, for example, Wilson, 1983). Offenders are seen as choosing crime and as responsible for their behavior. The only questions are the determination of the debt to society the offender must pay and the control of the offender so new crimes are prevented. Thus the focus is on retribution, deterrence, and incapacitation. None of these perspectives places primary emphasis on assistance to the offender.

Positivist theories of crime, on the other hand, contend that crime is not so simple. Biological, psychological, and sociological factors explain criminal behavior (Vold and Bernard, 1986). Human behavior reflects all sorts of influences, ranging from genetic makeup to parental upbringing to the availability of educational and job opportunities. Positivist perspectives imply that society has a responsiblity to assist the offender because societal factors are seen as having contributed to the criminal behavior. Thus there is a direct link between positivist perpsectives and programs to assist offenders in prison and in the community.

The ethical question is: Can society embrace a neoclassical perspective—assume offenders are totally free and responsible—and simply ignore any consideration of assistance to offenders? Or does society have some obligation to help offenders to some degree?

One answer to the question is that society does have a duty to provide assistance to offenders but that probation and parole should not attempt such a task. Embracing this solution, Rosecrance (1986) argues that other community agencies should provide assistance to offenders and that probation should be limited to investigations and monitoring of court-imposed sentence conditions. Much of the monitoring would be computer-assisted.

Rosecrance argues this drastic solution for several reasons. First, research and his own probation experience have convinced him that organizational priorities typically take precedence over concern for the needs of the offender. Both line officers and supervisors are more concerned with appearing effective rather than actually affecting clients. Thus reports of supposedly effective programs must be viewed skeptically. The effectiveness may well reflect organizational manipulations rather than true reformation of offenders. Second, offenders and officers come from different social worlds. As a result, neither party trusts the other and communication between the two often deteriorates into "patent mendacity" (Rosecrance, 1986, p. 28). Third, if service means counseling and advice, officers often have no particular expertise in these areas (Rosecrance, 1986). In fact, officers who attempt counseling may harm offender psyches (Dietrich, 1979).

One consideration in this area that many people forget is the state's obligation to the correctional worker to provide a humane working environment. Even if criminals are seen as deserving only warehouse prisons and some police-like form of probation and parole, some consideration must be given to the employee. What sort of individuals would want to work in sparse and spartan prisons? What sort of individuals would choose to be probation or parole officers if the job only required law enforcement activities? Because research has indicated that probation workers experience a sense of personal accomplishment from involvement with offenders (Whitehead, 1989), any proposal to divorce officers from assistance tasks raises the spectre of alienating a substantial number of line officers.

Thus recent developments in community supervision such as house arrest, electronic monitoring of offenders, intensive supervision, and calls for the elimination of parole raise important ethical considerations. Does society have any obligation to provide assistance to offenders? Does the introduction of increased emphasis on controlling offenders result in a work environment that would have negative consequences for officers? These are questions that need attention.

SUPERVISION FEES

Related to the issue of increasing emphasis on surveillance techniques in community supervision is the question of charging probationers and parolees supervision fees. This growing trend in community corrections raises important ethical considerations.

O'Leary and Clear (1984) argue against charging probationers a supervision fee for two reasons. "First, the attractiveness and measurability of 'dollars collected' and subsequent pressure to collect them can deflect the supervision officer from his or her main mission [of risk control]" (O'Leary & Clear, 1984, p. 18). By this they mean that administrators often prefer readily obtained measures of worker productivity, such as the percentage of supervision fees collected, rather than complex assessments of officer achievements in such matters as providing assistance to offenders. This is similar to the preference of college administrators to judge faculty productivity by simple counts of numbers of publications rather than by more difficult evaluations of what faculty do with students in the classroom. The second objection to such fees is that they would represent "a financial hardship for a large number of offenders" (O'Leary & Clear, 1984, p. 18).

Wheeler, Macan, Hissong, and Slusher (1989) strongly disagree with the arguments of O'Leary and Clear (1984). Based on their research of probation supervision fees in Houston, Texas, Wheeler and his associates found that "probation service fees offered more benefits than disadvantages to society" (1989, p. 22). For example, collection of fees had no negative impact on the service mission of the department and no adverse affect on the collection of restitution orders. Furthermore, fees were not used unfairly against those unable to pay. For example, revocations were not pursued against unemployed offenders if they were trying to find work. Instead, those who had their probation revoked were most likely "high risk probationers with previous criminal convictions, poor employment history, and serious felony property crimes" (Wheeler et al., 1989, p. 22).

Thus it appears that the objections of O'Leary and Clear (1984) and others to community supervision fees may not be well-founded. Nevertheless, they have raised possible ethical problems which probation officials must be wary of in any use of such fees.

ETHICAL ISSUES IN THE PRE-SENTENCE INVESTIGATION

Traditionally the pre-sentence investigation has been an important aid for judges in sentencing decisions. Research indicates that judges follow officer sentencing recommendations about 90% of the time (Carter & Wilkins, 1967; for a dissenting view, see Rosecrance, 1985). Several ethical issues arise concerning probation presentence reports.

One issue is possible deceptiveness. Officers attempt to establish rapport with defendants during interviews aimed at obtaining information for the reports. Officers then verify the information and summarize it for the court.

Several authorities have argued that the presentence investigation appears to be a straightforward inquiry into the defendant's legal and social situation when in fact it is really something else. Blumberg (1979), for example, has argued that the presentence report is really nothing more than a case of "cooling out" the mark. By this he means that most defendants have pled guilty and that the sentence has already been determined. Thus the probation officer's job is to prepare the defendant for the sentence that has already been decided. In other words, officers influence defendants to adjust to the fact that they have pled guilty and that the judge is going to impose some sanctions on them. This prevents outbursts in court. Furthermore, Blumberg argues that probation officers are not trained diagnosticians capable of accurately determining appropriate treatment plans. Instead they are occupational "voyeurs" who relish digging up intimate details about the lives of the defendants they investigate. Officers lead dull, middle class lives and allegedly enjoy examining the more exciting escapades of offenders.

Similarly, Rosecrance (1988) argues that the claim that the presentence report is a hallmark of individualized justice is blatantly inaccurate. In his research on California probation presentence investigators he found that officers made sentencing recommendations very early in the process based on the present offense and the prior record of the defendant (Rosecrance, 1988). Any additional information gathered during the investigation process reinforced the earlier recommendation decision and seldom changed the initial decision. Rosecrance also argues for a more recent version of Blumberg's cooling out the mark hypothesis. In other words, California's relatively recent determinate sentencing scheme has replaced whatever individualized justice may have existed under its old indeterminate system. Within the new determinate system the presentence report

allows defendants to feel that their case at least has received a considered decision. One judge admitted candidly that the "real purpose" of the presentence investigation was to convince defendants to feel that they were not getting "the fast shuffle." He observed further that if defendants were sentenced without such investigations, many would complain and would file "endless appeals" over what seems to them a hasty sentencing decision (Rosecrance, 1988, p. 253).

Rosecrance found that another function of the presentence report was to take judges off the hook for unpopular sentences. In such instances judges "deny responsibility for the sentence, implying that their 'hands were tied' by the recommendation" (Rosecrance, 1988, p. 254). Such claims are irresponsible because probation officers often merely recommend what they think the judge wants and because judges bear the ultimate responsibility for any sentence imposed.

Writing from a more objective viewpoint, Carter (1967) conducted some relevant research on the presentence process. He used actual presentence reports to determine the decision processes that probation officers use in arriving at sentencing recommendations. He found that officers required very little information to determine sentence recommendations. The offense and the prior record of the offenders substantially determined recommendations.

All of this raises some ethical questions. Is it appropriate for probation officers to delve into the lives of defendants for the alleged purpose of writing a presentence investigation report when most of the information is not even used in arriving at the recommendation or in determining the sentence? Is it appropriate for officers to feign concern and rapport when they are gathering ammunition for harsh judicial sentences? If a plea bargain has already been reached and the sentence worked out or if a state's determinate sentencing law dictates the outcome, is it appropriate for a probation officer to pry into an offender's life for details which have no impact on the sentence? Is it ethical for a judge to hide behind a probation presentence recommendation when it is actually the judge's responsibility for the sentence decision, no matter how unpopular?

Blumberg and Rosecrance would answer these questions negatively. From their perspectives the presentence investigation is a ritual which only serves organizational purposes such as "cooling out" defendants for sentences already determined by plea bargaining or allowing judges to hide behind recommendations of probation officers who simply anticipate what judges and probation supervisors want anyway.

The other side of the story, however, deserves further attention. First, Blumberg and Rosecrance neglect to mention that presentence reports serve other functions in addition to assisting judges in sentencing. The reports provide information that is useful to probation officers who supervise offenders sentenced to probation. The reports also convey such information to prison officials for incarcerated defendants. In both instances important details about the offender's educational background, intelligence, work experience, personality, health, drug history, and so forth are available so that correctional officials can plan appropriate intervention strategies. Prison officials, for example, do not have to waste time determining whether a defendant needs counseling; the presentence report contains that information.

Second, both Blumberg and Rosecrance paint an extreme picture. Others argue more dispassionately. Clear, Clear, and Burrell (1989), for example, acknowledge that many sentences are determined by plea bargain prior to the presentence report. Nevertheless, the presentence report can add two contributions. First, the investigation allows for a second look at the plea bargain by a less involved and less time-pressured official, the probation officer. This can counteract the tremendous pressure on defense attorneys and prosecutors to act hastily and thus point out "inappropriate plea bargains" (Clear, Clear, & Burrell, 1989, p. 54). Second, sometimes the reports do uncover information which simply was not available at plea bargaining, including reports from social workers, psychologists, and psychiatrists (Clear et al, 1989). Such information may indeed influence the sentence.

This is not to say that presentence reports are problem-free. It is disturbing that judges and others may be using the reports to maintain the myth of individualized justice (Rosecrance, 1988) in a new era of determinate sentencing. On the other hand, it is shortsighted to simply discard what can be a valuable tool simply because it bears the possibility of misuse.

WHISTLEBLOWING

Another ethical issue is whistleblowing making internal complaints outside the department. Rosecrance (1988) studied whistleblowing in probation and found that it followed a five-stage process "(1) internal criticism (within the department) of questionable activity, (2) state of instransigency, (3) external disclosure, (4) organizational reaction, and (5) aftermath" (p. 103). More importantly, he found that the whistleblowers were competent employees who had high self-esteem, an internal locus of control and were financially able to withstand a temporary loss of income.

Interestingly, the whistleblowers were not terrbily concerned with the efficacy of their actions. Instead they were personally driven to blow the whistle:

> The officers felt backed into a corner in which their option was either going along or blowing the whistle. By "doing something" the dissident was able to satisfy his conscience and to feel a sense of pride for "standing up for what I believe." Standing up and informing a source outside the department was not a well-conceived plan to bring about change but an act of personal redemption (Rosecrance, 1988, p. 108).

The organization was unresponsive to the complaints of the whistleblowers. After the whistleblowing, the departments moved to isolate the officers by transferring them to unimportant assignments; in effect, placing them in "Siberia" and "leaving the officers feeling powerless to effect change within the department." (Rosecrance, 1988, p. 109). Unfortunately, these isolating tactics had negative consequences within the department:

> ...other employees were deterred from speaking out or offering suggestions for department improvements. Probation officers were afraid that active dissent would cause them to be similarly ostracized and isolated. Thus, doing nothing in response to observed problems became the norm followed by probation workers (Rosecrance, 1988, p. 108).

Rosecance's (1988) research points out that probation administrators have often been unresponsive to line officers raising ethical concerns. As noted earlier, probation and parole have often been immersed in a "cover your _____" philosophy which is resistant to change or whistleblowing. The ethical challenge for admininstrators is to resist such paths of least resistance and instead pay attention to the whistleblowers to determine if they are calling attention to significant problems in the agency.

THE ROLE OF THE VICTIM

Another ethical issue is the proper role of the victim in probation and parole. Victims are involved in several stages of probation and parole.

Victims can and should enter into the presentence investigation process. Since they have been wronged, it is clear that the investigating officer should contact them about the extent of the harm the offender inflicted and ask if any restitution is in order. An officer can also ask about a sentence recommendation.

Although victims deserve sensitivity in any contacts from criminal justice personnel such as probation presentence investigators, investigators still need to attend to several concerns. One is that the victim verify in some way the amount of any physical harm or property damage for which the victim is seeking restitution. Despite concerns about the trauma a victim may have experienced at the hands of the offender, an investigating officer cannot simply take the victim's word about damages. In a bureaucratic society the victim must provide records of purchase, repair, insurance claims, and the like to verify claims for restitution. Otherwise the offender may feel that he has become the victim of a second crime: an unsubstantiated restitution order.

Another ethical concern is for the criminal justice system to keep victims informed about the status of the case. Victims deserve to know when perpetrators are sentenced, whether restitution has been ordered and whether the restitution is being paid or not. Several authorities contend that probation should take the lead in providing such information to crime victims (Galaway, 1983; McAnany, Thomson & Fogel, 1984). Others argue that the prosecutor's office should take the lead in these tasks. Clearly, if probation assumes such tasks, then officers should carry out their responsibilities.

A question that many do not consider is the ethical way to determine the amount of restitution. If a car is stolen and totally damaged or a stereo burglarized and fenced, the amount of restitution is not always simple to determine. As anyone who has tried to sell or trade in a used car knows, the car's value is extremely negotiable. If you take your current car to five auto dealers, chances are you will get five different estimates of the value of that car. Factors such as depreciation, market demand, condition, make and model make the determination of the value of a car extremely imprecise. Price estimation is as much an art or a game as it is an exact science.

A related issue is whether to consider depreciated value or replacement value. The depreciated value of a stolen auto or stereo set may be almost zero whereas the replacement value may be hundreds or thousands of dollars. A dealer might give you next to nothing for that clunker you drive to work or college, but that same dealer might charge you a hefty price for buying a replacement vehicle. Thus is it ethical for probation officers to consider the depreciated value or the replacement value when determining suggested restitution figures for presentence reports? Although Galaway (1988) argues that years of successful operation of restitution programs in numerous jurisdictions have proven that both the determination and the collection of restitution are relatively problem-free, it is important to recognize that care should be taken to ensure fairness (Klein, 1980).

One final issue in considering restitution amounts is the question of the victim's contribution, if any, to the crime. Does a victim who left his or her keys in the car deserve less compensation than a victim who locked his or her car before it was stolen? Certainly someone who leaves a car unlocked with keys in the ignition is acting foolishly. Do they deserve less restitution, however, than a completely conscientious car owner?

Galaway (1980) argues that there are two solutions. One is to attempt to consider victim contribution and reduce the restitution order accordingly. The second alternative is to assume offender responsibilty; "even in situations of high provocation, an individual has more than one alternative way of behaving" (Galaway, 1980, p. 278). He argues for the second approach because he fears the first approach would lead to "easy rationalizations...[which would] encourage irresponsible behavior" (Galaway, 1980, p. 278).

Another victim issue is the proper extent of victim involvement in parole release decisions. Several states now involve victims in the parole release decision. A 1982 California law, for example, allows victims to appear before the parole board when an offender is being considered for parole (Ranish & Shichor, 1985). Several issues arise about victim involvement in parole release.

One issue concerns how far victim involvement should go. Should victims merely be informed that the person who harmed them is being considered for parole or has been paroled, or should victims have some say in whether or not the offender is given parole? Ideally, victim involvement is justified on the grounds that justice demands consideration for the one who has been harmed and that it can be cathartic to allow victims to participate (Ranish & Shichor, 1985). More subtly, involvement often rests on "two unverified assumptions: that a lot of criminals get off easy and that a lot of victims are interested in appearing and testifying at various stages in the criminal justice process" (Walker, 1989, p. 174). Interestingly, research indicates that both of these assumptions are erroneous. Victims do not appear all that frequently and they do not have much impact on sentence and parole release decisions (Ranish & Shichor, 1985; Walker, 1989).

Such infrequent appearances and general lack of impact, however, raise an additional concern of disparity. One disparity is class bias since it is possible that "middle and upper middle class persons will be more inclined to participate in these proceedings" (Ranish & Shichor, 1985, p. 54). In California, for example, since many of the prisons are in central or northern California and since many victims reside in Los Angeles, only the more affluent can afford to travel to the parole hearings. A second disparity is that the notorious cases receive the most attention. As of the writing of this selection, for example, Sirhan Sirhan (the 1968 assassin of Senator Robert F. Kennedy) had just been denied parole for the tenth time (Germond & Witcover, 1989). Sirhan has served over twenty years for a murder when a murderer in a less publicized case might well have been paroled with little or no fanfare.

The more general question, however, is whether victim involvement introduces undue emotion, personality, and vengeance into the criminal justice system. Walker (1989) argues that if it does, then that represents "a major step backward" from our impersonal and professional system of justice which attempts to

> ensure fair and impartial treatment of all persons accused of crimes... A professional police officer enforces the law without regard to his or her personal feelings toward the offender. A lawyer has a professional obligation to provide the best defense for all clients, regardless of his or her personal feelings (p. 174).

Such detached determination of justice is a far cry from recent cases in California where victims and the public became so incensed at the decisions of correctional officials to release mandatory releasees to certain locales that in one case parole officials had to go from motel to motel in search of a release location at a cost of $3,776 a day (Barkdull, 1988).

There is no easy answer to the issue of victim involvement. Although victims deserve a voice, safeguards must be put in place to prevent any return to blatant vengeance.

USE OF VOLUNTEERS

Several ethical issues arise in the use of volunteers in probation and parole.

The basic ethical issue is whether it is responsible or irresponsible to use volunteers. If volunteers are sought merely to save the government agency from hiring needed probation or parole officers, this represents an unethical use of volunteers. Offenders, society, and officers are being shortchanged. Offenders are not receiving the professional supervision and assistance they need. Officers—actually would-be officers—are denied jobs because volunteers are being used instead of hiring additional officers. Finally, society is not getting the effective supervision it wants.

On the other hand, if volunteers are being used for tasks which officers cannot and should not be doing, then this represents a valid use of volunteers. An example of this type of volunteer activity is the establishment of a one-to-one relationship with the offender. Here the volunteer acts as a big brother or sister or friend in relation to the offender. Officers do not have the time to establish such personal relationships with offenders, nor would it be proper for officers to do so given their authority over offenders. Because such one-to-one relationships are the most frequent volunteer assignments (Shields, Chapmna, & Wingard, 1983), it appears that most volunteers are being used properly.

The critical issue is whether volunteers are doing what additional officers would be doing or whether they are making unique contributions to the department.

WORKPLACE CLIMATE

An issue that many ignore is the provision of a humane workplace climate for officers. Often little or no consideration is given to the effects of community supervision jobs on the employees. Correctional employees, however, just like all employees, deserve safe and humane working environments.

This section will examine what has been the working environment in community corrections and what adjustments should be made to make it more suitable.

Unfortunately probation and parole have frequently been unsuitable places to work. This might sound surprising, since images of unsuitable workplace environments usually involve unsafe coal mines or dirty and dangerous factories, but there are several problems which have plagued probation and parole. First, high caseloads, ranging from 200 offenders and beyond per officer, have placed inappropriate demands on officers. It is simply not realistic to ask one officer to supervise so many offenders. Second, the problems of ineffectiveness, lack of clear intervention strategies, and mission ambiguity discussed above have had negative effects on line officers. When you are not sure what you should be doing and are unclear whether what you are doing is effective, it is hard to feel positively about your efforts. Third, rewards in probation and parole have often been lacking or tied to seniority rather than effort and achievement with the result that "good performance remains virtually unrewarded, and the greatest available reward—promotion—is sometimes given to those whose work is perceived by colleagues as wanting in quality" (Clear, 1985, p 41). Given such outrageous conditions, it is hardly surprising that considerable numbers of officers have reported such problems as job dissatisfaction and burnout (see Whitehead, 1989, for a complete discussion of job burnout in probation). In fact, for many "probation is seen as an early-career position which most people eventually leave to take other jobs" (Clear, 1985, p. 40).

An obvious ethical issue is whether it is proper to allow this situation to continue. Is it right to allow probation to be the early-career position Clear has described? Is it right to hire young, idealist college graduates, use them for a few years and then let them burn out and move to other fields? Is it right for a state to fund probation at such low levels when it is clear that high caseloads and feelings of ineffectiveness often drive officers out after a few years? This author's ethical judgment is that inhumane work climates are wrong. Unfortunately, that opinion offers no relief to officers caught in such situations.

One recent workplace concern is the effect of new developments such as house arrest, electronic monitoring, and intensive supervision on officers. Some preliminary research on an intensive supervision program in Alabama, for example, indicated that officers were expected to monitor offender participation in community service work very early in the morning, put in a 9-to-5 day, and then also make evening and weekend curfew checks. Such stringent demands on the officers appeared to result in officer shortcuts such as telephone curfew checks instead of in-person evening monitoring (Whitehead & Lindquist, 1987). Thus it is shortsighted to suggest that community supervision embrace a new mission of increased surveillance without considering the implementation of that mission reform. A government official or a researcher sitting in an office can stipulate that officers make round-the-clock checks on offenders and then that official can go home at 5:00 pm. A line officer, however, has to leave his or her home and family at 11:00 pm to go to a high crime area to actually make the curfew checks. Unless officers are compensated and rewarded for such tasks, administrators are asking for shortcuts and noncompliance, if not resignations.

SUMMARY

This chapter has examined several of the ethical issues in probation and parole, ranging from the effectiveness of probation to workplace climate. Although the issues may not be as dramatic as some of the ethical issues in policing, nevertheless they are important issues. Given the high number of offenders on probation and parole, these issues are becoming more important.

REFERENCES

Barkdull, Walter L. (1988). Parole and the public: A look at attitudes in California. *Federal Probation*, 52 (3), 15-20.

Blumberg, Abraham S. (1979). *Criminal justice: Issues and ironies* (2 ed.). New York: New Viewpoints.

Carter, Robert M. (1967). The presentence report and the decision-making process. *Journal of Research in Crime and Delinquency*, 4, 203-11.

Carter, Robert M. and Leslie T. Wilkins (1967). Some factors in sentencing policy. *Journal of Criminal Law, Criminology and Police Science*, 58, 503-14.

Clear, Todd R. (1985). Managerial issues in community corrections. In L.F. Travis (Ed.), *Probation, parole, and community corrections: A reader* (pp. 33-46). Prospect Heights, IL: Waveland.

Clear, Todd R., Val B. Clear, and William D. Burrell (1989). *Offender assessment and evaluation: The presentence investigation report*. Cincinnati: Anderson.

Dietrich, Shelle G. (1979). The probation officer as therapist. *Federal Probation*, 43 (2), 14-19.

Erwin, Billy S. (1987). *Evaluation of intensive probation supervision in Georgia: Final report*. Atlanta: Georgia Department of Corrections.

Galaway, Burt (1980). Is restitution practical? In Martin D. Schwartz, Todd R. Clear, and Lawrence F. Travis III, *Corrections: An issues approach*, pp. 271-279. Cincinnati: Anderson.

Galaway, Burt (1983). Probation as a reparative sentence. *Federal Probation*, 47, (3), 9-18.

Galaway, Burt (1988). Restitution as innvoation or unfilled promise? *Federal Probation*, 52 (3), 3-14.

General Accounting Office (1976). *State and county probation systems in crisis*. Washington, DC: U.S. Government Printing Office.

Germond, Jack and Jules Witcover (June 1, 1989). Sirhan Sirhan, parole and the death penalty in the U.S. *Johnson City Press*, p. 4.

Klein, John F. (1980). Revitalizing restitution: Flogging a horse that may have been killed for just cause. In Martin D. Schwartz, Todd R. Clear, and Lawrence F. Travis III, *Corrections: An issues approach*, pp. 280-99. Cincinnati: Anderson.

McAnany, P.D., Thomson, D., & Fogel, D. (Eds.) (1984). *Probation and justice: Reconsideration of mission*. Cambridge, MA: Oelgeschlager, Gunn, & Hain.

McCarthy, Belinda R. (Ed.) (1987). *Intermediate punishments: Intensive supervision, home confinement and electronic surveillance*. Monsey, NY: Criminal Justice Press.

McCleary, R. (1978). *Dangerous men: The sociology of parole.* Beverly Hills, CA: Sage.

McFadden, R.D. (1982, November 21). City probation services for youth called "inadequate" by civic group. New York *Times,* p. 1.

McGaha, J., Fichter, M., and Hirschburg, P. (1987). Felony probation: A re-examination of public risk. *American Journal of Criminal Justice, 11* (1), 1-9.

National Institute of Justice (1986). *Probation: Crime File II Series.* Washington, DC: Author.

Newman, Graeme (1983). *Just and painful.* New York: Macmillan.

O'Leary, V. and Clear, T.R. (1984). *Directions for community corrections in the 1990s.* Washington, DC: National Institute of Corrections.

Pearson, Frank J. (1988). Evaluation of New Jersey's intensive supervision program. *Crime and Delinquency, 34,* 437-48.

Petersilia, Joan (1985). Probation and felony offenders. *National Institute of Justice Research in Brief,* March, 1985.

Petersilia, Joan, S. Turner, Kahan, J. and Peterson, J. (1985). Executive summary of Rand's study, "Granting felons probation: Public risks and alternatives." *Crime and Delinquency, 31,* 379-92.

Ranish, Donald R. and David Shichor (1985). The victim's role in the penal process: Recent developments in California. *Federal Probation, 49* (1), 50-57.

Rosecrance, John (1985). The probation officer's search for credibility: Ball park recommendations. *Crime and Delinquency, 31,* 539-54.

Rosecrance, John (1986). Probation supervision: Mission impossible. *Federal Probation, 50* (1), 25-31.

Rosecrance, John (1988). Maintaining the myth of individualized justice: Probation presentence reports. *Justice Quarterly, 5,* 235-256.

Shields, Patricia M., Charles W. Chapman, and David R. Wingard (1983). Using volunteers in adult probation. *Federal Probation, 46* (2), 57-64.

Studt, Elliot (1973). *Surveillance and service in parole: a report of the parole action study.* Washington, DC: National Institute of Corrections.

Vito, Gennaro F. (1986). Felony probation and recidivism. *Federal Probation, 50* (4), 17-25.

Vold, George B. and Thomas J. Bernard (1986). *Theoretical criminology* (3rd ed.). New York: Oxford University Press.

Walker, Samuel (1989). *Sense and nonsense about crime: A policy guide* (2nd ed.). Pacific Grove, CA: Brooks/Cole.

Wheeler, Gerald R., Therese M. Macan, Rodney V. Hissong, and Morgan P. Slusher (1989). The effects of probation service fees on case management strategy and sanctions. *Journal of Criminal Justice, 17,* 15-24.

Whitehead, John T. (1989). *Burnout in probation and corrections.* New York: Praeger.

Whitehead, John T. and Charles A. Lindquist (1987). Intensive supervision: Officer perspectives. in Belinda Rodgers McCarthy (Ed.), *Intermediate punishments: Intensive supervision, home confinement, and electronic surveillance* (pp. 67-84). Monsey, NY: Criminal Justice Press.

Wilson, James Q. (1983). *Thinking about crime* (rev. ed.). New York: Vintage Books.

IV.
ETHICAL ISSUES IN CORRECTIONS—
QUESTIONS AND SCENARIOS

CHAPTER ELEVEN

1. Pollock-Byrne describes a perspective on ethics that seems at first glance to be quite different from those described by Gold. Are there any similarities in these positions? Can the positions described by Gold be incorporated into the "moral development" perspective.

2. Mediation and moral development training are very different approaches to corrections than those proposed by retributivists. Can the objectives of these programs be accomplished within a retributivist framework?

3. How important are biological environmental and social factors in influencing a person's moral development?

4. Can a person who has achieved a high stage of moral development make an unethical decision?

CHAPTER TWELVE

1. What kinds of motivations might a correctional officer have for engaging in corruption? Are some forms of corruption worse than others?

2. Can correctional officers be expected to have moral careers comparable to other criminal justice officials? How might those careers differ from those already discussed? Are the employees themselves different, or is it the nature of job training or the nature of the job that is most influential in regard to ethical behavior?

3. Could some forms of correctional officer corruption be ethical? That is, could a jail or prison be administered in such a way that the ethical response was to violate some rules in an effort to assist inmates?

4. Is corruption an unavoidable result of discretion?

CHAPTER THIRTEEN

1. Whitehead writes that many probation or parole officers do not make much of an effort to do their jobs well. What factors might explain this response to job duties? Is this "do as little as possible" approach unethical? Do you think the problem is pervasive in other work areas as well?

2. Does society "owe" the offender anything? Is the probation officer (or correctional officer) "owed" humane working conditions? What are the consequences of answering these questions in the negative? In the affirmative?

3. Presentence reports often appear to be less than a skillfully developed tool to individualize justice. Does their use encourage unethical practices that erode the quality of justice, or are they just illustrations of a good idea poorly implemented?

4. How much involvement should victims have in judgments related to their offender, (e.g., restitution and parole release)? How can their involvement lead to unequal treatment of offenders? Is this inequality undesirable?

SCENARIOS

1. You are a counselor in a moral development program in a correctional institution. You feel that one of the inmates in your program is giving lip service to higher levels of morality but does not really understand the issues involved. Your recommendation is required for her placement on work release. What do you do?

2. You are a probation officer. One of your probationers is required to abstain from the use of drugs as a condition of his sentence. You have suspected that he is continuing to use cocaine, although he does seem to be making an effort to quit. Your visit to his home revealed that cocaine has been recently smoked in his house. He denies using the drug. What do you do?

3. You are a correctional officer. The conditions of the jail in which you work are terrible, food is poorly prepared, the place is overcrowded, and sanitation problems are on the increase. You have discovered that some of the inmates have contacted the local news media with plans to stage some event that will dramatize their plight. Do you inform on the inmates or keep quiet?

4. You are a guard at maximum security prison. Over the years, you have seen conditions gradually worsen where you work. Lately, however, you have also seen more and more corruption among your co-workers as well. It was much easier to overlook the smuggling of books, radios, cigarettes, and candies. The increased amount of drug smuggling has not only made you uneasy but has increased your stress level both at work and at home. You are torn between your duty as a guard and co-worker and your duty as a human being. Should there be a conflict between the two, and what do you do in this situation? Do you have an obligation to reveal what you know is going on?

V. ETHICAL ISSUES IN CRIMINAL JUSTICE RESEARCH

The scientific life provides no barrier to unethical conduct. The problem of employing unethical means to an otherwise desirable end is ever present in the research setting, where scientists are sometimes tempted to sacrifice the well-being of their subjects for the sake of scientific knowledge. Subjects can easily come to be viewed as the means to an end when the products of scientific research are equated with the utilitarian's "greater good."

In the name of scientific research, subjects may experience invasions of privacy, unknowing participation in simulated research experiments and physical and emotional stress. In experimental research designs, which systematically withhold an intervention from one group while exposing another, research subjects may be denied participation in programs offering medical, educational, or psychological treatment.

Sometimes research is designed so that every member of a specified group must participate in the project; such designs are employed to ensure that factors related to voluntary participation do not bias the research. The result of this design is that some persons may be coerced into participation.

277

Coercion is always an issue in research that does not rely on volunteers, but it becomes even more problematic when prison inmates or other persons in custody are involved in research. Is an inmate ever "free" to volunteer for research, or is subtle coercion to please authorities always a factor?

The study of deviant behavior and efforts to control deviance only add to the dilemmas confronting the researcher. What is the researcher's obligation to protect the identity of his or her subject? Criminal justice research often yields information on the criminal activities of subjects that is not known to police. Research on the police subculture similarly identifies unethical conduct on the part of law enforcement. Like the defense attorney, the researcher must weigh his obligation to protect his subjects versus the obligation to reveal misconduct to appropriate authorities.

Although the nature of the research task poses many ethical dilemmas, additional problems involve the political context of the research. No one wants to hear bad news about a popular new law enforcement or correctional program, least of all the people who administer the program. Researchers can find themselves in very difficult circumstances when results indicate that the program is not achieving its goals. Is the correct response to redo the results until a more palatable outcome is achieved, or to honestly report findings? How is this decision affected when the people administering the program are the same ones paying the researcher's salary?

To avoid unethical conduct among research scientists, grant proposals are required to specify the procedures the researchers will follow to ensure that subjects will be protected. Universities require faculty and research staff to submit research proposals for ethics reviews. These a priori steps are useful, but additional guidance may be necessary when researchers confront unforeseen dilemmas that arise after research is underway.

Researchers should police themselves, using standards of professional ethics and censure to provide appropriate guidance. It must be recognized, however, that there are significant pressures against the objective exercise of such standards. Competition for research funds is considerable—few universities or research centers are interested in forfeiting research funds on ethical grounds, and few scholars are interested in creating any more obstacles for their research efforts than necessary. It is therefore very important to establish a climate of high ethical standards in the graduate schools that produce researchers and in the organizations ultimately responsible for conducting research.

ETHICAL DILEMMAS IN THE RESEARCH SETTING: A SURVEY OF EXPERIENCES AND RESPONSES IN THE CRIMINOLOGICAL COMMUNITY 14

Dennis R. Longmire

Ethical dilemmas facing criminological researchers have become a topic of considerable interest in the recent literature. St. George and Martin (1979:143) describe a case in which a researcher engaging in "expert witness" testimony before a court examining the question of obscenity and pornography engaged in "outright charlatanism" through either gross methodological incompetence or the deliberate fabrication of data. Klockars and O'Connor (1979) edited a volume which—although offered under the aegis of the ethics of more general deviance research—focuses considerable attention upon ethical problems facing the criminological researcher. Sagarin (1980) provides us with a collection of essays addressing the specific question, "Are there taboo subjects in the scientific discipline of criminology?" Baunach (1980) discusses some ethical issues which the criminologist conducting an experimental research methodology must face. Roberg (1981) discusses ethical issues which face management researchers involved in criminal justice organizational analysis.

More recently, Inciardi and Siegal (1981) discuss some ethically questionable problems of a researcher engaged in contract research who is faced with a series of circumstances which liken the researcher to a prostitute: He or she must provide a fast, efficient service that focuses on short-term objectives and gives little concern to the development of a long-term relationship with the client. Toch (1981) also addresses the issue of research ethics in a more general vein, arguing that the issue of ethics is actually a weapon employed by opponents of the research community at large and/or by researchers themselves to cause conflict between partisan groups within the research community.

There are numerous instances in which some specific research has been identified as so ethically problematic that it captures the entire scientific community's attention. For example, the allegations that Sir Cyril Burt—a psychological researcher who provided evidence that intelligence is an inherited trait—fabricated his data and used fictitious co-authors to add credibility to his research publications are probably well known in most research circles (Diener and Crandall, 1978). Furthermore, some ethically questionable research is serious enough to capture the attention of the lay community as well. Milgram's (1963) study of "obedience to authority" is a classic example of this genre of research. More recently, a "scientific crime wave" involving the falsification of data by researchers at Cornell University, Yale School of Medicine and other highly prestigious institutions has received national attention (Golden, 1981).

It is interesting to note that among some of the most ethically infamous research there is a strong representation of criminologically based research. For example, one of the earliest and most visible instances of ethically questionable research that gained widespread public attention involved the "Wichita Jury Study," in which researchers tape-recorded federal jury deliberations without having gained informed consent of the jurors and in violation of some unspoken taboos against violating the sanctity of the jury room (Amrine and Sanford, 1956). The "Stanford Simulated-Prison Study" (Zimbardo, 1973) is another example of criminologically based research which has gained infamy as a result of ethical problems. Humphrey's (1970) study of homosexual tearooms also stands out as a classic example of criminologically based research that is often cited as exemplifying ethically questionable research practices (Diener and Crandall, 1978; Reynolds, 1979).

While these and other studies stand out as glaring examples of the possible ethical problems that could face contemporary criminological researchers, no systematic study has been undertaken to assess how much criminologists are actually faced with such problems in conducting research. There have been a few isolated attempts to estimate the frequency of unethical practices in biomedical research (Barber et al., 1973; Beecher, 1966) and in social psychological research (Striker, 1967; Seeman, 1969; Menges, 1973) that collectively suggest that ethically questionable research is not uncommon in either area. Biomedical researchers examined by Beecher (1966), for example, reveal that 12% of the articles published in a leading medical journal involved unethical research practices. Reynolds (1979:60) reports that sociopsychological studies are quite prone to the use of deceptive research practices—a technique that was employed with considerable frequency during the 1960's (e.g., 81% of the studies related to behavioral and attitudinal conformity relied upon deception). These studies, Reynolds argues, "support the argument that a substantial amount of unethical research occurs" (1979:67-68).

Another effort to examine the occurrence of ethically controversial practices in the social sciences was undertaken by Carroll and Knerr (n.d.), who focus specific attention upon how frequently confidentiality promised to research sources and/or data becomes difficult to maintain as a result of pressures by authorities (police, courts, legislators). Their study includes a survey of more than 300 social science researchers in a variety of fields and concludes that approximately 8% of these researchers experienced problems involving the confidentiality of their data. It is interesting to note that respondents in the Carroll and Knerr (n.d.:62) study, who identify themselves with the discipline of criminology or were engaged in criminology research, report the second highest number of confidentiality problems (psychiatrists report the highest incidence). Furthermore, 36% of all cases in which a subpoena was issued requesting that sources be identified involve criminological researchers (Carroll and Knerr, n.d.:82).

The prevalence of these and other ethical problems in the criminological community is the primary focus of this article. A corollary to this interest that must also be addressed involves assessing the viability of various approaches that have been offered in an effort to resolve ethical dilemmas. There have been several recent discussions about how the scientific community at large—and specifically how the social scientific disciplines—have attempted to prevent ethically controversial behavior among their researchers (Diener and Crandall, 1978; Douglas, 1979; Reiman, 1979; Reynolds, 1979; Toch, 1981). The primary approaches discussed—but not necessarily endorsed—in these works include

(1) professional associations and codes of ethics;
(2) governmental guidelines and administrative review processes;

(3) judicial intervention and legislative statutes; and
(4) the development of a humanistic morality among researchers.

The first of these approaches—developing professional codes of ethics—has received somewhat mixed reviews. Reynolds (1979), for example, suggests that such techniques do little to actually deter researchers from ethically controversial behavior. Douglas (1979:16) proposes that codes of ethics may provide a "monopolistic front" behind which professional elites can hide and avoid external scrutiny of their activities and profits. Toch (1981) agrees with both Reynolds and Douglas, but he seems to endorse adopting such codes precisely because they post no danger themselves and yet they provide the facade of internal control that may defuse the power of outsiders who would more viciously attack the professional community. Likewise, Diener and Crandall (1978) propose that professional associations provide guiding principles to the research community via codes of ethics but avoid the introduction of ethical canons that take the form of restrictive commandments.

The idea of instituting governmental guidelines and administrative review processes has also been the focus of mixed reviews. Reynolds (1979) examines the Institutional Review Board (IRB) procedures introduced by the Department of Health, Education and Welfare (DHEW) and similar IRB procedures introduced at the university level. He concludes that such procedures offer acceptable mechanisms for evaluating the ethicality of research endeavors involving human subjects on a case-by-case basis. Wilkins (1979), however, does not recognize such strictures as being broad enough to protect the general subject of all social research: humanity. Reiss (1979) suggests that the social sciences are better able to govern or police themselves, and that governmental regulations may cause more harm than good through lessened autonomy and regulated inquiry.

The innovation of judicial or legislative mechanisms that seek to resolve ethical dilemmas has most specifically focused on the protection of scientists from being forced to disclose the sources of their research. By arguing that scientists should be afforded the same protection against forced disclosure of data sources as that available to therapists, physicians, clergy, and journalists, there has been some suggestion that a national "Researcher's Shield Law" be introduced (Nejelski and Lerman, 1971; Nejelski and Peyser, 1975). Reynolds (1979) and Sagarin and Moneymaker (1979) point out that such suggestions are largely deflated when one recognizes that no group—including physicians, journalists, and clergy—is absolutely immune from subpoena and forced disclosure of information that is gained under the promise of confidentiality. Reynolds (1979) does not see this as a serious problem to the social sciences in general since few projects are actually subjected to the subpoena process, but he does recognize the problem as especially salient to those researching crime and the criminal justice system. Sagarin and Moneymaker (1979) also discuss the dilemma of researcher immunity and warn against any blanket immunity standards. They recommend instead that universities and professional associations clarify the limits of immunity from forced disclosures (such as the obstruction of justice).

The proposal to increase the research community's sensitivity to humanistic morality as a means of resolving ethical dilemmas is advanced in different forms by both Douglas (1979) and Reiman (1979). Douglas argues that ethical dilemmas confronting scientific researchers are the same as those faced by nonscientists in their day-to-day experiences, and that the logic employed to resolve such dilemmas ought to involve a general sense of morality—not some artificial, specialized code of conduct. Although Reiman seems to agree with the Douglas critique of utilitarian codes of ethics, he proposes that some general ethical standards need to be articulated to help guide social science researchers toward a basic respect for human dignity and individuality. The common ground shared by these authors is that ultimate ethical standards must come from within the individual researchers and be guided by a general sense of morality and not be special status proscriptions offered under the authority of "moral administrators" (Reiman, 1979:43) or scientific "fronts" (Douglas, 1979:16). In a similar vein, Diener and Crandall (1978:13) argue that "laws and codes serve as adjuncts to personal conscience as the major form of ethical control."

It is clear that there is little consensus in the social scientific or criminological literature as to which of the above approaches provides the most desirable and/or effective responses to the ethical dilemmas facing researchers. In addition to assessing the frequency of ethically controversial behavior in criminological research, the present study evaluates the attitudes expressed in the criminological community toward each of the above approaches. Before this examination is undertaken, however, a brief discussion of the types of ethical dilemmas to be studied must ensue.

Toch (1981) argues that identifying what is and is not ethical within the general scientific community is actually a subjective matter that varies from one researcher to another. His cursory elaboration of this point takes on a flavor much like the labeling theorists' proposal that no behavior is inherently deviant. While it must be acknowledged that the line separating the ethical from the unethical will be no easier to draw than the one distinguishing between the saint and sinner, the beautiful and ugly, the normal and the deviant, and so on, there are some general kinds of practices in the research arena that can be recognized as falling within the "ethical penumbra" (Toch, 1981:186). Whether or not any specific behavior in this area is ethical need not be predetermined. It is sufficient to note that these issues have been raised under the rubric of ethical dilemmas in the past.

While the items addressed in this study are not meant to serve as an exhaustive list of issues falling under the shadow of research ethics, it is worth noting that many of these issues are raised in this context in introductory research methods textbooks (Babbie, 1975; Black and Champion, 1976). The research community is warned that those who agree to participate in the research act ought to be reasonably certain that they are not going to experience physical or emotional harm as a result of their involvement in the research. Researchers are also urged not to coerce or deceive subjects into participating in a research project and that all subjects are to be fully informed of the nature of the research project. Subjects participating in social science research are also frequently promised that their identity and comments will be kept confidential.

In addition to the above admonishments regarding the handling of participants in the research act, scientific canons demanding truth and honesty in the research community are of critical importance. Researchers are strongly warned against the misrepresentation of their results, and those who have been identified as having tampered with their data are perhaps regarded as the most serious violators of ethical norms. Two final areas of concern to researchers involve practices that inhibit intellectual freedom and research autonomy (Diener and Crandall, 1978). Conditions that threaten to undermine freedom in choosing the nature of inquiry or in disseminating research results are of particular concern to applied social scientists (Alpert, 1958; Angell, 1967; Horowitz, 1971; Sjoberg, 1967). Furthermore, such conditions are discussed as being of special relevance to criminological researchers (Henshel, 1980; Wolfgang, 1976). Situational pressures such as funding patterns and publication decisions may be construed as informal mechanisms to control the production of knowledge (Bayles, 1981; Galliher, 1979). If such feelings are present in any specific discipline, the professional integrity of the scientific enterprise at large is undermined.

By way of summary, the present study examines the relative frequency with which the criminological community is confronted with two kinds of ethical dilemmas: (1) "participant issues" including any harm to subject, the lack of voluntary informed consent, confidentiality problems, and deception; and (2) "professional issues" such as misrepresentation of findings, tampering with data, undesired pressure to engage in a specific research project, and restrictions on the dissemination of findings.[1] Attitudes about the various approaches offered to resolve ethical dilemmas are also examined.

METHODOLOGY

The data were collected during the summer and autumn of 1980. A 10% random sample was drawn from the 1978-1979 *Membership Directory of the American Society of Criminology*. This resulted in the selection of 211 persons who, by virtue of their affiliation with the American Society of Criminology (ASC), were assumed to be interested in the general areas of criminological research. All of the sample members were mailed a 12-page, 40-item questionnaire asking about a variety of ethical issues including whether or not they had experienced any ethical problems during their research endeavors.[2] The respondents were instructed that participation was totally voluntary, and that their anonymity would be insured. Of the original mailings, 13 were "returned to sender" and 7 were returned by ASC members who did not speak English, thus reducing the actual sample pool to 191. Two waves of mailings resulted in a response rate of 74% (n = 142). The majority of the questionnaires were returned following the first mailing (57%, n = 110) and the remaining questionnaires (17%, n = 32) were returned following a second mailing approximately two months after the first.

Respondents represent a wide range of academic backgrounds with 34% identifying their backgrounds as "criminology," 35% as "sociology," 18% as "other social scientists" (e.g., economists, psychologists), and 13% as "applied scientists" (e.g., educators, social workers, public administrators). The majority of the respondents have earned a Ph.D. or its equivalent (68%), 25% have earned a masters degree, and 7% have earned a bachelors degree only. Of the respondents without a Ph.D., roughly 50% report that they are currently working toward their Ph.D. and expect to complete their studies in the general area of criminology. In this sample 60% classify themselves as being employed in an academic institution, 21% are engaged in nonacademic research capacities, and 19% are employed as "line-workers" in criminal justice agencies (including administrative personnel). Furthermore, approximately 33% of the respondents report that they are more interested in "pure research" (e.g., theory testing and construction), 39% report that they are more interested in "applied research" (e.g., program evaluation and research and development), and 28% report their research interests to be equally "pure" and "applied" in nature.

FINDINGS

There are actually two different research questions being raised in this study: (1) How frequently are criminologists confronted with ethical dilemmas in their research endeavors? (2) How strongly do researchers endorse the various mechanisms available to help resolve ethical dilemmas in general? Each of these questions will be addressed independently and followed by a close examination of the resolution mechanisms offered by researchers who have actually experienced one or more dilemmas during the course of their research.

FREQUENCY OF ETHICAL DILEMMAS

The data presented in Table 1 demonstrate that the number of researchers experiencing ethical dilemmas of either a "participant" or "professional" nature is quite high. While only 37.4% of the researchers report that they have not experienced any dilemma whatsoever, the remaining 62.6% have experienced some sort of ethical dilemma and most frequently of a "professional" nature. It is important to note that there are a total of 72 different incidents reported by the sample that, according to the respondents' standards, involve ethically questionable conduct. These incidents are reported by 68 different respondents; only 4 encountered more than one dilemma.

Although a total of 24.3% of those respondents who report recent (post-1975) research activity experienced some sort of "participant" related dilemma, and the incidence of any single problem is not extreme. The most frequently cited "participant issue," however, involves the issue of confidentiality. In light of the prior research in this regard (Carroll and Knerr, n.d.) this is not a total surprise.

The following vignettes are offered to illustrate the kinds of experiences reported under the aegis of each of the participant issues. Care has been taken to avoid disclosing any information that would be used to identify the source of these statements; in some instances the nature of the research project is fictitious to insure against any potential violation of anonymity.

Case 38: Our research team was responsible for the implementation and evaluation of an experimental treatment program for institutionalized adult offenders. Although participants in the program were "volunteers" and were informed that they would not be harmed in any way, they were routinely penalized with disciplinary reports by some correctional officers who resented their participation in the program (Harm experienced).

Case 20: While conducting a study designed to evaluate the frequency of victimization incidents in an institution for youthful offenders, subjects were not informed that I would ask them about their experiences as victims and perpetrators prior to agreeing to participate in the research (Informed consent lacking).

Case 26: Interviews had been conducted with several drug addicts living in the community regarding the extensiveness of their addiction and the methods whereby they acquire money to support their habits. Local law enforcement authorities learned of this research and applied considerable pressure on me to reveal the identity of my sources (Privacy or confidentiality jeopardized).

Case 49: In order to conduct research aimed at examining the kinds of practices common among vice officers, I told officers and departmental officials that I was really interested in studying prostitution. Department official allowed me to travel with vice officers as an observer (Deception used).

Case 55: While conducting research examining prison guards' perceptions of "jailhouse lawyers," I became aware that tension existed between those correctional officers who agreed to be interviewed and those who did not. This tension resulted in at least one fight between officers, and the identity of my data sources was subsequently requested by the warden of the prison (Harm to subjects and confidentiality problems).

The frequency of ethical dilemmas of a "professional" nature is quite extensive. There were 44 different incidents in which some "professional ethical dilemma" was encountered. These incidents represent 38.3% of all cases under study, thus indicating that a considerable proportion of the criminological community has experienced one of the problems listed under this label. The seriousness of this finding is somewhat limited by the fact that one kind of dilemma constitutes the great majority of the "professional issues;" 31 of those dilemmas (70.5% of all "professional problems" reported) involve researchers who have experienced unwanted pressure to engage in research considered by the respondent to be "undesirable."

The specific nature of this problem is almost identical from one case to another. In this dilemma, criminological researchers find themselves being pressured or "seduced" to conduct research simply because there are readily available funds. The interests of the researchers are secondary, and some other person (e.g., University Provost, Department Chair, Division Head) applies pressure to "go for the grant whether you are interested in the topic or not." The nature of this dilemma is nicely exemplified by the following statement made by a university professor with considerable experience in academia:

Case 4: The university has changed over the years so that it is now "par for the course" for a young assistant professor to be informed by the "powers that be" that they are more interested in profit margins than in quality and depth in research projects. The university can make money if you can pay your salary. You can do this by bidding on what looks winnable, rather than on what looks interesting.

This involves the kind of pressure discussed by Inciardi and Siegal (1981) as characteristic of private sector research firms. It is interesting to note that many academicians find similar pressures in the ivory towers as well. As federal and local funds available for criminological research are reduced, the frequency of this dilemma may decline.

Table 14.1
NUMBER OF DIFFERENT ETHICAL DILEMMAS EXPERIENCED*

Nature of Dilemma	(n)	%	Cumulative %
Participant Issues			
Harm to subjects	(5)	4.3	4.3
Informed consent lacking	(9)	7.8	12.1
Confidentiality problems	(10)	8.7	20.8
Deception used	(4)	3.5	24.3
Professional Issues			
Misrepresentation of findings	(6)	5.2	29.5
Tampering with data	(2)	1.8	31.3
Pressure to engage in undesired research	(31)	27.0	58.3
Restrictions on dissemination of findings	(5)	4.3	62.6
No Dilemma Experienced	(43)	37.4	100.0
Total	(115)	100	

*Only those respondents who had recently engaged in criminological research (post-1975) are included in this analysis (n = 111). It must be noted that four respondents reported experiencing two ethical dilemmas during their most recent research project. In this event, each dilemma was counted as a separate case for the present frequency distribution problem (see the vignette for Case 55 for an example of this).

The remaining "professional problems" reported in Table 14.1 occur with about the same frequency as the "participant problems." Although only two respondents report that they directly experienced tampering with data, such a finding is noteworthy nonetheless. Similarly, it is significant that 5.2% of the respondents misrepresented their findings and another 4.3% were unable to freely disseminate their findings. The typical cases of this nature are exemplified in the following vignettes; again, specific details may be fictitious to preserve anonymity.

Case 1: Research evaluating the effectiveness of a treatment program resulted in negative findings from the perspective of agency personnel. Our final report was accepted by the funding agency, and we were not allowed to publish any of our findings (Dissemination restricted).

Case 5: An evaluation of a training program was conducted, and the Project Director intentionally misrepresented the findings to make the program look more successful than it actually was (Misleading results).

Case 11: The Principal Investigator altered original data and in some instances fabricated data so that the "Final Report" could be completed under the required deadline (Data tampered with).

RESOLVING OR PREVENTING ETHICAL DILEMMAS

To measure the degree of the respondents' support for the four possible methods of resolving ethical dilemmas discussed earlier, four Likert-type scales have been constructed. Each scale reflects the respondents' attitudes about the acceptability of each resolution mechanism:

(1) professional codes (PROCODE);
(2) government regulations and administrative review processes (PROGVT);
(3) legal or judicial interventions (PROLAW); and
(4) humanistic morality (PROMORALITY).

All scales are coded so that higher scores indicate positive attitudes about the mechanisms. The number of different items included in each scale varies; however, the options for each item ranged from one to four. No neutral point was included. The number of items comprising each scale, along with other relevant information, is listed in Table 14.2.

The respondents indicate a fairly high level of support for professional codes of ethics (PROCODE) as an available mechanism that would potentially resolve or prevent ethical dilemmas. Almost 59% of the sample strongly support such codes. In fact, when specifically queried about whether or not the ASC needs to develop a code of ethics, 72% (n = 116) of the respondents strongly support such a development. Exactly what form such a code should take is not clearly identifiable from the present research. However, it is clear that there is a fairly strong sentiment among the general criminological community that a professional code of some sort is needed.

The second most strongly supported mechanism for the resolution of ethical dilemmas involves legislative or judicial maneuvers (PROLAW). The adoption of legislative standards that would help to clarify the researcher's legal rights is strongly supported by 42% of the respondents. Specific issues included in this scale include the need for a national "Researcher's Shield Law," the right to be subpoenaed to testify about research results, and the right of researchers to invoke constitutional standards (e.g., freedom of the press) to avoid the coerced disclosure of data sources.

Relying on governmental regulations and bureaucratic procedures such as IBRs as a viable mechanism for the resolution of ethical dilemmas receives the weakest support. Relying solely on the moral reasoning of the individual researchers also receives weak support—only 27% of the respondents suggest strong support for such a mechanism. The degree of correlation between each scale is presented in Table 14.3. This demonstrates fairly strong correlations between all of the scales except PROGVT. It might be implied from these correlations that the scales could be combined into a single Guttman scale due to the patterned level of support seen in Table 14.2 and the unidimensionality of the indexes that can be inferred from the strong product moment correlations in Table 14.3. A scalogram analysis was conducted using the same level of strong support as the one used in Table 14.2. The resulting coefficient of reproducibility (.79) and coefficient of scaleability (.39) suggest that the items do not combine to produce a unidimensional scale.

Table 14.2
Degree of Support for Each of the Possible Mechanisms
for the Resolution of Ethical Dilemmas

Mechanism (number of items)	$\bar{X}$	(SD)	Proportion of Respondents Strongly Supporting*	Rank Order of Support
PROCODE (5)	14.5	(3.7)	.59	1
PROGVT (2)	3.8	(1.6)	.20	4
PROLAW (3)	7.9	(1.8)	.42	2
PROMORALITY (3)	8.5	(1.9)	.27	3

*These figures reflect the proportion of respondents whose level of support for the respective mechanisms was stronger than the standard average score for each scale ($Z > .50$).

Table 14.3
Pearson Correlation Coefficients® Indicating Degree of
Association Between Level of Support for Various Methods
Available to Solve or Prevent Ethical Dilemmas

	PROCODE	PROGVT	PRO-LAW	PROMORALITY
PROCODE	1.00			
PROGVT	.01	1.00		
PROLAW	.34***	.06	1.00	
PROMORALITY	.68***	−.01	.44***	1.00

(***p < .001)

Table 14.4 reveals that those researchers who report having experienced one of the ethical dilemmas under study have significantly different feelings about two of the potential mechanisms available to resolve or prevent such dilemmas compared with researchers who do not report experiencing any dilemmas. Those respondents who report having experienced either a "participant" or "professional" dilemma are much more supportive of having ethical codes articulated by professional associations (PROCODE) and of focusing legislative or judicial activity on the clarification of the researcher's responsibilities and rights (PROLAW).[3] It is clear that those researchers most familiar with the dilemmas under study and the problems they entail are looking for some method to help prevent similar problems in the future. The most strongly supported resolution technique requires that professional associations representing criminological researchers adopt some form of ethical standards. This implies, as Toch (1980) has suggested, that researchers want to exercise self-control rather than suffer external control pressures.

Table 14.4
Summary Statistics from ANOVA of Mechanisms Available for
Resolution of Dilemmas and Whether or Not One of the Dilemmas
Had Been Experienced in Recent (post-1975) Research

			Experience with Dilemmas			
			Yes		No	
Mechanism	F Ratio	(Eta)	$\bar{X}$	(SD)	$\bar{X}$	(SD)
PROCODE	4.33**	(.18)	15.2	(3.7)	12.0	(3.5)
PROGVT	.08	(.03)	2.8	(1.6)	2.6	(1.5)
PROLAW	3.45*	(.15)	8.3	(1.8)	7.6	(2.0)
PROMORALITY	.03	(.01)	8.4	(2.0)	8.5	(1.7)

(*p < .05)
(**p < .01)

SUMMARY AND CONCLUSIONS

This research has demonstrated that a rather sizeable portion of the criminological community is engaging in research in which they experience some form of ethical dilemma. The most common problems facing criminological researchers involve undesirable pressures to engage in inquiries that have little or no value to the researcher, and difficulty in maintaining the confidentiality of data sources.

In their effort to prevent future dilemmas and/or help resolve present ones, the respondents strongly support both professional codes of conduct and legislative-judicial action. The focus of the desired legislative-judicial activity would be on the establishment and articulation of clear protections against forced disclosure of data sources. Professional associations such as the ASC are strongly urged to adopt some form of ethical guidelines to help researchers facing ethical dilemmas. While the present research cannot produce an exact list of "do's" and "don'ts" in criminological research, it is clear that a professional code of ethics, if developed, must address each of the ethical dilemmas discussed in this article. Most importantly, the way in which a researcher is to respond to undesirable pressures and attempts to coerce confidential information from the researcher must be addressed.[4] The more specific needs of the criminological research community must be discerned through more in-depth research and through the development of a more focused dialogue on this topic.

NOTES

1. Categorizing these problems into these two groups closely reflects the approach taken by Diener and Crandall (1978) in their more general discussion of ethical dilemmas.

2. Respondents were asked whether or not they had experienced any of the problems under review. If they answered in the affirmative, they were asked to elaborate on their experiences to make the nature of their research and the details of the problem clear. Each of the issues was approached independently. We relied upon open-ended questions that were content analyzed. Whether or not any one of the issues was considered "ethically problematic" was left for the respondent to decide subjectively.

3. It would be interesting to see how these respondents actually resolved their dilemmas, but the present data set does not include this information.

4. It might be argued that an ethical code of conduct cannot, in itself, resolve any of the dilemmas under study. Reynolds (1979:243) has argued, however, that researchers might benefit from codes that enable "them to seek competent advice when faced with complex and ambiguous research dilemma issues."

REFERENCES

Alpert, H. (1958) "Congressmen, social scientists, and attitudes toward federal support of social science research." Amer. Soc. Rev. 23 (December):682-686.

Amrine, M. and F. Sanford (1956) "In the matter of juries, democracy, science, truth, senators, and bugs." Amer. Psychologist 11 (January):65-60

Angell, R. (1967) "The ethical problems of applied sociology" in R. Lazarsfeld et al. [eds.] The Uses of Sociology. New York: Basic Books.

Babbie, E. (1975) The Practice of Social Research. Belmont, CA: Wadsworth.

Barber, B., J. Lally, J. Makarushika, and D. Sullivan (1973) Research on Human Subjects. New York: Russell Sage.

Baunach, P.J. (1980) "Random assignment in criminal justice research: some ethical and legal issues." Criminology 17 (February):435-444.

Bayles, M.D. (1981) Professional Ethics. Belmont, CA: Wadsworth.

Beecher, H. (1966) "Ethics and clinical research." New England J. of Medicine 274 (June):1354-1360.

Black, J.A. and D.J. Champion (1976) Methods and Issues in Social Research. New York: John Wiley.

Carroll, S. and C. Knerr (n.d.) "Confidentiality of social science research sources and data." Report of a research project sponsored by the American Political Science Association and funded by the Russell Sage Foundation. (unpublished)

Diener, E. and R. Crandall (1978) Ethics in Social and Behavioral Research, Chicago: Univ. of Chicago Press.

Douglas, J. (1979) "Living morality versus bureaucratic fiat," pp. 13-14 in C. Klockars and F. O'Connor [eds.] Deviance and Decency. Beverly Hills, CA: Sage.

Galliher, J.F. (1979) "Government research funding and purchased virtue: some examples from criminology." Crime and Social Justice (Spring/Summer):44-50.

Golden, F. (1981) "Fudging data for fun and profit." Time 118 (December):83.

Henshel, R. (1980) "Political and ethical considerations of evaluative research," pp. 231-236 in S. Talarico [ed.] Criminal Justice Research: Approaches, Problems and Policy. Cincinnati, OH: Anderson.

Horowitz, I. [ed.] (1971) The Use and Abuse of Social Science. New Brunswick, NJ: Transaction.

Humphreys, L. (1970) Tearoom Trade. Chicago: Aldine.

Inciardi, J. and H. Siegal (1981) "Whoring around: some comments on deviance research in the private sector." Criminology 19 (August):165-184.

Klockars, C. and F. O'Connor [eds.] (1979) Deviance and Decency: The Ethics of Research with Human Subjects. Beverly Hills, CA: Sage.

Menges, R. (1973) "Openness and honesty versus coercion and deception in psychological research." Amer. Psychologist 28 (December):1030-1034.

Milgram, S. (1963) "Behavioral study of obedience." Journal of Abnormal and Social Psychology 67 (April):371-378.

Nejelski, P. and L. Lerman (1971) "A researcher-subject testimonial privilege: what to do before the subpoena arrives." Wisconsin Law Rev. 4:1085-1148.

Nejelski, P. and H. Peyser (1975) "A researcher's shield statute: guarding against the compulsory disclosure of research data." Appendix B to Protecting Individual Privacy in Evaluation Research. Washington, DC: National Academy of Sciences.

Reiman, J. (1979) "Research subjects, political subjects, and human subjects," pp. 35-60 in C. Klockars and F. O'Connor [eds.] Deviance and Decency. Beverly Hills, CA: Sage.

Reiss, A. (1979) "Governmental regulations of scientific inquiry: some paradoxical consequences," pp. 61-98 in C. Klockars and F. O'Connor [eds.] Deviance and Decency. Beverly Hills, CA: Sage.

Reynolds, P. (1979) Ethical Dilemmas and Social Science Research. San Francisco, CA: Jossey-Bass.

Roberg, R. (1981) "Management research in criminal justice: exploring ethical issues." J. of Criminal Justice 9 (Spring): 41-49.

Sagarin, E. [ed.] (1980) Taboos in Criminology. Beverly Hills, CA: Sage.

_____ and J. Moneymaker (1979) "The dilemma of researcher immunity," pp. 175-196 in C. Klockars and F. O'Connor [eds.] Deviance and Decency. Beverly Hills, CA: Sage.

Seeman, J. (1969) "Deception in psychological research." American Psychologist 24(December):1025-1028.

Sjoberg, G. [ed.] (1967) Ethics, Politics, and Social Research. Cambridge, MA: Schenkman.

St. George, A. and P. Martin (1979) " 'Filthy pictures' or the case of the fraudulent social scientist: unmasking the phony expert." The Amer. Sociologist 14(August):142-149.

Striker, L. (1967) "The true deceiver." Psych. Bull. 58(July): 13-20.

Toch, H. (1981) "Cast the first stone? Ethics as a weapon." Criminology 19(August):185-194.

Wilkins, L. (1979) "Human subjects—whose subject?" pp. 99-124 in C. Klockars and F. O'Connor [eds.] Deviance and Decency. Beverly Hills, CA: Sage.

Wolfgang, M. (1976) "Ethical issues of research in criminology," in P. Nejelski [ed.] Social Research in Conflict with Law and Ethics. Cambridge, MA: Ballinger.

Zimbardo, P. (1973) "On the ethics of intervention in human psychological research: with special reference to the Stanford prison study." Cognition 22(March):243-246.

ETHICS AND CRIMINAL JUSTICE RESEARCH 15

Belinda R. McCarthy

No area of life or work is free of ethical dilemmas, and the field of research is no exception. In recent years a number of scandals surrounding the professional behavior of academic researchers have made newspaper headlines and stirred government inquiries. In 1989, an individual charged with the responsibility of reviewing an article prior to publication was charged with plagiarism—stealing the pre-publication results of the research reviewed and publishing them as the basis for his own work (*Chronicle of Higher Education*, 1989c). Another researcher, an award-winning scientist, was charged with falsifying laboratory records to indicate that tests never performed had been completed and publishing the results. The investigation of this event, including a review by the National Institute of Health and the eventual reprimanding of the Principal Investigator by his University, caused as much of an uproar as the allegations (*Chronicle of Higher Education*, 1989a). Because the research was federally funded, legislative inquiries were considered as a means of monitoring the investigation process.

In a very different vein, questions have been raised about the conduct of the two University of Utah professors, who went to the media with their discovery of cold fusion prior to the publication of their results. Subsequent efforts to replicate their findings have been unproductive (*Chronicle of Higher Education*, 1989b). A different problem was confronted by the Stanford University student of Anthropology who while doing field work in China reportedly witnessed the performance of many third-trimester abortions forced on pregnant women in an effort to control population growth. The student made the decision to go to the international press with his observations and was subsequently asked to leave the country (*New York Times*, 1983).

One might think that scientific endeavors, with their objective and unbiased approach to the world, would create fewer dilemmas than other occupational activities. Although most researchers are not faced with the same kind of corrupting influences confronting street level criminal justice officials, the pressures of "grantsmanship" and publication provide significant motivations. The dilemmas of working with human subjects in a political environment are equally challenging. And the goal of scientific purity, of unbiased objectivity, may be corrupting as well, as researchers are tempted to put scientific objectives before their concern for the welfare of others.

In this chapter we will examine the nature of ethical dilemmas confronting the criminal justice researcher. To a large degree these problems are comparable to those difficulties faced by other social scientists. Additional problems arise as a result of the particular focus of research on deviance and law-breaking.

PROBLEMS INVOLVING WORK WITH HUMAN SUBJECTS

Stuart Cook (1976) lists the following ethical considerations surrounding research with human subjects:

1. Involving people in research without their knowledge or consent
2. Coercing people to participate
3. Withholding from the participant the true nature of the research
4. Deceiving the research participant
5. Leading the research participants to commit acts which diminish their self-respect
6. Violating the right to self-determination: research on behavior control and character change
7. Exposing the research participant to physical or mental stress
8. Invading the privacy of the research participant

9. Withholding benefits from participants in control groups
10. Failing to treat research participants fairly and to show them consideration and respect (p. 202).

INVOLVING PEOPLE IN RESEARCH WITHOUT THEIR KNOWLEDGE OR CONSENT

Often the best way to study human behavior is to observe people in a natural setting without their knowledge. Self-reported descriptions of behavior may be unreliable, because people forget or are uncertain about their actions. Although most people might tell you that they would attempt to return a lost wallet, a hidden camera focused on a wallet lying on the sidewalk might reveal very different behaviors. People who know they are being watched often act differently, especially when unethical, deviant, or criminal behaviors are involved. For these reasons, studies of deviance often involve direct observation, which in scientific terminology involves listening as well as visual observation.

At times the observer participates to some degree in the activities being studied. Whyte's (1955) study of street corner society involved just this form of participant observation. Humphreys' (1970) examination of homosexual behavior in public rest rooms, Short and Strodtbeck's (1965) study of delinquency in Chicago, and Cohen's (1980) observations of female prostitutes in New York all involved the observation of persons who never consented to become research subjects.

Studies of persons on the other side of the criminal justice process have also been undertaken without the consent of those participating in the research. Meltzer (1953), for example, studied juror deliberations through the use of hidden microphones. The importance of discretion in the criminal justice process and the hidden nature of most decision-making support the greater use of such techniques in efforts to understand how police, prosecutors and correctional personnel carry out their duties.

The ethical dilemma, however, is a complicated one—is the value of the research such that persons should be turned into study "subjects" without their permission? The conditions of the research are extremely important to this deliberation. If the behaviors being studied would have occurred without the researcher's intervention, the lack of consent seems less troubling. Such studies involve little personal cost to unknowing subjects. Unintrusive research that involves only behaviors that occur in public view is also less questionable, because the invasion of personal privacy is not at issue.

But what about experiments that create situations to which subjects must react, such as those involving a "lost" wallet? Or a study of witness-response to crime that involves an actor or actress screaming and running from an apparent assailant down a crowded street? Observation might be the only method of determining how citizens would really respond, but the personal cost of being studied might be considerable.

Not only may such research be troubling for the persons involved, but when sensitive activities normally considered private or confidential are the subject of study, additional problems may arise. Cook (1976) reports that Meltzer encountered such difficulties in his study of jury deliberations:

> Members of Congress reacted to the jury recording as a threat to fundamental institutions. When the news of the study came out, a congressional investigation resulted. Following the investigation legislation was passed establishing a fine of a thousand dollars and imprisonment for a year for whoever might attempt to record the proceedings of any jury in the United States while the jury is deliberating or voting (p. 205).

Although the response might be less severe, one can anticipate similar objections to the taping of discussions involving police, attorneys, judges, correctional officials and probation and parole authorities.

COERCING PEOPLE TO PARTICIPATE

You have probably received a questionnaire in the mail at some time that offered you some small incentive for completing the form—a free pencil, a few quarters. This practice is a common one, reflecting the assumption that people who are compensated for their efforts may be more likely to participate in a research endeavor than those who receive nothing. Similarly, college students are often provided a grade incentive for participation in their instructor's research. But when does compensation become coercion? When is the researcher justified to compel participation? The issues here involve the freedom *not* to participate, and the nature and quantity of the incentives that can be ethically provided without creating an undue influence.

The person receiving the questionnaire in the mail is free to keep the compensation and toss away the form. Students may be similarly free not to participate in their instructor's research, but the instructor's power over the grading process may make students feel quite ill at ease doing so.

It might seem that the easiest way out of this dilemma is to simply rely on volunteers for research subjects. But volunteers are different from others simply by virtue of their willingness to participate. At a minimum they are more highly motivated than non-volunteers. So it is important to obtain a more representative sample of participants, a group that mirrors the actual characteristics of those persons to whom study results will be applied.

This problem becomes especially critical when research subjects are vulnerable to coercion. Although students might be considered a captive population, jail and prison inmates are clearly the most vulnerable of research subjects.

The history of inmate involvement in research is not a very proud one. Prisoners have been used as "guinea pigs" by pharmaceutical companies that set up laboratories at correctional institutions. For minimal compensation, or the possibility that participation might assist in gaining parole, inmates have participated in a variety of medical research projects.

In the United States, the first use of correctional subjects for medical experiments took place at the Mississippi state prison in 1914, when researchers attempted to discover the relationship between diet and pellagra. The Governor of Mississippi promised pardons to persons volunteering for the experiment. The situation may be contrasted to a more recent experiment in New York in which eight prisoners were inoculated with a venereal infection in order to test possible cures. For their voluntary participation the subjects, in their own words, "got syphilis and a carton of cigarettes." (Geis, 1980 p. 226).

Today, prisoners are forbidden to engage in such research efforts. But inmates are frequently required to participate in efforts to evaluate the impact of correctional treatment, work or education programs. The reason for requiring participation is the same as that stated above. Volunteers are sufficiently different from others that relying on their participation would probably produce more positive outcomes than the intervention alone would warrant.

Freedom of choice is highly valued in this society, but how much freedom of choice should prisoners have? Before denying a subject the opportunity to refuse participation, it should be clear that the overall value of the research outweighs the harm of coercion. In this consideration the nature of the participation must be carefully evaluated—coercion to participate in weekly group therapy is quite different from coercion to participate in eight weeks of paramilitary training. One must also assess whether coercion is the only or best means available to obtain research results. Confronting this dilemma requires a balancing of such matters with a concern for individual rights.

Withholding from the Participant the True Nature of the Research

Informed consent requires that subjects know fully the nature of the research, its possible effects, and the uses to be made of the data collected. However, even in the most benign circumstances written notification may deter further action. Full and complete notification has the added potential of prejudicing responses. Often more accurate assessments are achieved when the subject believes that one aspect of his behavior is the focus, when research interest is really on something else.

Researchers are understandably reluctant to provide too much information in this regard, especially in the early stages of a project, when the need to develop rapport and a willingness to cooperate are especially important. Ethically, informed consent should precede involvement in the study, so that individuals are given a meaningful opportunity to decline further participation.

Balancing research interests and respect for human dignity requires that subjects be informed about all aspects of the research that might reasonably influence their willingness to participate. Any risks that the subjects may expect to face should be fully discussed. Geis (1980) recommends that researchers remember the example of Walter Reed, who participated as a subject in his own experiments on yellow fever because he could ask no one to undergo anything that he himself was not willing to suffer (p. 227).

Deceiving the Research Participant

Perhaps the most flagrant example of deception in criminological research is provided by Humphreys' (1970) study *Tearoom Trade*. Humphreys assumed the role of lookout in public rest rooms so that strangers unaware of his research objective could engage uninterrupted in homosexual activity. He copied down the automobile license tags of the subjects and obtained their addresses. Later he went to their homes, explaining that he was conducting a health survey. He asked the respondents many personal questions that became part of his research on public homosexual conduct.

The rationale for such deception emphasizes the importance of the research and the difficulties of obtaining accurate information through other means. All deceptive acts are not equal. There are differences between active lying and a conscious failure to provide all available information. Deception may be considered an affront to individual autonomy and self-respect, or an occasionally legitimate means to be used in service of a higher value (Cook, 1976).

One alternative to deception is to provide only general information about the research project prior to the experiment and offer full disclosure after the research has been completed. Another technique relies on subjects to role play their behavior after the nature of the research project has been explained. There is mixed evidence, however, on the effectiveness of this technique (Cook, 1976).

In regard to deception, the researcher must evaluate the nature of the research and weigh its value against the impact of the deception on the integrity of participants. The degree to which privacy is invaded and the sensitivity of the behaviors involved are important considerations.

LEADING THE RESEARCH PARTICIPANTS TO COMMIT ACTS WHICH DIMINISH THEIR SELF-RESPECT

Research subjects have been experimentally induced into states of extreme passivity and extreme aggression. Efforts to provoke subjects to lie, cheat and steal have proven very effective. Cook (1976) describes a study in which students were recruited to participate in a theft of records from a business firm. The inducements described included an opportunity to perform a patriotic service for a department of federal government. A substantial number of students were significantly encouraged to take part in the theft, although ultimately the burglary was not carried out.

Research by Haney, Banks and Zimbardo (1973) involved the simulation of prison conditions, with 21 subjects assuming the roles of prisoners and guards. After a very short time, the guards began behaving in an aggressive and physically threatening manner. Their use of power became self-aggrandizing and self-perpetuating. The prisoners quickly experienced a loss of personal identity, exhibiting flattened affect and dependency; eventually they were emotionally emasculated by the encounters.

Because of the extreme nature of the subjects' responses, the project was terminated after only six days. The debriefing sessions that followed the research yielded the following comments:

Guards:

"They (the prisoners) seemed to lose touch with the reality of the experiment—they took me so seriously."

"...I didn't interfere with any of the guards' actions. Usually if what they were doing bothered me, I would walk out and take another duty."

"...looking back, I am impressed by how little I felt for them..."

"They (the prisoners) didn't see it as an experiment. It was real, and they were fighting to keep their identity. But we were always there to show them just who was boss."

"I was tired of seeing the prisoners in their rags and smelling the strong odors of their bodies that filled the cells. I watched them tear at each other, on orders given by us."

"...Acting authoritatively can be fun. Power can be a great pleasure."

"...During the inspection, I went to cell 2 to mess up a bed which the prisoner had made and he grabbed me, screaming that he had just made it, and he wasn't going to let me mess it up. He grabbed my throat, and although he was laughing, I was pretty scared. I lashed out with my stick and hit him in the chin (although not very hard), and when I freed myself I became angry."

Prisoners:

"...The way we were made to degrade ourselves really brought us down, and that's why we all sat docile towards the end of the experiment."

"...I realize now (after it's over) that no matter how together I thought I was inside my head, my prison behavior was often less under my control than I realized. No matter how open, friendly and helpful I was with other prisoners I was still operating as an isolated, self-centered person, being rational rather than compassionate."

"...I began to feel I was losing my identity, that the person I call _____, the person who volunteered to get me into this prison (because it was a prison to me, it *still* is a prison to me, I don't regard it as an experiment or a simulation...) was distant from me, was remote until finally I wasn't *that* person; I was 416. I was really my number, and 416 was really going to have to decide what to do."

"I learned that people can easily forget that others are human."

In Milgram's (1965) research, participants showed "blind obedience" to a white-coated "researcher" who ordered them to provide what appeared to be electric shocks of increasing severity to subjects who failed to respond correctly to a series of questions. Although they were emotionally upset, the subjects continued to follow their instructions as the "shocked" subjects screamed in agony.

Follow-up research revealed that Milgram's subjects experienced only minor and temporary disturbances (Ring, Wallston and Corey, 1970). One might argue that the subjects even benefited from the project as a result of their greater self-awareness, but the fact that the educational experience occurred without their initial understanding or consent raises ethical concerns.

To what degree should subjects be asked to unknowingly engage in activities that may damage their self-esteem? Again, the researcher is required to engage in a balancing act, reconciling research objectives and the availability of alternative methods with a concern for the integrity of subjects. At a minimum, such research efforts should provide means to address any possible harm to subjects, including debriefings at the conclusion of the research and follow-up counseling as needed.

VIOLATING THE RIGHT TO SELF-DETERMINATION: RESEARCH ON BEHAVIOR CONTROL AND CHARACTER CHANGE

The film "Clockwork Orange" provides an excellent illustration of the dilemmas of behavior-modifying research. In the film, a thoroughly violent and irredeemable individual named Alex is subjected to therapy which requires him to observe violent acts on film at the same time that the chemicals he has ingested make him physically ill. After a while, the acts that he has observed make him sick as well, and he is changed from a violent individual to one who avoids violence at all cost, including that required for his own self-defense. At the end of the film, the "powers that be" decide to reverse his treatment for political reasons.

Although there is little possibility of behavior modification being used to exact such effect in the near future, the question remains—to what extent should experimental efforts be made to alter human behavior against the will of the participant? Remembering the vulnerability of the inmate to coercion (in the film, Alex only participated in the violence control project because he thought it would help him gain early release), it becomes clear that the greatest desire to use behavior control strategies will be evident in areas involving those persons most vulnerable to coercion—criminals and persons with problems of substance abuse. Although research on crime prevention and control generally has only the most laudable aims, it should be remembered that it is often those well-intentioned actions that pose the greatest threat to individual freedoms.

EXPOSING THE RESEARCH PARTICIPANT TO PHYSICAL OR MENTAL STRESS

How would you evaluate the ethics of the following research project: an evaluation of a treatment program, in which persons convicted of drunk driving are required to watch and listen to hours of films depicting gory automobile accidents, followed by horrifying emergency room visits and interviews with grieving relatives? Would it matter whether or not the actions of the drunk drivers had contributed to similar accidents? If your answer is yes, you are probably considering whether or not the viewers deserve the "punishment" of what they are forced to observe on film.

This not-so-hypothetical scenario raises a difficult issue. Is it acceptable for a research project to engage in activities that punish and perhaps harm the subject? To test various outcomes, subjects in different settings have been exposed to events provoking feelings of horror, shock, threatened sexual identity, personal failure, fear, and emotional shock (Cook, 1976). The subjects in Zimbardo's and Milgram's research were clearly stressed by their research experiences. To what extent is it acceptable to engage in these practices for the objective of scientific inquiry?

In most situations, it is impossible to observe human reactions such as those described above in their natural settings, so researchers feel justified in creating experiments that produce these reactions. The extent of possible harm raises ethical dilemmas, however, because theoretically there is no limit to what might be contrived to create a "researchable" reaction. The balancing of research objectives with a respect for human subjects is a delicate undertaking, requiring researchers to dispassionately scrutinize their objectives and the value of their proposed studies.

INVADING THE PRIVACY OF THE RESEARCH PARTICIPANT

The issues of privacy and confidentiality are related concerns. Ethical questions are raised by research that invades an individual's privacy without questions are raised by research that invades an individual's privacy without his consent. When information on subjects has been obtained for reasons other than research, e.g., the development of a criminal history file, probation or prison records, there are questions about the extent to which data should be released to researchers. Some records are more sensitive than others in this regard, depending on how easily the offender's identity can be obtained, and the quantity and nature of the information recorded. Even when consent has been given and the information has been gathered expressly for research purposes, maintaining the confidentiality of responses may be a difficult matter when the responses contain information of a sensitive and/or illegal nature.

CONFIDENTIALITY

The issue of confidentiality is especially important in the study of crime and deviance. Subjects will generally not agree to provide information in this area unless their responses are to remain confidential. This may be a more difficult task than it appears. Generally it is important to be able to identify a subject, so that his or her responses can be linked to other sources of data on the individual. Institutionalized delinquents might be asked in confidence about their involvement in drug use and other forms of misconduct during confinement. An important part of the research would involve gathering background information from the offender's institutional files to determine what types of offenders are most likely to be involved in institutional misconduct. To do this, the individual's confidential responses need to be identifiable, so complete anonymity is unfeasible.

As long as only dispassionate researchers have access to this information, there may be no problem. Difficulties arise when third parties, especially criminal justice authorities, become interested in the research responses. Then the issue becomes one of protecting the data (and the offender) from officials who have the power to invoke the criminal justice process.

One response to this dilemma is to store identifying information in a remote place; some researchers have even recommended sending sensitive information out of the country. Because the relationship between the researcher and his informants is not privileged, researchers can be called upon to provide information to the courts.

Lewis Yablonsky, a criminologist/practitioner, while testifying in defense of Gridley White, one of Yablonsky's main informants in his hippie study, was asked by the judge nine times if he had witnessed

Gridley smoking marijuana. Yablonsky refused to answer because of the rights guaranteed him in the Fifth Amendment of the U.S. Constitution. Although he was not legally sanctioned, he said the incident was humiliating and suggested that researchers should have guarantees of immunity (Wolfgang, 1982, P. 396).

It is also important that researchers prepare their presentation of research findings in a manner that ensures that the particular responses of an individual cannot be discerned. Presentation of only aggregate findings was especially important for Marvin Wolfgang (1982), when he reinterviewed persons included in his earlier study of delinquency in a birth cohort. His follow-up consisted of hour-long interviews with about 600 youths. The subjects were asked many personal questions, including those about involvement in delinquency and crime. Four of his respondents admitted committing criminal homicide, and 75 admitted to forcible rape. Many other serious crimes were also described, for which none of the participants had been arrested.

At the time of the research, all of the respondents were orally assured that the results of the research would remain confidential, but Wolfgang raises a number of ethical questions surrounding this practice. Should written consent forms have been provided to the subjects, detailing the nature of the research? Wolfgang concludes such forms would have raised more questions than they answered. Could a court order impound the records? Could persons attempting to protect the data be prosecuted for their actions? Could the data be successfully concealed?

The general willingness to protect subjects who admit to serious crimes also requires close ethical scrutiny. Wolfgang (1982) takes the traditional scientific stance on this issue, proposing that such information belongs to science. Because the information would have not been discovered without the research effort, its protection neither helps nor hinders police. The ethical judgment here requires a weighing of interests—the importance of scientific research balanced against society's interest in capturing a particular individual.

It should be noted that if researchers began to routinely inform on their subjects, all future research relying on self-reports would be jeopardized. Thus the issue at hand is not simply that of the value of a particular study, but the value of all research utilizing subject disclosures. Researchers are generally advised not to undertake such research unless they feel comfortable about protecting their sources. This requires that all research involving the use of confidential information provide for controlled access to sensitive data and protect the information from unauthorized searches, inadvertent access, and the compulsory legal process (Cook, 1976).

WITHHOLDING BENEFITS TO PARTICIPANTS IN CONTROL GROUPS

The necessity of excluding some potential beneficiaries from initial program participation arises whenever a classical experimental design is to be used to evaluate the program. This research design requires the random assignment of subjects to experimental and control groups. Subjects in the control group are excluded from the program and/or receive "standard" rather than "experimental" treatment.

In a program evaluation, it is important that some subjects receive the benefits of the program while others do not, to ensure that the outcomes observed are the direct result of the experimental intervention and not something else (subject enthusiasm or background characteristics, for example). It is imperative that those who receive the intervention (the experimental group) and those that do not (the control group) be as identical in the aggregate as possible, so that a clear assessment of program impact, untainted by variation in the nature of subjects, can be obtained.

The best way to ensure that experimental and control subjects are identical is randomization. Randomization is to be distinguished from arbitrariness, in that randomization requires that every subject have an equal opportunity to be assigned to either the experimental or control group; arbitrariness involves no such equality of opportunity.

In many ways, randomization may be more fair than standard practice based on good intentions. Geis (1980) reports:

> For most of us, it would be unthinkable that a sample of armed robbers be divided into two groups on the basis of random assignment—one group to spend 10 years in prison, the second to receive a sentence of 2 years on probation. Nonetheless, at a federal judicial conference, after examining an elaborate presentence report concerning a bank robber, 17 judges said they would have imprisoned the man, while 10 indicated they favored probation. Those voting for imprisonment set sentences ranging from 6 months to 15 years (p. 221).

Randomization is also acceptable under law, because its use is reasonably related to a governmental objective, i.e., testing the effectiveness of a program intervention (Erez, 1986).

But although randomization is inherently fair, it often appears less so to the subjects involved. Surveys of prisoners have indicated that need, merit and "first come, first served" are more acceptable criteria than a method which the offenders equated with gambler's luck (Erez, 1986). Consider Morris' (1966) description of "the burglar's nightmare:"

> If eighty burglars alike in all relevant particulars were assigned randomly to experimental and control groups, forty each, with the experimentals to be released six months or a year earlier than they ordinarily would be and the control released at their regularly appointed time, how would the burglar assigned to the control group respond? It is unfair, unjust, unethical, he could say, for me to be put into the control group. If people like me, he might complain, are being released early, I too deserve the same treatment (cited in Erez, 1986, p. 394).

Program staff are also frequently unhappy with randomization, because it fails to utilize their clinical skills in the selection of appropriate candidates for intervention. Extending this line of thought, consider the likely response of judges requested to sentence burglary offenders randomly to prison or probation. While this might be the best method of determining the effectiveness of these sanctions, the judicial response (and perhaps community response as well) would probably be less than enthusiastic. This is because it is assumed, often without any evidence, that standard practice is achieving some reasonable objective, such as individualizing justice or preventing crime.

Randomization does produce winners and losers. Of critical importance in weighing the consequences of randomization are the differences in treatment experienced by the experimental and control groups. Six factors are relevant here:

1. Significance of the interest affected. Early release is of much greater consequence than a change of institutional diet.
2. Extent of difference. Six months' early release is of greater significance than one week's early release.
3. Comparison of the disparity with standard treatment. If both experimental and control group treatment is an improvement over standard treatment, then the discrepancy between the experimental and control group is of less concern.
4. Whether disparity reflects differences in qualifications of subjects. If the disparity is reasonably related to some characteristic of the subjects, the denial of benefits to the control group is less significant.
5. Whether the experimental treatment is harmful or beneficial to

subjects compared with the treatment they would otherwise receive. A program that assigns members of the experimental group to six weeks of "boot camp" may be more demanding of inmates than the standard treatment of six months' incarceration.

6. Whether participation is mandatory or voluntary. Voluntary participation mitigates the concern of denial of benefit, while coercion exacerbates the dilemma (Federal Judicial Center, 1981, pp. 31-40).

Similar to the management of other ethical dilemmas, an effort is required to balance values of human decency and justice with the need for accurate information on intervention effectiveness. Problems arise not in the extreme cases of disparity but in more routine circumstances.

Consider the following example:

...how do we judge a situation in which a foundation grant permits attorneys to be supplied for all cases being heard by a juvenile court where attorneys have previously appeared only in rare instances? A fundamental study hypothesis may be that the presence of an attorney tends to result in a more favorable disposition for the client. This idea may be tested by comparing dispositions prior to the beginning of the experiment with those ensuing subsequently, though it would be more satisfactory to supply attorneys to a sample of the cases and withhold them from the remainder, in order to calculate in a more experimentally uncontaminated manner the differences between the outcomes in the two situations.

The matter takes on additional complexity if the researchers desire to determine what particular attorney role is the most efficacious in the juvenile court. They may suspect that an attorney who acts as a friend of the court, knowingly taking its viewpoint as parens patriae and attempting to interpret the court's interest to his client, will produce more desirable results than one who doggedly challenges the courtroom procedure and the judge's interpretation of fact, picks at the probation report, raises constant objections, and fights for his client as he would in a criminal court. But what results are "more desirable" (Geis, 1980, pp. 222-223)?

It could be contended that little is really known about how attorney roles influence dispositions, and that without the project no one would have any kind of representation. Over the long term, all juveniles stand to benefit.

On the other hand, it could be argued that it is wrong to deprive anyone of the best judgment of his attorney by requiring a particular legal approach. What if there are only enough funds to supply half the juveniles with attorneys anyway? Is randomization more or less fair than trying to decide which cases "need" representation the most?

Randomization imposes a special ethical burden because it purposefully counters efforts to determine the best course of action with the element of chance. The practice is justifiable because the pursuit of knowledge is a desirable objective—as long as the overall benefits outweigh the risks. The balancing of risks and benefits is complicated by the fact that judgments must often be made in a context of ambiguity, attempting to predict the benefits of an intervention that is being tested precisely because its impact is unknown.

The Federal Judicial Center (1981) recommends that program evaluations should only be considered when certain threshold conditions are met:

> First, the status quo warrants substantial improvements or is of doubtful effectiveness. Second, there must be significant uncertainty about the value or effectiveness of the innovation. Third, information needed to clarify the uncertainty must be feasibly obtainable by the program experimentation but not readily obtainable by other means. And fourth, the information sought must pertain directly to the decision whether or not to adopt the proposed innovation on a general, non-experimental basis (p. 7).

Several conditions lessen the ethical burdens of evaluative research. Random assignment is especially acceptable when resources are scarce and demand for the benefit is high. Denying benefits to the control group is quite acceptable when members of the control group can participate at a later date. Finally, discrepancies between the treatment of experimental and control groups are decreased when the groups are geographically separated (Federal Judicial Center, 1981).

FAILING TO TREAT RESEARCH PARTICIPANTS FAIRLY AND TO SHOW THEM CONSIDERATION AND RESPECT

The basic tenets of professionalism require that researchers treat subjects with courtesy and fulfill the variety of commitments they make to subjects. In an effort to obtain cooperation, subjects are often promised a follow-up report on the findings of the research; such reports may be forgotten once the study has been completed. Subjects are often led to believe that they will achieve some personal benefit from the research. This may be one of the more difficult obligations to fulfill.

Researchers need to treat their human subjects with constant recognition of their integrity and their contribution to the research endeavor. This is especially important when subjects are powerless and vulnerable. Although such treatment may be a time-consuming chore, it is the only ethical way to practice scientific research.

BALANCING SCIENTIFIC AND ETHICAL CONCERNS

This discussion has emphasized the importance of balancing a concern for subjects against the potential benefits of the research. Cook (1976) identifies the following potential benefits of a research project:

1. Advances in scientific theory that contribute to a general understanding of human behavior.
2. Advances in knowledge of practical value to society.
3. Gains for the research participant, such as increased understanding, satisfaction in making a contribution to science or to the solution of social problems, needed money or special privileges, knowledge of social science or of research methods, and so on (p. 235).

The potential costs to subjects are considerable, however, and it is often difficult for the researcher to be objective in assessing the issues. For this reason, many professional associations have established guidelines and procedures for ethical research conduct. Generally the professional is honor-bound to follow these guidelines, as little active monitoring occurs.

To insure that their faculty follow acceptable procedures (and to protect themselves from liability), universities have established Institutional Review Boards to scrutinize each research project that involves the use of human subjects. These review boards serve a valuable function in that they review the specifications of each research project prior to implementation. These boards are also generally incapable of providing direct monitoring of projects, so again, the responsibility for ethical conduct falls on the researcher.

ETHICAL/POLITICAL CONSIDERATIONS

Applied social research, that is, research that examines the effectiveness of social policies and programs, carries with it additional ethical responsibilities. Such research influences the course of human events in a direct fashion—often work, education, future opportunities, and deeply held values and beliefs are affected by the outcomes. Researchers must be prepared to deal with a variety of pressures and demands as they undertake the practice and dissemination of research.

It is generally acknowledged that organizations asked to measure their own effectiveness often produce biased results. Crime statistics provide a notorious example of data that tend to be used to show either an effective police department (falling crime figures) or a need for more resources (rising crime figures). Criminal justice researchers are often asked to study matters that are equally sensitive. A correctional treatment program found to be ineffective may lose its funding. A study that reveals extensive use of plea bargaining may cost a prosecutor his election.

Often the truth is complicated. A survey that reveals that drug use is declining in the general population may prove troublesome for those trying to lobby for the establishment of more drug treatment facilities. The survey results may lead the public to believe that there is no problem at the same time that the need for treatment facilities for the indigent is substantial.

Such research has been known to produce unintended consequences. The publication of selected results of a study on the effectiveness of correctional treatment programs (Martinson, 1974) was used by many persons to justify limiting funds for education and treatment programs in correctional institutions. The research revealed that there was little evidence that correctional treatment programs were effective means of reducing recidivism (a finding that has been widely challenged). Rather than stimulating the development of more theoretically sound programs and rigorous evaluations of these efforts, the apparent product of the research was a decrease in the humaneness of conditions of confinement.

Sometimes research results conflict with cherished beliefs. Studies of preventive police patrol (Kelling, Page, Dieckman and Browne, 1974) and detective investigations (Chaiken, Greenwood and Petersilia, 1977) both revealed that these practices, long assumed to be essential elements of effective law enforcement, were of little value. Researchers can expect findings such as these to meet with considerable resistance.

Researchers may be asked to utilize their skills and their aura of objectivity to provide an organization or agency with what it wants. When the group that pays the bills has a direct interest in the nature of the outcome, the pressures can be considerable. Marvin Wolfgang (1982) reports:

> I was once invited to do research by an organization whose views are almost completely antithetical to mine on the issue of gun control. Complete freedom and a considerable amount of money to explore the relationship between gun control legislation and robbery were promised. I would not perform the research under those auspices. But the real clincher in the decision was that if the research produced conclusions opposite from that the organization wanted, the agency would not publish the results nor allow me to publish them. Perhaps their behavior, within their ideological framework, was not unethical. But within my framework, as a scientist who values freedom of publication as well as of scientific inquiry, I would have engaged in an unethical act of prostituting my integrity had I accepted those conditions (p. 395).

In-house researchers, who are employed by the organization for which the research is being conducted, face special problems in this regard, because they lack the freedom to pick and choose their research topic. These problems must balance their concern for rigorous scientific inquiry with their need for continued employment.

Generally the issues confronted are subtle and complex. Although researchers may be directly told to conceal or falsify results, more often they are subtly encouraged to design their research with an eye toward the desired results. The greatest barrier to such pressures is the development of a truly independent professional research unit within the organization. Such independence protects the researcher from political pressures, while at the same time promotes the credibility of the research being conducted. Without this protection, the individual is left to his own devices and standards of ethical conduct.

THE PURITY OF SCIENTIFIC RESEARCH

The ideal of scientific inquiry is the pure, objective examination of the empirical world, untainted by personal prejudice. But research is carried out by human beings, not automatons, who have a variety of motivations for undertaking the research that they do. Topics may be selected because of curiosity or perceived need to address a specific social problem, but the availability of grants in a particular field may also encourage researchers to direct their attention to these areas. This is critical if one is working for a research organization dependent upon "soft" money. The need for university faculty to publish and establish a name for themselves in a particular area may encourage them to seek "hot" topics for their research, or to identify an extremely narrow research focus in which they can become identified as an expert.

There is some evidence that the nature of one's research findings influences the likelihood of publication (*Chronicle of Higher Education*, 1989d). A curious author submitted almost identical articles to a number of journals. The manuscripts differed only in one respect—the nature of the conclusions. One version of the article showed that the experiment had no effect; the other described a positive result. His experiment produced some interesting findings—the article with positive outcomes was more likely to be accepted for publication than the other manuscript.

If research that concludes that "the experiment didn't work" or that "differences between Groups A and B were insignificant" are indeed less likely to see the light of day, then pressures to revise one's research focus or rewrite one's hypotheses to match the results produced can be anticipated.

None of the practices described above involve scandalous violations of ethical conduct. Their presentation should function, however, to remind us that actions justified in the name of scientific inquiry may be motivated by factors far less "pure" than the objective they serve.

PUBLIC POLICY PRONOUNCEMENTS AND TEACHING CRIMINAL JUSTICE

When is a researcher speaking from the facts and when is he or she promoting personal ideology? If there were any fully conclusive and definitive studies in the social sciences, this question would not arise. But research findings are always tentative, and statements describing them invariably require conditional language. On the other hand, researchers have values and beliefs like everyone else, and few of us want to employ the same conditional language required to discuss research when we state our views on matters of public policy and morality. Researchers thus have a special obligation to carefully evaluate their remarks and clearly distinguish between opinion and apparent empirical fact. This is not always an easy task, but it is the only way to safeguard the objectivity that is critically important to scientific inquiry.

CONCLUSION

Conducting scientific research in criminal justice and criminology in an ethical fashion is a difficult task. It requires a constant weighing and balancing of objectives and motivations. It would be nice to conclude that the best research is that which is undertaken in an ethical fashion, but such a statement would skirt the dilemma. This is the exact nature of the problem—those actions required to meet the demands of scientific rigor sometimes run counter to ethical behavior.

But evaluating rather than avoiding ethical dilemmas does provide a learning experience, the benefits of which can be expected to spill over into all aspects of human endeavor. Thinking and doing in an ethical fashion requires practice, and conducting research provides considerable opportunity for the development of experience.

REFERENCES

Chaiken, Jan, Peter Greenwood and Joan Petersilia (1977) "The Criminal Investigation Process: A Summary Report," *Policy Analysis*, 3:187-217.

Chronicle of Higher Education (1989a), January 25:A44.

(1989b), June 14:A44.

(1989c), July 19:A4.

(1989d), August 2:A5.

Cohen, Bernard (1980) *Deviant Street Networks: Prostitution in New York City*. Cambridge, Massachusetts: Lexington Books.

Cook, Stuart W. (1976) "Ethical Issues in the Conduct of Research in Social Relations" in *Research Methods in Social Relations*, 3rd ed., Claire Sellitz, Lawrence Rightsman and Stuart Cook, [eds.] New York: Holt, Rinehart and Winston.

Erez, Edna (1986) "Randomized Experiments in Correctional Context: Legal, Ethical and Practical Concerns." *Journal of Criminal Justice* 14, :389-400.

Federal Judicial Center (1981) Experimentation in the Law. Report of the Federal Judicial Center Advisory Committee on Experimentation in the Law Washington, D.C.: Federal Judicial Center.

Geis, Gilbert (1980) "Ethical and Legal Issues in Experiments with Offender Population, in *Criminal Justice Research: Approaches: Problems and Policy*, Susette Talarico, [ed.] Cincinnati: Anderson.

Haney, Craig, Curtis Banks and Phillip Zimbardo (1973) "Interpersonal Dynamics in a Simulated Prison," *International Journal of Criminology and Penology*, 1:69-97.

Humphreys, Laud (1970) *Tearoom Trade* Chicago: Aldine.

Kelling, George L., Tony Pate, Duance Dieckman and Charles E. Browne (1974) The Kansas City Preventive Patrol Experiment. Washington, D.C.: The Police Foundation.

Martinson, Robert (1974) "What Works?—Questions and Answers About Prison Reform," *Public Interest*, 35: 25-54.

Meltzer, B.A. (1953) "A Projected Study of the Jury as a Working Institution," *The Annals of the American Academy of Political and Social Sciences*, 287: 97-102.

Milgram, Stanley (1974) *Obedience to Authority: An Experimental View*. New York: Harper and Row.

Morris, Norval (1966) "Impediments to Penal Reform," *Chicago Law Review*, 33: 646-653.

New York Times (1983) February 26: p. 7.

Ring, K., K. Wallston and M. Corey (1970) "Mode of Debriefing as a Factor Affecting Subjective Reaction to a Milgram Type Obedience Experience: An Ethical Inquiry," *Representative Research in Social Psychology* 1: 67-88.

Short, James F., Jr. and Fred Strodtbeck (1965) *Group Processes and Gang Delinquency.* Chicago: University of Chicago Press.

Whyte, William F. (1955) *Streetcorner Society* Chicago: University of Chicago Press.

Wolfgang, Marvin (1982) "Ethics and Research," in *Ethics, Public Policy and Criminal Justice,* Frederick Elliston and Norman Bowie, eds. Cambridge, Massachusetts: Oelgeschlager, Gunn and Hain.

V.
Ethical Issues
in Criminal Justice Research–
Questions and Scenarios

Chapter Fourteen

1. Would you expect researchers to be more or less well prepared to handle ethical dilemmas in a responsible way than other criminal justice professionals?

2. What are the possible consequences for researchers, their subjects, and the field of criminal justice, if unethical conduct becomes accepted practice?

3. Every professional group tends to prefer self-control to control by an external body. What characteristics would identify a need for external review?

Chapter Fifteen

1. McCarthy notes several incidents in which the ethical conduct of researchers was either found lacking or proven negligent. Do you think that these incidents exemplify most research today? Does all research have an obligation to keep its goal of "scientific purity or unbiased objectivity"? Is there any way to be purely objective in a criminal justice system that focuses on the human element? How representative do you feel these incidents are regarding researchers today?

2. Do you feel that certain levels of deceit (e.g. withholding information or involving people without their knowledge) are acceptable, perhaps even necessary to criminal justice research? Can you think of any possible examples that might be acceptable?

3. Is a true balance possible between scientific and ethical concerns? Is there any benefit of research that would make you lean more toward one end of the continuum? If so, why?

4. McCarthy stated that "the need for university faculty to publish and establish a name for themselves" encourages them to seek "hot" topics or become experts in narrowly defined areas. Do you think that this tendency has contributed to or increased the level of unethical activity in research or lessened it? Why or why not?

SCENARIOS

1. You are a researcher who has been asked to testify before a Congressional Committee on the issue of drug treatment. Although you hope that effective treatment programs will be developed in the future, virtually all of the programs with which you are familiar have failed rates of over 50%. How do you present your testimony to congress? What if the failure rates were over 75%? 95%?

2. You are a famous researcher and you are almost positive that you are very close to developing a cure for AIDS. You've experimented on animals but you need human subjects to prove your point. You have been approved to do an experiment in a prison setting using prisoners who are paid for taking part in the experiment. After acquiring the first group to try the serum, one prisoner dies quite suddenly after the first injection. You are shocked but realize what the problem is and rapidly isolate the mistake in the serum. You feel the cure is amost ready. Is the death of the first man justified if someone does end up providing a cure for AIDS? Do you feel it will be worth risking other's lives with the revised serum? Why?

3. You have just been informed that one of your research subjects has been indicted by a grand jury for murder of an area black youth. In your recorded conversations with him, he had alluded to several incidents and you feel sure he has committed the crime. What is your duty as a human being and as a researcher? Would you testify, revealing what he told you, or would you remain silent because of the confidential nature of the conversation?

4. You are a university professor. Several students have been helping you in a rather large research project. You have worked long and hard on this project for several years. Nearing the end of your project, you find that one of your assistants falsified parts of a set of records. It is a very small group of data but crucial to your research. What do you do? Does it make any difference that you are currently being considered for tenure at your university?

VI. ETHICS AND CRIME CONTROL POLICY

How should we approach problems related to crime control? We are spending increasing sums of money in areas of law enforcement and corrections and we have continued to pass new legislation with an eye toward developing more effective crime control policies. Still, crime continues to increase. In addition, we have to contend with public perceptions regarding crime and the justice system's response which are largely shaped by the media. Newspaper headlines, television, and movies each try to attract readers or viewers. How much is fact and how much is fiction? Whether founded entirely on fact or not, many of our citizens' fear of crime is certainly real to them.

An increasing awareness of the scope and nature of corporate crime challenges the abilities and resources of our justice system on additional fronts. Our traditional approach to controlling crime seems more comfortable in addressing familiar criminal behavior in such areas as burglary, robbery, and assault. The "bad guys" are typically more clearly defined. This is not always the case with much of corporate crime. Problems involving consumer safety, pollution, and other related issues often involve business executives who are considered upstanding members of their respective communities, and with the rapid development of the computer, such crimes are increasingly difficult to track down. In some ways it seems that our traditional approach to administering justice is simply not adequate to

325

resolve the more sophisticated problems of much of the corporate world. Still, the demands of culture can encourage and stimulate us to develop new ways of thinking about crime and, as a result, more innovative responses to crime-related problems.

CRIME, CRIMINALS AND CRIME CONTROL POLICY MYTHS 16

Robert M. Bohm

INTRODUCTION

Despite recognition that the reality of crime is socially constructed, the task of debunking myths about crime, criminals and crime control policy has received only limited attention (Quinney, 1970; 1979; 1979b; Pearce, 1976; Milakovich and Weis, 1977; Reiman, 1979; Simon, 1981; Pepinsky and Jesilow, 1984; Walker, 1985). Myths continue to be perpetuated.[1] Moreover, some of them have become part of an ideology that informs, and is informed by, public interests in the area of social control in general and of crime and crime control in particular.[2] This has resulted in at least two undesirable consequences for the vast majority of Americans. First is a myopic focus on short-term interests of dubious value and a near total obliviousness to long-range interests which promise greater relief from criminal victimization. Obliviousness to future interests makes exploitation easier.[3] A second undesirable consequence for most Americans is the contradictions that occur when actions are based on myth-laden ideology. Though not inevitable, contradictions, when they arise, sometimes adversely affect both short- and

327

long-term interests. For many people, control policies based on myth-laden ideology result in an exacerbation of harm and suffering.

The focus of this essay, however, is not crime control ideology per se, but rather the myths that inform that ideology. Specifically, the purpose is three-fold: first, to identify some of the myths that inform the currently dominant crime control ideology in the United States; second, to examine some of the sources of and reasons for the perpetuation of the myths; and third, to consider some of the contradictions and consequences of beliefs and policies based on myths.

CRIME, CRIMINAL, AND CRIME CONTROL POLICY MYTHS

Due to space limitations, the following discussion considers only some of the myths that inform the prevailing "politically conservative," "law and order" ideology in the United States. Most of the myths examined are not new—testimony to both their enduring quality and their ability to be adapted to different, often opposing purposes.

CRIME MYTHS

The foundation of the entire crime mythology edifice is the definition of crime. The problem is a lack of clarity as to what the concept of crime refers. Historically, crime has been used to label an extraordinarily large and a seemingly unrelated number of actions and inactions. A legal definition of crime, moreover, does not solve the problem. The law is rather arbitrary about what kinds of phenomena are regarded as crime and has generally expanded and contracted depending on the interests of the dominant groups in the social struggle. All definitions of crime, legal or otherwise, include actions or inactions that arguably should be excluded and exclude actions or inactions that arguably should be included. This is inevitable, given the political nature of crime. Consequently, a critical issue is whether there is a socially unacceptable and generally unknown bias in including or excluding certain actions or inactions as crime. Considerable evidence indicates that there is (Pepinsky and Jesilow, 1984; Simon and Eitzen, 1982; Reiman and Headlee, 1981:43; Reiman, 1979; Quinney, 1979:62; Lieberman, 1974; Mintz and Cohen, 1971:25-26; American Friends Service Committee, 1971). For example, consider the crime of murder. According to the 1982 *Crime in the United States,* there were 21,012 murders and non-negligent manslaughters. These murders represent only a fraction of those killed intentionally or negligently. Conservative estimates indicate that each year at least 10,000 lives are lost to unnecessary surgeries, 20,000 to errors in prescribing drugs, 20,000 to doctors spreading diseases in hospitals, 100,000 to industrial disease, 14,000 to industrial accidents, 200,000 to environmentally caused cancer, and an unknown number from lethal industrial products (Reiman, 1979; Simon and Eitzen, 1982; Pepinsky and Jesilow, 1984). Yet, few of the latter actions or inactions are defined legally as murder or manslaughter. One reason is the myth that "white-collar crime" is nonviolent.

Another problem with criminal definitions that contributes to myths is the presumption that all laws are enforced and/or enforced fairly. Just as there is a socially unacceptable and generally unknown bias in the definition of crime, there is a similar bias in the enforcement of law. One reason so few white-collar crimes are brought to light, for example, is the inadequate enforcement mechanism. A myth that effectively obscures this inadequacy is that regulatory agencies can prevent white-collar crime. While there is little doubt that there would be more white-collar crime if regulatory agencies did not exist, it is not at all clear how much white-collar crime is prevented by their existence. In any event, the myth can be sustained only by ignoring the history of efforts at federal regulation of corporate crime. Humphries and Greenberg (1981:236) argue that "regulatory agencies were the Progressive Era's solution to the problem of controlling business in a manner that did not delegitimize capitalism by tarnishing capitalists with the stigma of criminality." Similarly, Pearce (1976:88) maintains that the state intentionally created agencies responsive to the interests of big business (also see Pepinsky and Jesilow, 1984;66-79). Furthermore, while the prosecution of corporate crime has increased dramatically in recent years, it may well be, as Pearce (1976:90) suggests, merely a symbolic effort to vindicate the myth that the state is neutral and to reinforce the myth that the law is applied uniformly to all persons. In the wake of lost legitimacy following Watergate and other scandals of the 1970s, an increase in the prosecution of elite criminality is not surprising. In any event, two problems lie at the heart of the myth of crime: the definitional problem and the enforcement problem.

Another myth is that crime in the United States is primarily violent. This myth is derived partly from the Uniform Crime Reports. These reports give the impression that the crime problem in the United States consists primarily of the eight "index offenses:" murder and non-negligent manslaughter, forcible rape, robbery, aggravated assault, burglary, larceny-theft, motor vehicle theft, and, beginning in 1979, arson. Three or possibly four of the eight "index crimes" are clearly "violent" (murder and nonnegligent manslaughter, forcible rape, aggravated assault and, possibly, robbery). Yet, according to recent Uniform Crime Reports, only about 10% of all the crime known to the police is violent. In addition, if the new arson category is excluded, no more than ten percent of all persons arrested are charged with *any* of the index crimes (Milakovich and Weis, 1977:339). It is hard to justify the crime problem, as conceptualized in the Uniform Crime Reports, as a problem of violence.

Another common myth is that crime is increasing. This myth is also sustained primarily by the data reported in the Uniform Crime Reports. However, if data in the Uniform Crime Reports are compared with the findings of the Census Bureau's National Crime Surveys from 1973 to 1980, one finds a major discrepancy. The Uniform Crime Reports show a substantial increase in the crime rate during the period, while the Census Bureau statistics indicate no increase in the proportion of victims reporting the same crimes. In some cases, the Census Bureau reports slight decreases (Paex and Dodge, 1982). Indeed, a careful examination of the historical record provides no basis for the belief that street crime, the type of crime most people fear, is rising: "People today are in no greater danger of being robbed or physically hurt than 150 years ago" (Pepinsky and Jesilow, 1984:22; also Ferdinand, 1977:353).

A final myth is that crime is an inevitable concomitant of complex, populous and industrialized societies. This myth has been advanced by Shelley in *Crime and Modernization: The Impact of Industrialization and Urbanization* (1981). Besides the serious problems with comparing crime statistics cross-culturally (cf. Sutherland and Cressey, 1974:25), there are at least four other problems with Shelley's proposition. First, it fails to account for the great variation in crime rates of different complex, populous and industrialized societies. For example, the crime rates of Japan and West Germany are much lower than those of the United States (Reiman, 1979:20; Martin and Conger, 1980; also see Clinard, 1978; Stack, 1984, especially Appendix 1). Second, the proposition fails to account for the great variation in crime rates within modern, complex, populous, and urbanized nations. For example, according to the 1984 Uniform Crime Report, the homicide rate in the United States varied from a low of one in New Hampshire to a high of 13.1 in Texas (per 100,000 persons). Similar variation is found for other crimes (cf. Lyerly and Skipper, 1981). Third, the proposition fails to account for the lack of correlation between a city's crime rate and its population and population density. According to the 1984 Uniform Crime Report, for example, the city with the highest homicide rate was Gary, Indiana. The three most populated cities in the United States—New York, Los Angeles, and Chicago—are not found among the top ten cities with the highest homicide rate (also see Reiman, 1979:21-23, especially Table 1). A fourth problem with the proposition is that the claim of inevitability in the social sciences is always tenuous and suspect.

CRIMINAL MYTHS

Several myths inform popular conceptions of criminals. For example, one myth holds that some groups are more law abiding than others (Pepinsky and Jesilow, 1984:47). Evidence indicates however, that over 90% of all Americans have committed some crime for which they could be incarcerated (Silver, 1968; Wallerstein and Wyle, 1947). The observation does not deny that crime may be more concentrated in some groups, but only that it is unlikely to be absent in others. The myth seems credible because the crimes of some (e.g., physicians or corporate executives) are not easily detected, or there is not as much effort exerted detecting them. These two problems sustain another myth: that most crime is committed by poor, young males between the ages of 15 and 24 (Pepinsky and Jesilow, 1984; Reiman, 1979). As noted, if law enforcement were able or willing to detect all crimes, it would be more evenly distributed among rich and poor and all age groups, though it may remain more highly concentrated in some groups. With regard to age discrimination, an additional problem with the myth is that "the crime rate is growing much faster than either the absolute number of young people or their percentage of the population" (Reiman, 1979:24).

CRIME CONTROL POLICY MYTHS

Myths about crime and criminals often form the basis of crime control policy. Historically, the use of myth in effecting crime legislation is perhaps the most transparent in the "educational campaign" mounted by the Federal Bureau of Narcotics to outlaw the consumption of marijuana (Grinspoon, 1977; Becker, 1973; Smith, 1970). Under the leadership of Commissioner H.J. Anslinger, the myth of the eleventh-century Persian Assassins was employed in the 1930s to substantiate a link between marijuana, violence, and crime. To obtain stiffer penalties in the 1950s, the attack on marijuana by Anslinger and the Federal Bureau of Narcotics shifted to the myth that marijuana use led to heroin use. Although there is speculation on the motives behind the campaign (cf. Helmer, 1975; Becker, 1973; Musto, 1973), suffice it to say that it was successful in achieving its ends. A result has been that somewhere between twelve and thirty-four million otherwise generally law-abiding citizens have been made criminals.

A number of myths inform public conceptions of law enforcement and law enforcement policy. One of the more pervasive myths is that the police are primarily crime-fighters. Nothing could be further from the truth. Only a small fraction of police time (perhaps less than 10%) is devoted to crime fighting. The vast majority of police time entails public service and traffic activities (Pepinsky, 1980:107; Manning, 1978; 1977:16; Bittner, 1975:42; 1967:700; Wilson, 1975:81; 1968:6; Garmire et al., 1972:25; Reiss, 1971:100).

Related to the myth of police as crime-fighters is one that holds that the police solve crimes. Evidence suggests otherwise (see sources cited in the paragraph above). According to recent editions of the Uniform Crime Report, the official overall clearance rate of the police in the United States is around 25%. The true rate, however, is probably closer to 13% (Walker, 1985:26).

A final myth of crime control policy to be considered is that eliminating injustices from the criminal justice system will reduce the level of serious crime. Eliminating injustices from the criminal justice system is certainly a worthwhile pursuit. However, it is unlikely to have an appreciable effect on serious crime. The causes of most crime are to be found in general social arrangements and not in the operation of the criminal justice system (Walker, 1985:206; Bohm, 1982).

The preceding list of myths is by no means exhaustive and is only intended as an indication of some of the myths that inform the now dominant "politically conservative," "law and order" ideology in the United States. Based largely on this ideology, crime prevention and enforcement resources have been expended recently on some of the following priorities: mandatory sentencing, habitual-criminal statutes, increased numbers of police officers, more effective police officers, changes in Miranda warnings, preventive detention, changes in plea bargaining, changes in the exclusionary rule, changes in the insanity defense, career criminal programs, prison industries and capital punishment. While each of these policies is intended to accomplish one or more bureaucratic goals (e.g., crime reduction, cost-effectiveness, or greater efficiency), none is likely to have a significant effect on the harm and suffering experienced by the vast majority of the American public. They do not adequately address the fundamental social structural elements of the crime problem (cf. Pepinsky and Jesilow, 1984; Walker, 1985; Bohm, 1982). The task now is to examine some of the sources of and reasons for the perpetuation of myths that do not contribute to pervasive harm and suffering.

SOURCES OF AND REASONS FOR THE MYTHS: CONTRADICTIONS AND CONSEQUENCES

Myths about crime, criminals and crime control policy are perpetuated because they serve a variety of interests. Among the interests served are those of the general public, the media, politicians, academic criminologists, criminal justice officials and social elites. One of the problems with previous discussions of crime-related mythology is the emphasis on the way elite interests are served (cf. Reiman, 1979; Quinney, 1979; 1979b). This emphasis is probably derived from the seminal observations of Marx and Engels, who wrote that "the ideas of the ruling class are in every epoch the full ideas..." (1970:64). They noted that in order for the ruling class to carry out its ideas, it is necessary for the ruling class "to represent its interests as the common interest of all the members of society, that is, expressed in ideal form: it has to give its ideas the form of universatility and represent them as the only rational, universally valid ones" (Marx and Engels, 1970:65-5). This, of course, includes ideas about crime.

A problem with Marx's and Engels' observations is that they failed to distinguish between short- and long-term interests. While in the long-run elite interests are served by myths about crime, criminals and crime control policy, and the general public is duped into believing that their long-run interests are also served, it is unlikely that the myths could find such universal appeal if they did not also serve real short-term interests of the general public. It is maintained here that myths about crime, criminals and crime control policy are perpetuated because they actually do serve the general short-term interest, as well as long-term elite interests.

This section examines some of the ways that myths serve both general and elite interests. It also considers some of the contradictions and consequences of beliefs and policies based on myths. While there is obvious overlap in groups served by myths (e.g., members of the media, politicians, academic criminologists, criminal justice officials and elites are also part of the general public), the ways that each group contributes to and is served by myths are a little different. For this reason, each group is considered separately.

THE GENERAL PUBLIC

The general public contributes to their own myth-laden conception of crime in at least four ways. The first is by overgeneralizing from personal experience. If people have been crime victims, they may consider their own experience typical or representative of crime in general. A problem is that it is unlikely that there is such a thing as "typical" crime, and the crime most people know and experience is not representative of crime in general. A second way the public contributes to myths is by relying on inaccurate communication. Some people embellish crime experiences and thus distort their own conceptions or the conception of those to whom they communicate. A third way the public contributes to myths is by relying on atypical information. For those who are not aware that they have experienced crime, part of their conceptions of crime may come from atypical and unrepresentative experiences, embellished or otherwise, of family or friends, who may or may not have been victims themselves. Finally, the public contributes to myths through a lack of consciousness. There are many cases where the general public has no knowledge of victimization. For example, in cases of consumer fraud or medical negligence, people may never know that a crime has been perpetrated against them. In such cases, it would be difficult to conceptualize such actions as criminal.

The public perpetuates myths about crime, criminals and crime control policy because they serve at least three short-term interests: 1) they offer identities, 2) they aid comprehension by creating order, and 3) they help forge common bonds and create and reinforce a sense of community. Implicit in each of these interests, however, are important contradictions. Myths about "criminals" and "law-abiding citizens" offer identities. For many people, it is comforting to conceive of themselves as law-abiding citizens. Given the daily temptations to violate the law, those who do not, even in the face of great material deprivation, demonstrate a moral courage and a self-control that often forms the basis of their self-identities. Additionally, abiding by the law is considered by many as aspect of patriotism. This does not mean that law-violators necessarily consider themselves unpatriotic, but only that to be law-abiding and patriotic is an important part of many people's identities. This facet of patriotism is an emotion that politicians find it advantageous to exploit. For these reasons, many people find it in their interests to believe in and perpetuate the myth of the criminal and law-abiding citizen.

In reality, however, many self-conceived law-abiding citizens are engaging in self-delusion. No doubt there are a few paragons of virtue, but not many. Most people manifest common human frailties. For example, evidence suggests that over 90% of all Americans have committed some crime for which they could be incarcerated (Silver, 1968; Wallerstein and Wyle, 1957). This is not to imply that most Americans are murderers or robbers, for they are not. Criminality is a relative (and political) phenomenon. In his discussion of delinquency, Matza (1964) captures this relativity when he writes that juveniles drift between law-abiding and law-violating behavior. Whether a juvenile actually engages in a delinquent act depends on a host of factors, not the least of which is available opportunity. There are few delinquents or criminals whose entire life orientation is centered around delinquent or criminal activities. Consequently, it makes little sense to label an individual a "delinquent" or a "criminal" who occasionally gets into a fight, steals from a store, exceeds the speed limit, or cheats on income taxes. While these are "criminal" acts, the people who perpetrate them are not "criminals."

A contradiction is that the criminal role offers a different kind of identity to another segment of the population. For some, the criminal label is actively sought. The literature on juvenile delinquency is replete with examples of juveniles whose identity is based on their "rep" (reputation) for toughness, sexual prowess, institutional experience, etc. Many of those who assissinate or attempt to assissinate famous people are likely seeking a public identity that could not be achieved legitimately. This applies as well to many "notorious" criminals. A problem with labeling theory, in this regard, is an overemphasis on the negative consequences of the label or stigma—that individuals actively seek to avoid it. In many cases, as noted above, individuals actively seek the label as a goal. Myths do offer identities, criminal or otherwise, real or imagined; and people find it in their interest to believe in and perpetuate the myth of the criminal and law-abiding citizen.

Another way in which myths about crime and criminals contribute to identity is through the reinforcement and perpetuation of the myth of the individual. The concept of "individual," as used here, does not deny "individualism" but only refers in a limited sense to the idea of the "free-willed" being who acts on society without being acted on by society. Although the myth of the individual has informed philosophical and criminological thought at least since the Enlightenment, it became a part of popular consciousness and identity through existentialism and the human potential and other movements of the 1960s. It began influencing crime control policy again significantly by the mid-1970s.

However, as Foucault (1977:194) explains, "The individual is no doubt the fictitious atom of the 'ideological' representation of society..." The idea of the individual, as used here and portrayed in existentialism, for example, is an illusion precisely because human beings are necessarily social. Not only are human beings social by virtue of the social nature of self-identity and of relations with others, but also because of the social component (e.g., language) in the ability of human beings to conceive of anything at all (Ollman, 1976; Mead, 1972).

The idea of the "free-willed individual" finds characteristic expression in the current politically conservative interpretation of the "criminal" and his or her behavior. In this view, the criminal is considered an isolated being whose social environment is generally inconsequential or, at least, legally irrelevant to his or her criminal actions. Kennedy (1976:39) maintains that the notion of the criminal as individual was the product of an historical transformation from "the ethic of shared responsibility for individual conduct (the cooperative ethic) to the ethic of individual responsibility." He adds that this transformation "was fundamental to the birth of crime and penal sanction" and "to political, economic, religious, and familistic transformation generally..." Thus, states Kennedy (1976:38), "individualism as an attitude of self is basic to guilt, and as a premise of both civil and criminal law it is elemental to the whole legal practice of incrimination." A consequence is that the belief that the individual alone is responsible for his or her conduct diverts attention away from the structural elements in society that inevitably contribute to criminal behavior. (This last point will be discussed further in another context later.)

Another reason that myths find popular support is that they aid comprehension by creating order. Myths aid comprehension in two ways. They reduce contradictions and simplify complex phenomena.

As previously noted, myths about crime and criminals create a simple dichotomy that separates the "good guys" from the "bad guys." Quinney (1977:14) maintains that the myth of crime "provides the metaphor for our human nature; crime represents human nature in its 'less attractive form'." Consequently, for many people, the "criminal" is conceived as abnormal, irrational, evil or untrustworthy, while the "law-abiding citizen" is normal, rational, good and trustworthy. While dichotomies such as these can be useful heuristic devices, they necessarily abstract and distort reality.

Myths also aid comprehension by reducing contradictions, which is especially important when it comes to public conceptions about crime and crime control. One of the major contradictions that confronts American society is that one of the wealthiest and technologically advanced countries in the world contains widespread poverty, unemployment and crime. Historically, a myth that has been perpetrated to resolve this contradiction is that crime is an individual problem, the result of personal defect—especially of poor, young males between the ages of 15 and 24. Conceived of in this way, it follows that there is no social or structural solution to the problem of crime.

Another contradiction that perplexes many Americans is that at a time when more effort was expended and more money spent on crime control, the worse the problem got. Myths help people cope with the knowledge that crime control efforts have not lived up to expectations. For example, during the heyday of LEAA, when billions of dollars were presumably spent on crime control, crime became, in the minds of many, epidemic. However, when LEAA was disbanded and the monies expended on crime control were greatly reduced, the crime problem, according to official statistics, decreased. No doubt other factors were operating, but the impression given to many people must have been that the more we do, the worse we fail, which for many is a very disconcerting observation. It is likely that the current punitive attitude of a large segment of the public and the call for a result to the punishment model in crime control can be attributed at least in part to the simple solution that the punishment model offers to a seemingly intractable problem. A result is that the United States currently holds the distinction of incarcerating more of its citizens than any other country in the world with the exception of the Soviet Union and South Africa, and it is among one of the last countries outside of Africa and Asia to impose the death penalty.

Finally, crime myths contribute to public fear which helps forge common bonds and creates and reinforces a sense of community. Fear of crime makes people feel that they share the same boat. Crime crosses social barriers. In reality, however, the chance of actual victimization from the crimes most people fear is very unevenly divided among social groupings. Nevertheless, that matters little, since it is the abstract fear that helps unite people. Fear of crime also creates and reinforces a sense of community. Recent enthusiasm over neighborhood watch programs and the recent increase in vigilantism are two examples of the way that fear of crime brings people together.

A contradiction is that fear of crime also inhibits community. Because of fear, people are afraid to leave their homes and are suspicious of strangers. It is fear of crime, moreover, that politicians play upon in their "law and order" campaigns. Weighted together, it is likely that factors that inhibit community are more influential than those that create community.

In sum, the public perpetuates myths about crime, criminals or crime control policy because they serve at least three short-term interests:

1) they offer identities;
2) they aid comprehension by creating order; and
3) they help forge common bonds and create and reinforce a sense of community.

THE MEDIA

Perhaps the most important source of common conceptions and myths of crime, criminals and crime control policy is the media. As Vold observed, "crime waves are now and probably always have been products of newspaper headlines" (1935:803; also see Fishman, 1978). One thing is certain: the media presents a distorted crime picture to the public. According to one study, the factors that influence crime news selection are the seriousness of the offense, whimsical or unusual elements, sentimental or dramatic aspects and the involvement of famous or high-status persons (Roshier, 1973:34-35; also see Graber, 1980; Sheley and Ashkins, 1981).

The entertainment media has a particularly distorting effect on public conceptions of crime, criminals and crime control policies. Crime-related television programs have been estimated to account for about one-third of all television entertainment shows (Dominick, 1978). Information that the public receives from these shows is anything but accurate. Studies have indicated that

1) the least committed crimes, such as murder and assault, appear more frequently than those crimes committed more often, such as burglary and larceny;
2) violent crimes are portrayed as caused by greed or attempts to avoid detection rather than by passion accompanying arguments as is more typical;
3) the necessary use of violence in police work is exaggerated;
4) the use of illegal police tactics is seemingly sanctioned;
5) police officers are unfettered by procedural law; and
6) the police nearly always capture the "bad guys," usually in violent confrontations (Dominick, 1973; Pandiani, 1978; Gitlin, 1979).

Perhaps the principal reason why the entertainment media perpetuates such myths is that they attract a large viewing audience which, in turn, sells advertising. Whether more accurate presentations would be less appealing, however, is an empirical question yet to be answered. In any event, whether intentional or not, crime myths perpetuated by the media often do serve elite interests by, among other things, portraying crime in a particular manner. (Other ways in which crime myths serve elite interests are examined in a later section). The fact that most of the mass media in the United States are either owned by large corporations or are dependent on corporate advertising has been taken as evidence of a conspiracy among the elite to control public consciousness (Miliband, 1969; Halberstam, 1979; Dreier, 1982; Evans and Lundman, 1983). While such a view has a certain intuitive appeal and some empirical evidence to support it, the fact remains that the mass media, particularly of late, has been at the vanguard at exposing elite malfeasance. Whether the effort is sincere or merely an attempt to legitimate the media as an institution that serves the interests of the general public, as was the case with the federal regulation of corporate crime, is not clear. Intentions aside, there is no question that the mass media perpetuates a false conception of crime to the general public.

Another, though subtle, way the media affects common conceptions about crime, criminals and crime control policy is through public opinion polls. Erskine (1974) argues that the public's conception of crime may be the result of categories selected by pollsters. Erskine reports that 1965 was the first year (since 1935 when Gallup polled his first respondent) that crime appeared as a response to the question: "What do you think is the most important problem facing this country today?" The crime response, however, did not appear alone as a single category but was grouped in a category that included "immorality, crime and juvenile delinquency." Crime did not appear again as a response when the same question was asked until 1968 when it was grouped in a category of "crime and lawlessness, including riots, looting, and juvenile delinquency." The importance of the category in which crime is grouped in generating a response in underscored by Erskine who notes, "When categories such as unrest, polarization, student protest, moral decay, drugs, and youth problems began to be itemized separately, crime 'per se' began to rank relatively lower than it had previously" (1973:131). Furthermore, in response to the Harris Survey question—"In the past year, do you feel the crime rate in your neighborhood has been increasing, decreasing, or has it remained about the same as it was before?"—the conception of crime appears to be tied to a variety of events such as racial violence, assassination, war protest and campus unrest, as well as criminal activity (Erskine, 1974:131-2). In short, it is conceivable that people who were polled in both Gallup and Harris Surveys were responding either to non-criminal problems (e.g., unrest, polarization, student protest, moral decay, etc.) arbitrarily grouped together in a category that also included crime or to dramatic social events that artificially raised people's conceptions of the crime rate.

POLITICIANS

A third source of crime-related myths is politicians. As members of the public, politicians derive much of their knowledge in the same way as does the rest of the public. However, unlike much of the public, politicians also get knowledge about crime, criminals and crime control policy from academic criminologists and especially criminal justice officials. Since "law and order" rhetoric is often politically advantageous (for reasons already discussed), many politicians find it difficult not to disseminate popular myths.

ACADEMIC CRIMINOLOGISTS AND CRIMINAL JUSTICE OFFICIALS

A fourth source of crime-related myths is academic criminologists and criminal justice officials. Like politicians, they are members of the public and

and thus derive part of their conception of these subjects from their own experiences. However, if blame is to be leveled at any one group for perpetuating myths, then it should fall here, because academic criminologists and criminal justice officials should and often do know better. They are in the best position to dispel the myths. There are several reasons why they do not.

Many academic criminologists find it in both their short- and long-term interests to perpetuate myths. These interests, moreover, may be either cognitive or structural. Regarding the former, many academic criminologists, like other members of the general public, have internalized the myths as part of their social "reality." To challenge the myths would be, for many, to undermine long-established and fundamental conceptions of society. For many academic criminologists, what has been considered here as myth simply makes sense or attunes with preconceived ideas. To question the myths might create cognitive dissonance.

Other academic criminologists perpetuate myths because it is in their structural interests to do so. Platt (1975:106-7) suggests that this is because of academic repression and cooptation. My impression is that prestigious university appointments and promotions in general typically go to those academics whose work does not fundamentally challenge myths supportive of the status quo. It appears that prestigious journals rarely publish articles that radically deviate from an accepted, often myth-laden perspective (though this may reflect considerations other than ideology). Similarly, major research grants generally seem to be awarded to academics whose proposals do not fundamentally undermine privileged positions or deviate from preconceived, often myth-laden wisdom. Whether or not myths are perpetuated because of academic repression and cooptation, academic life is generally more pleasant for those who do not make waves.

Criminal justice officials perpetuate myths for at least four reasons. First, employment and advancement often depend on a responsiveness to the interests of political and economic elites. Administrators, in particular, are generally either elected to their positions or appointed to them by political electees. Since political election or appointment often depends on the support of political and economic elites, those who would dispel myths that serve interests of political and economic elites are not likely to find support forthcoming.

Second, in case of the police, the myth of increasing crime is used to justify larger budgets for more police officers and higher pay (Pepinsky and Jesilow, 1984:16-17 and 30). Third, as was the case with the general public, myths also provide order to the potentially chaotic role of the police officer. They allow police officers to believe that they can do the job (i.e., prevent or control crime). Finally, as was also the case with the general public, myths provide police officers with a basis of solidarity, common purpose and collective unity in the face of a hostile and potentially threatening environment.

SOCIAL ELITES

As part of the general public, social elites contribute to the perpetuation of myths in much the same way as do other members of the general public. It is doubtful, moreover, that political and economic elites conspire to perpetuate myths primarily because it is unnecessary for them to do so. Because myths serve at least the short-term interests of virtually all members of society, myths of crime, criminals and crime control policy probably would be perpetuated whether they served the interests of social elites or not. Nevertheless, social elites receive more significant and long-lasting advantages from the myths than any other social grouping. Social elites are also affected by the adverse consequences of the myths.

The principal way that myths about crime, criminals and crime control policy serve elite interests is by helping to secure and legitimate the social status quo with its gross disparities of wealth, privilege and opportunity. Two interrelated means by which myths help to accomplish this are by providing a scapegoat and by redirecting the defusing dissent.

In the first place, the "crime problem" in general has been used as a scapegoat for increasing political and economic distress (Quinney, 1977:6). Secondly, by focusing public attention on particular forms of crime (e.g., crimes of the poor), the belief that such crime is the basic cause of social problems obscures "the conditions of inequality, powerlessness, institutional violence, and so on, which lie at the bases of our tortured society" (Liazos, 1977:155).

In effect, almost every type of "reported crime" has served as a "scapegoat" for political and economic contradictions. Examples include: organized crime (Galliher and McCartney, 1977:376; Pearce, 1976; Simon, 1981), street crime (Center for Research on Criminal Justice, 1977:14), rape (Griffin, 1976:237), and juvenile delinquency (Platt, 1977:192; Foucault, 1977). Even the occasional prosecution of corporate crime has its advantages for social elites. It serves as a symbolic gesture that reinforces the belief that the law is applied uniformly to all persons (Pearce, 1976:90).

A major result of scapegoating is the polarization of the population into a "confident and supportive majority" and an "Alienated and repressible minority" (Clements, 1974). By creating a readily identifiable criminal group through scapegoating, willing obedience and popular support of the "noncriminal" majority are made less problematic, thus reducing the need for compulsion. If polarization were not accomplished, or if people (e.g., the poor) were not divided through a fear of being criminally victimized, for example, then they might unite to the detriment of social elites to press for the realization of their common interests (Wright, 1973:21; Chambliss, 1976:7; Pearce, 1976:90; Quinney, 1979).

Another result of scapegoating and another way that myths serve the interest of social elites is by redirecting or defusing dissent. One means by which dissent is redirected is the perpetuation of the myth that crime is primarily the work of the poor. Belief in this myth diverts the attention to the poor from the social and economic exploitation they experience to the criminality of their own class (Chambliss, 1976:8). Furthermore, the myth "deflects the discontent and potential hostility of middle America away from the classes above them and toward the classes below them" (Reiman, 1979:5; also see Pepinsky and Jesilow, 1984:42). In both cases, myth has the effect of directing attention away from the sources of crime that have the most detrimental consequences for society.

A primary way that dissent is defused is by supervising or institutionalizing potential dissidents. As Gordon (1976:208) relates, "If the system did not effect this neutralization, if so many of the poor were not trapped in the debilitating system of crime and punishment, then they might otherwise gather the strength to oppose the system which reinforces their misery." Thus, the criminalization of the poor negates their potential "for developing an ideologically sophisticated understanding of their situation...and by incarcerating them it is made difficult for them to organize the realize their ideas" (Pearce, 1976:81).

Ultimately, the success or failure of redirecting or defusing dissent depends on the degree to which the public accepts myths of crime, criminals and crime control policy as accurate descriptions of reality. Fortunately for social elites, myths are likely to be critically accepted by the public for the following reasons (besides those already noted): First, the ethic of individual responsibility, a "legal fiction" which is both socially and psychologically insupportable, obscures the state's causal role in crime (Kennedy, 1976:48). Second, most individuals have been socialized, to varying extents, to behave in conformity with the law (Schumann, 1976:292). Third, most criminal behavior represents impulsive reactions to unspecific social conflicts which rarely victimize the opponent in the underlying conflict, thus obscuring the "real" sources of social conflict (Schumann, 1976:292). Ironically, for the exploited, "much, if not most, crime continues to victimize those who are already oppressed...and does little more than reproduce the existing order" (Quinney, 1977:103). Fourth, most individuals who commit crimes attempt to conceal their illegal behavior from others, and, thus, remain isolated instead of attempting to develop solidarity with others (Schumann, 1976:292). Finally, most individuals are insulated from any abridgment of justice so that interpretations of justice made by the state are credible. For example, "systematic elimination or incarceration of a certain 'criminal element' must always be the objective and professional pursuit of the role of law..." (Clements, 1974:176).

CONCLUSION

As the preceding discussion shows, common conceptions of crime, criminals and crime control policy are to a rather large degree informed by myths. The myths are perpetuated not only because they serve elite interests, but also because they serve short-term interests of much of the general public.

Because myths serve elite interests by helping to secure and to legitimate the social status quo, and because social elites are less affected by the crimes most people fear, social elites have little incentive to dispel myths or to reduce crime. Ironically, social elites are the one group that could have a profound effect on changing the system that creates these problems (cf. Reiman, 1979).

The real irony is that the rest of the public helps perpetuate myths that inhibit the reduction of those actions or inactions that cause them harm and suffering. While myths do serve, in a perverted way, short-term interests of the general public, in the long-run, they inhibit comprehension of the fundamental changes necessary to bring about a reduction in harm and suffering. The poor, as a result, bear the bulk of the blame while continuing to be the most victimized; and the middle class, also victimized, must bear the bulk of the costs of policies that would not provide them the protection and the security they are seeking.

There are people who would like to perpetuate the myth that nothing can be done to significantly reduce crime in the United States. If the ameliorative reforms of the past are the sole indication, they may be right. However, there remains the possibility that a significant reduction can be achieved through, as yet tried, fundamental social change. Although the details of such a program are beyond the scope of this essay,[4] a first step is demystifying the myths that inform the ideology that inhibits fundamental social change. A promising means by which to achieve this goal is the development and the employment of a self-reflexive critical theory grounded in justifiable human interests (cf. Gouldner, 1976:292).

According to Ollman (1976), "reflexivity" may be distinguished by three characteristics. First is an awareness of oneself as an individual active in pursuing his own ends (Ollman, 1976:82). Evidence of this endowment include: 1) the ability to choose whether or not to act in any given situation (this includes the ability to forego gratification of short-term interests for achievement of long-term interests); 2) a purposefulness or an ability to plan actions before engaging in them; and 3) a mental and physical flexibility in regard to one's tasks (Ollman, 1976:110-112). Second is an awareness that actions of others have aims similar to, and even connected to, one's own (Ollman, 1976:82). For this reason, human activity is always social: "Even when it is not done with or for other men, production is social because it is based on the assumptions and language of a particular society" (Ollman, 1976:112). The last characteristic is an awareness of a past, which is the record of one's successes and failures in attaining one's aims and of the possibilities which constitute one's failure (Ollman, 1976:82). In sum, "reflexivity" is the "conscious, willed, purposive, flexible, concentrated and social facets which enable man to pursue the unique demands of his species" (Ollman, 1976:112).

Critical theory involves the critique of contemporary society; especially "the system of information publicly available through the concretely organized mass media" (Gouldner, 1976:159). Critical theory makes problematic generally unquestioned traditional belief. In this sense, critical theory is similar to traditional sociology, except in two important respects: 1) in the emancipatory values it explicitly seeks and 2) in the reflexive relation it has toward its own value commitments (Gouldner, 1976:292).

A self-reflexive critical theory, then, does not transcend ideology because of the assumption that nearly all human actions, and ideologies that inform them, are necessarily grounded in partisan interests. Since ideology cannot be transcended, it can only be reconstituted around other interests. Consequently, self-reflexive critical theory grounds its ideology in justifiable human interests and makes these interests problematic or subject to examination in their own right. Ultimately, self-reflexive critical theory seeks to demonstrate connections between knowledge, belief and human interests. It is hoped that this essay has contributed to that effort.

NOTES

1. According to Nimmo and Combs (1980:6), "at best, myths are simplistic and distorted beliefs based upon emotion rather than rigorous analysis; at worst, myths are dangerous falsifications." Specifically, a "myth" is:

    ...a credible, dramatic, socially constructed re-presentation of perceived realities that people accept as permanent, fixed knowledge of reality while forgetting (if they were ever aware of it) its tentative, imaginative, created, and perhaps fictional qualities (Nimmo and Combs, 1980:16).

    For examples of myths of crime, criminals, and crime control policy, see especially Reiman, 1979; Pepinsky and Jesilow, 1984; Walker, 1985.

2. For Gouldner (1976:30), "ideology" is "a call to action—a 'command' grounded in social theory," Ideology "presents a map of 'what is' in society; a 'report' of how it is working, how it is failing, and also how it could be changed" (Gouldner, 1976:30). "Interests," on the other hand, refer to "what it makes sense for people to want and do, given their overall situation" (Ollman, 1976:122). Although ideologies are partly legitimated by their claim to represent the "public interest," in practice, they nearly always represent private interests. This does not necessarily forbode undesirable social consequences, however, because there is often hidden public value in vested private interests (Gouldner, 1976:282).

3. "Exploitation," in this context, refers to the activity of one group preventing another group from "getting what they may as yet have no idea of, and therefore do not desire, but would prefer to their present condition if only they knew about it" (Plamenatz, 1963:322).

4. For some interesting "new" ideas, see Pepinsky and Jesilow, 1984.

References

American Friends Service Committee Working Party (1971) Struggle for Justice. New York: Hill and Wang.

Becker, H.S. (1973) Outsiders: Studies in the Sociology of Deviance. New York: Free Press.

Bittner, E. (1967) "The Police on Skid Row: A Study of Peace-Keeping." American Sociological Review 32:699-715.

——— (1975) The Functions of the Police in Modern Society. New York: Jason Aronson.

Bohm, R.M. (1982) "Radical Criminology: An Explication." Criminology 19:565-589.

Center for Research on Criminal Justice (1977) The Iron Fist and the Velvet Glove. Berkeley: Center for Research on Criminal Justice.

Chambliss, W.J. (1976) "Functional and Conflict Theories of Crime: the Heritage of Emile Durkheim and Karl Marx." In W.J. Chambliss & M. Mankoff [eds.], Whose Law What Order? New York: Wiley.

Clements, J.M. (1974) "Repression: Beyond the Rhetoric." In C.E. Reasons [ed.], The Criminologist: Crime and the Criminal. Pacific Palasades, CA: Goodyear.

Clinard, M.B. (1978) Cities with Little Crime: The Case of Switzerland. Cambridge, England: Cambridge University Press.

Dominick, J.R. (1973) "Crime and Law Enforcement on Prime-time Television." Public Opinion Quarterly 37:241-250.

Dreier, P. (1982) "The Position of the Press in the U.S. Power Structure." Social Problems 29:298-310.

Erskine, H. (1974) "The Polls: Fear of Violence and Crime." Public Opinion Quarterly, (Spring) 131:145.

Evans, S.S. and R.J. Lundman (1983) "Newspaper Coverage of Corporate Price-Fixing: A Replication." Criminology 21:529-541.

Ferdinand, T.N. (1977) "The Criminal Patterns of Boston Since 1849." In J.F. Galliher and J.L. McCartney [eds.], Criminology: Power, Crime and Criminal Law. Homewood, IL: Dorsey.

Fishman, M. (1978) "Crime Waves as Ideology." Social Problems 25:531-543.

Foucault, M. (1977) Discipline and Punish. New York: Pantheon.

Galliher, J.F. and J.L. McCartney (1977) Criminology: Power, Crime and Criminal Law. Homewood, IL: Dorsey.

Garmire, F., J. Rubin, and J.Q. Wilson (1972) The Police and the Community. Baltimore: Johns Hopkins University Press.

Gitlin, T. (1979) "Prime Time Ideology: The Hegemonic Process in Television Entertainment." Social Problems 26:251-266.

Gordon, D.M. (1976) "Class and the Economics of Crime." In W.J. Chambliss and M. Mankoff [eds.], Whose Law What Order? New York: Wiley.

Gouldner, A.W. (1976) The Dialectic of Ideology and Technology: The Origins, Grammar, and Future of Ideology. New York: Seabury.

Graber, D.A. (1980) Crime News and the Public. New York: Praeger.

Griffin, S. (1976) "Rape: the All-American Crime." In W.J. Chambliss and M. Mankoff [eds.], Whose Law What Order? New York: Wiley.

Grinspoon, L. (1977) Marijuana Reconsidered, Second Edition. Cambridge, MA: Harvard University Press.

Halberstam, D. (1979) The Powers That Be. New York: Knopf.

Helmer, J. (1975) Drugs and Minority Oppression. New York: Seabury.

Humphries, D. and D.F. Greenberg (1981) "The Dialectics of Crime Control." In D. Greenberg [ed.] Crime and Capitalism. Palo Alto, CA: Mayfield.

Kennedy, M.C. (1976) "Beyond Incrimination." In W.J. Chambliss and M. Mankoff [eds.], Whose Law What Order? New York: Wiley.

Liazos, A. (1977) "The Poverty of the Sociology of Deviance: Nuts, Sluts, and Perverts." In J.F. Galliher & J.L. McCartney [eds.], Criminology: Power, Crime and Criminal Law. Homewood, IL: Dorsey.

Lieberman, J.K. (1974) How the Government Breaks the Law. Baltimore: Penguin.

Lyerly, R.R. and J.K. Skipper, Jr. (1981) "Differential Rates of Rural-Urban Delinquency: A Social Control Approach." Criminology 19:385-399).

Manning, P. (1977) Police Work. Cambridge, MA: MIT Press.

_____ (1978) "Dramatic Aspects of Policing." In P. Wickman and P. Whitten [eds.], Readings in Criminology. Lexington, MA: D.C. Heath.

Martin, R.G. and R.D. Conger (1980) "A Comparison of Delinquency Trends: Japan and the United States." Criminology 18:53-61.

Marx, K. and F. Engels (1970) The German Ideology. New York: International Publishers.

Matzo, D. (1964) Delinquency and Drift. New York: Wiley.

Mead, G.H. (1972) On Social Psychology. Chicago: The University of Chicago Press.

Milakovich, M.D. and K. Weis (1977) "Politics and Measures of Success in the War on Crime." In J.F. Galliher and J.M. McCartney [eds.], Criminology: Power, Crime and Criminal Law. Homewood, IL: Dorsey.

Miliband, R. (1969) The State in Capitalist Society. New York: Basic Books.

Mintz, M. and J.S. Cohen (1971) American Inc.: Who Owns and Operates the United States? New York: Dial.

Musto, D.F. (1973) The American Disease: Origins of Narcotic Control. New Haven: Yale University Press.

Nimmo, D. and J.E. Combs (1980) Subliminal Politics: Myths and Mythmakers in America. Englewood Cliffs, N.J.: Prentice-Hall.

Ollman, B. (1976) Alienation (2nd Ed.). Cambridge: Cambridge University Press.

Paez, A.L. and R.W. Dodge (1982) "Criminal Victimization in the U.S." Bureau of Justice Statistics Technical Report. U.S. Department of Justice (July).

Pandiani, J.A. (1978) "Crime Time TV: If All We Know is What We Saw..." Contemporary Crises 2:437-258.

Pearce, F. (1976) Crimes of the Powerful. London: Pluto Press.

Pepinsky, H.E. (1980) Crime Control Strategies: An Introduction to the Study of Crime. New York: Oxford University Press.

Pepinsky, H.E. and P. Jesilow (1984) Myths that Cause Crime. Cabin John, MD: Seven Locks.

Plamenatz, J. (1963) Man and Society, Vol. 2 New York: McGraw Hill.

Platt, T. (1975) "Prospects for a Radical Criminology in the USA." In I. Taylor, P. Walton and J. Young [eds.] Critical Criminology. Boston: Routledge and Kegan Paul.

———— (1977) The Child Savers. Chicago: The University of Chicago Press.

Quinney, R. (1970) The Social Reality of Crime. Boston: Little, Brown.

———— (1977) Class, State and Crime. New York: David McKay.

———— (1979) Criminology (2nd Ed.) Boston: Little, Brown.

———— (1979b) "The Production of Criminology," Criminology 16:445-457.

Reiman, J.H. (1979) The Rich Get Richer and the Poor Get Prison: Ideology, Class and Criminal Justice. New York: Wiley.

———— and S. Headlee (1981) "Marxism and Criminal Justice Policy." Crime and Delinquency 27:24-47.

Reiss, A. (1971) The Police and the Public. New Haven: Yale Univesity Press.

Roshier, B. (1973) "The Selection of Crime News by the Press." In S. Cohen and J. Young [eds.], The Manufacture of News. Beverly Hills: Sage.

Schumann, K.F. (1976) "Theoretical Presuppositions for Criminology as a Critical Enterprise." International Journal of Criminology and Penology 4:285-294.

Sheley, J.F. and C.D. Ashkins (1981) "Crime, Crime News, and Crime Views." Public Opinion Quarterly 45:492-506.

Shelley, L.I. (1981) Crime and Modernization: The Impact of Industrialization and Urbanization on Crime. Carbondale, IL: Southern Illinois University Press.

Silver, I. (1968) Introduction to The Challenge of Crime in a Free Society. New York: Avon.

Simon, D.R. (1981) "The Political Economy of Crime." In S.G. McNall (eds.), Political Economy: A Critique of American Society. Glenview, IL: Scott, Foreman.

Simon, D.R. and D.S. Eitzen (1982) Elite Deviance. Boston: Allyn & Bacon.

Smith, R.C. (1970) "U.S. Marijuana Legislation and the Creation of a Social Problem." In D.E. Smith [ed.], The New Social Drug: Cultural, Medical, and Legal Perspectives on Marijuana. Englewood Cliffs, N.J.: Prentice-Hall.

Stack, S. (1984) Income Inequality and Property Crime: A Cross-National Analysis of Relative Deprivation Theory." Criminology 22:229-257.

Sutherland, E.H. and D.R. Cressey (1974) Criminology, 9th Ed. Philadelphia: J.B. Lippincott.

Vold, G.B. (1935) "The Amount and Nature of Crime." American Journal of Sociology 40:496-803.

Walker, S. (1985) Sense and Nonsense About Crime: A Police Guide, Monterey, CA: Brooks/Cole.

Wallerstein, J.S. and C.J. Wyle (1947) "Our Law-Abiding Lawbreakers." Probation 25:107-112.

Wilson, J.Q. (1968) Varieties of Police Behavior. Cambridge, MA: Harvard University Press.

_____ (1975) Thinking About Crime. New York: Vintage.

Wright, E.O. (1973) The Politics of Punishment. New York: Harper Colophon.

THE FORD PINTO CASE AND BEYOND: ASSESSING BLAME   17

Francis T. Cullen, William J. Maakestad & Gray Cavender

In 1968 the President's Commission on Law Enforcement and Administration of Justice concluded that "the public tends to be indifferent to business crime or even to sympathize with the offenders who have been caught" (1968:84). Now some might question the accuracy of the commission's assessment; indeed, it appears that the public has never been quite so sanguine about white-collar crime as governmental official and academicians have led us to believe (see Braithwaite, 1982a:732-733). Nevertheless, it would be too much to assert that the commission's evaluation of the views of the American citizenry was fully without empirical referent. For if the commission underestimated the willingness of the public to punish criminals of any sort, it was perhaps more correct in sensing that citizens had yet to define white-collar and corporate criminality as anything approaching a social problem.

By contrast, few social commentators today would seek to sustain the notion that the public considers upperworld illegality as "morally neutral conduct" (Kadish, 1963). To be sure, there are now and undoubtedly will continue to be calls for citizens both to sharpen their awareness of the dangers posed by the lawlessness of the rich and to demand that the state take steps to shield them from this victimization. Nonetheless, public awareness of white-collar and corporate crime has reached the point where the concept has become part of the common vernacular. Further, survey data indicate that the public judges such criminality to be more serious than ever before, is quite prepared to sanction white-collar offenders, and is far more cognizant of the costs of upperworld crime than had been previously imagined (Cullen, Clark, et al., 1982; Cullen et al., 1982, Cullen et al., forthcoming).

In light of the events of the past decade and a half, the finding that upperworld crime has emerged as an increasingly salient social issue is not surprising. Indeed, during this time we have witnessed what Katz (1980) has termed "the social movement against white collar crime" (Clinard and Yeager, 1978:258-262; 1980:12-15). Thus with Watergate and Abscam representing the more celebrated examples, prosecutions for political corruption have climbed markedly (Katz, 1980:161-164). Similarly, consumer groups have scrutinized corporate activities and asked what officials planned to do to put a halt to "crime in the suites" (Nader and Green, 1972). Meanwhile, investigative news reporters and news shows such as "60 Minutes" have told us much about improprieties ranging from kickbacks to the illegal dumping of chemical wastes that endanger lives (Brown, 1980). Mistrust has run so deep that physicians are now suspected of fraudulent Medicaid schemes, and hence states have moved to establish enforcement agencies to combat this possibility (Cullen and Heiner, 1979; Pontell et al., 1982). In 1977 the notion that white-collar crime is a serious problem received further reification when U.S. Attorney General Griffin Bell remarked that he would make such illegality his "number 1 priority."

It is clear, then, that consciousness about upperworld lawlessness rose, perhaps substantially, since the President's Commission on Law Enforcement and Administration of Justice [President's Commission] (1968) characterized public opinion about such matters as essentially disinterested. However, it is equally important to be sensitive to the particular content that this consciousness came to assume. On the one hand the social movement Katz speaks of alerted people to the enormous costs incurred by white-collar crime (Conklin, 1977; Schrager and Short, 1978) yet it did much more than this: It provided the additional message that the rich and powerful could exact these harms with impunity. Consequently, questions of justice and moral right were immediately suggested. The matter was thus not merely one of preventing victimization but of confronting why crime allows "the rich to get richer and the poor to get prison" (Reiman, 1979). As Katz (1980:178-179) has observed:

> The demand supporting the movement to date has been much more than a utilitarian concern for the efficient deterrence of antisocial conduct...In order to understand the expansion of "white collar

crime," we must understand the demand that unjust enrichment and unjustly acquired power be made criminal; not just that it be made unprofitable but that it be defined officially as abominable, that it be treated as qualitatively alien to the basic moral character of society.

In short, a core element of the movement against white-collar crime was to assert that the harms committed by the more and less advantaged be subject to the same moral mandates, particularly within our courts. Of course the very attempt to reshape moral boundaries is itself a manifestation of broader changes in the social context of any historical era (Erikson, 1966; Gusfield, 1967; Farrell and Swigert, 1982:27-51). While a complicated matter, two circumstances would appear to have done much to encourage and structure the nature of the attack on upperworld criminality that has emerged in recent times.

First, the unfolding of the civil rights movement focused attention on the intimate link between social and criminal justice. Pernicious patterns of racism and class discrimination were thus seen to be reproduced within the legal system. In turn it became incumbent upon political elites to explain why such inequities were allowed to prevail in our courts. Significantly, a second circumstance made answering this charge of perpetuating injustice an essential task for those in government: the "legitimacy crisis" facing the state (Friedrichs, 1979). Indeed such poignant happenings as Attica, Kent State, Vietnam, and Watergate, as well as the failure of the "Great Society" programs to fulfill promises of greater distributive justice, all combined to shake people's trust in the benevolence of the government (Rothman, 1978). In response, elected officials (like Jimmy Carter) felt compelled to campaign on their integrity and to claim that they would not show favor to criminals of any class. That is, political elites, under the press of the call for "equal justice," were placed in the position of having to publicly support the notion that the harms of the rich be brought within the reach of the criminal law. And as Piven and Cloward (1971, 1977) have demonstrated, when necessity moves political elites to define existing arrangements as unfair, the possibility of a social movement to refashion the social order is greatly enhanced. It would thus appear that, at least in part, elite definitions lent legitimacy and helped give life to the movement against white-collar crime.

Now, in this social climate, the behavior of corporations took on new meaning. The world of big business was seen to suffer, in Durkheim's (1951) terms, from "chronic anomie," a breakdown of any sense of ethical regulation. It was thus common to encounter articles which first asked, "How lawless are big companies?" and then answered that "a surprising number of them have been involved in blatant illegalities" (Ross, 1980). What is more, these infringements of existing legal and administrative standards not only involved enormous and ostensibly intentional harm, but also were seen to be greeted only rarely with the full force of the criminal law. Corporate actors were thus depicted as readily sacrificing human well-being for unjustly acquired profits with little worry over paying any real price; meanwhile those who had the misfortune of stealing lesser amounts through more customary means could anticipate no immunity from state sanction.

Notably, such imagery helped to precipitate not only public discussion and popular accounts about corporate malfeasance (e.g., Vandivier, 1972; Rodgers, 1974; Stern, 1976; Caudill, 1977; Dowie, 1979; Wright, 1979), but a proliferation of scholarship on the topic as well (e.g., Fisse, 1971, 1973, 1981; Geis, 1972; Geis and Edelhertz, 1973; Coleman, 1975; Stone, 1975; Elkins, 1976; Kriesberg, 1976; Duchnick and Imhoff, 1978; Yoder, 1979; Braithwaite, 1979, 1982b; Kramer, 1979; Braithwaite and Geis, 1982). Typically these academic writings followed a pattern of initially identifying the large costs of corporate illegality and lamenting the failure of existing enforcement strategies to diminish this pressing problem. The commentary would then turn to a consideration of whether such activity should be brought under the umbrella of the criminal law. In particular, two issues were debated: (1) Should corporations and their executives be held responsible for unlawful acts just as street criminals are? (2) Will efforts to use criminal sanctions really result in a reduction of corporate illegality?

These latter concerns as well as those discussed previously furnish a context for understanding both the very occurrence and importance of Ford Motor Company's prosecution for reckless homicide by the State of Indiana. It appears that the Ford Pinto case was very much a child of the times; succinctly stated, it is doubtful that Ford would have been brought to trial during a previous era. Yet is the case is best seen as a manifestation of the broad movement against white-collar crime—and, in particular, against corporate crime—it is also unique in the legal precedent it set, the publicity it received, and in the opportunity it provides to examine how more theoretical insights on corporate responsibility and control are shaped by the realities of the courtroom.

With these issues in mind the current endeavor attempts to present a case study of Ford's prosecution.[1] To be more exact, four matters are discussed below: Why was an indictment brought against Ford in Indiana? Why did the courts permit a corporation itself to be tried for a criminal offense? What transpired at the trial? And what will be the meaning of the case in the time ahead?

ASSESSING BLAME

On August 10, 1978, Judy and Lyn Ulrich and their cousin visiting from Illinois, Donna Ulrich, set out to play volleyball at a church some twenty miles away. While on U.S. Highway 33 in northern Indiana, the yellow 1973 Pinto they were driving was struck in the rear by a van. Within seconds their car was engulfed in flames. Two of the teenagers, trapped inside the vehicle, died quickly; the driver, Judy was thrown clear of the blazing Pinto with third-degree burns on more than 95% of her body. Though conscious following the accident, she died at a hospital eight hours later (Strobel, 1980).

As might be anticipated, the accident stunned those who witnessed the aftermath of the crash and soon sent shock waves throughout the local community of Elkhart. Yet, like many other fatal collisions, this might have been defined exclusively as a tragedy. Or, if wrongdoing was involved, law enforcement officials might have prosecuted the driver of the van. Indeed, as a 21-year-old who had just recently reacquired a suspended license and who was driving a van which was labeled "Peace Train" and contained half-empty beer bottles as well as the remains of marijuana cigarettes scattered on the floor, he would have made a likely candidate to take the rap.

However, both the particulars of the accident and the tenor of the times led the blame to be placed elsewhere. In particular the observations of State Trooper Neil Graves were crucial in determining that this was not a "normal crime" (Sudnow, 1965). After arriving at the scene of the crash, Graves discovered that gasoline had somehow soaked the front floorboard of the car. He found as well that the van had sustained only minor damage, and its driver, Richard Duggar, was only mildly injured. By contrast, the Ulrichs' Pinto was viciously crushed in the rear and, of course, badly charred. This oddity was made even more poignant when eyewitnesses reported that the van was not speeding and that it looked initially like the accident was going to be nothing more than a fender-bender (Strobel, 1980).

These inconsistencies might have been set aside had it not been that Trooper Graves recalled reading an exposé about the Pinto some months before. This piece, written by Mark Dowie (1977) and entitled "Pinto Madness," alleged that the placement of the gas tank on the Pinto constituted a lethal hazard. Specifically, Dowie noted that the location of the tank adjacent to the rear bumper made it highly susceptible to puncture by the fender's bolts during a rear-end collision. In turn, this meant that the Pinto would experience considerable fuel leakage and hence fires when hit even at low speeds.

Yet this is not all that Dowie claimed. Far more controversial was his assertion that Ford was fully aware of this problem in the initial stages of production but chose not to fix the Pinto's defect because it was not cost efficient. To bolster this conclusion, he presented secret Ford memoranda which revealed that the financial loss of a recall exceeded the loss incurred as the result of injuries and fatalities "associated with crash-induced fuel leakage and fires." In the name of profit, Dowie believed, "for seven years the Ford Motor Company sold cars in which it knew hundreds of people would needlessly burn to death."[2]

Sensitized to the potential dangers of the Pinto, Graves was thus aware that the blame for the accident might rest with Ford. This sentiment was reinforced when he began to receive calls from news reporters around the country inquiring about the crash and the possibility that the fuel tank defect may have been responsible for the deaths of the three teenagers. Meanwhile, Michael A. Cosentino, Elkhart County's State's Attorney, was apprised of the accident. When he had an opportunity to review photographs of the crash, he too was troubled by the discrepancy between the minimal damage to the van and the wreckage of the Ulrich girls' Pinto. And then there was the emotional, human side to the accident: the pictures of the charred remains of the victims and the reality that three teenagers had suffered a terrible death (Strobel, 1980; Cosentino interview).

As a 41-year-old conservative Republican county prosecutor, Cosentino was an unlikely candidate to try to bring Ford Motor Company within the reach of the criminal law. Like many people at this time, he had heard about the problems associated with the Pinto and about the recall of the car that Ford had begun earlier in the summer. However, he had not read Dowie's article, and he was not inclined to attack corporations because of an ideological persuasion that they constituted a menace to society. Indeed, even now, Cosentino is convinced that the civil law should be used to deal with "99 percent" of all cases involving alleged corporate misbehavior (Cosentino interview).

Yet in light of the facts surrounding the accident and of conversations with Neil Graves (who by this time had called and talked with Mark Dowie), Cosentino could not easily put the matter aside. He was aware as well that Indiana's revised criminal code, which had become effective on October 1, 1977, less than a year before the accident, contained a provision for the offense of "reckless homicide." Section 35-42-1-5 of the Indiana Code thus read: "A person who recklessly kills another human being commits reckless homicide." Taken together, these considerations led Cosentino to wonder whether the Ford Motor Company could or should be criminally prosecuted. Because of the novelty of the case, the power of Ford, and the difficulty of piercing the corporate veil, Cosentino did not seriously consider prosecuting individual Ford executives (Cosentino interview).

Cosentino, however, did not want to act precipitously. Therefore, he set out to explore whether Ford could in fact be prosecuted under Indiana law. Since Section 35-41-1-2 of the penal code included "corporation" under its definition of "person," his staff reported that a prosecution was legally permissible. This conclusion was corroborated by William Conour of the Indiana Prosecuting Attorney's Office, who had been involved in drafting the reckless homicide statute (Strobel, 1980).

But even though the potential for prosecution seemed to exist, the question remained whether Ford really should be charged with a criminal offense. Research conducted by Cosentino and his staff suggested that it should be. Particularly influential were the conversations with and documents supplied by those involved in civil judgments against Ford. The prosecutor was in contact, for example, with automobile experts who had testified against Ford in civil hearings and with Mark Robinson, who was the lawyer in the Alan Grimshaw case.[3] As the evidence from these varied sources who had been close to the Pinto scene accumulated, it became clear that Ford knew that its Pinto was defective and chose to risk human life by not moving quickly to fix it. Thoughts of criminal culpability did not seem out of place in this context (Maakestad, forthcoming).

It is important to note here that, without the mounting attention concerning Ford's handling of the Pinto, it would have been unlikely that Cosentino would have come to blame Ford for the deaths of the three teenagers. Had the accident occurred several years before, he might have been forced, perhaps reluctantly, to put aside the peculiarities of the crash and move on to other cases. Yet now the social climate worked against this option and, alternatively, made a criminal prosecution seem plausible, if not obligatory. By August of 1978 the attack against Ford and its Pinto had emerged as a "symbolic crusade" (Gusfield, 1967), a movement aimed at showing that Ford, like other powerful corporations, felt comfortable in operating outside accepted moral boundaries in its irresponsible pursuit of profit. Ford's handling of the Pinto thus came to symbolize what was wrong with corporate America.

In general terms Dowie's (1977) "Pinto Madness" article, its release trumpeted at a press conference sponsored by Ralph Nader, signaled the beginning of the "crusade" against Ford. With concern over corporate crime running high, Dowie's article earned national exposure. In February of 1978 the movement intensified still further with the announcement of the exorbitant financial damages awarded in the Grimshaw civil case. At the same time the National Highway Traffic Safety Administration (NHTSA), a federal regulatory body, had undertaken tests on the Pinto. In May of 1978, NHTSA notified Ford that there had been "an initial determination of the existence of a safety-related defect" (quoted in Strobel, 1980:23). Denying any wrongdoing but faced with pressure on all sides, Ford subsequently issued a recall of all Pintos manufactured from 1971-1976 and all 1975-1976 Bobcats, a total of 1.5 million cars (Strobel, 1980). As might be expected, this series of events sparked a marked escalation in the focus placed by the media on Pinto issues (Swigert and Farrell, 1980-1981). Indeed, it was clear that reporters had come to view the Ford Pinto matter as a fascinating and eminently newsworthy upperworld scandal.

Thus it is significant that Mike Cosentino confronted the Ulrichs' tragic accident in the midst of a general crusade against Ford, for in several ways this necessarily shaped what the case could and did come to mean to him. First, unlike the traffic fatalities he had processed in the past, the numerous calls that his office and Neil Graves received from reporters across the nation alerted him, if only vaguely at the start, to the fact that any Pinto crash was potentially of national concern. Second, the movement against Ford, while certainly informal and unorganized, nevertheless created invaluable informational networks. This meant that in a matter of days Cosentino acquired revealing documents and expert feedback from parties who harbored strong sentiments against Ford. Under normal circumstances, such material would have either been unavailable or taken months to uncover, a task beyond the resources of a county prosecutor. Third, the ideological framework of the Pinto crusade provided the conservative state's attorney with a vocabulary about the case that encouraged a response by the criminal law. As Swigert and Farrell (1980-1981) have demonstrated, accounts of the Pinto appearing at this time increasingly characterized Ford as willfully and without repentance inflicting harm on innocent citizens. In a sense, then, Ford was being designated as a sociopath which knew no social responsibility.

In short Cosentino quickly learned that the death of the Ulrich girls was not a local or isolated occurrence and that Ford, like the worst of criminals, endangered its victims not inadvertently but intentionally. He was aware as well that evidence existed that made a prosecution feasible. Taken together, these considerations personally convinced Cosentino that Ford had acted recklessly and should be prosecuted. Again he did not wish to initiate a campaign calling for the use of criminal sanctions to deal with all corporate wrongdoing. However, it was manifest to him that Ford had been largely unaffected by traditional forms of control; after all, Ford's conduct surrounding the Pinto had already triggered nearly every legal response possible other than criminal prosecution: civil cases involving compensatory damages, civil cases involving both compensatory and punitive damages, and federal administrative agency actions. In absence of effective regulation and where corporate behavior is so outrageous as to affront moral sensibilities, Cosentino could see the application of the criminal law as appropriate. And from what he knew of the Pinto case, it seemed that this was just such an instance, where justice demanded that a corporation be held criminally responsible for its behavior (Cosentino interview; Maakestad, forthcoming).

However, the very novelty of this idea caused Cosentino to exercise caution. While he believed that Ford should be indicted and that he possessed the authority to do so, he was not certain that the community would support such a prosecution. Consequently, he convened a grand jury to consider an indictment under the reckless homicide statute. From the beginning of the hearing, Cosentino consciously made every effort not to sway the grand jury one way or the other (Cosentino interview). Nevertheless, after entertaining testimony from both Ford officials and safety experts who had previously served as witnesses in civil cases against Ford, the grand jury unanimously returned indictments against Ford Motor Company for three counts of reckless homicide. In essence, the six-member panel agreed with Cosentino that there was sufficient evidence to believe that Ford had acted with moral irresponsibility. Swigert and Farrell (1980-1981:180) captured this point when they wrote:

> The indictment against Ford may be viewed as an attempt on the part of the state to assert moral integrity in the face of enemy deviation. In its decision to contest civil suits, the corporation refused to recognize that moral boundaries had been transgressed. This opened the way to a definition of the manufacturer as a force against whom the power of the law must be directed.[4]

GETTING TO TRIAL

Word of Ford's indictment immediately received front-page attention in newspapers across the nation. It now appeared that Ford Motor Company, at that moment the fourth largest corporation in the world (Clinard et al., 1980:3), would go to trial for reckless homicide. While a guilty verdict would bring only a $30,000 fine ($10,000 on each count), company officials viewed the prospect of a trial with considerable consternation. With Pinto sales already down 40%, due to the recent recall, a lengthy, highly publicized criminal case could only serve to erode still further consumer confidence in the car and, more generally, in the corporation. Equally troubling was that a prosecution could encourage state's attorneys elsewhere to bring criminal charges against the company and alert other Pinto victims (or surviving families) to the fact that Ford should be held civilly liable for burn injuries occurring in rear-end collisions (Strobel, 1980). Moreover, executives realized that a criminal conviction would be powerful evidence of Ford's culpability in any subsequent civil suits. With the potential costs of a prosecution running high, Ford thus quickly mobilized to see that the case would never come before a jury.

The task of preventing a trial was given to the prestigious Chicago law firm of Mayer, Brown, and Platt. With a ten-member team assigned to the case, the result of the firm's efforts was a 55-page motion which argued that the criminal indictment should be dismissed on both conceptual and constitutional grounds. In fashioning a response to this attack, Cosentino and his small staff realized that they could well benefit from additional assistance. However, all such help would have to come from volunteers. Cosentino had asked Elkhart County for a special fund of $20,000 to try the case, and he had promised not to request any additional moneys. This figure would have to be stretched far in the fight against Ford; in fact, Cosentino would eventually spend money of his own to defray expenses (Strobel, 1980). Yet, given the prevailing social context, finding law professors to join the prosecution's team did not prove overly difficult. After all, corporate liability and the criminal law was a "hot topic," and the Pinto case obviously possessed both important national and legal ramifications. Again, whether a local prosecutor could have so readily acquired such expert assistance in a previous decade or on a different case is questionable. Bruce Berner, one of the two law professors who worked full time on the case,[5] wrote that "originally, of course, I got involved because of the novel legal questions presented by the indictment." However, it should also be realized that, after agreeing to become part of the prosecution's staff, the appeal of legal novelties was not all that sustained the commitment of volunteers to the case. There was also and always the reality of the horrible deaths of the Ulrich girls. In Berner's words (letter to author, February 21, 1982):

> It was only after I became involved that I saw the photographs [of the girls following the crash] and met the families of the girls. It is nevertheless hard for me to separate the motivating force of the legal issues from that of the personal aspect of the tragedy... Part of what we were saying is that a corporation like all other persons must be forced at all times to look at the very personal tragedies it causes. It seems to me that Ford's whole effort in keeping the pictures of the girls out of evidence, including the pictures of them while they were alive, was in part a way to disconnect themselves from what they had wrought to some very nice people. All I can say about the "Car Wars" photos was that they made me ill and that I cannot, to this day, get them out of my head.[6]

While numerous arguments were voiced in the debate over whether Ford could be brought to trial, the continued vitality of the indictment hinged on two central issues (Maakestad, 1980, 1981, forthcoming). To begin with, Ford's legal brief contended that conceptually the reckless homicide statute could not be applied to corporate entities. For one thing the statute defines the offense as "a person who recklessly kills another human being." Ford claimed in turn that the meaning of "another" was "one of the same kind." Consequently, since the victim is referred to as "another human being," it followed that the perpetrator of the crime must also be human (Clark, 1979). For another thing, the brief asserted that the use of the word "person" in other places in the criminal code clearly is not meant to apply to corporations. Conceptual consistency thus would preclude corporations from being charged with violently oriented offenses like reckless homicide. Quoting Ford's memorandum:

> There are numerous examples in the Criminal Code where the legislature has used the word "person" to refer exclusively to human beings. See, e.g., the section prohibiting rape... ("A person who knowingly or intentionally has sexual intercourse with a member of the opposite sex...") Thus, although corporations may generally be covered by the definition of "persons," there are clearly crimes— essentially crimes of violence against other human beings—where it is irrational to read the statutes as applying to corporations.

In response to this line of reasoning, the prosecution initially turned to the penal code itself. First, it observed that the code distinguishes between a "person" ("a human being, corporation, partnership, unincorporated association, or governmental entity") and a "human being" ("an individual who is born and alive"). Because the statute defines reckless homicide as a "person who recklessly kills another human being," rather than as a "human being who recklessly kills another human being," it is evident that the legislative intent here is to encompass corporate behavior. Second, the prosecution noted that the Indiana criminal code explicitly reads that a corporation "may be prosecuted for any offense...if it is proved that the offense was committed by its agent within the scope of his authority." Finally, the state's brief dismissed the idea that "corporations" cannot physically commit violent crimes like rape and homicide by emphasizing the realities of the corporation as a legal fiction:

> The major premise that "person" cannot include corporation in the rape statute is simply incorrect. This argument patently exploits the

corporate fiction. It attempts to show corporate inability to commit rape... Of course, a corporation cannot itself engage in sexual intercourse; a corporation cannot itself do anything. As it is a fictional person, it can act only through its natural-person agents. A corporation has no genitals, to be sure, but neither does it have a trigger finger, a hand to forge a check, an arm to extend a bribe nor mind to form an intent or to "consciously disregard" the safety of others. Nevertheless, a corporation is liable for all crimes of its agents acting within their authority. The unlikelihood of corporate rape liability is because sexual intercourse by its agents will almost always be outside the scope of their authority—not because the crime is definitionally ridiculous.

Apart from conceptual considerations Ford maintained that there were two constitutional barriers to its being brought to trial. First, there was the matter that the National Traffic and Motor Vehicle Safety Act had already created a federal apparatus to supervise the automobile industry. Consequently, Ford argued, Congress intended that this system would preempt any state, including Indiana, from regulating the same field. In rebuttal, the prosecution argued that the federal measure was not invoked to deprive states of their police power, and they observed that Ford was unable to cite "a single case where a traditional, general criminal statute was found to have been preempted by a federal regulatory scheme."

Yet there was a second, more serious constitutional matter raised by Ford's lawyers: the ex post facto provision of both the Indiana and U.S. Constitutions. As may be recalled, the revised Indiana code which contained the new reckless homicide crime category became law only on October 1, 1977. Moreover, it was not until July 1, 1978—41 days prior to the Ulrichs' crash—that the reckless homicide offense was amended to include acts of omission as well as commission. Significantly, it is the amended version of the statute which was employed to indict Ford. In light of these two dates, Ford reminded the court that it was being charged with recklessly designing and manufacturing a car that was a 1973 model. It was thus being prosecuted for an act that had transpired several years before enactment of the very law under which it was being charged. Even if its acts were reckless, such ex post facto application of the law constitutionally barred prosecution.

The prosecution assaulted Ford's logic on two fronts. First, issue was taken with Ford's interpretation of when its offense occurred. Contrary to Ford's assertions, the prosecution argued that it is the date the offense is completed, not the date of the first element of the crime, that determines whether ex post facto provisions have been violated. Thus, since the accident postdated the reckless homicide law, the company was potentially subject to criminal sanction. Second, the prosecution maintained that the defendant's omissions in regard to its obligation to either repair the Ulrichs' 1973 Pinto or warn them of the car's hazards were important elements of the offense. That is, Ford was being charged with reckless homicide not only for an act of commission (building a dangerous vehicle), but for an act of omission (ignoring its duty to protect owners from the Pinto's known dangers). The prosecution then went on to propose that once either proscribed acts or omissions are shown to have taken place after a criminal statute is enacted, all of the defendant's prior acts and omissions can properly and constitutionally be considered by the court.

On February 2, 1979, Judge Donald W. Jones succinctly rendered his decision: "There are substantial factors in this case for which there are no precedents. The indictment is sufficient. I therefore deny the motion to dismiss" (quoted in Strobel, 1980:55). In large part Judge Jones embraced the prosecution's reasoning, agreeing that Indiana law does permit a corporation to be charged for reckless homicide and that federal regulatory statutes did not in this instance preempt the state's rights to seek retributive and deterrent goals unique to the criminal sanction. However, he was only partially persuaded by the prosecution's thoughts on the ex post facto aspects of the case, and thus he attempted to clarify exactly what Ford could and could not be tried under.

In essence Jones's ruling declared that since the vehicle was marketed in 1973, Ford could not be charged for recklessly designing and manufacturing the Pinto. Instead, its actions with regard to the actual production of the Pinto were relevant only to the extent that they constituted antecedents for Ford's alleged recklessness in repairing the vehicle. Alternatively, Ford could be charged with failure to fulfill its obligation to repair, because such recklessness could potentially have occurred in the 41 days between the enactment of the omission amendment to the reckless homicide statute on July 1 and the Ulrich girls' deaths on August 10.

The problems surrounding the ex post facto issue clearly complicated the prosecution's case. At least in theory it would no longer be sufficient to convince the jury that Ford had recklessly assembled the Pinto. To be sure, this much would have to be proven in order to show that Ford knew its product was unsafe and thus had a duty to warn its customers, including the Ulrichs, of this fact. However, Ford could now only be convicted if it could also be revealed that the company had recklessly ignored its duty to inform the Ulrichs of the Pinto's dangers in the period following July 1.

In sum, with the help of law professors and other volunteers, Cosentino had succeeded in getting Ford to trial. However, the legal constraints on his case, the realities of the courtroom, and the resources at his opponent's disposal would make getting a conviction another matter.

TRYING FORD

Ford's failure to quash the indictment taught the company that their foes were perhaps more formidable than initially imagined. It was now manifest that nothing could be spared in order to avert the shame of a criminal stigmatization. In particular, Ford's lawyers would be given a blank check; they would be free to craft the best defense money could buy.

For Ford two orders of business were immediately at hand. First, there was the crucial matter of whom to select to head the defense team. The choice proved to be a wise, if expensive, one; James J. Neal, a former special prosecutor during Watergate.[7] The second pressing concern was to move Cosentino off his home turf by securing a change of venue. Based on evidence gathered from a survey of Elkhart residents about the case (commissioned by Ford) and the testimony of $1000-a-day consultant Hans Zeisel (co-author with Harry Kalven of The American Jury), Ford argued that it could not receive a fair trial in Elkhart.[8] Judge Jones agreed, and the case was moved to Winamac, a town of 2450 located in Pulaski County some 55 miles southwest. Sixty-year-old Judge Harold Staffeldt would preside over the trial (Strobel, 1980).

The move to Winamac and the additional living expenses this entailed further strained the prosecution's budget; Cosentino himself would shoulder much of this new burden. However, as would become evident throughout the trial, there appeared to be no limit to the resources that Ford was able and willing to devote to its defense. The cost of the survey employed to justify the change of venue itself approximated the entire Cosentino budget. Other facts are equally revealing. For instance, after the place of the trial became known Ford quickly made an attractive offer to and succeeded in retaining a local Winamac lawyer who was a close friend of Judge Staffeldt and who had practiced with the judge for 22 years. Similarly, the bill for housing the Ford defense team, which at times reached 40, ran to $27,000 a month. Later they would undertake additional crash tests on Pintos at a cost of around $80,000. Importantly, they were also able to purchase daily transcripts of the trial at $9 a page, with the total expenditure for the trial transcripts being $50,000 (Strobel, 1980). Since the complexity and length of the trial meant that a private firm supplied the court stenographers and thus that the transcripts were not available free to the prosecution, budgetary constraints precluded Cosentino from having access to this material. In his opinion the inability to review previous testimony (e.g., to prepare for cross-examination) was one of the largest disadvantages plaguing the prosecution (Cosentino interview). In the end it is estimated that Ford may have spent anywhere from $1.5 million to $2 million on its defense.

In launching its case, the prosecution wanted to impress upon the members of the jury that they were not merely dealing with statistical casualties; like other homicide cases, they were being asked to assess whether Ford should be held responsible for the horrible burn deaths of three vibrant teenagers. James Neal, however, fully realized that it would be important to neutralize this emotional factor. In a skillful maneuver he thus submitted a document which first admitted that the Ulrich girls had died as a result of burns and then declared that there was no need for the jury to see the grotesque pictures of or hear testimony about the girls' charred bodies. The prosecution countered that Neal was endeavoring to "sanitize" the girls' deaths and that it is common practice to present evidence on cause of death in a homicide trial. Somewhat amazingly, Judge Staffeldt agreed with Neal and prevented the jury from seeing or hearing about what the reality of the crash entailed. Stymied on this front, the emotional advantage of the prosecution was largely confined to the remarks of the victims' mother, Mrs. Mattie Ulrich, who told the court that she would have gotten rid of the Pinto had she known of its dangers. She then remarked that she had in fact received notice of the Pinto recall; however, it came to her house in February of 1979, several months after the crash in which her two daughters and niece had perished (Strobel, 1980).

Despite this setback the prosecution remained optimistic. After all, the foundation of its case was not erected upon the angle of playing on the jurors' sympathies. Instead, Cosentino felt that the Pinto had a defective fuel tank placement. This material included internal Ford memos and documents commenting on the Pinto's safety as well as the results of crash tests on 1971 and 1972 models, conducted by Ford and the government, showing that the vehicle exploded in flames at low impact speeds. These tests would be crucial, Cosentino reasoned, because they revealed that in planning the production of the 1973 Pinto, Ford had concrete evidence of the car's defects yet chose not to rectify them. Moreover, Cosentino did not have crash tests at low speeds for the 1973 model, and his tight budget precluded his conducting them at this stage.

Recognizing the damaging nature of this evidence, Neal moved quickly to challenge the admission of any testimony or tests that were not directly related to the 1973 Pinto, the model year of the Ulrichs' car. In a series of rulings over the course of the trial, Judge Staffeldt concurred with Neal and barred nearly all materials that predated 1973. Needless to say, this had the result of seriously undermining the state's case. In the end, only a small percentage, perhaps as low as 5 percent, of the documents the prosecution had compiled were admitted as evidence (Anderson, 1981:370, n.20).

The judge's reluctance to permit the jury to consider the totality of the prosecution's case points up the difficulty of transporting what has traditionally been a product liability case from civil into criminal court. To a large extent it appears that the rural judge was never fully comfortable in knowing how this was to be done. Indeed, his grabbing onto 1973 as his evidentiary standard reveals that he either did not fully comprehend the logic of the prosecution's case or did not embrace the legal theory on which it was based. It seems that he wished to treat the 1973 Pinto as he would any other weapon in a homicide case: Since it was this weapon that caused the crime, evidence on other weapons was irrelevant. Of course, at the heart of the prosecution's case was the understanding that Ford's recklessness with regard to the 1973 Pinto was intimately contingent on what the corporation had done in its product development of the car line in the previous years. Whether rightly or wrongly, Judge Staffeldt failed to appreciate this distinction between the recklessness of corporate decision-making and that involved in more traditional forms of criminality.

Now with much of its case set aside, the prosecution presented two major lines of argument to the jury. First, it called in auto safety experts, including a former Ford executive who testified that the fuel tank on the Pinto was placed in a potentially lethal position. Second, Cosentino relied upon eyewitnesses to prove that Duggar's van was traveling at 50 miles per hour or less and that the Ulrichs' Pinto was still moving when hit from behind. Taken together, these facts indicated that the speed differential at the moment of impact was around 30. In turn, establishing this low differential was crucial to the prosecution's case because it explained both why so little damage was done to the van and why the girls died from their burns but not from injuries sustained in the crash, as would be expected in a high-velocity collision. Most importantly, however, it showed that the Pinto the girls were driving exploded despite being hit at a relatively low speed. The implication was thus clear: Because of Ford's reckless construction of the Pinto, three girls died in an accident that should have been little more than a fender-bender.

Having done much to diminish the force of the prosecution's case, James Neal began Ford's defense by vigorously rejecting the claim that the Pinto was an unsafe vehicle. For instance, Neal brought his own automotive experts before the jury to testify that the 1973 Pinto met prevailing federal automotive standards and was just as safe as comparable subcompacts manufactured at that time. He also produced Ford executives who testified that they had such faith in the car that they had purchased Pintos for members of their own families. Neal then challenged the prosecution's version of the speed differential between the van and the Ulrichs' Pinto. Crucial in this regard were the dramatic accounts of two surprise witnesses; both claimed that prior to her death in the hospital Judy Ulrich had said that her car was stopped on the highway. If so, the speed at impact would have been 50 miles per hour, a collision that no small car could have withstood. This reasoning was given added credence when Ford presented newly conducted crash tests which showed that at 50 miles per hour a van would sustain only minimal damage despite the large crushing effect it exerted on the rear of the Pinto. Neal thus concluded from this that the small front-end wreckage of Duggar's van was not evidence of a low-impact accident but was normal, even at speeds exceeding 50 (Strobel, 1980).

The defense also took pains to remind the jurors that Ford itself had voluntarily agreed to recall the Pinto two months before the Ulrich accident and thus during all 41 days following the enactment of the omission amendment to the reckless homicide statute. Ford employees testified that during this period the company had pressured them to contact Pinto owners about the recall as quickly as possible. To accomplish this task, workers were given overtime pay, and airplanes were used to hurry recall kits across the nation. With 1.5 million customers it was not surprising, though of course terribly regrettable, that the Ulrichs' notification did not arrive until February 1979. Indeed, Ford had done everything feasible to warn Pinto owners; it certainly had not been reckless in this duty (Strobel, 1980).

After four days of exhausting deliberations, the jurors returned their verdict: not guilty. The initial vote was 8-4 to acquit. Twenty-five ballots later, the final holdout changed his mind and joined the majority. Some on the jury felt that the hazards of the Pinto were basically inherent in all small cars and that owners took certain risks when they chose a vehicle that was less costly and consequently less sturdy. A number of other jurors, however, were convinced that Ford had marketed a defective automobile, but that the prosecution simply had not proven that the corporation was reckless in its recall efforts during the 41 days in which it was criminally liable (Strobel, 1980). Regardless, the ten-week Ford Pinto trial was now over. As might be anticipated, there was much jubilation and relief at Ford headquarters in Dearborn, Michigan (Time, 1980). Meanwhile, Cosentino and his staff were left to contemplate the bitterness of an unsuccessful crusade and to wonder what might have occurred had a different judge presided over the case and the prosecution not been burdened by a tight budget and ex post facto considerations.

CONCLUSION: BEYOND THE FORD PINTO CASE

The Ford Pinto trial was regularly hailed in the media as "one of the most significant criminal court trials in American corporate history" (Newsweek, 1980). This notoriety clearly signifies the uniqueness of the case. While Ford's prosecution was not totally devoid of legal precedents (Maakestad, 1981), it was certainly the most poignant example of a corporation being brought within the reach of the criminal law for allegedly visiting violence upon innocent citizens (Anderson, 1981). In this light it thus provided a rare and concrete glimpse of the power that corporations can bring to bear in order to avoid conviction. Similarly, it revealed that prosecution of corporations for offenses of a product liability type will necessarily involve legal theories with which participants in the criminal justice system are only vaguely familiar and perhaps find inappropriate for their arena. Indeed, from an ideological standpoint, the potential for irony here is pronounced: We can expect conservative jurists now to be inclined to look favorably on the rights of the defendant (the corporation) and their more liberal brethren to furnish a more generous interpretation of the prerogatives enjoyed by the state. Finally, the very fact of prosecution is notable not merely for its role in bolstering formal legal precedent but in breaking psychological barriers. The legal community is now sensitized to the possibility that companies that recklessly endanger the physical well-being of the public may, even by a local state's attorney, be held criminally responsible for their conduct.

Yet the special character of the Pinto case should not mask the realization that Ford's prosecution was very much a social product. As argued earlier, the more general crusade against the Pinto, itself a manifestation of a broader movement attacking corporate crime that sought to question the appropriate moral boundaries of corporate behavior, was integral in creating the opportunity for Cosentino to prosecute Ford. In turn this perspective suggests that the ultimate, long-range meaning of the Pinto trial may depend less on the legal precedent that has been set and more on the nature of the social context that comes to prevail. That is, will the time ahead sustain the movement against corporate crime and thus encourage attempts to build upon the Pinto prosecution, or will concern with upperworld illegality diminish any interest in criminally sanctioning corporations commensurately decline?

At present the answer to the question is by no means certain. To be sure, the Reagan Administration has moved to reinterpret the moral character of corporate America and to officially clarify what "real" crime is (Reiman, 1979). Thus Reagan's loosening of regulatory controls on business has been accompanied by a renewed concern over violent street crimes and the trafficking of drugs; meanwhile, white-collar and corporate criminality has been placed on the back burner (Gordon, 1980; Cullen and Wozniak, 1982). Notably, like many of his other social policies, Reagan's crime control agenda is informed by his implicit view of human nature; the productive response to incentives (opportunities for profit), while the unproductive respond to punishments, thus the need for harsh sanctions for the crimes of the poor (Piven and Cloward, 1982:39).

However, these policies and the sentiments that underlie them may very well have the unanticipated consequence of fueling the public's concern over upperworld lawlessness. The ostensible failure of the president's domestic programs to effect promised benefits for working people has made his administration susceptible to charges of injustice, an image that Democrats across the nation are constantly trying to make more salient. In this climate sensitivity to collusion between government and big business, as in the EPA incident involving the dumping of chemical wastes, should run high (Time, 1983). Corporate conduct should thus remain a matter of continuing public concern, and in turn it will be difficult for the state to retain legitimacy if it chooses to ignore flagrant affronts to existing moral boundaries. If this analysis is correct, we should see additional, if only intermittent, criminal prosecutions within the immediate future of corporations who persist in recklessly endangering the public's well-being.

REFERENCES

Anderson, D. (1981) "Corporate homicide: the stark realities of artificial beings and legal fictions." Pepperdine Law Rev. 8:367-417.

Braithwaite, J. (1979) "Transnational corporations and corruption: towards some international solutions." International J. of Sociology of Law 7:125-142.

——— (1980) "Inegalitarian consequences of egalitarian reforms to control corporate crime." Temple Law Q. 53:1127-1146.

——— (1982a) "Challenging just deserts: punishing white collar criminals." J. of Criminal Law and Criminology 73(Summer): 723-763.

——— (1982b) "Enforced self-regulation: a new strategy for corporate crime control." Michigan Law Rev. 80(June): 1466-1507.

Braithwaite, J. and G. Geis (1982) "On theory and action for corporate crime control." Crime and Delinquency 28(April): 292-314.

Brown, M. (1980) Laying Waste: The Poisoning of America by Toxic Chemicals. New York: Pantheon.

Caudill, H. (1977) "Manslaughter in a coal mine." Nation 224 (April 23):492-497.

Clark, G. (1979) "Corporate homicide: a new assault on corporate decision-making." Notre Dame Lawyer 54(June): 911-924.

Clinard, M. and P. Yeager (1978) "Corporate crime: issues in research." Criminology 16(August):255-272.

——— (1980) Corporate Crime. New York: Free Press.

——— J. Brissette, D. Petrashek, and E. Harries (1979) Illegal Corporate Behavior. Washington DC: Government Printing Office.

Coleman, B. (1975) "Is corporate criminal liability really necessary?" Southwestern Law J. 29:908-927.

Conklin, J. (1977) Illegal but Not Criminal: Business Crime in America. Englewood Cliffs, NJ: Prentice-Hall.

Cullen, F. and K. Heiner (1979) "Provider Medicaid fraud: a note on white-coat crime." Presented at the annual meeting of the American Society of Criminology.

——— and J. Wozniak (1982) "Fighting the appeal of repression." Crime and Social Justice 18(Winter):23-33.

———, B. Link, and C. Polanzi (1982) "The seriousness of crime revisited; have attitudes toward white collar crime changed?" Criminology 20(May):82-102.

———, R. Mathers, G. Clark, and J. Cullen (forthcoming) "Public support for punishing white collar crime: blaming the victim revisited?" J. of Criminal Justice.

_____, G. Clark, B. Link, R. Mathers, J. Lee, and M. Sheahan (1982) "Dissecting white collar crime: offense-type and punitiveness." Presented at the annual meeting of the Academy of Criminal Justice Sciences.

Dowie, M. (1977) "Pinto madness." Mother Jones (September-October):18-32.

_____ (1979) "The corporate crime of the century." Mother Jones (November): 23-38, 49.

Duchnick. J. and M. Imhoff (1978) "A new outlook on the white collar criminal as it relates to deterring white collar crime." Criminal Justice J. 2(Winter):57-76.

Durkheim, E. (1951) Suicide. New York: Free Press.

Elkins, J. (1976) "Corporations and the criminal law: an uneasy alliance." Kentucky Law J. 65:73-129.

Erikson, K. (1966) Wayward Puritans. New York: John Wiley.

Farrell, R. and V. Swigert (1982) Deviance and Social Control. Glenview, IL: Scott, Foresman.

Fisse, B. (1971) "The use of publicity as a criminal sanction against business corporations." Melbourne Univ. Law Rev. 8(June):107-150.

_____ (1973) "Responsibility, prevention, and corporate crime." New Zealand Univ. Law Rev. 5(April):250-279.

_____ (1981) "Community service as a sanction against corporations." Wisconsin Law Rev. (September):970-1017.

Friedrichs, D. (1979) "The law and the legitimacy crisis: a critical issue for criminal justice," pp. 290-311 in R. Iacovetta and D. Chang [eds.] Critical Issues in Criminal Justice. Durham, NC: Carolina Academic Press.

Geis, G. (1972) "Criminal penalties for corporate criminals." Criminal Law Bull. 8(June):377-392.

_____ and H. Edelhertz (1973) "Criminal law and consumer fraud: a sociological view." Amer. Criminal Law Rev. 11(Summer): 989-1010.

Gordon, D. (1980) Doing Violence to the Crime Problem: A Response to the Attorney General's Task Force. Hackensack, NJ: NCCD.

Gusfield, J. (1967) "Moral passage: the symbolic process in public designations of deviance." Social Problems 15(Fall):175-188.

Kadish, S. (1963) "Some observations on the use of criminal sanctions in enforcing economic regulations." Univ. of Chicago Law Rev. 30(Spring):423-449.

Katz, J. (1980) "The social movement against white collar crime," pp. 161-184 in E. Bittner and S. Messinger [eds.] Criminology Review Yearbook, Volume 2. Beverly Hills: Sage.

Kramer, R. (1979) "The Ford Pinto homicide prosecution: criminological questions and issues concerning the control of corporate crime." Presented at the annual meeting of the American Society of Criminology.

Kriesberg, S. (1976) "Decisionmaking models and the control of corporate crime." Yale Law J. 85(July):1091-1129.

Maakestad, W. (1980) "The Pinto case: conceptual and constitutional problems in the criminal indictment of an American corporation." Presented at the annual meeting of the American Business Law Association.

———— (1981) "A historical survey of corporate homicide in the United States: could it be prosecuted in Illinois?" Illinois Bar J. 69(August):2-7.

———— (forthcoming) "Constitutional, utilitarian, and moral perspectives on the State of Indiana v. Ford Motor Company." St. Louis Univ. Law J.

Nader, R. and M. Green (1972) "Crime in the suites: coddling the corporations." New Republic 166(April 20):18.

Newsweek (1980) "Ford's Pinto: not guilty." Volume 95(March 24): 74.

Piven, F. and R. Cloward (1971) Regulating the Poor: The Functions of Public Welfare. New York: Pantheon.

———— (1977) Poor People's Movements: Why They Succeed, How They Fail. New York: Pantheon.

———— (1982) The New Class War: Reagan's Attack of the Welfare State and Its Consequences. New York: Pantheon.

Pontell, H., P. Jessilow, and G. Geis (1982) "Policing physicians: practitioner fraud and abuse in a government Medicaid program." Social Problems 30 (October):117-125.

President's Commission on Law Enforcement and Administration of Justice (1968) Challenge of Crime in a Free Society. New York: Avon.

Reiman, J. (1979) The Rich Get Richer and the Poor Get Prison. New York: John Wiley.

Rodgers, W. (1974) "IBM on trial." Harper's Magazine 248(May): 79-84.

Ross, I. (1980) "How lawless are big companies?" Fortune 102 (December 1):56-64.

Rothman, D. (1978) "The state as parent: social policy in the progressive era," pp. 67-96 in W. Gaylin et al., Doing Good: The Limits of Benevolence. New York: Pantheon.

Schrager, L. and J. Short (1978) "Toward a sociology of organizational crime." Social Problems 25(April):407-419.

Stern, G. (1976) The Buffalo Creek Disaster. New York: Vintage.

Strobel, L. (1980) Reckless Homicide? Ford's Pinto Trial. South Bend, IN: And Books.

Sudnow, D. (1965) "Normal crimes: sociological features of the penal code in a public defender's office." Social Problems 12(Winter):255-276.

Swigert, V. and R. Farrell (1980-1981) "Corporate homicide: definitional processes in the creation of deviance." Law & Society Rev. 15,1:171-182.

Time (1980) "Three cheers in Dearborn." (March 24):24.

_____ (1983) "Superfund, supermess." (February 21):14-16.

Vandivier, K. (1972) "The aircraft brake scandal." Harper's Magazine 244(April):45-52.

Wright, J. (1979) On a Clear Day You Can See General Motors: John A. DeLorean's Look Inside the Automotive Giant. New York:Avon.

Yoder, S. (1979) "Criminal sanctions for corporate illegality." J. of Criminal Law and Criminology 69(Spring):40-58.

NOTES

1. The account of the Pinto case presented here was drawn from four sources: (1) several telephone interviews by the authors with prosecutor Michael Cosentino; these were conducted in late February 1983; (2) the personal observations of one of the authors, William J. Maakestad, who served as Special Deputy Prosecuting Attorney during the case; (3) the detailed information compiled by newsman Lee Strobel (1980) in his fascinating chronicle of the case; and (4) news reports and scholarly commentary written about the trial. Please note that data taken from the talks with Cosentino is cited in the text as "Cosentino interview."

2. The estimated cost of fixing the fuel tank defect has generally been placed at $11, though the price has at times been set as low as $6. Also it should be noted that the memo printed by Dowie in which Ford calculated the costs of fixing the Pinto versus the financial loss due to death and injury pertained to problems in the fuel tank during rollover tests conducted by Ford and not during rear-end crash tests. Nevertheless, the mode of thinking suggested by the memo vividly reinforces Dowie's point that, with regard to the Pinto, profit was more important to Ford than consumer safety.

3. In this latter instance, Grimshaw, who had undergone over 50 operations to correct burn injuries suffered during a Pinto crash-turned-inferno, was awarded $2.8 million in compensatory damages and $125 million in punitive damages (reduced to a total of $6.6 million two weeks after the trial).

4. Interestingly, Swigert and Farrell reached this conclusion without talking with Cosentino. Thus, while their observations were drawn from a broad understanding of the social meaning of the case, their comments captured much of what was going on inside prosecutor Consentino's mind.

5. Berner was on the law faculty at Valparaiso. The second professor working full time on the case was Terry Keily of DePaul University. A few other lawyers, including author William Maakestad, also volunteered substantial amounts of time at points in the case. Finally, Berner and Kiely recruited up to 15 law students to conduct research and otherwise assist the prosecution.

6. During the course of the trial, tired members of the prosecution's team, especially the law students helping with research, would look at the post-crash photographs of the girls in order to remember what the case was really about and hence bolster their resolve to continue working.

7. As Strobel (1980:60) noted, Neal's salary in other cases is reputed to have been as much as $800,000.

8. The survey showed that 56% of the residents sampled felt that Ford was either guilty or probably guilty (Strobel, 1980:66). Interestingly, Cosentino believed that about half his community initially supported the idea of prosecuting Ford, while the other half thought he was "crazy." However, by the time of the trial, it was his perception that the vast majority of his constituents were in his camp (Cosentino interview).

VI.
ETHICS AND CRIME CONTROL POLICY—
QUESTIONS AND SCENARIOS

CHAPTER SIXTEEN

1. When most people talk about crime, they are referring to street crime. How did the common usage of the term "crime" come to refer to what is in fact a small portion of all criminal activity?

2. It appears that myths about the criminal justice system are as pervasive as those that affect crime. How do these myths simplify our views of reality?

3. It has been said that we have nothing to fear but fear itself. It appears that fear of crime and the beliefs and actions promoted by fear may be as dangerous to most of us as crime itself. Explain this position.

4. Myths about crime and criminal justice serve a great many interests. Whose interests are served by the destruction of these myths?

CHAPTER SEVENTEEN

1. The 1968 President's Commission concluded that "the public tends to be indifferent to business crime or even to sympathize with the offenders who have been caught." Do you think that this statement is true? If so, what are its implications for the future of crime control policy?

2. Cullen et al says that there will be calls for citizens to "sharpen their awareness of the dangers posed by the lawlessness of the rich and to demand that the state take steps to shield them from this victimization." Do you see a need to "sharpen" the public's awareness? What role do you foresee the state taking in addressing such concerns?

3. What features are shared by both organized and white-collar crime? How does the ideology of criminal justice policy work to obscure these similarities?

4. In recent years, many of the law enforcement strategies previously applied against organized crime have come to be used against white-collar criminals (insider trading, for example). Do these actions represent a shift in ideology?

SCENARIOS

1. You are a police officer who agrees with Bohm about crime and criminal justice myths. How can you justify enforcing the laws against street crime, knowing the ideological bias inherent in this enforcement? How do you reconcile your actions with your beliefs?

2. You are a prosecutor in a community in which anti-abortion demonstrations have become an everyday occurence. The number of persons arrested for trespassing is swamping the local jail and the court system and making it difficult to carry out routine business. Up until this time you have been diverting these arrestees from prosecution. What factors will influence your future policy on the matter?

3. You have just been given the job of warden of one of the toughest maximum security prisons in your state. After your first week on the job, you see and hear things that are going on behind the scenes: payoffs, thefts, beatings, and even murders. To top that off, you find that most of the so-called "treatment" programs are a joke. However, the prison has a name as one of the more stable, treatment-oriented institutions. In other words, from the outside it looks as though things are running smoothly and this is a model institution. You know that things are bound to be shaken up if you try to curb the hidden violence and smuggling. What is your moral obligation, and what do you do to fulfill it?

4. You are the CEO of a large corporation. Your job involves the supervision of hundreds of individuals. Your corporation provides many services, one of which is drug testing and research. This particular company is competing with another for a new drug which, when marketed, could corner the market as a possible cure for AIDS. You are only a short step ahead of the competition on perfecting the drug. However, you know that it is possible to pass the FDA standards now, market it, and perfect it later on. You feel reasonably certain that the side effects are no worse than many of the other drugs on the market. Do you market the drug? If so, what are your justifications? If not, what are your reasons?

VII. ETHICS AND THE FUTURE

When thinking about the future of our institutions of justice and other processes that are related to them, a number of questions come to mind. What philosophical model or models will guide us personally and professionally? How will we attempt to balance the rights of the individual with the needs of the larger community? How will these same models help to define and redefine the roles of the courts, policing, and corrections? The heart and mind of our system of justice from which our policies and programs spring forth is composed of our personal and professional philosophical models. Will our collective heart and mind of justice use its long arms of the law to simply keep the peace or will it begin to try to encourage and contribute to the peace? And how will all the interrelated aspects of this process be evaluated? How will we define success in the future?

It seems evident that as we come to the last section of this book, there are many more questions than answers. Perhaps that is as it should be. As we look to our future, we may find the beginnings of the answers we seek through the asking of clear, accurate, meaningful questions about our personal sense of justice and how it is expressed through our formal justice process.

CRIMINAL JUSTICE: AN ETHIC FOR THE FUTURE   18

Michael C. Braswell

Now that we have come to the end of this volume, we would like to finish by once again considering its beginning. The first chapter was concerned with developing a philosophical framework through which we could consider the ethical implications of a variety of criminal justice issues. Now that we have attempted to examine contemporary issues within this framework, we are challenged to look toward the future of criminal justice, a future which is found hidden in its present. How are we to find the eyes to see such a future? a vision which can empower us to contribute to its promise? Will our contributions as individuals and institutions be expressed in the context of a community of hope or a community of fear and apathy? Will we protect and serve the status quo—focus on the criminal, or will we move ahead, riding the crest of a long shot—that the larger sense of justice is what will be accentuated and that the possibility of social peace can increasingly become a reality? Are we only to be engaged in colorful, crisis-minded rhetoric, or can we translate contemporary justice dilemmas into opportunities for encouraging more substantial policies and practical applications toward restitution and reconciliation.

If we choose to commit to seeking justice and peace in a community of hope, we will need to begin acting on an enlarged vision which includes an ethic for the future. Of course, to some this sort of thinking may seem to be too romantic a notion, undergrounded in the hard realities of today's justice problems. Still, it would appear that an attitude of hope which empowers us on a personal as well as systemic level and is anchored in something more than another blue-ribbon task force or budget increase is worth pursuing. Whether in reference to offenders, victims, citizens, or criminal justice professionals, it seems to be in our best interests to recognize and encourage an attitude of personal empowerment; that perhaps we need to restore the balance of our interaction with our environment—that problems and solutions come from the inside-out as well as from external means—from the outside-in. Thich Nhat Hanh writes, "The problem is to see reality as it is. A pessimistic attitude can never create the calm.. But, in fact, when we are angry, *we ourselves* are anger. When we are happy, we ourselves are happiness. When we have certain thoughts, *we are those thoughts*... In a family, if there is one person who practices mindfulness, the entire family will be mindful... And in one class, if one student lives in mindfulness, the entire class is influenced" (pp. 40, 52, 64).

THE NEED FOR MINDFULNESS

If we are to develop an ethic for the future of criminal justice, we need to become more mindful and conscious of ethical truths concerning justice which are found in the present. For example, the utilitarian's priority for community good and the individual integrity of the deontologist become conscious of one another in the context of connectedness and, more importantly, reconciled in an ongoing response of active care. At some point in our lives, we are inclined to become aware that no matter how strong our personal needs and interests are, no one is an island. We need to be with other people in community to survive and grow.

Whether we live in suburbia, the inner city, or rural America, we begin to realize that we are connected: parents to children, teachers to students, guards to prisoners, and offenders to victims. We like the ideas of "one for all and all for one" and "one nation under God with liberty and justice for all," yet we are also connected to our environment. Drought, acid rain, forest fires and oil spills all raise our consciousness of our interdependence with our physical environment as well.

To demonstrate this dynamic interaction between the community and the individual along a continuum of connectedness and care in a more specifically criminal justice context, we may still find it necessary to remove an offender from society. We may decide to place this person in prison "for the good of the community;" yet, even in prison, we need to realize that offenders are entitled to certain rights of basic care and safety. In other words, we need to see that they are treated humanely on ethical and moral grounds even if in some cases we may feel they are not deserving because of the crimes they have committed or that our correctional treatment efforts have little effect on their behavior.

Although the offender may be inside prison and we may be outside, in the community, we are still connected in a number of ways. We are bound together from the past by direct fear and suffering of the victim and the vicarious feelings and perceptions of our citizens. There is also the fear and suffering of the offender and the offender's family, who may also be victims. We are brought together in the present through the quality of life of the prison staff who are also members of the community and are tied to the offenders they supervise and with whom they interact. The promise of the future connects us in the knowledge that most offenders, especially with current overcrowding problems, will eventually return to our communities. We might even consider the notion that how we, as a community, allow prisoners to be treated in prison and in the correctional programs may say a lot about how we see ourselves and expect to be treated when they return to us. Becoming more mindful can allow us, as individuals and communities, to take greater care in seeing and responding more meaningfully to the connections that bind us together in relationships.

ORDER-KEEPING AND PEACE-MAKING

Hans Mattick (in Conrad, 1981) once said, "If I could sum up my entire education experience and reflection in a single sentence, it would be" 'Things are not what they seem' (p. 14)." Yet, often in our haste to find and keep order, we try to do just the opposite of what Mattick suggests: we try to eliminate the ambiguity and paradox from human behavior—we try to "make things be as they seem." If we limit our search for justice to crime and criminals, we are likely to miss the larger truth of Mattick's point. Our search for justice can instead become subverted to a search for order. It is even possible that the ambiguity that is an inevitable part of democracy's birthright can, over time, be replaced by the certainty and predictability of a totalitarian society.

Too much emphasis on order-keeping encourages us to view problems or failures in the justice process as technological difficulties which through sound engineering can be corrected rather than fundamental problems of design. We imagine that if we can just do things more efficiently, crime and justice problems can eventually be solved or at least reduced to an insignificant level (Braswell and Lafollette, 1988). Unfortunately, an order-keeping focus may inhibit us from expanding our area of concern to include the impact of the interaction within the larger social arena, which addresses more specific crime and justice issues. It is worth remembering that if we have not asked the right questions which include a variety of diverse perspectives, our solutions, no matter how efficiently implemented, are no solutions at all; rather, they simply add another layer to the confusion and difficulty that already exists and end up creating additional problems and suffering.

The importance of viewing criminal justice and related issues from a variety and diversity of perspectives is well illustrated by a Sufi writer: "What is fate?" Nasrudin was asked by a scholar. "An endless succession of intertwined events influencing each other." "That is hardly a satisfactory answer. I believe in cause and effect." "Very well," said the Mulla, "look at that." He pointed to a procession passing in the street. "That man is being taken to be hanged. Is that because someone gave him a silver piece to bury the knife with which he committed murder, or because someone saw him do it, or because nobody stopped him?" (Meredith, 1984, p. 48).

While keeping the order is important, keeping the peace is more than that. Peace-keeping represents a larger vision with potentially profound implications for the individual and the community. Peace keeping can in fact emerge into a practice of peace-making. Such a practice requires that we encourage a greater sense of mindfulness which allows us to remain conscious that human behavior is not an either/or proposition but a continuum which includes and connects offenders, victims, and non-offenders. Order keeping focuses on the "guilty few" while the mindfulness of peace-keeping and peace-making remind us that "few may be guilty, but all are responsible" (Quinney, 1980).

Isaiah (32:17) states, "Justice will bring about peace, right will produce calm and security." Is that what is happening in our crime and justice conscious culture? Are our citizens experiencing a greater sense of peace, calm, and security? How can we in a meaningful and balanced way maintain that order yet keep and even contribute to the peacefulness, calm, and security in our communities? Such existential questions seem challenging at best and overwhelming at worst. It is easy enough to think and talk about peace-making, but quite another thing to put it into mindful action. Hubert Van Zeller (in Castle, 1988) adds yet another twist when he writes, "Thinking about interior peace destroys interior peace. The patient who constantly feels his pulse is not getting better (p. 180)." Van Zeller would lead us to believe that if we are able to contribute to the peacefulness, calm, and security of our community, we must learn to be more peaceful, calm, and secure within ourselves. Can we offer calm if we are angry, security if we are fearful, or hope if we are cynical? It seems that if we are to contribute to a more just society, we must not simply think, talk, or write about peace-keeping and peace-making but personally struggle to increasingly *be* peace. Quinney (1987) writes, "Rather than attempting to create a good society first, and then trying to make ourselves better human beings, we have to work on the two simultaneously... Without peace within us and in our actions, there can be no peace in our results (p. 19, 23)." Critics of peace-making as a viable way to improve our justice process would point to its impracticality. Such an approach seems to have little in common with the popular notions, such as "Getting tough on crime." Unfortunately, while such popular notions may get people elected to political office and make many of us feel better emotionally, their practical applications have done little to reduce crime or increase the calm and security of citizens. Although perhaps requiring an alternative mindset, peace-making may not be as impractical as many critics would suggest. Dass and Perlman (1985) offer an account by a police officer who struggled to see himself primarily as a peacekeeper and peacemaker:

> Now there are two theories about crime and how to deal with it. Anti-crime guys say, "You have to think like a criminal." And some police learn that so well they get a kind of criminal mentality themselves.
>
> How I'm working with it is really pretty different. I see that man is essentially pure and innocent and of one good nature. That's who he is by birthright. And that's what I'm affirming in the course of a day on the job. In fact, that is my job. The "cop" part of it...well, they call us "cops", to me, my job is *I'm a peace officer.*
>
> So I work not only to prevent the crime but to eliminate its causes—its causes in fear and greed, not just the social causes everyone talks about.
>
> Even when it gets to conflict. I had arrested a very angry black man who singled me out for real animosity. When I had to take him to a paddy wagon, he spit in my face—that was something—and he went after me with a chair. We handcuffed him and put him in the truck. Well, on the way I just had to get past this picture of things, and again I affirmed to myself, "This guy and I are brothers... When I got to the station, I was moved spontaneously to say, "Look, if I've done anything to offend you, I apologize." The paddy wagon driver looked at me as if I was totally nuts.

The next day I had to take him from where he'd been housed overnight to criminal court. When I picked him up, I thought, "Well, if you trust this vision, you're not going to have to handcuff him." And I didn't. We got to a spot in the middle of the corridor which was the place where he'd have jumped me if he had that intention, and he stopped suddenly. So did I. Then he said, "You know, I thought about what you said yesterday, and I want to apologize." I just felt deep appreciation.

Turned out on his rap sheet he'd done a lot of time in Michigan and had trouble with guards in jail. I symbolized something. And I saw that turn around, saw a kind of healing, I believe.

So what really happens if you're going to explore whether or not this vision of nature really has power? Maybe people will say you're taking chances. But you're taking chances without any vision; your vision is your protection. Maybe they'll say you're sentimentalizing people. But it's not about people. It's about principle and truth. It's about how the universe is. Maybe they'll think it's idealistic; things could never be this way. Well, for me, things are this way already; it's just up to us to know that more clearly.

I see that my work is to hold to an image of who we all truly are and to be guided by that. And I have been guided by that, to greater strength and security...within myself and on the street.

SOME SUGGESTIONS FOR CRIMINAL JUSTICE

If we are to look to the future of criminal justice with some measure of hope rather than a growing sense of cynicism, we must seek out fresh possibilities rather than defend traditional certainties. We need not be naive to remain open to creative alternatives concerning justice philosophy, policy and programming. As Geis (1984) suggests, we need to "stand apart from the parade" to see old problems with a new perspective. Nettler (1982) exhorts us to spend more time and energy in asking the right questions *before* seeking answers. We need reflection before action. Lozoff puts our dilemma in perspective when he writes, "We all want to know the way, but very few of us are willing to study the maps (p. 3)."

It seems more important than ever for us to look past our individual and agency interests into the larger community of which we are a part. The corporate body of this larger community includes both the best and the worst that we have to offer. The sinner and saint, offender and victim all share the consequences of our formal and informal responses to matters of crime and justice. Prevention, intervention or no response at all holds meaning for each part of our community as well as the whole. We have to keep trying to look at the problems of crime and justice with fresh eyes, through the eyes of overworked bureaucrats, prison guards, caseworkers, through the eyes of the victims and offenders as well. We need to look beyond the next career opportunity and try to see through the eyes of our children and even their children, for we are responsible to them as well.

The following suggestions are offered as observations to consider, as food for thought:

LAW AND JUSTICE

Can legal statutes or the justice system make up for our lack of community, for our feelings and experiences of fragmentation? Can morality or a responsible and caring community be legislated? The answer to both questions is, of course, no. However, the way we define laws and the way our justice system enforces them can enhance or diminish our opportunities for more peaceful and orderly communities. While conflict and ambiguity are an inevitable part of how social ills are connected to problems of crime and justice, intervention (in the form of prevention efforts) must occur before as well as after crimes are committed. Health care and opportunities for meaningful work are as or more important than simply improving the efficiency of the criminal justice process. As we consider how laws must be changed and our justice system needs to be improved, an expanded vision can allow us to create a space where we can more honestly address differences between how we view the justice process ideally and how it often functions in reality. Myths such as a) white-collar crime is nonviolent, b) the rich and poor are equal before the law, c) that the punishment can fit the crime, and d) that law makes people behave can be examined and responded to in a more enlightened context of community.

There are also issues of law and justice that must be struggled with on a personal basis both in terms of our being criminal justice professionals and as members of families and social communities. For example, it seems that many persons have come to believe that a legal act and a moral act are essentially the same. Politicians or corporate executives charged with crimes typically declare to the press and the public that they have done nothing illegal and indeed, they may often be correct. But does that make it right? Can legal behavior be immoral and illegal behavior moral? Were Martin

Luther King, Jr. and Mahatma Ghandi criminals or heroes? In a society where success is measured primarily in terms of money and prestige, are we encouraged to do whatever is necessary within (and sometimes outside) the law to be successful (Braswell & LaFollette, 1988)? We are appalled when public figures are convicted of large-scale fraud, yet we may consider cheating on our income taxes or college exams acceptable. It seems as if we are saying, "It's alright to do something wrong as long as we don't get caught at it." Of course, in life or in criminal court, when we do get caught our plea is for mercy. From minor greed to major fraud, when we are the victim we are inclined to want retribution, yet when we are the offender we want mercy. This contrasting desire seems true in personal relationships as well as in a professional or criminal justice context.

Policing

With more minorities and women entering police work, the opportunity exists for a greater openness in defining and redefining police roles and function. In addition, as issues surrounding the family such as domestic violence and child abuse are translated into law and criminal justice policies, a clearer focus concerning the need for police officers to possess meaningful communication and interpersonal skills should become more apparent. It seems ironic that police officers are expected to intervene with families who are in crisis, while few, if any, helping services are available to many of them when they experience family crisis situations (Braswell & Meeks, 1978). Shift work and a closed professional system are just several of the factors that can contribute to difficulties regarding family life. To make matters worse, in some instances a stigma perceived as weakness is identified with those officers who do seek professional help for family related problems.

Police agencies are also responsible for detaining offenders in jails until courts dispense with them. Current problems associated with prison overcrowding have also spilled over into jails, turning many of them into little more than institutions for extended incarceration. Most jails are operated by law enforcement agencies more inclined toward enforcement and order maintenance strategies than correctional intervention with offenders. And the offenders who end up in jail are typically from the underclass and represent the least in the community since they often cannot afford bail. Suggestions for more creative options such as pretrail release, diversion programs, and speedier trials have long been a possibility, but they are often not utilized. Such an attitude of neglect has additional implications for one of the criminal justice systems most missed opportunities, its potential impact on first-time offenders who have their initial contact with the system at the jail. It seems ironic that the point in the justice process where the first-time offender is usually the most open to intervention is also the place where the least resources are allocated.

Are police officers tough, unyielding crime fighters, or are they much more than that? Many police officers consider social services calls as "garbage calls," not worthy of their time and effort, yet, the majority of their typical work day is spent dealing with human service situations. And paradoxically, the more mindful they are with the ethic of care as translated through effective communication and interpersonal skills, the less likely they are to have to get tough with the people with whom they come in contact. Still, the image persists: Dirty Harry, crime fighter, or peacemaker? It is interesting to note that an informal survey of introductory criminal justice students, given each semester consistently reveals that the overwhelming majority of them, would prefer, all things being equal (i.e., job responsibilities, pay, etc.), to be identified as a police officer or deputy sheriff rather than as a public safety officer. How can we enlarge vision of police work to include a primary emphasis on peace-making as well as law enforcement? It is not just a matter of knowing "how" to shoot well but also knowing "when" to shoot and also being open to possible nonviolent alternatives. Given the litigious nature of today's world, such an orientation has pragmatic as well as peace-making advantages. It is unfortunate that the nature and tradition of contemporary police work would make the previous example of a police officer who saw himself as primarily a peace officer seem so unusual (Dass & Perlman, 1985). With so much research focused on police corruption and deviance, we might find it worthwhile to follow A.H. Maslow's (1954) example and turn our attention to what motivates well adjusted, creative, and psychologically healthy police officers. Given the discretion and immediacy of response police officers utilize in the community setting, there is perhaps no other criminal justice professional who is as connected to the community and who has as great an opportunity to contribute to the community's sense of care and well-being.

CORRECTIONS

Corrections directly addresses the "least of the community;" the two-time losers, the nuisance factor, the disenfranchised and the violent ones. Along the continuum of connectedness, offenders appear to be the least useful to the community. They have demonstrated their disdain or inability to do their duty as citizens, adequately contribute to the common good, or provide meaningful care. As a result, the larger community often retributively feels that such persons themselves are deserving of the least care. Ironically, while we want them to pay for crimes and be corrected, we are not particularly supportive of their feeling good about themselves. The paradox "be good, but don't feel good about it" can often put our correctional process at odds with itself. Is our priority to be corrections or punishment? Is our emphasis to repair the connection and restore both offender and victim to our community or to disconnect and distance one or the other or both from community? Are we to be more interested in restitution and reconciliation whenever possible or retribution? Thomas Merton writes, "You cannot save the world with merely a system. You cannot have peace without charity" (In Quinney, 1988, p. 71).

While the effectiveness of correctional treatment is a worthy and important topic for debate between the pro- and anti-rehabilitation factions in criminal justice (Gendreau & Ross, 1980; Cullen & Gilbert, 1983; Lipton et al., 1975; Whitehead & Lab, 1989), is it the only or even most important basis for funding and providing correctional treatment services for offenders? Are the moral and ethical grounds for treating offenders at least as important, if not more so, than the utilitarian demands for effectiveness? Perhaps we need to more clearly develop and articulate a treatment ethic that is restorative in nature and one that more honestly addresses the community's (including its least members) sense of duty to itself. Such a turn of focus also allows us to pay closer attention to the art of correctional treatment rather than strictly to its scientific aspect, to the creation as well as the operation of correctional process.

It is interesting that when we think of correctional treatment interventions we are inclined to think of them more as treatment systems or clinical approaches to be evaluated and less as existential processes to be experienced. And while this tendency may also be true of our psychotherapeutic colleagues, they are more among them that are sensitive to and grounded in a vital sense of the existential that makes the philosophy and science of theory come alive in the art and process of relationship (Satir, 1973; Rogers, 1980; Whitaker, 1976). It seems worth noting the substantial research Robert Carkhuff and his associates (1969a & b) conducted which is continuing to evolve (1987) that indicates the further graduate students progressed in clinical help professions, the more proficient they became in diagnostic, assessment-juand evaluation skills but seemed to become less effective in demonstrating meaningful and effective communication skills. To put the "art of treatment" perspective into a more specifically correctional context, we can turn to the ground-breaking work of John Augustus and Alexander Maconochie. We can become so enamored of their innovative approaches, that we can easily forget or at least take for granted, the personal, inner aspect of who they were which made their approaches come alive in experience. David Dressler (1959) writes of John Augustus' interaction with offenders in a police court: "It is probable that some of them know him, for as he walks to the box two or three turn their blood-shot eyes toward him with eager glances... In a moment he is with them, gently reproving the hardened ones, and cheering...those in whom are visible signs of penitence (p. 25)." Dressler continues in commenting on Maconochie's restorative impact on an incorrigible and disturbed inmate; "He was out of touch with reality most of the time, unaware of what was going on about him, but when Maconochie, his wife, or their children, visited him, he returned to reality, recognized his callers. He showed affection for them to the day he died (p. 67)." It is true that evaluating treatment effectiveness is important, as is educating and training competent clinical professionals in diagnostic, assessment, and evaluation skills. However, the art of helping requires more than cognitive or affective sensitivity; it requires a synthesis of both these dimensions and more—emerging from within and lived out in experience with others. "A staff person who's calm and strong and happy is worth his or her weight in gold. People who are living examples of truthfulness, good humor, patience, and courage are going to change more lives—even if they're employed as janitors—than the counselors who can't get their own lives in order (Braswell, 1989, 52).

Perhaps we can begin to rethink our attitude regarding corrections. Do we really want it to work or not? Is corrections to be little more than an opportunity for an incomplete community to express its feelings of retribution or can it be more than that? Can we realize the possibility that corrections, even with its need for punishment, can also include restitution and rehabilitation as a means of the community of which we are all a part experiencing reconciliation? After speaking to local Kiwanis groups about juvenile crime and corrections in their community, the speaker was asked by one of the Kiwanians what could they do to help? His response: "Create recreation opportunities for the least of their community and for themselves—join the local PTA."

JUSTICE AS A WAY RATHER THAN A DESTINATION

It is in our best interests to begin to see justice as an evolutionary way of service rather than as an efficiently engineered technological destination. We need an ethic for our future that will empower us to act on an enlarged vision of what justice is about; a vision that will include the community of which we are all a part; the best of us and the worst of us—the best in each of us and the worst in each of us. We need a prophetic vision to energize the empowerment of such an ethic. The passion of prophetic vision resounds in the words of Amos (5:24) and is repeated by Martin Luther King, Jr. in a striking address: "Let justice roll down like waters. And righteousness like a mighty stream." Quinney (1980) adds, "For the prophets, justice is like a mighty stream, not merely a category or mechanical process. In contrast, the moralists discuss, suggest, counsel; the prophets proclaim, demand, insist (p. 25)."

Justice as a way of service requires more than just the passionate zeal of the visionary, it also requires the mindfulness of quiet compassion. Creative and humane policies and plans are one thing, but making them work is something else. It is the compassionate professionals in public schools, courts, law enforcement, corrections, and other human service agencies that make the ethic of care come alive in the community. Such persons are mindful of the suffering crime and social injustice creates for victims and offenders. Their mindfulness is born of their own suffering as well. Dietrich Bonhoeffer, himself incarcerated and finally executed in a NAZI prison camp, writes (In Castle, _____), "We must learn to respond to people less in the light of what they do or omit to do, and more in the light of what they suffer." Seeing a Ted Bundy or Charles Manson through the eyes of compassion keeps us from closing ourselves off from the terrible suffering they have given and received. Their acts are not excused, nor is our irresponsibility in choosing not to commit our collective resources and energies toward preventing the creation of future Bundys or Mansons. Compassionate professionals realize it is not how much they do, but rather how mindfully they do whatever they do. To put it another way, as Mother Teresa suggests, "It is not how much you do, but how much you do with love." From a compassionate way of services comes a sense of peace and well-being.

Success, happiness, even justice are all preludes at best and second-rate substitutes at worst to what we really seek—peace. Only peace has the potential to remain calm and resolute even in the midst of suffering which is an experience that connects each of us to the other in community. Peace comes from the inside/out. It cannot be implemented organizationally from the top/down. People at peace with themselves create peaceful organizations which can then become instruments for peacemaking in the larger community. To reiterate Dass and Gormans' (1985) cogent observation: "If we ourselves cannot know peace, *be* peaceful, how will our acts disarm hatred and violence?" (p. 165). And to borrow once again from Isaiah (32:17): "How else will our justice system bring about peace, produce calm and security for our people?"

REFERENCES

Amos 5:24.

Braswell, Michael C. (1989) "Correctional Treatment and the Human Spirit: A Focus on Relationship," *Federal Probation*, June 49-60.

Braswell, Michael and Hugh Lafollette (1988) "Seeking Justice: The Advantages and Disadvantages of Being Educated," *American Journal of Criminal Justice* (Spring): 135-147.

Castle, Tony (1988) *The New Book of Christian Quotations*. New York: Crossroad.

Conrad, John (1981) *Justice and Consequences*. Lexington, MA: Lexington Books.

Carkhuff, Robert (1987) *The Art of Helping III*. Amherst, MA: Human Resource Development Press.

Carkhuff, Robert (1969) *Helping Human Relations, Vol. II*. New York: Holt, Rhinehart, and Winston.

Cullen, Francis and Karen Gilbert (1982) *Reaffirming Rehabilitation*. Cincinnati, OH: Anderson.

Dass, Ram and Paul Gorman (1985) *How Can I Help?* New York: Alfred A. Knopf.

Dressler, David (1959) *Practice and Theory of Probation and Parole*. New York: Columbia University Press.

Geis, Gilbert (1984) "Foreword" *Myths that Cause Crime* (Harold Pepinsky and Paul Jesilow). Cabin John, MD: Seven Locks Press.

Gendreau, Paul and Robert Ron (1987) "Revivification of Rehabilitation: Evidence from the 1980's." *Justice Quarterly* 4:349-409.

Hahh, Thich That (1987) *Being Peace*. Berkeley, CA: Parollox Press.

Isaiah 32:17.

Lozoff, Bo and Michael Braswell (1989) *Inner Corrections*. Cincinnati, OH: Anderson.

Lozoff, Bo (1989) "Editorial," *Human Kindness Foundation Newsletter*, p. 3.

Lozoff, Bo (1987) *We're All Doing Time*. Chapel Hill, NC: Human Kindness Foundation.

Maslow, Abraham (1970) *Motivation and Personality*. New York: Harper and Row.

Meredith, Nikki (1984) "The Murder Epidemic," *Science*. (December) p. 48.

Nettler, Gwynn (1982) *Explaining Criminals*. Cincinnati, OH: Anderson.

Pepinsky, Harold and Paul Jesilow (1984) *Myths That Cause Crime*. Cabin John, MD: Seven Locks Press.

Quinney, Richard (1988) "Crime, Suffering, and Service: Toward a Criminology of Peacemaking," *The Quest* (Winter) p. 71.

——(1987), "The Way of Peace: On Crime, Suffering, and Service," unpublished paper, (November) p. 19 & 23.

——(1980) *Providence: The Reconstruction of Social and Moral Order.* New York: Longman.

Rogers, Carl (1980) *A Way of Being.* Palo Alto, CA: Houghton-Mifflin.

Satir, Virginia (1972) *Peoplemaking.* Palo Alto, CA: Science and Behavior Books.

Whitehead, John and Steve Lab (1989) A Response to "Does Correctional Treatment Work?" unpublished paper.

VII.
Ethics and the Future—
Questions and Scenarios

Chapter Eighteen

1. What are some potential dangers in our criminal justice system's maintaining too narrow a focus on "order-keeping" without becoming more mindful of its connection to the larger social environment?

2. How is one's personal sense of justice, order, and peace related to the effectiveness or ineffectiveness of the system's response to justice and crime-related problems?

3. Why is mindfulness important to one's personal and professional life? Can you think of any personal example? How could becoming too enmeshed with a professional agency or organization discourage mindfulness?

SCENARIOS

1. You are the head of a committee appointed by the Governor to recommend some ways to produce a greater sense of "peace, calm and security" for the people of your state regarding crime and justice issues. What types of resistance might you expect from lawmakers and police corrections officials? What would your recommendations be? How do you feel they would be received?

2. You are the new Director of Probation and Parole in your state. The state decided it wanted fresh talent to implement some new ideas. You are much younger than most of those under your supervision. After being chosen for the position, you decide an extensive inspection of the different regions and their respective probation officers would be in order. What you find is disheartening. Your officers are tired and burned out. They no longer have the zeal for helping others that they once had. They have received empty promises for better pay and working conditions. You are at a loss. You cannot believe the state of your department but you realize something must be done to revitalize it, to give those under you something to live and work for. What do you do?

3. The year is 2074 and things are quite different. All prisions have been merged into one huge prison complex in upstate Texas that encompasses approximately 250 square miles of land. As expected, the prison population is at an all-time high with hundreds of thousands of persons incarcerated. Rehabilitation has been forfeited completely in favor of custodial pursuits. Conditions have worsened to a point whereat prisoners are released only at mealtime and for one short outdoor visit. The visits are short, due to the shift changes, to let everyone go out at least once a day. Disturbances continue to escalate to an average of 75 inmates seriously injured or killed each month. An average of six correctional staff are injured each month, most of a minor nature. During the last three, staff members were killed and 300 inmates lost their lives. You have been appointed warden and you are a strong advocate of justice in the true sense of the word. What will your actions be, and what are the reasons behind those actions?

Index